Sustainable Universities and Colleges

NEW HORIZONS IN SUSTAINABILITY AND BUSINESS

Books in the New Horizons in Sustainability and Business series make a significant contribution to the study of business, sustainability and the natural environment. As this field has expanded dramatically in recent years, the series will provide an invaluable forum for the publication of high-quality works of scholarship and show the diversity of research on organizations and the environment around the world. Global and pluralistic in its approach, this series includes some of the best theoretical and analytical work with contributions to fundamental principles, rigorous evaluations of existing concepts and competing theories, stimulating debate and future visions.

For a full list of Edward Elgar published titles, including the titles in this series, visit our website at www.e-elgar.com.

Sustainable Universities and Colleges

Sustainability Advances in Institutions of Higher Education

Edited by

Mark Starik

Senior Lecturer, Sustainability Management Program, University of Wisconsin Extended Campus, Madison, Wisconsin, and Contributing Faculty Member, College of Health Sciences and Public Policy, Walden University, Minneapolis, Minnesota, USA

Paul Shrivastava

Professor, Department of Management and Organization, The Pennsylvania State University, University Park, Pennsylvania, USA and Co-President, The Club of Rome, Switzerland

NEW HORIZONS IN SUSTAINABILITY AND BUSINESS

Edward Elgar
PUBLISHING

Cheltenham, UK • Northampton, MA, USA

Published by
Edward Elgar Publishing Limited
The Lypiatts
15 Lansdown Road
Cheltenham
Glos GL50 2JA
UK

Edward Elgar Publishing, Inc.
William Pratt House
9 Dewey Court
Northampton
Massachusetts 01060
USA

A catalogue record for this book
is available from the British Library

Library of Congress Control Number: 2024934181

This book is available electronically in the **Elgar**online
Business subject collection
http://dx.doi.org/10.4337/9781035314737

ISBN 978 1 0353 1472 0 (cased)
ISBN 978 1 0353 1473 7 (eBook)

Printed and bound in Great Britain by
TJ Books Limited, Padstow, Cornwall

Contents

List of figures		vii
List of tables		viii
List of contributors		ix
Acknowledgments		xv

1   Introduction   1
Mark Starik and Paul Shrivastava

2   Needs and opportunities for sustainability programs
in higher education: insights from the Global Council
for Science and the Environment's *Pathways toward
Accreditation* initiative   15
Jordan King, Katja Brundiers and Krista Hiser

3   Sustainable practices as innovation adoption on campus   38
Jason C. Senjem

4   Higher education institutions can do more to lead society
toward resilience and sustainability   58
Thomas S. Benson

5   Transition 2026: stakeholder engagement and the
co-construction of a climate strategy in a French business school   82
María Castillo, Susana Esper, Gustavo Birollo and Frank
G.A. de Bakker

6   Crystallization of a university's sustainability efforts
around Laudato Si': a case study of opportunities and challenges   105
Michael J. Pawlish

7   A student-driven approach to establishing sustainability
programs at colleges and universities: lessons from the
Green Office Movement in Europe   120
Jean Wu

8   How universities enable sustainable solutions to persistent
     social problems in Africa: the case of a Pan African
     university alliance   132
     Alessia Argiolas and Said Benamar

9   Schools of management making an impact:
     operationalization mechanisms and methods for
     contributing to organizational change   160
     Bart van Hoof and Sjors Witjes

10   Sustainable transformation in business and management
     higher education: an analysis of global and European
     collaborative initiatives for positive impact   184
     Julia Wolny

11   Disrupting the business curriculum for sustainability and
     the common good: the Glasgow Caledonian New York
     College experiment   207
     Jacqueline LeBlanc and Gastón de los Reyes

12   Education for climate change: an andragogical approach
     with a transdisciplinary framework   225
     Younsung Kim

13   Enlightened education: advancing the sustainability of
     schools, colleges, and universities by deployment of solar
     photovoltaic infrastructure   249
     Kenneth A. Walz

14   Decolonizing post-secondary sustainability education in
     the Anthropocene   275
     Kimberly M. Post

Index   297

Figures

1.1 ROOTS of sustainable universities   5

2.1 Change drivers and change areas for sustainability
     programs in higher education   19

5.1 Process timeline   89

8.1 Summary of E4Impact alliance indicators and results   139

8.2 Structure of the MBA program   140

9.1 Categories of RML Literature   162

9.2 The framework for operationalization of TD for schools of
     management contributing to societal challenges   166

9.3 RedES operating structure indicating the roles of various
     stakeholders   168

11.1 Sustainability Impact Loop   218

12.1 One-group pretest-posttest design for the impact of four
     climate change modules on student knowledge increase
     and personal support for climate policy   231

12.2 An application of a transdisciplinary framework   241

13.1 View of the 1.85 MW solar PV system at Madison
     College's Truax Campus   251

13.2 The 10-kW instructional sub-array for the Madison
     College solar PV system (top), and the associated
     ADA-compliant doorway and ramp (bottom)   260

Tables

3.1   Meaningful sustainable practices on college campuses listed by ease of adoption   55

8.1   Key sectors for impact entrepreneurship   143

8.2   The practices of sustainability knowledge orchestration   146

10.1   Names and roles of interviewees   186

11.1   GCNYC curricula revisions for M.S. business for social impact & sustainability   216

11.2   Curriculum revision for M.S. in sustainable fashion   217

11.3   Recommendations to leaders in higher education   221

12.1   Climate change learning modules from climate science to policy   230

12.2   Pre-assessment and post-assessment of students' understanding of global warming   233

12.3   Pre-assessment and post-assessment of students' understanding of global policy   235

13.1   Useful solar and energy modeling software resources for schools seeking to implement solar PV projects   255

13.2   Madison College's solar roadmap team rankings of motivations for solar energy   265

13.3   Stakeholder table for Madison College's solar roadmap   267

13.4   Ten steps to complete a solar roadmap strategic plan   269

Contributors

Alessia Argiolas is a Post-doctoral Researcher at the Technical University of Munich, Germany, and Research Coordinator at the TUM SEED Center, and holds a Ph.D. in Management from the Catholic University of Milan, Italy. Her research focuses on sustainable entrepreneurship and social impact, primarily in the Global South. She has published in the *Journal of Business Venturing* and *Business Research Quarterly*. Her professional experience is in fostering global academic collaboration between the north and south.

Said Benamar (Ph.D.) lectures and consults in organizational behavior and educational leadership. He works as the Academic Director of Executive Education at the International University of Casablanca in Morocco and contributes as a research fellow at the INTI International university in Malaysia. He obtained his doctorate in Education, from Walden University. His involvement in international academic transformative projects and his travels to Africa have helped him support his research on how to reshape education in the 21st century.

Thomas S. Benson is a Postdoctoral Research Associate at Pacific Northwest National Laboratory, and his research focuses on: energy, environmental, and intergenerational justice; decision-making models and community engagement; energy security and resilience; and planning, siting and permitting renewable and nuclear technologies. In 2023, Thomas received the EDF Climate Corps Environmental Justice Award and, in 2022, he received the AASHE Student Sustainability Award. Thomas earned his Ph.D. in Political Science and International Relations from the University of Delaware in 2023.

Gustavo Birollo (Ph.D.) is an Associate Professor in the Department of Management at the Faculty of Business Administration at Laval University. His research focuses on strategy implementation, strategy-as-practice, and middle managers and has been published in leading academic outlets such as the *European Journal of Management* and *International Journal of Project Management*. Prior to joining the academia, he worked as a project manager in the agro-industry in South America, North America and Europe.

Katja Brundiers is a Clinical Associate Professor at the School of Sustainability, College of Global Futures, at Arizona State University. Dr.

Brundiers, holding a doctorate degree in sustainability science, researches how to design professional education that integrates sustainability education and disaster management seeking to reduce disaster risk while advancing sustainability and resilience. In her teaching, she explores how key competencies in sustainability can be fostered through whole-person and project-based courses in collaboration with practitioners.

María Castillo is the Social and Environmental Impact Director at IESEG School of Management, and Assistant Professor in the Management and Society Department. She received her Ph.D. from Kedge Business School in France and is responsible for the development and implementation of the sustainability strategy at IESEG. Her research interests include sustainability in higher education, change management for sustainability, and the role of technology and innovation as a driver for sustainability.

Frank G.A. de Bakker is a full Professor at IÉSEG School of Management in Lille, France. He earned his Ph.D. at the University of Twente, the Netherlands. He studies interactions between activist groups and firms on issues of corporate social responsibility. He also studies firms' responses to such interactions, examining corporate political activity and the role of sustainability managers within firms. His research appeared in journals such as the *Academy of Management Review*, *Journal of Management Studies*, and *Business & Society and Organization Studies*.

Gastón de los Reyes studies and teaches international business and strategy with particular interest in questions of sustainability, governance, and ethics at Northeastern University's D'Amore-McKim School of Business. Previously, Dr. de los Reyes was Glasgow Caledonian New York College's first full-time faculty member, helping to update and expand GCNYC's innovative M.S. programs. Before earning his Ph.D. in Business Ethics from the Wharton School, he practiced corporate law and studied philosophy.

Susana Esper is an Assistant Professor at IESEG School of Management. She received her Ph.D. from HEC Montreal. Her research interests lie at the intersection of sustainability, strategic management, and organizational theory. She focuses on how the role of governments affects CSR, and on how individuals participate in the implementation of CSR and sustainability strategies in their organizations.

Krista Hiser (Ph.D.) currently serves as the Senior Lead and Advisor for Sustainability Education at the Global Council for Science and the Environment. Formerly the director of the University of Hawai'i System Center for Sustainability Across the Curriculum, she teaches writing and literature at Kapi'olani Community College, with an emphasis on sustainability, climate education, and community resilience. She received her doctoral degree in Educational Administration from the University of Hawai'i at Mānoa.

Younsung Kim (Ph.D.) is a Professor at George Mason University's Department of Environmental Science and Policy. Her research primarily focuses on environmental policy, business sustainability, and climate and energy policy. She has published her work in reputable journals, including the *Public Administration Review* and *Business and Politics*. Additionally, she has edited a book called *Foundational Readings in Environmental Policy*. With her interest in environmental education, she also studies innovative teaching methods for environmental policy and climate change.

Jordan King is a Ph.D. Candidate at Arizona State University in the School of Sustainability and College of Global Futures, where he explores ways to design, facilitate, and evaluate innovations in transdisciplinary sustainability-focused teaching, learning, and assessment. In connection with his scholarship, Jordan is a Graduate Research Fellow for the Global Council for Science and the Environment and a founding member of the Greater Phoenix Regional Center of Expertise on Education for Sustainable Development.

Jacqueline LeBlanc (Ph.D.) is an experienced leader in higher education with expertise in academic affairs, accreditation, assessment, and strategic planning. Dr. LeBlanc's broad experience and expertise in higher education has developed through her work with the Middle States Commission, the New York State Education Department, and the American Council on Education. As Vice President & Provost of Glasgow Caledonian New York College, she built a comprehensive strategy to focus the college mission on social justice and sustainability.

Michael J. Pawlish is an Assistant Professor of Management at the School of Business and Digital Media at Georgian Court University in New Jersey. He holds a Ph.D. from Montclair State University in New Jersey. He completed an MBA from San Francisco State University and an MS in International Environmental Science from Lund University in Sweden. His research interests are in organizational culture and the intersection of business and sustainability.

Kimberly M. Post (Ph.D.) is the Associate Dean of Environmental Graduate Studies at Unity Environmental University. Throughout her career in higher education, she has supported faculty and students with sustainability-focused community-based learning and research projects. Her peer-reviewed work has been published in various academic journals, including *Sustainability: The Journal of Record* and *Sustainability and Climate Change*. She authored the seminal curriculum guide *A Settled Mind* (2007) and has contributed to several anthologies. Her research interests include sustainability education, ecopeda-gogy, trans-systemic knowledge systems, and human–nature relational values assessment.

Jason C. Senjem, Ph.D., is Professor and Chair of the Management Department at St. Ambrose University in Davenport, IA, US. His work focuses on entre-preneurship and sustainability, especially on how organizations can use inno-vative work practices to make the world a better place. He enjoys connecting students to the local community with service learning, offering real-life sus-tainability projects, leading students on study abroad to Italy, and partnering with organizations in pursuing sustainability goals.

Paul Shrivastava (Ph.D.) is Professor of Management and Organizations at the Smeal College of Business at The Pennsylvania State University. Until July 2022 he was also the university's Chief Sustainability Officer and Director of the Sustainability Institute. Prior to this he served as the first Executive Director of Future Earth global research platform. He is the Co-President of the Club of Rome. At the ICN Business School, Nancy, France, he founded the UNESCO Chair on Integrating Arts and Science for Implementing the SDGs. He was advisor to the Research Institute for Humanity and Nature, Kyoto, and Network for Education and Research in Peace and Sustainability at Hiroshima University. Paul has over 40 years' experience as an academic, advisor, and entrepreneur. He was part of the team that founded Hindustan Computer Ltd., one of India's largest computer companies. He founded the journal *Organization and Environment* (published by Sage Publications). He was founding President and CEO of eSocrates, Inc., a knowledge management software company, and the founding Chair of the Organizations and the Natural Environment Division of the Academy of Management. He has published 19 books and over 110 peer-reviewed papers in research and scholarly journals.

Mark Starik (Ph.D. University of Georgia) is Senior Lecturer for the University of Wisconsin Extended Campus, teaching both graduate and undergraduate courses in its Sustainability Management Program, is a Contributing Faculty member of the Walden University School of Health Policy and Administration doctoral program, and is the Editor of its *Journal of Sustainable Social Change*. He has published dozens of academic and practitioner articles, books, cases, editorials, curated volumes and special journal issues, and other works on the topics of sustainability, corporate social responsibility, and climate action, was a co-Editor-in-Chief of the journal *Organization & Environment* and was a founding co-organizer and subsequent Chair of the Academy of Management Organizations and the Natural Environment (ONE) Division. Mark has founded and directed several university-related sustainability insti-tutes, centers, and programs and has advised multiple sustainability-oriented student groups. In addition, he has served in management and energy researcher capacities for a half-dozen US business, government, and nonprofit organizations, has been an active volunteer in several sustainability-oriented organizations, and has provided financial and other support to numerous international sustainability causes.

Bart van Hoof is Associate Professor at the School of Management of the Los Andes University, Colombia. He holds a Ph.D. in Industrial ecology. His research and teaching interests are focused on dissemination of environmental management practices in industrial and grid-food systems in emerging markets. He has served as senior advisor of the national struggles on circular economy of several Latin American governments, and used to be the environmental director of Ecopetrol.

Kenneth A. Walz (Ph.D.) teaches Science, Engineering, and Renewable Energy at Madison Area Technical College, where he serves as the Director of the CREATE Energy Center funded by the National Science Foundation. He earned his doctorate in Environmental Chemistry and Technology at the University of Wisconsin, and has conducted research in solar photovoltaics, lithium-ion batteries, and other clean energy applications with Rayovac, the University of Rochester, Argonne National Laboratory and the National Renewable Energy Lab.

Sjors Witjes (Ph.D.) is Associate Professor of Organizational Sustainability and Circularity at Radboud University in the Netherlands. Sjors has been part of corporate sustainability and innovation processes applying transdisciplinary approaches resulting in research and education that supports organizations to reflect on their contribution to a more sustainable society.

Julia Wolny (Ph.D.) is Associate Professor in Responsible Marketing Strategy and Director of Impact Initiatives at EADA Business School Barcelona. Her expertise lies in responsible marketing, sustainable transformation and digital innovation for good. She has published in the field of marketing strategy and participatory digital ecosystems in top journals (e.g., Journal of Marketing Management) and books (e.g., SAGE Handbook of Digital Marketing). Through her international experience she worked on a portfolio of transformative research and advisory projects in education, retail, publishing, creative and cultural industries.

Jean Wu (J.D.) is founding Director of the Green Office Sustainability Programs at Franklin University Switzerland, where she leads a team of Green Office Scholars in implementing projects and programs that range across curricular, co-curricular and organizational sustainability efforts. Jean received her Juris Doctorate from the University of California at Berkeley

School of Law, with a specialization in environmental law. She graduated with highest honors, was inducted into the Order of the Coif and was twice awarded the American Jurisprudence Award. Beyond Franklin, Jean serves on the Advisory Council of the Association for the Advancement of Sustainability in Higher Education. Jean's current research interests include Environmental, Social and Governance (ESG) strategy and the evolving area of sustainability reporting.

Acknowledgments

We, the co-editors, acknowledge all of our author/contributors, reviewers, employers/universities, students, faculty colleagues, family members, and friends, and anyone else in our respective networks who have incorporated significant sustainability actions into their lives and who assisted us in developing and publishing this book.

1. Introduction

Mark Starik and Paul Shrivastava

INTRODUCTION

Welcome to our co-edited book on *Sustainable Universities and Colleges*! We are pleased to have been involved in crafting this book with a wide range of contributors, including contributing authors, informed contacts, former academic and professional co-authors, participating reviewers, and the staff of Edward Elgar Publishing, Inc. We want to express our appreciation and admiration to them and to all university and college stakeholders who have attempted and, to whatever extent, succeeded in advancing sustainability within and/or beyond their respective institutions of higher education! Though many definitions of sustainability have been forwarded, we define sustainability as the ability to achieve and maintain long-term quality of life for all humans in current and future generations and for life, in general, on our planet, short-, medium-, and long-term.

With each passing day, month, and year, the need for both environmental and socio-economic sustainability appears more urgent and vital than ever. Numerous climate change impacts and crises, continuing extinctions of a wide variety of species, socio-economic displacement, discrimination, and inequality, human overconsumption and overpopulation, and multiple other unsustainable conditions continue unabated, worsening over time. If one considers how society is progressing on the 17 United Nations Sustainable Development Goals (SDGs), according to the UN 2023 Midpoint Report:

> **At the midpoint of the 2030 Agenda, all of the SDGs are seriously off track.** From 2015 to 2019, the world made some progress on the SDGs, although this was already vastly insufficient to achieve the goals. Since the outbreak of the pandemic in 2020 and other simultaneous crises, SDG progress has stalled globally. In most high-income countries (HICs), automatic stabilizers, emergency expenditure, and recovery plans mitigated the impacts of these multiple crises on socioeconomic outcomes. Only limited progress is being made on the environmental and biodiversity goals, including SDG 12 (Responsible Consumption and Production), SDG 13 (Climate Action), SDG 14 (Life Below Water), and SDG 15 (Life on Land), even in countries that are largely to blame for the climate and biodiversity crises.

The disruptions caused by these multiple crises has aggravated fiscal-space issues in low-income countries (LICs) and in lower-middle income countries (LMICs), leading to a reversal in progress on several goals and indicators. (bolded emphasis added by co-editors) (Sachs, Lafortune, Fuller, & Drumm, 2023)

Never before has it seemed so imperative that "(u)niversities and colleges, as institutions of knowledge acquisition, development, utilization, and dissemination, are uniquely positioned to advance the important values of their respective societies" (Starik, Schaeffer, Berman, & Hazelwood, 2002, p. 335), especially sustainability values. Universities/colleges, perhaps uniquely, have the knowledge, the legitimacy, and the resources needed to make significant transformative impacts on individuals and systems in their respective communities (Shrivastava, 2020). Some universities have annual budgets greater than the GDP of many countries. Their own ecological footprints need serious reduction. Our hope is that the chapter contributions in this book help to propagate that societal value and transformation to spark and disseminate an ever-increasing number of potential approaches to that end.

THE LAY OF THE LAND OF UNIVERSITIES AND COLLEGES: SIGNIFICANT BREADTH AND VARIETY

Sustainability, in the many ways it has been defined over the last several decades, appears to be undergoing a kind of "coming of age" metamorphosis in the present decade. In Western thought, one could trace its roots back to at least the Transcendental era, with its attention to nature, both human and other (Caradonna, 2016). But, of course, many cultures, including indigenous cultures, have given significant attention to the long-term health and well-being of human individuals and collectivities, as well as of the many living species with whom we share this planet (Haraway, 2016).

Before we describe the chapters in this book, we want to acknowledge the breadth and diversity of the topic of sustainable universities and colleges. We recognize the thousands of institutions of higher education around the world, including recent startups and centuries-old establishments in all three sectors (public, non-profit, and for-profit). We acknowledge that higher education institutions exist in multiple countries on every continent (including one in Antarctica which has a botanical garden!). There are many different types of such entities, including both standalone and affiliated universities and colleges, vocational and technical colleges, online-only institutions, and those with a highly specialized mission, such as those serving religious, military, and other special interests. Higher education institutions also differ in the type, length, and level of educational programs they offer. We highlight this institutional variety to emphasize that a wide variety of sustainability approaches are likely possible in the education sector. Therefore, we generally support a similarly wide variety of sustainability goals, strategies, and results in that sector.

Yet another aspect of this sectoral diversity are the multiple functions with which all of these institutions serve, including research, education, endowment/investment, community membership, facilities, operations, and maintenance, goods and services consumption, and waste management, all of which could have sustainability connections. Finally, we also want to highlight the grand diversity and breadth of the set of stakeholders connected to this sector's actual and potential sustainability. In addition to present-day and near-term future multiple types of students (and their families), faculty, alumni, administrators and trustees, staff, suppliers, vendors, funding sources, neighbors, and actual and potential employers of their students, we suggest all due attention to the longer-term future of these and perhaps additional university and college stakeholders.

The most obvious internal variation of potential sustainability advancement in the higher education institutional space is the variability of disciplines or educational subject areas. While all disciplines might have at least some orientation or connection to environmental and/or socio-economic sustainability, others such as the natural and social sciences and other disciplines that cover those general areas likely address them in some depth. For, while environmental and/or socio-economic sustainability could conceivably be incorporated into virtually any higher education discipline, for some, these might be core and, for others, supplemental. The goal here should be educating future generations to live sustainable lives. Hence, we advocate incorporating sustainability in both concentrated and distributed approaches, even a combination of the two, given the urgent imperative of advancing sustainability as much and as soon as possible.

Speaking of variety, while we co-editors cast a very wide net for submissions on sustainable university and colleges, we received an array of submission topics which clustered into several interesting sub-groupings. First, we are pleased to lead off with two chapter contributions related to sustainability systems and strategies that focus on the big picture of leading toward sustainability in higher education institutions. Second, several accepted submissions focused on a wide assortment of stakeholders involved in the movement of universities and colleges in more sustainable directions. Third, though we distributed our initial Call for Submissions very broadly across multiple disciplines, sectors, and other categories, the business and management fields, with which we co-editors have long been associated, attracted more contributor attention than any other disciplines or sectors. Our last category is sustainability education, which includes three highly differentiated contributions. [Regarding these last two topics of sustainability in Management/Business and in Education, we want to commend readers to another co-edited source that integrates those topics (Arevalo & Mitchell, 2017)]. As broad as the swath of these submissions and categories are, many sustainable university and college topics that we suggested in our initial Call for Submissions are still available (and needing) to be addressed by our readers and others. These include sustainable university and college research, investments, community, suppliers, vendors, and career services.

ROOTS OF A SUSTAINABLE UNIVERSITY/COLLEGE?

Given the vast breadth of higher education institutions, defining those that are sustainable is a daunting task and we co-editors have our own separate and joint ideas on both that definition and on how those entities should act ideally. As indicated earlier, institutions of higher education present themselves as a wide array of types, missions, operations, and other factors, and those that might be described as sustainable exhibit the same diversity. In addition to the obvious differences in location, student/faculty/staff makeup, size, and culture, sustainable universities and colleges include a wide breadth of specializations, combinations, missions, values, structures, practices, and impacts.

Despite the extensive differences in geography, mission, governance, disciplinary focus, educational programs, operations, etc., colleges and universities have in common the mandate to create new knowledge and to educate. In doing so, most universities and colleges operate within the five root elements of research, operations, outreach to community, teaching, and students and other stakeholders. Integrating sustainability into each of these five entities is both possible and desirable (Shrivastava, 2020). The Times Higher Education has created a universities' ranking system that measures them on how these functions help achieve the Sustainable Development Goals (The Times Higher Education World University Rankings[1]).

If human society and HEIs are to become truly sustainable on this planet, the higher education sector needs to make its ROOTS (Research, Outreach, Operations, Teaching, and Students and other stakeholders) or core activities, sustainable. The general public and a host of rating organizations periodically assess if these institutions are sustainable enough, and, if not, what more needs to be done, such that educational institutions do not just follow society's actions but also help lead it toward sustainability.

Sustainable universities and colleges certainly at least need a strong focus on the future. They need to project what and how many students, faculty, and staff they will need to attract, at least a generation ahead in time. What career and professional tracks will students need to master, and what faculty and other staff knowledge bases and skills will be available to meet those career preparation needs in a climate- and sustainability-challenged world? Importantly, universities in high-income countries must question whether it is sustainable to

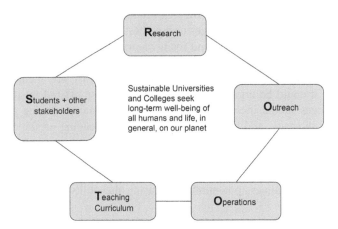

Figure 1.1   *ROOTS of sustainable universities*

continue producing students who as citizens will have a carbon footprint that is many times the world average.

Those questions will likely also be relevant regarding sustainability-centered careers. Sustainable universities and colleges could contribute to the formation and cultivation of those sustainability-centered career tracks and sustainable lifestyles. For instance, it appears obvious that those careers involving climate change mitigation and adaptation, such as renewable energy engineers and wildlife protection/relocation specialists, will be in high demand in the next few generations. The same could be said for human relations and health specialist careers that focus on race relations, refugee resettlement, community health, human–animal health interactions, and traditional and social media and communications management. Sustainable universities and colleges in the near- and mid-term futures will likely need to be better integrated into their communities to play a more active role in shaping community health and welfare. They must sustainably engage all other university and college stakeholders, such as alumni, suppliers, and potential employers of their students, perhaps especially considering AI (artificial intelligence) and other technologies that will likely be available in those timeframes that could be used to help advance the sustainability of many universities and colleges and their respective stakeholders.

From a building and facilities perspective, the progressive digitalization of education and commerce calls for sustainable institutions of higher education to shrink their ecological footprints and increase their fostering of greater community inclusion. Similarly, for transportation footprints – universities need to ask how many of their students, faculty, and staff will be traveling to and from their campuses, and how many will be using air travel or video conferencing for their institution's (or their own career-building) business? How can the land these universities or colleges occupy best serve the values, practices, and results of both environmental and socio-economic sustainability?

Given the significant breadth of the sustainability topic, especially when both environmental and socio-economic sustainability are included in the concept, it could be argued that nearly every course offered by universities and colleges should include some sustainability content, varying in amount, duration, intensity, and other curricular factors depending on the course and instructor. Doing so would likely broaden and raise student awareness of the multiple aspects of the concept's values, practices, and impacts. It can also encourage holistic understanding that connects and integrates across course topics and disciplines, potentially increasing the utility and applications of sustainability.

Essentially, what is needed is the development of one or more internal sustainability cultures, however those cultures are defined (by location, sub-organization, stakeholder group, or some other collective recognition) with a mission of helping to promote sustainability both internally and externally to wider-scoped cultures. We co-editors have both been actively involved for a number of years in, for instance, promoting sustainability in the Academy of Management (AOM) in the initial form of the organizing of a sustainability-centered interest group, called Organizations and the Natural Environment (ONE), and subsequently as a division within the AOM. Members of that group not only researched and presented on sustainability topics, but they also were active in promoting sustainability research and practice within the larger organization. They examined the advisability of holding online, as opposed to in-person conferences, "greening" the in-person conferences, and encouraging wide participation, diversity, and leadership by academics from around the world.

Considerations of universities and colleges, given their size, typically focus on more macro-level concerns, such as campus buildings, the entering freshman and exiting graduate classes, faculty senate resolutions, and alumni association activities. But they could also include attention to more micro-level topics, such as individual sustainability, including that of their students, faculty, staff, suppliers, and alumni. Higher education institutions could promote sustainability values, practices, and impacts among individuals in each of these groups, perhaps after assessing their current sustainability orientations, attitudes, and behaviors. Individuals could then develop their own sustainability plans, request assistance from the institution in implementing those plans, and join with other individuals in refining, expanding, and implementing those plans.

However, certain likely individuals are key sustainability practitioners and proponents. These include top university and college administrators, highly visible institutional spokespersons, and, of course, faculty, particularly those in departments associated with sustainability. Sustainability leaders, like leaders, in general, need to "model the behavior" that they expect their stakeholders to follow. Indeed, this was the theme that emerged from a previous co-edited volume on *Personal Sustainability Practices* (Starik & Kanashiro, 2021). The faculty who submitted chapters to that volume appeared to generally hold the opinion that their own sustainability practices helped influence their students (and perhaps other stakeholders) to also adopt and promote sustainability practices.

We co-editors have also attempted to set personal sustainability examples for our respective stakeholders in a number of ways. These actions have included the selection and promotion of numerous energy efficiency practices in the transportation, buildings, and general consumption areas in our employer universities. Each of us has been actively and visibly engaged in promoting sustainability in our courses, departments, schools, and universities, as well as in external organizations with which we have worked. Our individual and collaborative research follows this same sustainability track.

Primarily, we contend that universities and colleges need to adopt and inspire sustainability-centered worldviews and values, by developing and implementing strategies that advance both environmental and socio-economic sustainability. These goals and strategies must create structures and advance processes that highlight leading-by-example. Institutional sustainability strategies and practices should cover the areas of infrastructure sustainability, research and curriculum integration, and internal and external stakeholder/community engagement. Finally, of course, these higher education institutions should be held accountable for setting and meeting the highest sustainability standards. Universities can help reduce the deficit in sustainable development mentioned earlier, by adopting a never-ending-improvement approach and leading a global sustainability revolution.

WHAT HAVE OUR AUTHORS CONTRIBUTED TO THE SUSTAINABLE UNIVERSITIES AND COLLEGES CONVERSATION?

Our very broad Call for Submissions resulted in the accepted submissions (chapters) found in this book, which were double-blind reviewed, and have been organized in the following four Sustainable University and College sustainability themes or categories: systems/strategies; stakeholders; business/management; and, education. Below is a listing of those chapters and a brief description of each.

Sustainability Systems/Strategy

In Chapter 2, Needs and Opportunities for Sustainability Programs in Higher Education: Insights from the Global Council for Science and the Environment's *Pathways toward Accreditation* Initiative, Jordan King, Katja Brundiers, and Krista Hiser address the micro, meso, and macro aspects and dimensions of changes they recommend to sustainability change leaders in higher education institutions. They suggest a number of positive strategies that include more experimentation and innovation, the integration of sustainability curricula with other sustainability higher education efforts, and the continued operationalization of successful sustainability practices.

In Chapter 3, Sustainable Practices as Innovation Adoption on Campus, Jason C. Senjem examines two case study small colleges' sustainability efforts, finding that one innovative approach, called The Idea Journey, and a multi-level sustainability model helped these organizations realize a number of their sustainability achievements. He also highlights the opportunities and challenges related to sustainability entrepreneurial and structural influencers.

Sustainability Stakeholders

In Chapter 4, Higher Education Institutions Can Do More To Lead Society Toward Resilience and Sustainability, Thomas Benson forwards seven institutional goals to help universities and colleges advance both environmental and socio-economic sustainability, including emphasizing interdisciplinary approaches and facilitation of student, faculty, and staff sustainability leadership. The author uses his own graduate student and Office of Sustainability staff experiences and the practices at other universities to develop a set of stakeholder-oriented best practices that serve to promote and integrate those goals, using devices such as a campus-wide cross-disciplinary survey of all faculty, to assess sustainability integration across all of his university's programs.

In Chapter 5, Transition 2026: Stakeholder Engagement and the Co-Construction of a Climate Strategy in a French Business School, María Castillo, Susana Esper, Gustavo Birollo, and Frank G.A. de Bakker describe an interesting and instructive stakeholder engagement process that involves significant climate sustainability considerations in the curricula, research, and operations of a French business school. The institution's transformation and planning processes include the engagement and empowerment of internal and external stakeholders who represented both proponents and opponents of strategic sustainable change. Finally, they offer a potentially useful list of lessons learned that would likely be relevant to sustainability efforts in other higher education institutions.

In Chapter 6, Crystallization of a University's Sustainability Efforts around Laudato Si': A Case Study of Opportunities and Challenges, Michael J. Pawlish highlights the Laudato Si' ("Praise Be") efforts and results in a case study of a Catholic university. That institution focuses on three main internal stakeholders – students, faculty, and staff – and their sustainability opportunities and challenges.

In Chapter 7, A Student-driven Approach to Establishing Sustainability Programs at Colleges and Universities: Lessons from the Green Office Movement in Europe, Jean Wu examines that student stakeholder program, including campus infrastructure and curricula. She believes the sustainability skills and experience students gain in this program warrants the Movement's expansion beyond Europe.

Sustainability and Management (and Business)

Though we distributed our initial Call for Submissions widely, the sector from which we received the most submissions was the Management/Business discipline. We accepted four quality submissions that focused on that category of higher education institutions and summarize them briefly below.

In Chapter 8, How Universities Enable Sustainable Solutions to Persistent Social Problems in Africa, Alessia Argiolas and Said Benamar present the case of the Pan African University Alliance, focusing on its "impact entrepreneurship" MBA program and its efforts to scale up that program to the continental level. One unique feature of this effort is the active involvement of alumni in several parts of this interesting collaborative program.

In Chapter 9, Schools of Management Making an Impact: Operationalization Mechanisms and Methods for Contributing to Organizational Change, Bart van Hoof and Sjors Witjes assess the need of schools of management to take a transdisciplinary approach to, what they call, responsible management learning. They forward three mutually reinforcing mechanisms of legitimacy, resource supply, and capacity-building and advocate combining these with several learning approaches, including experience-based learning, to foster sustainable change at multiple levels of society.

In Chapter 10, Sustainable Transformation in Business and Management Higher Education: An Analysis of Global and European Collaborative Initiatives for Positive Impact, Julia Wolny provides descriptions of several collaborative initiatives whose purposes revolve around higher education sustainability. She forwards a "Collaborative Canvas" tool for these and other sustainability collaborations to use to assist such organizations in fully achieving the multiple benefits, including sustainability benefits, of higher education collaboration.

In Chapter 11, Disrupting the Business Curriculum for Sustainability and the Common Good: The Glasgow Caledonian New York College Experiment, Jacqueline LeBlanc and Gastón de los Reyes describe the issues experienced by and the particular strategic features of a sustainable business school startup in New York City. They particularly focus on the unique professionalism aspects of the sustainability students and the practitioner experiences and orientations of their faculty.

Sustainability Education

Of course, education is typically the main sub-mission of universities and colleges, so we selected three submissions on sustainability education to conclude this book. In Chapter 12, Education for Climate Change: An Andragogical Approach with a Transdisciplinary Framework, Younsung Kim explores the use of a modular approach on different, though related, climate topics to gauge both adult-student understanding of sustainable climate issues and student support for regulatory climate policies. Transdisciplinary modular approaches, she found, increased adult-student levels of understanding of both climate science and climate policy.

In Chapter 13, Enlightened Education: Advancing the Sustainability of Schools, Colleges, and Universities by Deployment of Solar Photovoltaic Infrastructure, Kenneth A. Walz presents the potential opportunities and means of utilizing solar photovoltaic technology to benefit educational institutions, their students, and the general public in the study of a number of sustainability subjects. He forwards a "Solar Road Map" for educational institutions, once again, that could benefit both the institutions (with lower cost renewable energy) and their stakeholders (with "up-close" information on those technologies).

In Chapter 14, Decolonizing Post-Secondary Sustainability Education in the Anthropocene, Kimberly M. Post explores the evolving nature of Sustainability Education in its movement away from Anthropocentrism toward Ecocentrism, with increased recognition of indigenous worldviews. She advocates that universities begin to change to become "pluriversities", providing real-world, high-impact learning experiences as active and participatory community hubs.

RECOMMENDATIONS FOR FURTHER RESEARCH ON SUSTAINABLE UNIVERSITIES AND COLLEGES

Building on the collection of works in this book, the overall message that emerges is that many universities and colleges are moving toward becoming more sustainability oriented. They need to envision those types of systems and to develop strategies, preferably in collaboration with stakeholders. They need to co-create related structures and processes to realize sustainability visions and values. Along those lines and focusing on climate sustainability, we recommend to our readers an excellent source of sustainability education institutional visions in *Universities on Fire: Higher Education in the Climate Crisis*, by Bryan Alexander. One of many of those imaginings has been labeled "solarpunk", which is an emerging Sci-Fi genre and social movement, that includes beneficial technologies and healthful relationships both for humans and for other life on Earth. Hopefully, taking into account some of the sustainability opportunities and challenges mentioned throughout this book, both the individual higher education institutions and the sector overall will realize the need for and the calling to become society's sustainability leaders rather than followers. Given the scope of the sustainability challenge, leading society toward sustainability is such a vital but daunting challenge that every one of us at every level will need to step up to that existential responsibility (Starik, Rands, & Deason, 2023).

Though our contributing authors presented a good deal of excellent, useful information on the topic of sustainable universities and colleges, we want to conclude this introductory chapter with several issues we raised in our initial Call for Submissions that we think deserve even more attention from both researchers and practitioners, in fact, from all stakeholders, who are interested in advancing the state of knowledge and practice regarding sustainable universities and colleges. While several of our contributing authors touched on a number of these topics, we, the co-editors, think these subjects bear some additional consideration from all of our readers, as well, so we are including those (or variants of those) same questions from our Call below.

How can and should transdisciplinary, activist, and/or transformative mindsets and results-oriented game-changing strategies be developed and employed, especially by university and college administrators and trustees who are charged with governing these institutions?

How can higher education curricula, research, and external stakeholder outreach functions be both more sustainability-focused and better integrated to help resolve or at least address sustainability crises?

How might large public universities collaborate not only with one another but also with smaller specialized colleges, such as technical, community, and on-line colleges, and/or with other types of organizations, such as associations, thinktanks, and consultancies, to advance sustainability both internally and externally?

How can these institutions serve as model sustainability organizations, including in their physical operations, to help other societal entities learn how to contribute more to sustainability solutions and less to sustainability problems?

What will the university or college of the future look like, do, and/or achieve if it is to become society's sustainability role model?

What transitional steps would be necessary to achieve that sustainability leadership result and status?

While we did not mention it in our Call, among the more inventive ways to foster attention to sustainability in academia is to start and continue to offer the opportunity for stakeholders to participate in one or more sustainability book clubs in which either sustainability non-fiction or sustainability fiction books (or both types) are selected, read, and discussed. One model to follow is the AASHE Ultimate Cli-Fi book club, which is led by one of our contributors (Krista Hiser) and in which one of the co-editors (Mark Starik) has been a member for several years (A Cli-Fi Book Club for College Educators and Sustainability Advocates (aashe.org)[2]). Individual and institutional sustainability experiences and ideas are often discussed in such clubs with the potential for motivating sustainability action and follow-through. Of course, multiple media, in addition to books, could be a club's communication centerpiece and another of this book's co-editors (Paul Shrivastava) is actively involved in a podcast he curated, called Managing Sustainable Futures,[3] focusing on the contributions of climate fiction to climate science and policy. Video and many other media could play similar "club" roles in sparking sustainability in academia (and elsewhere). However, before we move on from the subject of books, we want to encourage readers of this book to consider several excellent sustainability-oriented books that could be used to advance sustainability in higher education institutions. These include *The Climate Book* created by Greta Thunberg, *Drawdown*, edited by Paul Hawken, *The Uninhabitable Earth* written by David Wallace-Wells, *The Ministry for the Future* written by Kim Stanley Robinson, *The Book of Hope: A Survival Guide for Trying Times* co-written by Doug Adams and Jane Goodall, *Being the Change: Live Well and Spark a Climate Revolution* written (and lived by) Peter Kalmus, and *This Changes Everything: Capitalism and the Climate,* written by Naomi Klein, any of which would be excellent selections for a sustainability book (or other media) club.

Along those same lines, considering regional and/or national sustainability centers, collaborative groups of sustainable universities and colleges that are co-located or are focused on particular sustainability topics, might combine to share resources, information, and plans to advance sustainability both within and outside their institutions. Such centers could use various social media to share sustainability information, such as the United Nations Principles of Responsible Management Education (PRME) online Climate Literacy Training program. These centers could also develop programs to encourage both traditional and non-traditional cultural attention on sustainability topics, with the intent of garnering more attention to sustainability in all media, in the arts, and in public gathering locations.

Numerous other higher education sustainability topics to consider include land management, including the development and cultivation of arboreta and community organic gardens; water usage; building restoration; circular economy participation; travel alternatives; green sanctuaries; animal welfare; vendor, contractor, supplier, and athletic event footprints; student green investment funds; green labs; indigenous programs; and hosting sustainability conferences, online or in-person. Many more possible sustainability topics associated with dozens of universities and colleges can be found in the Association for the Advancement of Sustainability in Higher Education, or AASHE, STARS (Sustainability Tracking, Assessment & Rating System) sustainability assessment program.

In sum, we co-editors of this book hope readers have been motivated to start, join, and/or strengthen efforts to advance sustainability in higher education institutions, and we welcome all reader feedback and strongly recommend all readers join us and those institutions in participating in the advancement of the concept and practice of sustainable universities and colleges.

NOTES

1. https:// www . timeshighe reducation .com/ world -university -rankings/ 2023/ world-ranking
2. https://www.aashe.org/calendar/cli-fi-2022/
3. https://msfutures.net/#Homepage

REFERENCES

Adams, D. & Goodall, J. (2021). *The book of hope: A survival guide for trying times*. Celadon Books.

Alexander, B. (2023). *Universities on fire: Higher education in the climate crisis*. Johns Hopkins University Press.

Arevalo, J.A. & Mitchell, S.F. (Eds.) (2017). *Handbook of sustainability in management education: In search of a multidisciplinary, innovative, and integrated approach*. Edward Elgar Publishing.

Caradonna, J. (2016). *Sustainability: A history*. Oxford University Press.

Haraway, D. (2016). *Staying with the trouble: Making kin in the Chthulucene*. Duke University Press.

Hawken, P. (2017). *Drawdown: The most comprehensive plan ever proposed to reverse global warming*. New York, New York: Penguin Books.

Kalmus, P. (2017). *Being the change: Live well and spark a climate revolution*. New Society Publishers.

Klein, N. (2014). *This changes everything: Capitalism and the climate*. Simon & Schuster.

Robinson, K.S. (2020). *Ministry for the future*. Orbit Books.

Sachs, J.D., Lafortune, G., Fuller, G., & Drumm, E. (2023). *Implementing the SDG stimulus. Sustainable development report 2023*. Dublin University Press. 10.25546/102924. https://dashboards.sdgindex.org/chapters/executive-summary

Shrivastava, P. (2020). Global sustainability in the Anthropocene: The role of universities. In G. MaGill (Ed.), *The global sustainability challenge*. Cambridge Scholar's Publishing.

Starik, M. & Kanashiro, P. (2021). *Personal sustainability practices: Faculty Approaches to walking the sustainability talk and living the U.N. SDGs*. Edward Elgar Publishing.

Starik, M., Rands, G.P., & Deason, J.P. (2023). Introduction. In Starik, Rands, Deason, and Kanashiro, P. (Eds.), *The handbook of multi-level climate action: Sparking and sustaining transformative approaches*. Edward Elgar Publishing.

Starik, M., Schaeffer, T., Berman, P., & Hazelwood, A. (2002). Initial environmental project characterizations of four U.S. universities. *International Journal of Sustainability in Higher Education, 3*(4), 335–345.

Thunberg, G. (2022). *The Climate Book*. Penguin Press.

Wallace-Wells, D. (2019). *The uninhabitable Earth: Life after warming*. Penguin Random House.

2. Needs and opportunities for sustainability programs in higher education: insights from the Global Council for Science and the Environment's *Pathways toward Accreditation* initiative

Jordan King, Katja Brundiers and Krista Hiser

INTRODUCTION

The sustainability challenges faced by societies around the world continue to intensify and expand, amplifying the pressure for viable solutions and comprehensive action (Engler et al., 2021). In addressing these challenges, education can play a vital role in operationalizing transformational strategies to advance individual and institutional capacities to achieve sustainability goals (Sachs et al., 2019). Higher education institutions have increasingly recognized this pivotal responsibility, seeking to develop knowledge for public benefit, advance equity, and strengthen connections to societal impacts such as sustainability (Guzmán-Valenzuela et al., 2020). As a result, sustainability-focused learning opportunities have intensified in their importance to prepare students as emergent professionals and change agents (SDSN, 2020). This has led to a proliferation of sustainability and sustainability-related degree programs and certificates (AASHE, 2023). But with the heightened attention and increased spread of sustainability-related teaching and learning has come a need to better understand the scope and scale of sustainability programs in higher education, as well as their quality, accessibility, and impact in fostering more sustainable futures. If higher education institutions are to shift from following societal trends that emphasize sustainability goals to serving as leaders in stewarding these ambitions for society, they will need to examine their existing needs and leverage opportunities to enhance innovation and resilience in sustainability programs and beyond.

The question of how to define these programs has persisted over the past two decades, with a series of reports by the Global Council for Science and the Environment (GCSE) tracking the evolution from 13 relevant programs in 2010 to 2,361 in 2017 (Vincent, 2010; Vincent et al., 2012; 2017). Today, the Carnegie Classification of Instructional Programs defines sustainability programs as "focused on the concept of sustainability from an interdisciplinary perspective", which covers areas such as "sustainable development, environmental policies, ethics, ecology, landscape architecture, city and regional planning, economics, natural resources, sociology, and anthropology" (NCES, 2023). This wide-reaching definition has led to an even greater diversity of topically focused approaches to sustainability education in higher education. By 2023, the Association for the Advancement of Sustainability in Higher Education's community hub database contained 647 programs specifically focused on sustainability studies or science, which expands to 3,271 sustainability-related programs across different disciplines such as environmental studies and sciences, resilience, energy, and others (AASHE, 2023).

This profusion of approaches to sustainability in higher education has resulted in challenges in defining the parameters, features, goals, and outcomes of programs in the field. Approaches to sustainability-related teaching and learning commonly take several different strategies, such as integrating sustainability across the curriculum, through specialization degrees in different disciplines (e.g., Sustainable Architecture, Fashion Design and Sustainability), or Sustainability Science programs that seek to support students to develop as sustainability professionals capable of solving problems across a range of sectors (government, nonprofit, corporate, and academic) by integrating environmental, social, and economic concerns (Kates, 2011; Miller et al. 2014). This diversity has led to the diffusion of sustainability as a key topic and focus in higher education, yet lingering questions remain about quality standards for sustainability programs, their accessibility to diverse and marginalized populations, and how they contribute to local and global impact by cultivating citizens and professionals who can address complex sustainability challenges. As a result, the field remains unconsolidated and incoherent, with its full realization across diverse institutions unfulfilled (O'Byrne et al., 2015). Establishing cross-cutting best practices for sustainability programs would help administrators, faculty, students, employers, and other university and community stakeholders to act as leaders in advancing societal change for sustainability by better understanding and articulating the value of these programs across a range of program design and evaluation approaches.

A close examination is warranted as to how sustainability programs in higher education are defined and developed to strengthen their *design* and *evaluation*.

The purpose of this chapter is to present a synthesis of the fundamental *needs* and emergent *opportunities* for sustainability programs in higher education in order to outline potential strategies to enhance their *quality*, *accessibility*, and *impact*. To do so, we consider different *drivers* and *areas* of change to better understand how transformation can be facilitated across program, institutional, and systemic levels. We draw from an analysis of the literature and our practical experience with the Global Council for Science and the Environment's *Pathways toward Accreditation* initiative. This initiative provides an example of how best practices in program design and evaluation can be facilitated through a network of program leaders and other stakeholders to address the needs and opportunities of sustainability programs in higher education. We hope that the insights and visions that we share can be adapted by program leaders in navigating the complex landscape of designing and evaluating their sustainability programs, while meeting the needs of stakeholders from students to administrators to employers. By presenting a set of needs and opportunities we illustrate potential pathways for advancing strategic and systematic change in strengthening sustainability programs and the ways that they generate transformative outcomes for higher education institutions and society.

FACILITATING CHANGE FOR SUSTAINABILITY IN HIGHER EDUCATION

Change in higher education occurs through actions across different levels in order to create systemic transformation that reorients the educational, research, operations, leadership, and engagement dimensions of higher education institutions (Wals, 2014), particularly through an emphasis on justice, equity, diversity, and inclusion (NASEM, 2020). Building on transition theories for transformative change related to sustainability in higher education (Stephens et al., 2008) and social change more broadly (Geels, 2004), recent work has further explored this area. Bamberg and colleagues (2021) have described a model for how these transformations can occur, where innovations start at the *micro*-level (individual sustainability programs) and gain momentum, beginning to influence the *macro*-level (the field of sustainability in higher education) and create pressures on the *meso*-level (higher education institutions) that destabilize structures and norms in order to create windows of opportunity for niche innovations to be tested and implemented, contributing to systemic transformation (the reorientation of higher education towards sustainability).

Changes across micro-, meso-, and macro-levels are driven by three primary *change drivers* that compel transformations in higher education, specifically as embodied in sustainability programs. First, the myriad complexities, uncertainties, and challenges of *sustainability issues* such as climate change, biodiversity loss, social injustice, and overconsumption urge changes in how higher education institutions operate as well as the abilities of the graduates that they produce (Shephard, 2015). Second, *broader trends in higher education*, especially around social responsibility, tether institutions to contributing to public good and how global agendas, such as sustainability, are pursued in corporations, communities, and beyond (Barnett & Guzmán-Valenzuela, 2022). Third, *societal stakeholders* motivate responses from higher education, such as employers who increasingly face a "skills gap" between the emergent professional positions focused on sustainability and the capabilities of graduates, due to misalignment and misapprehension of the rigor, availability, and outcomes of sustainability-related learning opportunities (Boone & Seto, 2023). These three forces act as *change drivers*, mediating the *change areas* that program leaders – such as directors, instructors, and staff – negotiate in order to translate needs and opportunities into actionable strategies for program design and evaluation.

Based on our experience with the GCSE *Pathways toward Accreditation* initiative, and derived from an analysis of the literature, we have identified four *change areas* that program leaders can address to promote greater quality, accessibility, and impact for sustainability programs in higher education. These change areas entail *needs* (gaps or limitations that impede the advancement of programs towards their goals or potential) and *opportunities* (possible developments in the scope, scale, and significance of programs) related to *program design* and *evaluation*. The change areas focus on:

1. emphasizing *justice, equity, diversity, and inclusion* in the curriculum, structure, management, and accessibility of programs;
2. operationalizing the shared reference framework on *key competencies in sustainability* in contextualized tools, practices, and standards;
3. facilitating *synergistic connections* between teaching and learning with sustainability initiatives and operations across campus and into the wider community; and
4. generating *organizational change* through institutional support and implementation of sustainability as a core purpose of teaching, learning, campus operations, and other endeavors.

Figure 2.1 portrays the ways that these *change drivers* and *change areas* interact with needs and opportunities in the design and evaluation of sustainability programs in higher education to enhance their quality, accessibility, and impact. We next consider insights from our experience with the Global Council for Science and the Environment's *Pathways toward Accreditation* initiative to describe approaches to facilitating change across levels. Then, we reflect on visions for change presented in the literature to advance strategies for improving quality, accessibility, and impact across the four change areas.

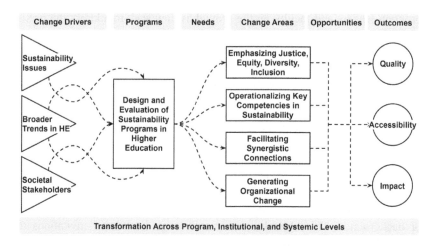

Figure 2.1   Change drivers and change areas for sustainability programs in higher education

SYSTEMIC CHANGE THROUGH THE *PATHWAYS TOWARD ACCREDITATION* INITIATIVE

The Global Council for Science and the Environment, with support from the Cynthia and George Mitchell Foundation, has developed an initiative that engages with each of the four change areas. Building from a history of work with interdisciplinary sustainability and environmental education and research in higher education, GCSE launched the *Pathways toward Accreditation* initiative in 2021. The initiative aims to address the needs and opportunities of sustainability programs in higher education by exploring strategies to strengthen program design and evaluation (micro-level) as a leverage point for advancing institutional (meso-level) and systemic (macro-level) transformation. Motivated by the complexity and lack of clarity in articulating the features and value of sustainability programs in higher education, the initiative entails a set of interconnected activities with the aim of developing a flexible, inclusive, and innovative process and set of dynamic best practice standards for program accreditation to support the transformation of the quality, accessibility, and impact of sustainability programs in higher education. GCSE engages in these activities through an approach centering justice, equity, diversity, and inclusion as fundamental principles in guiding both the initiative and sustainability programs in higher education. This approach translates to close engagement with a variety of stakeholders from over 90 US and international GCSE member institutions, who help to describe the realities faced by program leaders and faculty on the ground as they seek to address the needs and opportunities of their own context in the program development process.

For the first change area of *emphasizing justice, equity, diversity, and inclusion*, GCSE strives to expand the transformative potential of sustainability programs by including both aspirational language and tangible actions around justice, equity, diversity, inclusion, and accessibility. In its own mission and values, GCSE has focused on becoming an anti-racist organization, demonstrating this intention with an anti-racist oath published on its website and read at staff, board, and public meetings. GCSE has also achieved progress in facilitating inclusive participation in the initiative, particularly for populations underrepresented in sustainability fields. In establishing a Sustainability Education Leadership Advisory Council, GCSE set an internal metric of 50% of the council to be composed of leaders from underrepresented institutions or backgrounds. This objective was met through intentional invitations to leaders from Hispanic-Serving Institutions, Historically Black Colleges and Universities, Asian American and Native American Pacific Island-Serving Institutions, Tribally Controlled Colleges and Universities, and community colleges, as well as research universities and others representing indigenous or international perspectives. The hope is that diversity in high-level decision making will permeate to systemic changes by informing actions and next steps in the initiative. Another aspect of GCSE's approach to inclusive participation in the *Pathways toward Accreditation* initiative is the Sustainability Education Community of Practice, which facilitates discussion on program design and evaluation across a range of program leaders, faculty, staff, and other stakeholders from within and outside of academia in monthly convenings.

As the GCSE *Pathway toward Accreditation* initiative looks to develop an approach to program accreditation, it has considered practical implications for these transformative concepts as well. Specifically, the initiative has aimed to take a flexible and inclusive approach to the development of potential accreditation standards and processes in order to invite diversity and innovation as drivers to increased access to quality sustainability programs in higher education. This intentionality is especially important to consider in the initiative as accreditation processes and quality standards have been demonstrated to commonly reinforce inequities or present barriers to diversity, inclusion, equity, and justice in program design and evaluation (Ferreira et al., 2014; Nora, 2021). While the initiative's efforts in this change area are in their formative stages, an emphasis on justice, equity, diversity, and inclusion as core purposes can contribute to further maturation of the partnerships, principles, and practices through which these fundamental priorities are enacted in sustainability programs in higher education. While tangibly engaging with each of these transformational concepts is challenging within an individual program, the goal of GCSE's efforts is to infuse them across programmatic elements (such as faculty hiring or curricular content) and support change at institutional and systemic levels.

In addressing the second change area of *operationalizing key competencies in sustainability*, GCSE developed a *Proposal Statement on Key Competencies in Sustainability* to provide guidance for sustainability programs in higher education. The statement presents the growing convergence around the shared reference framework on key competencies in sustainability (Brundiers et al., 2021), describing four foundational features and functions in its relationship to program design and evaluation. A public input process in 2023 affirmed convergence around the utility of the shared reference framework on key competencies in sustainability among stakeholders of higher education programs, including administrators, faculty, staff, students, and employers. The public input process also highlighted the lead role of values-thinking competency in orienting the application of the other competencies towards engagement with normative sustainability goals as well as principles and practices related to justice, equity, diversity, and inclusion. Additional activities as part of the *Pathways toward Accreditation* initiative, such as participatory research and workshops to deliberate best practices, are exploring ways to operationalize the framework in order to identify potential quality standards for accrediting programs. These activities aim to provide recommendations and professional development resources that support program leaders in developing their programs in coherent and comprehensive ways to meet the needs of students and employers.

For the third change area of *facilitating synergistic connections*, the *Pathways toward Accreditation* initiative has aimed to address the gap between sustainability-focused academic activities and initiatives in several ways. As a part of their Sustainability Education Community of Practice, GCSE facilitated a discussion around sustainability across campus and the curriculum. This discussion explored different strategies for integrating sustainability throughout the institution, as well as how connections can be drawn between learning experiences and sustainability-focused research and operations. GCSE has expanded these discussions through partnerships with organizations such as the Association for the Advancement of Sustainability in Higher Education and the Campus as a Living Lab Network North America, which explore sustainability activities across different aspects of higher education institutions. GCSE has also hosted a "Roundtable on Workforce Perspectives", in which employers and program leaders highlighted the value of linking student learning with the practical and technical aspects of campus and community sustainability. Roundtable panelists emphasized the need for applied and real-world learning experiences that can help better prepare students to apply their skills in meeting workforce needs, suggesting the need for multifaceted and interconnected sustainability initiatives that support student learning.

In relation to the fourth change area of *facilitating organizational change*, the *Pathways toward Accreditation* initiative has aimed to enhance the credibility and rigor of sustainability programs to advance momentum for institutionalization. A guiding principle for the initiative in pursuing this aim has been to target activities towards program leaders and administrators, as they often serve as leverage points for advancing curricular integration and facilitating change among different actors (Barth & Rieckmann, 2012). Leaders of these change processes have to face not only internal pressures and conflicts, but manage external forces related to efficiency and accountability, such as how they serve employers, community stakeholders, and accreditors who do not fully comprehend the relevance of sustainability (Wals, 2014). GCSE is approaching program accreditation as a lever to generate organizational learning and scale transformative change related to sustainability in higher education. Specifically, the initiative targets these areas by setting aspirational quality standards with context- and place-based implementations, describing best practices across different programs, and developing professional resources such as faculty development tools, evaluation metrics, and networking opportunities.

VISIONS OF CHANGE IN THE LITERATURE

To examine how the efforts of GCSE have drawn from, and could be furthered by, insights from the field of sustainability in higher education, we now consider visions of change presented in the literature that respond to the needs and opportunities for program design and evaluation. Then, we recommend strategies for advancing the quality, accessibility, and impact of sustainability programs in higher education as a way to facilitate transformation across program, institutional, and systemic levels.

Change Area 1: Emphasizing Justice, Equity, Diversity, and Inclusion

In response to broader social movements, as well as the concerns and aspirations of faculty and students, higher education leaders have increasingly engaged with issues related to justice, equity, diversity, and inclusion (Mahdavi, 2022). However, the field of sustainability education in higher education has struggled to fully engage with these areas as both thematic foci and concrete practices (Maina-Okori et al., 2018), even with previously identified conceptual relationships between justice and equity with sustainability principles (Agyeman et al., 2002). Forging stronger and more tangible engagements with diverse perspectives and populations, while integrating justice and equity into problem-solving approaches remains a fundamental endeavor for the present and future of the field of sustainability (Clark & Harley, 2020). Despite these challenges and the commonly perceived white, elite nature of sustainability discourse (Taylor, 2015), trends suggest that change is occurring as the population, and more specifically sustainability professions, becomes more diverse (Mak, 2021). This compels programs and higher education institutions to determine ways to remain relevant for a changing population with changing demands related to climate change, sustainability, and the culture of academic programs in higher education.

In the context of sustainability programs in higher education, this suggests the critical need to: (1) incorporate diverse ontologies, epistemologies, and value sets (Demssie et al., 2020), (2) support the inclusion of marginalized communities by addressing systemic barriers (Garibay & Vincent, 2018), (3) integrate equity into the design, implementation, and evaluation of programs (Valley et al., 2020), and (4) advance institutional and community justice through teaching, research, administration, operations, and outreach (Kinol et al., 2023). Examples of how to address these needs include taking an intersectional approach to learning about and addressing sustainability challenges (Kaijser & Kronsell, 2014) as well as investigating power dynamics and how they restrict or can be addressed to promote social change (Avelino, 2021). These actions are especially significant in analyzing program design and evaluation where practices and standards can enact barriers to learning and professional advancement in inequitable ways (Denaro et al., 2022). In addition to addressing these areas as part of the curricula or through critical, emancipatory pedagogical approaches (Sandri, 2020), the relevance of justice and equity as core tenets of sustainability integration in higher education has been demonstrated in relation to research (Menton et al., 2020), engagement (Agyeman, 2005), leadership (Aung & Hallinger, 2023) and operations (Eby & Rangarajan, 2023).

Change Area 2: Operationalizing the Key Competencies in Sustainability Framework

The shared reference framework on key competencies in sustainability describes the knowledge, skills, and dispositions needed by sustainability professionals to address complex problems and create change (Wiek et al., 2011). These include the following key competencies: systems-thinking, futures-thinking, values-thinking, strategic-thinking, interpersonal, intrapersonal, implementation, and integrated problem-solving (for a deeper description of these key competencies than is possible here, please see Brundiers et al., 2021; Redman & Wiek, 2021; and Wiek et al., 2011; 2016). As convergence around the interrelated set of key competencies in sustainability has been established over the past 20 years, the framework has come to provide dynamic guidance on potential learning objectives for sustainability programs in higher education (Brundiers et al., 2021). However, efforts to translate the key competencies into quality teaching and curriculum practices have been disparate, often resulting in miscomprehension of concepts and inattention to implications for pedagogies and assessments (Sterling et al., 2017). Thus, the next step in advancing the application of the framework to support program design and evaluation is to operationalize it in learning standards, teaching approaches, and assessment tools across a variety of programs and institutional contexts (NASEM, 2020).

International research programs, such as the "Educating Future Change Agents" project involving Leuphana University of Lüneburg in Germany and Arizona State University in the US, have made initial efforts to advance the operationalization of the shared reference framework. This research examined change processes within programs that facilitate the operationalization of the framework, identifying design strategies for program leaders (Weiss et al., 2021a; Weiss et al., 2021b; Weiss & Barth, 2019) as well as connections between curricula and the key competencies in sustainability (Birdman et al., 2022). Research efforts also explored approaches for faculty and instructors related to pedagogies for cultivating specific competencies such as inter-personal competency (Konrad et al., 2020; Konrad et al., 2021), assessment procedures (Redman et al., 2021), and the outcomes of project-based learning experiences (Birdman et al., 2021).

Further work might explore ways to promote greater intentionality and alignment between learning objectives, teaching approaches, and assessment methods to ensure that students cultivate and are able to apply their competencies in relevant personal and professional settings (Shephard et al., 2019). In this pursuit, established approaches such as constructive alignment (Biggs, 1996) and backward design (Wiggins & McTighe, 1998) could prove helpful. The connection of the key competencies in sustainability with justice and equity also requires more attention to determine conceptual overlap and practical applications. Anderson (2013) suggests that in operationalizing the key competencies in sustainability framework in relation to justice and equity, programs should: (1) place greater emphasis on historical analysis of oppressive systems and structures, (2) highlight intercultural competencies, (3) recognize the intimate place- and culture-based nature of sustainability problems and solutions that intersect with diverse and often marginalized populations, and (4) more explicitly outline and operationalize the justice- and equity-oriented values needed for sustainability professionals.

Change Area 3: Facilitating Synergistic Connections Between Academics and Initiatives

As the integration of sustainability in higher education has evolved, efforts have focused on several areas beyond teaching and learning, such as research, operations, leadership, and engagement. However, cultivating holistic organizational sustainability that creates synergies among these areas has proved challenging (Menon & Suresh, 2020). The lack of alignment between academics (i.e., education and research) and campus initiatives or community engagement related to sustainability hinders the ability of programs and institutions to meet their critical responsibility to fully engage with this topic in tangible ways (SDSN, 2020).

Stronger connections between teaching and learning with other sustainability-focused initiatives are needed to strengthen educational experiences and create a culture of sustainability that can promote benefits for programs, institutions, and communities (Adams et al., 2018). These benefits can be observed in increased institutional capacity to link sustainability across facets of the university, contributions to change in local communities, and experiences that support students to develop the capacities to address complex, real-world sustainability problems (Yarime et al., 2012). Through experiential learning opportunities, which provide a tangible approach for integrating sustainability in teaching, learning, research, and operations, students engage with stakeholders and project partners from different sectors to situate the campus as a living laboratory for experimenting with sustainability solutions (Brundiers et al., 2010). These applied learning projects leverage participatory, collaborative, and action-oriented pedagogical approaches to position students as changemakers that can contribute to strategic and systematic processes for scaling and sustaining supportive institutional pathways for collective innovation and impact (Beaudoin & Brundiers, 2017). Practicing equity and seeking to promote justice through integrative and synergistic approaches can produce benefits for community members (Hurd & Stanton, 2022). These equity- and justice-focused efforts are often driven by, and further accelerate, student-led action to advance sustainability across areas, highlighting the fundamental need for emphasis of equitable, justice-oriented approaches (Murray, 2018).

Change Area 4: Generating Organizational Change Through Institutionalizing Sustainability

The previous three change areas culminate in this fourth change area, which is about expanding program-level change towards the institutionalization of sustainability as a core purpose that facilitates shifts in organizational approaches and priorities. Taking a whole-institution approach is needed to fully realize the potential for the quality, accessibility, and impact of sustainability programs in higher education (UNESCO, 2014a). This approach recognizes that integrating sustainability into teaching and learning requires transformation across all aspects of the institution including operations, organizational culture, leadership and management, student participation, community engagement, and research (UNESCO, 2014b). Sterling (2004) describes this full integration of sustainability across areas of the institution as triple-loop organizational learning in which institutions advance past "bolt-on" or "built-in" approaches to actually redesigning the purposes and processes of the university in transformative ways. More comprehensive institutionalization processes occur in a variety of ways, including top-down (presidential mandates) or bottom-up (student- and faculty-led) change, externally driven initiatives (through policies or supported through international networks like Regional Centers of Expertise), and collaborative paradigm changes that bring together different stakeholders in participatory partnerships to reorient institutional cultures (Weiss et al., 2021a). These different processes demonstrate the interconnectedness of change across micro-, meso-, and macro-levels, as well as how innovations in programs can stimulate actions in other areas of the institution and beyond.

Despite these areas and strategies for change, the process of institutionalizing sustainability by promoting organizational learning and change remains complex and contested, often faced with resistance and ambiguity (Sylvestre & Wright, 2016). A recent review of efforts to implement sustainability at an institutional level discovered that progress has been narrow and disparate (Kohl et al., 2022), which limits the full potential of universities to act as drivers of societal transformation (Purcell et al., 2019). Challenges for institutions in integrating sustainability typically center around a lack of awareness or confusion about sustainability concepts and practices among the campus community that results in a lack of motivation, coordination, and vision to implement innovations, particularly among leadership (Veiga Ávila et al., 2019). These challenges are sometimes exacerbated by bureaucratic barriers as well as tentativeness in decision making that emerges from engaging with the complex, normative, and transformative aspects of sustainability that are commonly at odds with institutional structures (Thomas, 2016). This highlights the need for supportive policies, sufficient resources, compatible collective mindsets, and individual advocates willing to champion organizational learning and culture change (Blanco-Portela et al., 2017).

The preceding three change areas can be seen as actionable building blocks that amplify the progress of institutionalization, situating programs as spaces for negotiating and facilitating transformations across different areas and levels of the institution. In order to move forward, institutions need to ensure not only that they have robust approaches to teaching sustainability in academic programs, but have in place the organizational structures, processes, and finances to fully incorporate sustainability and position the university as a change agent in engaging with the community to address the dominant sustainability challenges of the region (Stephens et al., 2008). Inclusive approaches to organizational change are needed that aim to not only inform the institutional community about sustainability but engage and empower diverse stakeholders to take agency in embedding sustainability in transformative ways (Cebrián, 2018). In these efforts, leadership that engages with power dynamics to advance justice-oriented, participatory organizational change processes can garner collective support (Shriberg & MacDonald, 2013) that contributes to implementing sustainability across areas in comprehensive plans that enable change through shared visions and collaboration (Swearingen White, 2014). While more work is needed to articulate concrete evidence and strategies to guide organizational change, this section provides some guideposts to target within this dynamic process.

Strategies for Quality, Accessibility, and Impact

To address the slow change and associated challenges to institutionalize sustainability in higher education, we envision – for each of the change areas – potential strategies to engage with needs and opportunities to advance quality, accessibility, and impact in program design and evaluation. In this endeavor, prioritizing the first change area related to *emphasizing justice, equity, diversity, and inclusion* is important for sustainability programs in higher education both in how they engage with these transformational concepts as key curricular themes, but also in the accessibility, structure, and management of these programs. Emphasizing justice and equity in teaching approaches and learning experiences can enhance the *quality* of teaching and learning by creating more meaningful, critical, and potentially transformative outcomes for students that enable them to analyze structural elements that further oppression while articulating their positionalities and developing agency to act in constructive ways (Cachelin & Nicolosi, 2022). For example, the key competencies in sustainability framework offers conceptual and methodological links to justice (in values-thinking competency), equity (in strategic-thinking competency), diversity (in futures-thinking and systems-thinking competencies), and inclusion (in interpersonal competency) that can be emphasized and evolved through a range of techniques in different settings (Brundiers et al., 2021). Diversity and inclusion can be enacted by creating greater *accessibility* to sustainability programs for diverse and marginalized populations (Garibay & Vincent, 2018). Historically, sustainability- and environmentally focused programs in higher education, as well as professional organizations in these areas, have demonstrated stark gender and racial gaps in representation (Taylor,

2015; 2018). In order to generate more equity in sustainability initiatives and outcomes, as well as within higher education programs, a focus on inclusion for marginalized and underrepresented populations is needed (NASEM, 2020).

Prioritizing diversity of perspectives, inclusion of marginalized populations, and enabling justice and equity through program principles, practices, and processes can also enhance the *impact* of sustainability programs across the curriculum, management, and structure of programs. Curriculum that integrates learning, research, and community partnerships can contribute to the advancement of intertwined social justice and sustainability benefits that extend beyond the institution, while developing students' awareness, knowledge, and skills related to these areas (Habron, 2022). In relation to the management of programs, equity- and justice-focused approaches can contribute to addressing white supremacy and other forms of oppression in not only educational content but administrative practices, leading to outcomes such as greater representation of marginalized communities among faculty, staff, and administration (Bratman & DeLince, 2022; Coleman & Gould, 2019). Justice-oriented initiatives related to program structure, such as multi-stakeholder and participatory planning committees, can create more inclusive and equitable organizational structures and contribute to transformative learning and impact (Cronin et al., 2021).

For the second change area, *operationalizing the key competencies in sustainability* framework can strengthen the design and evaluation of sustainability programs in higher education in several ways. Drawing from the framework can improve the *quality* of program design and evaluation by providing the foundation for relevant and rigorous learning objectives for students (Wiek et al., 2016). Developing pedagogical strategies and assessment tools related to the key competencies can enrich student learning experiences and ensure that students engage with the concepts, methods, and motivational factors entailed in each key competency (Wiek & Redman, 2022). Efforts in this area can also support greater *accessibility* for sustainability programs by providing a framework that can be operationalized across different contexts, programs, pedagogies, and populations (e.g., Levesque & Wake, 2021; Richard et al., 2017). The framework can also contribute to the *impact* of sustainability programs in higher education by providing a reference for what students need to learn and how they can apply their emergent key competencies in iterative and collaborative sustainability problem-solving processes in professional and personal settings (Redman & Wiek, 2021). Recent research has demonstrated the value of the key competencies for alumni of sustainability programs across a range of professional settings and tasks, in particular in their justice-oriented transformative activities (Salovaara & Soini, 2021).

Strategies for the third change area of *facilitating synergistic connections* focus on integrating teaching and learning into sustainability activities in other areas of the institution. Applied learning projects can enhance the *quality* of both student learning in sustainability programs as well as campus sustainability initiatives by supporting students to act as agents of change in addressing sustainability problems on campus and in the community (Beaudoin & Brundiers, 2017). Fostering synergistic experiences can also increase the *accessibility* of sustainability learning opportunities by integrating different groups of students (e.g., from different disciplines) to collaborate with different stakeholders (e.g., campus sustainability managers) through a variety of techniques that can advance education, research, and capacity-building (Wals et al., 2016). Linking academics and initiatives also enhances the potential *impact* of sustainability programs in higher education by bringing together faculty, students, staff, and community members to integrate knowledge and action for the mutual benefit of all partners by promoting co-learning, transferable practices, and opportunities for further innovation that can serve the needs of marginalized communities (Rowe & Hiser, 2016).

For the fourth change area of *generating organizational change*, a variety of strategies present potentially transformative opportunities to strengthen sustainability programs. Institutionalizing sustainability contributes to program *quality* by cultivating shared visions and collaborative, participatory action driven by diverse stakeholders to ensure that programs meet the needs of the populations and communities they serve and work towards realizing local and global sustainability goals that advance equity and justice (Fia et al., 2022). Organizational change can also increase *accessibility* to sustainability learning experiences across different areas of the university (academic offerings, informal learning, campus operations), providing a range of ways for students with various professional aspirations to participate in sustainability-oriented activities (Yarime et al., 2012). Promoting organizational change to reorient institutional purposes and processes towards sustainability can also contribute to greater *impact* by enabling the scaling of sustainability programs, activities, and ultimately actionable knowledge and solution strategies for a range of stakeholders (Barth, 2014). In this context, scale can be defined as not only increasing the size of a program, but as strengthening the depth of implementation, ensuring the endurance of organizational change, promoting spread to other areas within the institution (and to other institutions), and enabling a shift in agency of the scaling process, for example, from a dedicated department of staff to university administration (Coburn, 2003).

CONCLUSION

The work of GCSE's *Pathway toward Accreditation* initiative has focused on programs as an intervention point to create institutional and systemic transformation. To enhance the quality, accessibility, and impact of these programs, interconnected actions are needed across micro-, meso-, and macro-levels to support program, institutional, and systemic transformation. At the *micro*-level, we suggest that programs experiment with new approaches to sustainability in higher education in order to focus on garnering momentum and support in achieving sustainability-oriented objectives in teaching and learning, campus initiatives, and organizational change, guided by principles and practices that center justice, equity, diversity, and inclusion. At the *meso*-level, we suggest that institutions pursue innovations to become more responsive to the needs and desires of students, employers, and diverse communities to support just and equitable transitions towards liberatory, regenerative futures. At the *macro*-level, we suggest that the field of sustainability in higher education seeks to focus on strategies that operationalize the theoretical and practical knowledge that the field has already generated, specifically with a focus on applying a justice, equity, diversity, and inclusion lens to strengthening program design and evaluation.

We believe that the four change areas that we have described can inform actions across these three levels by suggesting priorities and tactics for navigating the needs and opportunities facing sustainability programs in higher education. More specifically, we hope that program leaders can build from the change framework that we have provided to specify and enhance the efficacy of their program design and evaluation approaches in advancing quality, accessibility, and impact. In this pursuit, we have offered practical experiences and insights from the literature to support others in realizing the potential of their goals through changes in their own contexts. For instance, a program director might apply the framework in evaluating needs related to "facilitating synergistic connections between academics and initiatives" and then designing strategies, such as applied learning projects, that increase program impact by promoting quality and accessibility in this area. Using the framework to develop these niche innovations might support further breakthroughs for sustainability endeavors at program and institutional levels while translating into new practices and perspectives in higher education and beyond. Amidst a variety of change drivers – such as sustainability issues, broader trends in higher education, and the needs and desires of societal stakeholders – we are at a moment with potential for the destabilizing of the norms and functions of the dominant paradigm in higher education. Actions by the leaders of sustainability programs to address the proposed four change areas can place pressure on institutions around the globe to prioritize sustainability and position higher education as a leader in driving society towards systemic transformations for justice, resilience, and social-ecological vitality.

REFERENCES

Adams, R., Martin, S., & Boom, K. (2018). University culture and sustainability: Designing and implementing an enabling framework. *Journal of Cleaner Production, 171*, 434–445. https://doi.org/10.1016/j.jclepro.2017.10.032

Agyeman, J. (2005). Alternatives for community and environment: Where justice and sustainability meet. *Environment: Science and Policy for Sustainable Development, 47*(6), 10–23. https://doi.org/10.3200/ENVT.47.6.10-23

Agyeman, J., Bullard, R.D., & Evans, B. (2002). Exploring the nexus: Bringing together sustainability, environmental justice and equity. *Space and Polity, 6*(1), 77–90. https://doi.org/10.1080/13562570220137907

Anderson, M.D. (2013). Higher education revisited: Sustainability science and teaching for sustainable food systems. In R. Braun, J. Pippig, F. Mari, & Z. Heuschkel (Eds.), *Future of food: State of the art, challenges and options for action* (pp. 179–188). UIT Cambridge.

Association for the Advancement of Sustainability in Higher Education (2023). *Academic programs*. AASHE Campus Sustainability Hub. https://hub.aashe.org/browse/types/academicprogram/

Aung, P.N., & Hallinger, P (2023). Research on sustainability leadership in higher education: A scoping review. *International Journal of Sustainability in Higher Education, 24*(3), 517–534. https://doi.org/10.1108/IJSHE-09-2021-0367

Avelino, F. (2021). Theories of power and social change: Power contestations and their implications for research on social change and innovation. *Journal of Political Power, 14*(3), 425–448. https://doi.org/10.1080/2158379X.2021.1875307

Bamberg, S., Fischer, D., & Geiger, S.M. (2021). Editorial: The role of the individual in the great transformation toward sustainability. *Frontiers in Psychology, 12*, 710897. https://doi.org/10.3389/fpsyg.2021.710897

Barnett, R., & Guzmán-Valenzuela, C. (2022). The socially responsible European university: A challenging project. *International Journal of Sustainability in Higher Education, 23*(4), 752–766. https://doi.org/10.1108/IJSHE-03-2021-0100

Barth, M. (2014). *Implementing sustainability in higher education: Learning in an age of transformation*. Routledge.

Barth, M., & Rieckmann, M. (2012). Academic staff development as a catalyst for curriculum change towards education for sustainable development: An output perspective. *Journal of Cleaner Production, 26*, 28–36. https://doi.org/10.1016/j.jclepro.2011.12.011

Beaudoin, F.D., & Brundiers, K. (2017). *A guide for applied sustainability learning projects: Advancing sustainability outcomes on campus and in the community*. Association for the Advancement of Sustainability in Higher Education.

Biggs, J. (1996). Enhancing teaching through constructive alignment. *Higher Education, 32*, 347–364. https://doi.org/10.1007/BF00138871

Birdman, J., Redman, A., & Lang, D.J. (2021). Pushing the boundaries: Experience-based learning in early phases of graduate sustainability curricula. *International Journal of Sustainability in Higher Education, 22*(2), 237–253. https://doi.org/10.1108/IJSHE-08-2019-0242

Birdman, J., Wiek, A., & Lang, D.J. (2022). Developing key competencies in sustainability through project-based learning in graduate sustainability programs. *International Journal of Sustainability in Higher Education, 23*(5), 1139–1157. https://doi.org/10.1108/IJSHE-12-2020-0506

Blanco-Portela, N., Benayas, J., Pertierra, L.R., & Lozano, R. (2017). Towards the integration of sustainability in Higher Education Institutions: A review of drivers of and barriers to organisational change and their comparison against those found of companies. *Journal of Cleaner Production, 166*, 563–578. https://doi.org/10.1016/j.jclepro.2017.07.252

Boone, C., & Seto, K.C. (2023). Green jobs are booming, but too few employees have sustainability skills to fill them – here are 4 ways to close the gap. *The Conversation.* https://theconversation.com/green-jobs-are-booming-but-too-few-employees-have-sustainability-skills-to-fill-them-here-are-4-ways-to-close-the-gap-193953

Bratman, E.Z., & DeLince, W.P. (2022). Dismantling white supremacy in environmental studies and sciences: An argument for anti-racist and decolonizing pedagogies. *Journal of Environmental Studies and Sciences, 12*, 193–203. https://doi.org/10.1007/s13412-021-00739-5

Brundiers, K., Barth, M., Cebrián, G., Cohen, M., Diaz, L., Doucette-Remington, S., Dripps, W., Habron, G., Harré, N., Jarchow, M., Losch, K., Michel, J., Mochizuki, Y., Rieckmann, M., Parnell, R., Walker, P., & Zint, M. (2021). Key competencies in sustainability in higher education: Toward an agreed-upon reference framework. *Sustainability Science, 16*, 13–29. https://doi.org/10.1007/s11625-020-00838-2

Brundiers, K., Wiek, A., & Redman, C.L. (2010). Real-world learning opportunities in sustainability: From classroom into the real world. *International Journal of Sustainability in Higher Education, 11*(4), 308–324. https://doi.org/10.1108/14676371011077540

Cachelin, A., & Nicolosi, E. (2022). Investigating critical community engaged pedagogies for transformative environmental justice education. *Environmental Education Research, 28*(4), 491–507. https://doi.org/10.1080/13504622.2022.2034751

Cebrián, G. (2018). The I3E model for embedding education for sustainability within higher education institutions. *Environmental Education Research, 18*(2), 153–171. https://doi.org/10.1080/13504622.2016.1217395

Clark, W.C., & Harley, A.G. (2020). Sustainability science: Toward a synthesis. *Annual Review of Environment and Resources, 45*, 331–386. https://doi.org/10.1146/annurev-environ-012420-043621

Coburn, C.E. (2003). Rethinking scale: Moving beyond numbers to deep and lasting change. *Educational Researcher, 32*(6), 3–12. https://doi.org/10.3102/0013189X032006003

Coleman, K., & Gould, R. (2019). Exploring just sustainability across the disciplines at one university. *The Journal of Environmental Education, 50*(3), 223–237. https://doi.org/10.1080/00958964.2019.1582471

Cronin, J., Hughes, N., Tomei, J., Couto, L.C., Ali, M., Kizilcec, V., Adewole, A., Bisaga, I. Broad, O., Parikh, P., Eludoyin, E., Hofbauer, L., Machado, P.G., Butnar, I., Anandarajah, G., Webb, J., Lemaire, X., & Watson, J. (2021). Embedding justice in the 1.5°C transition: A transdisciplinary research agenda. *Renewable and Sustainable Energy Transition, 1*, 100001. https://doi.org/10.1016/j.rset.2021.100001

Demssie, Y.N., Biemans, H.J.A., Wesselink, R., & Mulder, M. (2020). Combining indigenous knowledge and modern education to foster sustainability competencies: Towards a set of learning design principles. *Sustainability, 12*, 6823. https://doi.org/10.3390/su12176823

Denaro, K., Dennin, K., Dennin, M., & Sato, B. (2022). Identifying systemic inequity in higher education and opportunities for improvement. *PloS One, 17*(4), e0264059. https://doi.org/10.1371/journal.pone.0264059

Eby, R.F., & Rangarajan, N. (2023). Campus sustainability plans: Past, present, and future. *International Journal of Higher Education*. https://doi.org/10.1108/IJSHE -03-2022-0063

Engler, J., Abson, D.J., & von Wehrden, H. (2021). The coronavirus pandemic as an analogy for future sustainability challenges. *Sustainability Science, 16*, 317–319. https://doi.org/10.1007/s11625-020-00852-4

Ferreira, C., Vidal., J., & Viera, M.J. (2014). Student guidance and attention to diversity in the processes of quality assurance in higher education. *European Journal of Education, 49*(4), 575–589. https://doi.org/10.1111/ejed.12098

Fia, M., Ghasemzadeh, K., & Paletta, A. (2022). How higher education institutions walk their talk on the 2030 agenda: A systematic literature review. *Higher Education Policy*. https://doi.org/10.1057/s41307-022-00277-x

Garibay, J.C., & Vincent, S. (2018). Racially inclusive climates within degree programs and increasing student of color enrollment: An examination of environmental/ sustainability programs. *Journal of Diversity in Higher Education, 11*(2), 201–220. https://doi.org/10.1037/dhe0000030

Geels, F.W. (2004). From sectoral systems of innovation to socio-technical systems: Insights about dynamics and change from sociology and institutional theory. *Research Policy, 33*(6–7), 897–920. https://doi.org/10.1016/j.respol.2004.01.015

Guzmán-Valenzuela, C., Barnett, R., & Labraña, J. (2020). Consensus and dissensus: Changing perceptions of the public dimension of universities in a marketised environment. *Journal of Higher Education Policy and Management, 42*(1), 49–66. https://doi.org/10.1080/1360080X.2019.1658850

Habron, G. (2022). Applied & engaged learning for equitable sustainability & social justice. In M. Urbanski (Ed.), *No sustainability without justice: An anthology on racial equity & social justice* (pp. 21–30). Association for the Advancement of Sustainability in Higher Education.

Hurd, C., & Stanton, T.K. (2022). Community engagement as community development: Making the case for multilateral, collaborative, equity-focused campus-community partnerships. *Community Development*. https://doi.org/10.1080/15575330.2022 .2121297

Kaijser, A., & Kronsell, A. (2014). Climate change through the lens of intersectionality. *Environmental Politics, 23*(3), 417–433. https://doi.org/10.1080/09644016.2013 .835203

Kates, R.W. (2011). What kind of a science is sustainability science? *Proceedings of the National Academy of Sciences, 108*(49), 19449–19450. https://doi.org/10.1073/ pnas.1116097108

Kinol, A., Miller, E., Axtell, H., Hirschfeld, I., Leggett, S., Si, Y., & Stephens, J.C. (2023). Climate justice in higher education: A proposed paradigm shift towards a transformative role for colleges and universities. *Climatic Change, 176*, 15. https:// doi.org/10.1007/s10584-023-03486-4

Kohl, K., Hopkins, C., Barth, M., Michelsen, G., Dlouhá, J., Razak, D.A., Abidin Bin Sanusi, Z., & Toman, I. (2022). A whole-institution approach towards sustainability: A crucial aspect of higher education's individual and collective engagement with the SDGs and beyond. *International Journal of Sustainability in Higher Education, 23*(2), 218–236. https://doi.org/10.1108/IJSHE-10-2020-0398

Konrad, T., Wiek, A., & Barth. M. (2020). Embracing conflicts for interpersonal competence development in project-based sustainability courses. *International Journal of Sustainability in Higher Education, 21*(1), 76–96. https://doi.org/10.1108/IJSHE -06-2019-0190

Konrad, T., Wiek, A., & Barth. M. (2021). Learning processes for interpersonal competence development in project-based sustainability courses. *International Journal of Sustainability in Higher Education, 22*(3), 535–560. https://doi.org/10.1108/IJSHE -07-2020-0231

Levesque, V.R., & Wake, C.P. (2021). Organizational change for sustainability education: A case study of one university's efforts to create and implement institution-wide sustainability competencies. *International Journal of Sustainability in Higher Education, 22*(3), 497–515. https://doi.org/10.1108/IJSHE-09-2019-0285

Mahdavi, P. (2022). Social justice in, through and beyond higher education. *Times Higher Education.* https://www.timeshighereducation.com/campus/social-justice -through-and-beyond-higher-education

Maina-Okori, N.M., Koushik, J.R., & Wilson, A. (2018). Reimagining intersectionality in environmental and sustainability education: A critical literature review. *The Journal of Environmental Education, 49*(4), 286–296. https://doi.org/10.1080/ 00958964.2017.1364215

Mak, H. (2021). *The state of equity, diversity and inclusion in sustainability.* Diversity in Sustainability.

Menon, S., & Suresh, M. (2020). Synergizing education, research, campus operations, and community engagements towards sustainability in higher education: A literature review. *International Journal of Sustainability in Higher Education, 21*(5), 1015–1051. https://doi.org/10.1108/IJSHE-03-2020-0089

Menton, M., Larrea, C., Latorre, S., Martinez-Alier, J., Peck, M., Temper, L., & Walter, M. (2020). Environmental justice and the SDGs: From synergies to gaps and contradictions. *Sustainability Science, 15*, 1621–1636. https://doi.org/10.1007/s11625 -020-00789-8

Miller, T.R., Wiek, A., Sarewitz, D., Robinson, J., Olsson, L., Kriebel, D., & Loorbach, D. (2014). The future of sustainability science: A solutions-oriented research agenda. *Sustainability Science, 9*, 239–246. https://doi.org/10.1007/s11625-013-0224-6

Murray, J. (2018). Student-led action for sustainability in higher education: A literature review. *International Journal of Sustainability in Higher Education, 19*(6), 1095–1110. https://doi.org/10.1108/IJSHE-09-2017-0164

National Academies of Sciences, Engineering, and Medicine (2020). *Strengthening sustainability programs and curricula at the undergraduate and graduate levels.* The National Academies Press. https://doi.org/10.17226/25821

National Center for Education Statistics (2023). *Detail for CIP Code 30.3301: Sustainability studies.* The Classification of Instructional Programs. https://nces.ed .gov/ipeds/cipcode/cipdetail.aspx?y=55&cipid=89257

Nora, L.M. (2021). Using accreditation to transform diversity, equity, and inclusion efforts into diversity, equity, and inclusion systems. *Academic Medicine, 97*(1), 25–29. https://doi.org/10.1097/ACM.0000000000004377

O'Byrne, D., Dripps, W., & Nicholas, K.A. (2015). Teaching and learning sustainability: An assessment of the curriculum content and structure of sustainability degree programs in higher education. *Sustainability Science, 10*, 43–59. https://doi.org/10 .1007/s11625-014-0251-y

Purcell, W.M., Henriksen, H., & Spengler, J.D. (2019). Universities as the engine of transformational sustainability toward delivering the sustainable development goals: "Living labs" for sustainability. *International Journal of Sustainability in Higher Education, 20*(8), 1343–1357. https://doi.org/10.1108/IJSHE-02-2019-0103

Redman, A., & Wiek, A. (2021). Competencies for advancing transformations towards sustainability. *Frontiers in Education, 6*, 785163. https:// doi .org/ 10 .3389/ feduc .2021.785163

Redman, A., Wiek, A., & Barth, M. (2021). Current practices of assessing students' sustainability competencies: A review of tools. *Sustainability Science, 16*, 117–135. https://doi.org/10.1007/s11625-020-00855-1

Richard, V., Forget, D., & Gonzalez-Bautista, N. (2017). Implementing sustainability in the classroom at Université Laval. In W. Leal Filho, M. Mifsud, C. Shiel, & R. Pretorius (Eds.), *Handbook of theory and practice of sustainable development in higher education* (pp. 133–147). Springer. https://doi.org/10.1007/978-3-319-47895 -1_9

Rowe, D., & Hiser, K. (2016). Higher education for sustainable development in the community and through partnerships. In M. Barth, G. Michelsen, M. Rieckmann, & I. Thomas (Eds.), *Routledge handbook of higher education for sustainable development* (pp. 315–330). Routledge.

Sachs, J.D., Schmidt-Traub, G., Mazzucato, M., Messner, D., Nakicenovic, N., & Rockström, J. (2019). Six transformations to achieve the Sustainable Development Goals. *Nature Sustainability, 2*, 805–814. https://doi.org/10.1038/s41893-019-0352 -9

Salovaara, J.J., & Soini, K. (2021). Educated professionals of sustainability and the dimensions of practices. *International Journal of Sustainability in Higher Education, 22*(8), 69–87. https://doi.org/10.1108/IJSHE-09-2020-0327

Sandri, O. (2020). What do we mean by "pedagogy" in sustainability education? *Teaching in Higher Education.* https://doi.org/10.1080/13562517.2019.1699528

Shephard, K. (2015). *Higher education for sustainable development.* Palgrave Macmillan.

Shephard, K., Rieckmann, M., & Barth, M. (2019). Seeking sustainability competence and capability in the ESD and HESD literature: An international philosophical hermeneutic analysis. *Environmental Education Research, 25*(4), 532–547. https:// doi .org/10.1080/13504622.2018.1490947

Shriberg, M., & MacDonald, L. (2013). Sustainability leadership programs: Emerging goals, methods & best practices. *Journal of Sustainability Education, 5*(1), 1–21.

Stephens, J.C., Hernandez, M.E., Román, M., Graham, A.C., & Scholz, R.W. (2008). Higher education as a change agent for sustainability in different cultures and contexts. *International Journal of Sustainability in Higher Education, 9*(3), 317–338. https://doi.org/10.1108/14676370810885916

Sterling, S. (2004). Higher education, sustainability, and the role of systemic learning. In P.B. Corcoran & A.E.J. Wals (Eds.), *Higher education and the challenge of sustainability: Problematics, promise, and practice* (pp. 47–70). Springer. https:// doi .org/10.1007/0-306-48515-X_5

Sterling, S., Glasser, H., Rieckmann, M., & Warwick, P. (2017). "More than scaling up": A critical and practical inquiry into operationalizing sustainability competencies. In P.B. Corcoran, J.P. Weakland, & A.E.J. Wals (Eds.), *Envisioning futures for environmental and sustainability education* (pp. 153–168). Wageningen Academic.

Sustainable Development Solutions Network (2020). *Accelerating education for the SDGs in universities: A guide for universities, colleges, and tertiary and higher education institutions.* Sustainable Development Solutions Network.

Swearingen White, S. (2014). Campus sustainability plans in the United States: Where, what, and how to evaluate? *International Journal of Sustainability in Higher Education, 15*(2), 228–241. https://doi.org/10.1108/IJSHE-08-2012-0075

Sylvestre, P., & Wright, T. (2016). Organisational change and organisational learning for promoting higher education for sustainable development. In M. Barth, G. Michelsen, M. Rieckmann, & I. Thomas (Eds.), *Routledge handbook of higher education for sustainable development* (pp. 301–314). Routledge.

Taylor, D.E. (2015). Gender and racial diversity in environmental organizations: Uneven accomplishments and cause for concern. *Environmental Justice, 8*(5), 165–180. http://doi.org/10.1089/env.2015.0018

Taylor, D.E. (2018). Racial and ethnic differences in students' readiness, identity, perceptions of institutional diversity, and desire to join the environmental workforce. *Journal of Environmental Studies and Sciences, 8*(2), 152–168. https://doi.org/10.1007/s13412-017-0447-4

Thomas, I. (2016). Challenges for implementation of education for sustainable development in higher education institutions. In M. Barth, G. Michelsen, M. Rieckmann, & I. Thomas (Eds.), *Routledge handbook of higher education for sustainable development* (pp. 56–71). Routledge.

UNESCO (2014a). *Shaping the future we want: UN Decade of Education for Sustainable Development (2005–2014). Final report.* UNESCO.

UNESCO (2014b). *UNESCO roadmap for implementing the Global Action Programme on Education for Sustainable Development.* UNESCO.

Valley, W., Anderson, M., Blackstone, N.T., Sterling, E., Betley, E., Akabas, S., Koch, P., Dring, C., Burke, J., & Spiller, K. (2020). Towards an equity competency model for sustainable food systems education programs. *Elementa: Science of the Anthropocene, 8*, 33. https://doi.org/10.1525/elementa.428

Veiga Ávila, L., Neuron, T.A., Brandli, L.L., Damke, L.I., Pereira, R.S., & Klein, L.L. (2019). Barriers to innovation and sustainability in universities: An international comparison. *International Journal of Sustainability in Higher Education, 20*(5), 805–821. https://doi.org/10.1108/IJSHE-02-2019-0067

Vincent, S. (2010). *Interdisciplinary environmental education on the nation's campuses: Elements of field identity and curriculum design.* National Council for Science and the Environment.

Vincent, S., Bunn, S., & Stevens, S. (2012). *Interdisciplinary environmental and sustainability education: Results from the 2012 census of U.S. four year colleges and universities.* National Council for Science and the Environment.

Vincent, S., Rao, S., Fu, Q., Gu, K., Huang, X., Lindaman, K., Mittleman, E., Nguyen, K., Rosenstein, R., & Suh, Y. (2017). *Scope of interdisciplinary environmental, sustainability, and energy baccalaureate and graduate education in the United States.* National Council for Science and the Environment.

Wals, A.E.J. (2014). Sustainability in higher education in the context of the UN DESD: A review of learning and institutionalization processes. *Journal of Cleaner Production, 62*, 8–15. https://doi.org/10.1016/j.jclepro.2013.06.007

Wals, A.E.J., Tasson, V.C., Hampson, G.P., & Reams, J. (2016). Learning for walking the change: Eco-social innovation through sustainability-oriented higher education. In M. Barth, G. Michelsen, M. Rieckmann, & I. Thomas (Eds.), *Routledge handbook of higher education for sustainable development* (pp. 25–39). Routledge.

Weiss, M., & Barth, M. (2019). Global research landscape of sustainability curricula implementation in higher education. *International Journal of Sustainability in Higher Education, 20*(4), 570–589. https://doi.org/10.1108/IJSHE-10-2018-0190

Weiss, M., Barth, M., & von Wehrden, H. (2021a). The patterns of curriculum change processes that embed sustainability in higher education institutions. *Sustainability Science, 16*, 1579–1593. https://doi.org/10.1007/s11625-021-00984-1

Weiss, M., Barth, M., Wiek, A., & von Wehrden, H. (2021b). Drivers and barriers of implementing sustainability curricula in higher education: Assumptions and evidence. *Higher Education Studies*, *11*(2), 42–64. https:// doi .org/ 10 .5539/ hes .v11n2p42

Wiek, A., Bernstein, M.J., Foley, R.W., Cohen, M., Forrest, N., Kuzdas, C., Kay, B., & Withycombe Keeler, L. (2016). Operationalising competencies in higher education for sustainable development. In M. Barth, G. Michelsen, M. Rieckmann, & I. Thomas (Eds.), *Routledge handbook of higher education for sustainable development* (pp. 241–260). Routledge.

Wiek, A., & Redman, A. (2022). What do key competencies in sustainability offer and how to use them. In P. Vare, N. Lausselet, & M. Rieckmann (Eds.), *Competencies in education for sustainable development* (pp. 27–34). Springer.

Wiek, A., Withycombe, L., & Redman, C.L. (2011). Key competencies in sustainability: A reference framework for academic program development. *Sustainability Science*, 6, 203–218. https://doi.org/10.1007/s11625-011-0132-6

Wiggins, G.P., & McTighe, J. (1998). *Understanding by design*. Association for Supervision and Curriculum Development.

Yarime, M., Trencher, G., Mino, T., Scholz, R., Olsson, L., Ness, B., Frantzeskaki, N., & Rotmans, J. (2012). Establishing sustainability science in higher education institutions: Towards an integration of academic development, institutionalization, and stakeholder collaborations. *Sustainability Science*, 7, 101–113. https://doi.org/10.1007/s11625-012-0157-5

3. Sustainable practices as innovation adoption on campus

Jason C. Senjem

SUSTAINABLE PRACTICES AS INNOVATION ADOPTION ON CAMPUS

Many organizations have announced commitments to adopting sustainable environmental practices only to realize the difficulty in implementing these in a consistent and meaningful way. This has led to a wide distribution in how effective organizations are at becoming sustainable. This chapter will examine the role that innovation, entrepreneurial behavior, and structural practices play in explaining why some but not all colleges and universities successfully adopt environmental practices and suggests implications for practice. This chapter will highlight common experiences of firsthand cases of two small US midwestern Catholic universities in their pursuit of adopting sustainable practices and how they deal with challenges such as getting the Trustees on board, going beyond the "low-hanging fruit", avoiding distractions, and creating true community engagement. Major findings at what works include having a building and grounds champion, committee leadership, bias toward action, collaboration between the sciences and business, consistent meetings and community interactions, network engagement at the edges, less is more influencing, and bringing in ideas and knowledge from outside the US.

Why do sustainable practices matter for higher education institutions? Sustainability is about balancing the social, economic, and environmental aspects of development. It means meeting the needs of the present without compromising the ability of future generations to meet their own needs. Sustainability is important for higher education institutions because they have a significant impact on society and the environment through their teaching, research, operations, and outreach activities. By adopting sustainability practices on campus, higher education institutions can not only fulfill their moral duty, but also enhance their quality, relevance, and reputation.

Colleges and universities have been responding to calls to make a meaningful organization by committing to adopt environmental practices as part of its sustainability and social responsibility efforts (Barnett, Henriques, & Husted, 2020; Hoffman, 2001; Ones & Dilchert, 2012). The case study examples come from two small US midwestern Catholic universities that had active sustainability committees. These cases offer a variety of undergraduate and graduate programs in arts and sciences, business, health and human services, and education. A majority of students are athletes. The examples include involvement from students (undergraduate and graduate), faculty, staff, administrators, alumni, local community, and businesses. Identifying information is left out so the focus is on the behaviors that were successful as well as challenges they faced. Based on the case studies, inferences are drawn as to how colleges and universities innovate as they adopt sustainable practices.

An innovation perspective identifies the ability to recognize opportunities and enact resources, two key aspects of entrepreneurship (Shane & Venkataraman, 2000), and examines their role in creating unique solutions to improving environmental performance through the adoption of sustainable practices. As organizational researchers grapple over whether environmentally and socially sustainable practices lead to performance gains or not, some have instead looked at how and why organizations have adopted specific sustainable practices (Bansal & Roth, 2000; Etzion, 2007; King & Lenox, 2000).

But how do these practices come about? Who are the actors and factors that influence the adoption of sustainability practices on campus? A combination of innovation and sustainability frameworks and case examples illustrate the arguments. Evidence of entrepreneurial and structural influences provides the key roles they play in adoption of practices of sustainability on campus. Opportunities and challenges imply key lessons learned from this evidence. The lessons benefit higher education institutions who want to adopt or improve their sustainability practices on campus.

The Role of Innovation in Adopting Sustainable Practices

Sustainability is a pressing and complex challenge that demands innovative and collaborative solutions from diverse actors and sectors. However, implementing sustainability practices is not a simple task, as it entails multiple dimensions and levels of analysis, as well as various stakeholders and interests. Moreover, sustainability practices need to be able to adapt and evolve in response to changing conditions. Therefore, achieving sustained success of adopting sustainability practices requires not only generating and implementing creative ideas, but also developing and maintaining competencies that enable continuous learning and improvement. In other words, adopting sustainable practices reflects many aspects of the innovation process.

The strategic attribute of innovation is essential to the identification of opportunities for sustainability (Cohen & Winn, 2007; Dean & McMullen,

2007; Hart & Milstein, 1999) as well as to improve sustainable operations and value chain activities (Christmann, 2000; Etzion, 2007). Viewing environmental issues as opportunities has been shown to positively influence more progressive environmental strategies (Sharma, 2000). Therefore, an entrepreneurial and innovation perspective that involves opportunity recognition is helpful in understanding the adoption of sustainable practices.

Applying a model of innovation, such as the Idea Journey model, to the adoption of sustainability practices produces a process-oriented perspective that focuses on how to generate and implement creative ideas for sustainability practices at different levels and phases (Perry-Smith & Mannucci, 2017; Perry-Smith, 2022). The Idea Journey model is a four-phase model that describes how individuals and teams can generate and implement creative ideas in organizations. The four phases are: idea generation, idea elaboration, idea championing, and idea implementation. Each phase involves different social network drivers that influence the creativity and innovation outcomes. The Idea Journey contributes to the sustained success of adopting sustainability practices by addressing the importance of creating competencies, coming up with a quantity of ideas, creating cumulative advantage, and managing path dependence.

First, the Idea Generation phase involves coming up with novel and useful ideas for sustainability practices, such as reducing waste, saving energy, or promoting awareness. This phase contributes to the sustained success of adopting sustainability practices by creating competencies that enable the identification and exploitation of opportunities for improvement in the sustainability system. By generating novel and useful ideas for sustainability practices, creative teams can develop competencies such as opportunity recognition, problem-solving, or creativity.

Consequently, this phase also contributes to the sustained success of adopting sustainability practices by coming up with a quantity of ideas that increase the chances of finding high-quality ideas. According to the quantity breeds quality principle (Diehl & Stroebe, 1987), generating more ideas increases the probability of producing more original and diverse ideas. By coming up with a quantity of ideas for sustainability practices, individuals and teams can increase their pool of potential solutions and explore different alternatives.

Second, the Idea Elaboration phase involves refining and developing the ideas for sustainability practices by testing their feasibility, viability, and desirability. This phase contributes to the sustained success of adopting sustainability practices by creating competencies that enable the evaluation and improvement of ideas for sustainability practices. By elaborating on the ideas for sustainability practices, creative teams can develop competencies such as critical thinking, decision making, or feedback seeking.

This phase further contributes to the sustained success of adopting sustainability practices by achieving cumulative advantage that enhances the quality and attractiveness of ideas for sustainability practices. According to the cumulative advantage principle (Merton, 1968), early success leads to more resources, recognition, and support, which in turn leads to more success. By elaborating on the ideas for sustainability practices, creative teams can improve their quality and attractiveness, which in turn can increase their chances of gaining more resources, recognition, and support for their ideas.

Third, the Idea Championing phase involves persuading and mobilizing others to support the ideas for sustainability practices, such as decision makers, stakeholders, or customers. This phase contributes to the sustained success of adopting sustainability practices by creating competencies that enable the communication and diffusion of ideas for sustainability practices.

By championing the ideas for sustainability practices, creative teams can develop competencies such as persuasion, influence, or networking. Furthermore, this phase contributes to the sustained success of adopting sustainability practices by avoiding path dependence that limits the adaptability and evolution of ideas for sustainability practices.

According to Justin Berg's path dependence concept (2016), the creativity of the sustainability practices at the time of their initial implementation influences their later ability to sustain success in changing markets. Creativity is defined as the degree to which a product is novel (different from existing products) and varied (different from other products in the same portfolio). Relatively creative portfolios (those that are novel or varied) give creators more options for adapting to market changes and increasing their odds of additional hits.

However, there is a tradeoff between the likelihood of initial and sustained success, such that building a relatively creative early portfolio is a risky bet that can make or break a creator's career. By championing the ideas for sustainability practices, individuals and teams can avoid path dependence by balancing the tradeoff between initial and sustained success and choosing the optimal level of creativity for their sustainability practices.

Lastly, the Idea Implementation phase involves executing and evaluating the ideas for sustainability practices, such as organizing and coordinating the tasks and resources. This phase contributes to the sustained success of adopting sustainability practices by creating competencies that enable the execution and evaluation of ideas for sustainability practices. By implementing the ideas for sustainability practices, creative teams can develop competencies such as project management, teamwork, or performance measurement. As a result, this phase contributes to the sustained success of adopting sustainability practices by achieving cumulative advantage that enhances the outcomes and impacts of the sustainability practices.

By implementing the ideas for sustainability practices, creative teams can improve their outcomes and impacts, such as environmental, economic, social, cultural, or spiritual aspects of sustainability, which in turn can increase their chances of gaining more resources, recognition, and support for their sustainability practices.

In brief, the Idea Journey model elaborates the achievement of sustained success in adopting sustainability practices by providing a process-oriented perspective that focuses on how to generate and implement creative ideas for sustainability practices at different levels and phases. Each phase of the Idea Journey contributes to the sustained success of adopting sustainability practices by addressing the importance of creating competencies, coming up with a quantity of ideas, cumulative advantage, and Justin Berg's path dependence. By applying the Idea Journey model to the sustainability context, organizations enhance their ability to plan and implement sustainability practices that are not only novel and useful, but also adaptable and evolving.

Connecting to the Integrated Sustainability Model

Starik, Stubbs, and Benn (2016) proposed a sustainability model that is a multi-level approach integrating environmental and socio-economic sustainability concepts and practices for different types of entities, such as individuals, organizations, or societies. The model consists of micro-, meso-, and macro-levels, systems, culture, and structure along three phases of sustainability progress.

This model's structure, culture, and systems interact with the Idea Journey phases from the previous section. Examples illustrate how a Catholic university that follows Laudato Si' might work.

Starik et al. (2016) identify structure, culture, and systems as three aspects of the organizational context in their integrated sustainability model. These aspects can influence and be influenced by the Idea Journey phases. Structure refers to the formal and informal arrangements and mechanisms that organize and coordinate the tasks and resources of the organization. Culture refers to the shared values and norms that guide and motivate the behavior and performance of the organizational members. Finally, systems refer to the set of components and interactions that constitute the organizational environment and processes.

A university that follows Laudato Si' is a university that aligns its mission and values with the encyclical letter by Pope Francis that calls for care for our common home and ecological conversion. It critiques the current model of development that exploits and destroys nature and human dignity and proposes an integral ecology that respects the interconnectedness of all creation and the dignity of each person. It also appeals for a global dialogue and action to address the environmental and social crisis (Pope Francis, 2015).

Structure, culture, and systems interact with the Idea Journey phases especially with a university that follows Laudato Si' in the following ways:

1. Idea generation: This phase involves coming up with novel and useful ideas for sustainability practices on campus. Structure, culture, and systems can interact with this phase by providing or constraining the resources, incentives, and opportunities for generating ideas. For example, a university that follows Laudato Si' has a structure that encourages cross-disciplinary collaboration and participation among different stakeholders; a culture that fosters curiosity, experimentation, and risk-taking; and a system that integrates environmental, economic, social, cultural, and spiritual dimensions of sustainability.

2. Idea elaboration: This phase involves refining and developing the ideas for sustainability practices on campus. Structure, culture, and systems can interact with this phase by supporting or hindering the testing and improvement of ideas. For example, a university that follows Laudato Si' has a structure that provides feedback and validation for the ideas; a culture that values learning from failure and diversity of perspectives; and a system that simulates the dynamics and complexity of the sustainability system under different conditions or interventions.

3. Idea championing: This phase involves persuading and mobilizing others to support the ideas for sustainability practices on campus. Structure, culture, and systems can interact with this phase by facilitating or obstructing the communication and diffusion of ideas. For example, a university that follows Laudato Si' has a structure that enables access and influence on key decision makers and stakeholders; a culture that promotes trust, commitment, and solidarity; and a system that measures and reports the outcomes and impacts of the sustainability practices on campus.

4. Idea implementation: This phase involves executing and evaluating the ideas for sustainability practices on campus. Structure, culture, and systems can interact with this phase by enabling or disabling the execution and evaluation of ideas. For example, a university that follows Laudato Si' has a structure that allocates roles, responsibilities, resources, and rules for implementing and managing the sustainability practices; a culture that recognizes and appreciates the contributions and achievements of the sustainability actors; and a system that tracks and audits the progress and performance of the sustainability practices on campus.

Case Study 1: Green College

Green College demonstrates its dedication to sustainability in various ways. The college is a top-ranked Catholic liberal arts college in the Midwest that values environmental stewardship and education. The college has several initiatives and groups that support sustainable practices on campus, such as the zero-food waste program, the campus garden, the student environmental club, and the Environmental Sustainability Advisory Committee (ESAC). Green College aims to help its communities achieve environmental integrity and social justice.

Their sustainability strategy began with signing the American College & University Presidents' Climate Commitment (ACUPCC) that focused on measuring and mitigating the campus carbon emissions. This helped spur some very innovative ideas that were not adopted due to cost. However, progress was still made. For example, though LEED certification was deemed too expensive, a new library was built to LEED standards. Though sustainability was not in the initial design process, once it was identified as important the architect was more than happy to oblige. This suggests a need for policies that have architects and engineers put forth sustainable plans rather than hold back.

Structurally, a sustainability committee was formed with representation across campus including students. The ACUPCC signing was an official support from administration. Members of the committee also crossed over to the community sustainability committee so synergies could be created there. For example, the college created a community engagement day highlighting the campus and local sustainable businesses where learning and relationships were developed.

From a systems perspective, several projects had been implemented successfully and had also saved the college money. The sustainability committee thought the money should be paid forward to fund future sustainable initiatives. Due to certain fiscal difficulties in making that happen, a student green initiative fee was developed and charged to students. Students may propose green projects that use those funds to promote sustainability on campus. This is an excellent student engagement and an implicit promise that the college is doing something by "putting money where its mouth is".

Culturally, the campus wanted to better leverage its mission emphasis on social justice. It had a peace and justice center, campus ministry, and many student life clubs all doing a variety of service as well as a significant number of courses using academic service learning. Unfortunately, faculty all got in each other's way and were starting to wear out the local non-profits. A systematic effort was made to consolidate and organize the service projects. A needs analysis and proposal were made. Then a donor was identified as well as key individuals to create a center for service learning that leveraged everyone's time and efforts to be more effective and efficient. This center was then able to leverage and organize connections across the college and into the community to be a more effective and efficient partner for environmental and social impact. Faculty leading service-learning courses could then better serve the mission as "contemplatives in action".

Case Study 2: Blue University

Blue University is a Catholic regional comprehensive university with several graduate programs in the Midwest that values sustainability as an individual and collective responsibility. The university has a sustainability committee that leads various initiatives to protect the environment and educate the community, such as community litter cleanup events, leadership workshops, and community gardens. The university also has a student club that organizes campus-wide cleanups, food drives, pollinator gardens, and roundtable discussions on climate change. The university offers academic programs that equip students with the skills and knowledge to become sustainability champions in fields such as biology, environmental studies, and public health. The university also demonstrates its commitment to sustainability through its physical plant practices, such as using biodiesel-fueled vehicles, creating stormwater retention tanks, installing water bottle filling stations, and prioritizing energy efficiency in new construction. Furthermore, the university embraces diversity, equity, and inclusion as core priorities that respect the dignity and worth of every individual in pursuit of social justice. Blue University is committed to stewardship of natural resources and protection of the rest of creation.

The Idea Journey relates to sustainable practices such as those that relate to the Sustainable Development Goals (SDGs) 2, 3, and 11 or zero hunger, good health and well-being, and sustainable cities. Blue U has a service and justice coordinator who was contacted by a local leader who was looking to expand their food pantry to distribute an extra time or two a month. The coordinator brought this to a professor who was involved in doing service-learning work and who was on the sustainability committee. In the Idea Generation phase, they discussed some ideas together with the local leader and then took the idea to a student club whose goal was to improve peoples' lives through pursuing the SDGs. More talks took place and a management course that the professor was teaching was enlisted to help organize and support the labor efforts of this new venture. With input from other faculty, they decided they wanted the focus to be on healthy food for families.

During the Idea Elaboration phase, which is still ongoing, students decided they wanted to have some ownership of this and gave the food pantry its own name and identified officers who would help plan things. Students were given office space to work. They learned how to place an order the week before from the local food bank. They scheduled students to prepare the receiving room for the palates from the delivery truck. They planned and organized how the food would be broken down and placed in refrigerators and freezers and sorted into boxes. Finally, they determined how to distribute food to the families. Students contacted various afterschool programs to recruit and educate families about the food pantry. Three afterschool programs had joined making 36 families that would be fed several boxes of dry goods, frozen meat, and produce. More layers to the program were added, including a partnership with a local TV chef who is making recipes for the families based on the food the pantry gives them. A partnership with a local food rescue is expanding the kind of food given as well as the food drive partnership with the campus food vendor.

Idea Champions come from local leaders, professors, and student leaders. They committed to coming in at 6am and working very hard for several hours. They developed several partnerships that acted as champions financially, mentoring-wise, and educationally as previously discussed. There are key local organizations supporting the recipients and key student clubs, courses, and athletic clubs supporting the planning and service needs.

This food pantry was implemented monthly, repeated, and applied learning each time. Students created goals and learned the vision of what was being achieved, including a social justice perspective that helped them understand why there is the need here. They learned about historic redline districts and how they line up with the food deserts in the city. This was launched in conjunction with an aligned academic theme which enhanced the students' learning and motivation.

The Role of Entrepreneurial Influences

The role of entrepreneurial influences plays a role throughout the Idea Journey in adopting sustainability practices on college campuses. Evidence will be given from both Green College and Blue University in this section. Entrepreneurial influences are those individuals or groups who initiate, create, or lead sustainability projects or initiatives on campus, using their creativity, passion, and skills to overcome barriers and seize opportunities. Entrepreneurial influences can come from students, faculty, staff, alumni, or external partners who have a vision and a mission to make a positive difference for the environment and society through their actions. They are called champions or influencers.

Entrepreneurial influencers can have a significant impact on campus sustainability by generating innovative ideas and solutions that address environmental or social issues. They can also inspire, educate, and mobilize others to join their cause and create a culture of sustainability on campus. Entrepreneurial influencers can be role models, mentors, advocates, or leaders for sustainability.

The entrepreneurial influencer tends to use entrepreneurial bricolage (Baker & Nelson, 2005). This would include the following: finding new use or value in forgotten, discarded, worn, or presumed valueless materials; involving volunteers to work on projects, permitting or encouraging the use of amateur and self-taught skills that would otherwise go unapplied in an organization; providing services that would otherwise be unavailable to students, faculty, staff, or alumni; and refusing to be limited by internal and external norms and standards.

One illustrative example of an entrepreneurial influencer or champion is the Grounds and Maintenance Director. Having someone in this position that cares about the environment is key to getting practices and policies adopted. In this position, the director uses their innovation, communication, collaboration, and impact skills to influence sustainability practices on campus. He generated novel ideas and solutions for reducing energy usage on campus, such as swapping out light bulbs for LEDs and proposing cutting-edge technology that used garbage for fuel. He communicated his vision and passion for sustainability by providing data from prototype projects and being practical at implementation. For example, the college could not afford to purchase a new boiler system for campus, so instead he took a long-term phased approach that implemented upgrades over time that proved to be well received by administrators, did not entail huge costs each year, but did improve efficiency over time. Finally, he cooperated with other actors who shared his vision or supported his cause to achieve maximum impact.

Benefits for campus sustainability

Entrepreneurial influencers have a significant positive impact on campus sustainability efforts and results in the case study campuses. First, they create value for themselves and others by solving real-world problems with sustainable solutions. For example, student-led clubs or organizations have organized events or campaigns that raised awareness, educated, and mobilized others to act on sustainability issues, such as waste reduction, energy conservation, or social justice. These activities have positive impacts on the environment and society, as well as on the personal and professional development of the students involved.

Second, they leverage their networks and resources to access funding, mentorship, support, or recognition for their projects or initiatives. For example, internal sustainability committees have applied for grants, awards, or fellowships from internal or external sources that support sustainability research or innovation. These opportunities provide financial, technical, or academic assistance, as well as visibility and credibility for the faculty and their projects.

Third, they develop their skills, knowledge, competencies, and confidence as entrepreneurs and change-makers. For example, staff-led initiatives have implemented sustainability practices or policies in campus operations, infrastructure, or administration that improve efficiency, performance, or quality.

These initiatives enhance the skills and knowledge of the staff involved in areas such as project management, problem-solving, communication, or collaboration. They also boost their confidence and motivation as they see the results and benefits of their actions.

Fourth, they contribute to the reputation and attractiveness of their campus as a leader in sustainability. For example, holding community roundtables and events like Earth Day and Sustainability Week allows the university to engage with others in what it offers and what the community network offers in terms of sustainable initiatives. These touchpoints showcase the excellence and impact of their campus education and culture on sustainability. They also attract potential students, faculty, staff, partners, or donors who share the same interests and goals.

Challenges for campus sustainability

Entrepreneurial influencers also face significant challenges for campus sustainability initiatives. First, they may encounter resistance or skepticism from some campus stakeholders who are not supportive of or familiar with sustainability issues or practices. For example, student-led clubs or organizations have faced difficulties in getting approval, funding, space, or participation for their events or campaigns from campus administrators, faculty, staff, or peers who do not see the relevance or importance of sustainability. These challenges discourage and hinder the students from pursuing their projects or initiatives.

Second, they may face competition or conflict with other entrepreneurial influencers who have different visions or approaches for sustainability. For example, faculty-led projects or initiatives sometimes clash with other faculty members who have conflicting research agendas, methodologies, or perspectives on sustainability. These conflicts create tension or hostility among the faculty community and affect their collaboration and productivity.

Third, they may struggle with balancing their academic or professional responsibilities with their entrepreneurial endeavors. For example, staff-led initiatives often require extra time, effort, or resources that go beyond their regular duties and expectations. These demands cause stress, fatigue, or burnout for the staff involved and affect their work performance or quality.

Fourth, they may experience uncertainty, risk, or failure in their projects or initiatives. For example, many ideas are simply experiments to try new things and these will often fail and not meet the mark. One initiative unplugged water fountains across campus to save energy on cooling the water. That was met with resistance from the users as people were being encouraged at the same time to fill their water bottles instead of buying plastic water bottles and storing them in an energy-using mini fridge. This failed experiment of energy conservation was useful to learn from as an adaptation was then made by installing water bottle filling stations at the water fountains that remained plugged in for fresh cool water for people to use. The initial failure in one area, energy conservation, then led to success in another area, reduction of plastic use.

Lessons learned in fostering entrepreneurial action for sustainability
Individuals such as the director of grounds and maintenance on a college campus may face some major challenges in implementing and promoting sustainability. However, there are also many possible ways to overcome these challenges. One challenge is the cost and time required to upgrade and maintain the campus facilities and infrastructure to meet the sustainability goals. One solution is to seek external funding and partnerships with various departments that share an interest as well as local businesses, organizations, and government agencies that support sustainability. Another solution is to use student research and innovation to test and implement new sustainability technologies and practices on campus. For example, the sustainability committee wanted to renovate a building courtyard to house pollinator gardens, an outdoor teaching area with seating, and teaching stations with a handicap-accessible entrance. A donation seemed out of reach, so students applied to their student fund to help finance this and multiple student organizations, the Engineering Club, and other volunteers helped build the gardens and seating areas without having to use nearly as much money as they had originally budgeted. So instead of a project getting stopped in its tracks, discussion across multiple areas combined with innovative ideas and hard work resulted in realizing the vision.

Another challenge is the lack of awareness and engagement among the campus community about the benefits and importance of sustainability. A solution to overcome this is to educate and empower the campus community about the benefits and importance of sustainability through various channels and events. The sustainability committee reintroduced Earth Day to help build awareness. What seemed to work best is including community partners such as local water, garbage, and recycling centers as well as several other sustainability businesses such as solar, political advocacy, peace and justice, food rescue, and a food pantry. Another solution is to incentivize and recognize the campus community for their sustainability efforts and achievements. The sustainability committee implemented a Sustainability Hero award for faculty, staff, and students that is voted on by the environmental club. In addition, a monthly newsletter and website recognizes what others are doing in the social and justice areas as well as the environment.

A third challenge is the complexity and interconnectedness of the sustainability issues and solutions, which demand a multidisciplinary and collaborative approach. A solution to address this is to adopt a holistic and systemic approach to sustainability that considers the environmental, social, and economic impacts of each decision and action. For example, an educational speaker series addressed the Sustainable Development Goals and engaged with students so they could learn about systemic issues and receive a certificate from it. Another solution is to collaborate and coordinate with other campus departments, units, and stakeholders to ensure alignment and integration of sustainability goals and strategies. The committee meets monthly and various subcommittees meet even more often. The committee share out all information in written form as well, so the right hand knows what the left hand is doing.

A final challenge is the uncertainty and variability of the environmental conditions and regulations, which may affect the feasibility and effectiveness of the sustainability initiatives. A solution to deal with this challenge is to use data and evidence to monitor and evaluate the progress and outcomes of the sustainability initiatives on campus, as well as to adapt and improve the sustainability initiatives based on the feedback and changing conditions. The sustainability committee make comparisons to what they did before, whether it is previous event turnout or amount of water saved in the cafeteria. They assess as things happen and afterwards so trends can be tracked to determine improvements.

Making a system of reporting, information sharing, and relationship-building has helped make the campus feel supportive for taking on any new project just as an entrepreneur would.

Structural Influences

In contrast to entrepreneurial influences are structural influences on college campuses. These include institutional policies, physical infrastructure, organizational culture, or stakeholder networks that could influence adoption of sustainability initiatives. Evidence will be given from both Green College and Blue University in this section.

Benefits of structural influences

Institutional policies are the rules and regulations that govern the campus operations and activities. They can set goals and standards for sustainability performance, such as reducing waste, water, and energy consumption, increasing recycling and composting, promoting renewable energy sources, etc. They can also provide incentives and rewards for sustainable practices, such as grants, scholarships, recognition, etc. For example, many universities have a sustainability plan that outlines its goals and strategies for various aspects of campus sustainability. More examples of institutional policies for sustainability include using recycled materials for production, integrating the highest standards of sustainability in building design, limiting the use of nonrenewable resources, and collaborating with other stakeholders to address environmental challenges.

Physical infrastructure refers to the design and layout of the campus buildings, facilities, transportation, etc. It can influence the environmental impact and efficiency of the campus, as well as the health and comfort of students and staff. It can also provide opportunities and resources for sustainability education and action, such as water bottle refill stations, bike racks, solar panels, green roofs, etc. For example, many campuses have installed recycling bins next to trash cans to make recycling more convenient and visible. Other examples of physical infrastructure for sustainability include installing energy-efficient equipment, utilizing renewable energy sources, implementing green building materials and construction techniques, and improving waste management.

Organizational culture is the shared values, beliefs, norms, and practices that shape the campus community and identity. It can influence the attitudes and behaviors of students and staff toward sustainability issues and initiatives. It can also foster a sense of responsibility and commitment to sustainability among different groups and individuals. For example, many campuses participate in Earth Day activities every April to raise awareness and engagement on sustainability topics. Further examples of organizational culture for sustainability include fostering a sense of purpose and responsibility, promoting innovation and learning, encouraging collaboration and diversity, and rewarding ethical and sustainable practices.

Stakeholder networks are the relationships and collaborations among different groups and individuals who have an interest or influence on campus sustainability. They can include students, faculty, staff, alumni, administrators, donors, community partners, etc. They can provide support and feedback for sustainability initiatives, as well as share ideas and best practices. They can also advocate for sustainability issues and policies at different levels. For example, many campuses have student-led sustainability clubs or organizations that organize events and projects on campus. Other examples of stakeholder networks for sustainability include engaging with customers and suppliers to reduce environmental footprint, partnering with investors and regulators to access finance and incentives, working with civil society and academia to address social issues, and communicating with media and public to enhance reputation and trust.

Lessons learned for improvement and alignment of structural influences
Some of the negative structural challenges college campuses face involve conflict, resistance, or inertia when adopting sustainable practices. There are some effective strategies for overcoming the challenges of sustainability in higher education.

One structural challenge is lack of awareness and engagement among students, faculty, staff, and administrators about the importance and benefits of sustainability, as well as the opportunities and resources available for sustainability initiatives. Students, faculty, staff, and administrators raise awareness and engagement by providing information, education, training, incentives, recognition, and opportunities for participation and leadership in sustainability initiatives. Getting people's attention is increasingly more difficult, however, faculty have had students get course credit for designing engaging games and activities during sustainability events on campus and that has seemed to have gotten students engaged.

Another structural challenge is lack of institutional support and commitment from the leadership and governance structures of the colleges, such as insufficient funding, policies, incentives, accountability, and recognition for sustainability efforts. The committee can secure institutional support and commitment from the leadership and governance structures of the college by developing and implementing clear and coherent sustainability policies, plans, goals, indicators, budgets, and accountability mechanisms. Showing that the committee is thinking practically as well shows good faith with administrators as the example of the phased updating of the boiler shows.

A third structural challenge is lack of integration and collaboration across disciplines, departments, units, and stakeholders within and outside the colleges, such as difficulty in incorporating sustainability principles and practices into the curriculum, research, community service, and campus operations. The university can work to enhance integration and collaboration across disciplines, departments, units, and stakeholders within and outside the colleges by fostering interdisciplinary and transdisciplinary curriculum, research, service, and operations that address sustainability issues and solutions. For example, sustainability committees should be made up of people from all different departments and levels of staff, faculty, and administration. The sustainability committees in these cases have been very inclusionary and this has allowed for more innovative thinking and information sharing that has led to serendipitous relationships.

A final structural challenge is lack of innovation and adaptation to the changing needs and expectations of the society and the environment, such as reluctance to adopt new technologies, methods, models, and paradigms that can enhance sustainability performance and outcomes. This can be dealt with by trying things out, so they do not create fear in people. On one campus, the university has adopted a practice of prototyping or trying something out before it is adopted. This strategy has the commitment from the President on down. This can make it easier to see what works and what doesn't as well as get people on board. The first time one makes a proposal, people think you are crazy, the second time they are skeptical, and the third time they thought it had already been adopted. Persistence driven by a vision can make things happen.

FUTURE RESEARCH

Two primary constructs of entrepreneurship research, opportunity recognition and enactment of resources (Shane & Venkataraman, 2000), are essential to connecting research to the practice of improving sustainability performance in organizations. Furthermore, how entrepreneurial behaviors can help construct organizational processes and systems that lead to the adoption of environmental practices to create meaningful environmental performance should be explored. It may be that designing work structures is enabling for bricolage activities. Bricolage may be more than enacting resources but also responding in a purposeful way to defy socially constructed institutional or cultural conventions. Future research should focus on how to enable this entrepreneurial behavior to suggest ways for organizations to improve their environmental performance as they face increasing pressures and incentives to do so. Connecting these findings to micro-foundations of sustainability and an ethic of care (Aragòn-Correa, Marcus, & Vogel, 2020; Carmeli, Brammer, Gomes, & Tarba, 2017) could help everyone understand broader connections between these behaviors and the organizational context.

CONCLUSION

What is next? Damon Centola, Professor at the University of Pennsylvania, who has conducted research on complex contagions and change, may have an answer (Centola, 2021). Centola's research on complex contagions suggests that social influence is not always as simple as the spread of a single idea or behavior. Instead, he argues that some behaviors require exposure to multiple sources before they can be adopted. This is known as a "complex contagion". In his book *Change: How to Make Big Things Happen*, Centola explores how complex contagions work and how they can be used to create positive change in society.

In terms of college campuses using this theory to spread the adoption of sustainability practices, Centola suggests that it is important to target groups of people who are already interested in sustainability and have strong social ties with others who are interested in sustainability. This is because people are more likely to adopt behaviors when they see others around them doing the same thing.

One way to do this is by creating social networks that connect people who are interested in sustainability. These networks can be used to share information about sustainability practices and encourage people to adopt these practices. He suggests that reaching 25% involvement in people on the edge of networks is a tipping point that can lead to 100% adoption. Certainly, creating more opportunities for multiple spheres of influence to intersect is creating more energy and momentum. For example, the university expanded from one event at Earth Day to Earth Week in the spring and from Sustainability Fest to Sustainability Week and now Sustainability Month in the fall. Add to that a roundtable of community members at Sustainability Fest to a roundtable series and now year-round programming develops multiple connections with multiple nodes. Instead of just a few people having access to key members there are a significant number who can access and collaborate with each other.

With that network you do not need to rely on just a key champion such as the building and grounds director as mentioned earlier. But those champions can set the tone for inclusivity and openness to innovation. A suggestion for adopting sustainable practices is having an overall strategy that aligns with policies and the institution itself. At one institution it was decided to sign a sustainability commitment that had the approval at the top and then they went about measuring the carbon footprint. At another institution, they decided not to do what can be soul-crushing work of measurement and instead started with action and "low-hanging fruit". However, they were determined to make meaningful adoptions and make significant change. Progress happened due to spreading to all corners of the university so that they could act strategically even if a bit at a time.

Another way of creating complex contagion to get support for sustainable practice adoption is by keeping the message simple. "Less is more" should be the rule according to Sivanathan and Kakkar (2017) who studied argument dilution. When promoting a point of view, use only the best arguments or else people will anchor to the weakest evidence and average out the strength of the argument.

In terms of entrepreneurial influencers, the building and grounds directors, committee chairs, student leaders, faculty leaders, dean of students, student life, residence hall directors all acted entrepreneurially in making things happen. In terms of structural policies, listed in the table below are the most meaningful practices adopted judged by how difficult they are to achieve. So far, a "green" fund that is a student fee for sustainable practices and a Solar Fund Initiative aimed at donors are two of the bigger catalyzing practices that have begun. It is certain through the community they are building they will continue to see progress and success in becoming sustainable. It is hoped these frameworks and retelling of these stories is useful.

So, are universities and colleges leading or following society toward resilience? The evidence from the two Catholic higher education institutions would suggest that they are leading through the process of innovation. The university environment is one of learning and experimentation, which is the most important aspect for sustainable innovations to eventually be successful. Some of these innovations take longer and are more difficult than others to adopt (See

Table 3.1). Faculty, staff, and students are bound up in the culture of learning on the campus that does not necessarily occur in other environments. This chapter has shown how the structures, cultures, and systems of colleges have adapted to pursue sustainability strategies. In addition, innovation on college campuses follows the Idea Journey to implement sustainable practices. While ideas may initially come from outside of campus, the innovation process on campus ensures that experimentation and learning create new practices. Furthermore, these institutions of higher learning are hubs where businesses and the community interact to share knowledge and ideas for sustainability. Consequently, universities lead the way for society and will continue to do so for the foreseeable future.

Table 3.1   Meaningful sustainable practices on college campuses listed by ease of adoption

Sustainable Practice	Ease or Difficulty
Buying local food	Easy
Promoting green transportation	Easy
Installing water-saving devices	Easy
Encouraging recycling and litter pick up competitions	Easy
Creating waste sorts and educational signage	Easy
Forming sustainability committees, groups, and advisories	Easy
Hosting sustainability events and campaigns	Easy
Supporting green student organizations and clubs	Easy
Recognizing and rewarding sustainability achievements	Easy
Getting BeeCampus USA certification	Moderate
Creating a Bike Rental on campus	Moderate
Reducing waste	Moderate
Offering sustainability degree programs	Moderate
Creating green spaces and pollinator habitat	Moderate
Implementing composting programs	Moderate
Creating and caretaking of gardens	Moderate
Educating students and staff on sustainability	Moderate
Participating in sustainability ratings and competitions	Moderate
Engaging with local communities on sustainability issues	Moderate
Developing Beehives on campus	Moderate
Providing green career services and opportunities	Moderate
Creating a food pantry in the community	Moderate

Sustainable Practice	Ease or Difficulty
Providing funding from student fees	Moderate
Creating targeted donor funding	Moderate
Implementing renewable energy sources	Difficult
Achieving carbon neutrality	Difficult
Supporting green research and innovation	Difficult
Developing sustainability policies and plans	Difficult

REFERENCES

Aragòn-Correa, J.A., Marcus, A.A., & Vogel, D. (2020). The effects of mandatory and voluntary regulatory pressures on firms' environmental strategies: A review and recommendations for future research. *Academy of Management Annals, 14*(1), 339–365.

Baker, T., & Nelson, R.E. (2005). Creating something from nothing: Resource construction through entrepreneurial bricolage. *Administrative Science Quarterly, 50,* 329–366.

Bansal, P., & Roth, K. (2000). Why companies go green: A model of ecological responsiveness. *Academy of Management Journal, 43,* 717–736.

Barnett, M.L., Henriques, I., & Husted, B.W. (2020). Beyond good intentions: Designing CSR initiatives for greater social impact. *Journal of Management, 46*(6), 937–964.

Berg, J.M. (2016). Balancing on the creative highwire: Forecasting the success of novel ideas in organizations. *Administrative Science Quarterly, 61*(3), 433–468.

Carmeli, A., Brammer, S., Gomes, E., & Tarba, S.Y. (2017). An organizational ethic of care and employee involvement in sustainability-related behaviors: A social identity perspective. *Journal of Organizational Behavior, 38*(9), 1380–1395.

Centola, D. (2021). *Change: How to make big things happen.* Little, Brown Spark.

Christmann, P. (2000). Effects of 'best practices' of environmental management on cost advantage: The role of complementary assets. *Academy of Management Journal, 43,* 663–680.

Cohen, B., & Winn, M.I. (2007). Market imperfections, opportunity and sustainable entrepreneurship. *Journal of Business Venturing, 22,* 29–49.

Dean, T.J., & McMullen, J.S. (2007). Toward a theory of sustainable entrepreneurship: Reducing environmental degradation through entrepreneurial action. *Journal of Business Venturing, 22,* 50–76.

Diehl, M., & Stroebe, W. (1987). Productivity loss in brainstorming groups: Toward the solution of a riddle. *Journal of Personality and Social Psychology, 53*(3), 497–509.

Etzion, D. (2007). Research on organizations and the natural environment, 1992–present: A review. *Journal of Management, 33,* 637–664.

Hart, S.J., & Milstein, M.B. (1999). Global sustainability and the creative destruction of industries. *Sloan Management Review, 41*(1), 23–33.

Hoffman, A.J. (2001). *From heresy to dogma: An institutional history of corporate environmentalism.* Stanford University Press.

King, A., & Lenox, M. (2004). Prospects for developing absorptive capacity through internal information provision. *Strategic Management Journal, 25,* 331–345.

Merton, R.K. (1968). *Social theory and social structure* (1968 enlarged). Free Press.

Ones, D.S., & Dilchert, S. (2012). Environmental sustainability at work: A call to action. *Industrial and Organizational Psychology*, *5*(4), 444–466.

Perry-Smith, J.E. (2022). How collaboration needs change from mind to marketplace. *MIT Sloan Management Review*, *63*(2), 22–31.

Perry-Smith, J.E., & Mannucci, P.V. (2017). From creativity to innovation: The social network drivers of the four phases of the Idea Journey. *Academy of Management Review*, *42*, 53–79.

Pope Francis. (2015). *Laudato Si'* [On Care for Our Common Home] [Encyclical letter]. Retrieved from: http://www.vatican.va/content/francesco/en/encyclicals/documents/papa-francesco_20150524_enciclica-laudato-si.html

Shane, S., & Venkatamaran, S. (2000). The promise of entrepreneurship as a field of research. *Academy of Management Review*, *25*, 217–226.

Sharma, S. (2000). Managerial interpretations and organizational context as predictors of corporate choice of environmental strategy. *Academy of Management Journal*, *43*, 681–697.

Sivanathan, N., & Kakkar, H. (2017). The unintended consequences of argument dilution in direct-to-consumer drug advertisements. *Nature Human Behaviour*, *1*(11), 797–802.

Starik, M., Stubbs, W., & Benn, S. (2016). Synthesising environmental and socio-economic sustainability models: A multi-level approach for advancing integrated sustainability research and practice. *Australasian Journal of Environmental Management*, *23*(4), 402–425.

4. Higher education institutions can do more to lead society toward resilience and sustainability

Thomas S. Benson

INTRODUCTION

Higher education institutions (HEIs) – universities and colleges – are beginning to recognize their role as leading societal institutions in the movement toward resilience and sustainability by empowering their students as sustainability stakeholders and leaders and recognizing the value of faculty and staff as facilitators in this mobilization toward a more sustainable future. This mobilization is essential in the Anthropocene era, which is characterized by the dual crises of climate change and ecological collapse. To address the environmental and socio-economic challenges posed by these crises, such as depleted landscapes and oceans, food and water insecurity, destructive resource extraction and overconsumption, and pollution, HEIs must build change inside and outside the classroom to prepare its students for a brighter, greener future (Hörisch et al., 2014, p. 329; Weber & Tascón, 2020, p. 858).

As "institutions of knowledge acquisition, development, utilization, and dissemination", HEIs are expected to "advance the important values of their respective societies" (Starik et al., 2002, p. 335). Beside bestowing students with these values, HEIs must recognize that students have played and will continue to play integral roles in supporting the pursuit of sustainability goals and they must harness their enthusiasm, knowledge, experiences, and appetite for change. In doing so, HEIs can achieve a triple-win – wins for student learning, wins for faculty and staff development and organizational sustainability, and wins for institutional image. Beside student success, however, HEIs are also involved in managing real estate, procurement contracts, endowments, consumption of goods and services, different roles in local and regional communities, cultivation of knowledge, the shaping of behaviors and carbon habits, and defining sustainability.

To foster student leadership in sustainability and support faculty and staff in facilitatory roles, HEIs must focus on seven goals that have been identified by reviewing academic literature. These goals include: (1) emphasize interdisciplinary approaches; (2) promote critical thinking and problem-solving skills; (3) advocate for justice, diversity, equity, and inclusion; (4) collaborate with diverse stakeholders; (5) encourage research and innovation for resilience and sustainability; (6) highlight the relationship between mental health, well-being, and resilience; and (7) become and facilitate sustainability leaders and environmental stewards. These seven goals can have varying degrees of progress, and activities across the goals are not exclusive to one another. For example, collaborative efforts with diverse stakeholders can be made to improve critical thinking skills in students by developing experiential learning opportunities. In turn, these opportunities can help to create student leaders, and the overlap between these goals – as illustrated in this example – demonstrates the synergistic connection between the seven goals.

By adopting stakeholder theory and conducting an integrated case study assessment, this chapter identifies undergraduate and graduate students as primary stakeholders, and faculty and staff as secondary, facilitatory stakeholders in achieving these seven goals. Existing literature regarding sustainability and resilience in HEIs, however, has focused predominantly on sustainability in the classroom environment or the establishment of living labs. Although valuable, these insights do not capture the broader capacity of HEIs to be leaders in resilience and sustainability, nor how HEIs can draw on the strengths of its internal stakeholders (students, faculty, staff) to lead sustainable change at the societal level. Thus, there is a need for a stronger focus on students as primary stakeholders at HEIs in improving sustainability and resiliency, especially across the seven aforementioned goals. By shedding light on student leadership in sustainability and the facilitatory role played by faculty and staff in establishing student leaders, existing research is expanded upon to recognize the value of students *outside* of the classroom environment.

Alongside a review of extant literature – which helps to identify the seven goals – the University of Delaware (UD) is assessed to illustrate how it has made progress toward the seven goals and how there remains room for improvement. This sustainability profile is illuminated by the author's observations and experiences at UD as a graduate student from 2017–2023, and as a graduate fellow for the university's Sustainability Council and Office of Sustainability from 2021–2023. These observations are supplemented by existing literature to identify opportunities and challenges for HEIs to do more to lead society toward improved resilience and sustainability. Thus, the aim of this chapter is threefold: (1) to develop a stronger understanding of sustainability and resilience; (2) to identify best practices for empowering student leaders and to better understand the facilitatory role played by faculty and staff in achieving the seven goals; and (3) to offer further insights through a reflective case study of UD. Finally, this chapter calls for HEIs to capitalize on their students and perceive them as an asset in improving organizational sustainability and by recognizing that bottom-up support from students can help advance society toward resilience and sustainability.

SUSTAINABILITY AND RESILIENCE

As powerful institutions, HEIs can define sustainability. A definition of sustainability, however, needs to transcend traditional conceptualizations that are often anthropocentric in their lens, whereby sustainability is often perceived as exclusively focusing on human needs. To further compound the challenges in defining sustainability, there were approximately over 100 definitions by the mid-1990s, and these challenges and definitions include: a lack of foresight of economic activity on the environment (Chen et al., 2008, p. 187); a lack of clear indicators to measure sustainability (Somogyi, 2016, p. 338); avoidance in defining sustainability altogether or presumption of a definition (Somogyi, 2016, p. 339); and adoption of sustainability as a "widely used buzzword" (Scoones, 2007, p. 589).

Sustainability typically characterizes the environment as a form of "natural capital", whereby nature is perceived only in terms of its quantifiable economic value (Callicott & Mumford, 1997, p. 32; Somogyi, 2016, pp. 338, 342). In 1987, the World Commission on Environment and Development defined sustainable development as "development that meets the needs of the present world, without compromising the ability of future generations to meet their own needs" (Chen et al., 2008, p. 187). Some scholars extend this definition to further incorporate concerns about equitable access to resources within and amongst countries (Agyeman, 2008, p. 753).

Agyeman draws attention to the equity component of sustainability. He argues that "just sustainability" calls for the "the need to ensure a better quality of life for all, now and into the future, in a just and equitable manner, whilst living within the limits of supporting ecosystems" (Agyeman, 2008, p. 753). In practice, just sustainability requires equitable citizen participation, a long-term vision, and the recognition of how social and economic justice are intertwined with environmental well-being and sustainability (Agyeman, 2008, p. 754). Byrne et al. (2002) add that with the "embrace of modernity, civilization seeks to act without normative constraint" and has led to the commodification of "social and ecological relations" (pp. 263, 287). Thus, the seven goals that this chapter articulates are designed to help HEIs recognize that there are ways that they can lead society to a more just, equitable, sustainable, and resilient future.

However, whilst beneficial for scholars to understand the relationship between equity and sustainability, sustainability has been criticized as anthropocentric. In turn, the concept of ecological sustainability was conceived. Ecological sustainability is predominantly concerned with conservation and biodiversity, including the conservation of the "biota of ecosystems that are humanly inhabited and economically exploited" (Callicott & Mumford, 1997, p. 33). The emphasis in ecological sustainability lies with the notion of "sustainable living" which is understood as "human economic activity that does not seriously disrupt ecological processes and functions" (Callicott & Mumford, 1997, p. 35). This conceptualization of sustainability recognizes the intrinsic value of nature as well as meeting the needs of the "world's people" (Byrne & Rich, 1992, pp. 271–272). Thus, ecological sustainability has been considered a "long-missing piece of the sustainability puzzle" because it is often omitted by scholars and economists who instead prioritize sustainable development that is oriented toward capitalist economic demands and consumption (Chen et al., 2008, p. 187). HEIs, in the face of neoliberalism, must lead society in this transition toward ecological sustainability (Szulevicz & Feilberg, 2018, p. 322).

The concept of ecological sustainability is broader in its range and scope than "sustainability" is traditionally interpreted because it acknowledges the intrinsic value of nature and incorporates concepts like just sustainability. From this perspective, humans are understood to be one component of a life system and are dependent on nature for the provision of clean water and air, and fertile soil to grow nutritious food (Byrne et al., 2002, p. 271; IPBES, 2019, pp. 4, 6). Accordingly, the broad scope of ecological sustainability underpins the need for a wide-ranging approach adopted by HEIs in the form of the seven goals to increase resiliency and sustainability. Benchmarking tools like the Association for the Advancement of Sustainability in Higher Education's (AASHE) Sustainability Tracking, Assessment and Rating System (STARS) can be leveraged by institutions to monitor progress toward the seven goals, alongside other frameworks.

Defining resilience is similarly challenging because of the "diversity in conceptualizations" (Borquez et al., 2017, p. 164). Many scholars highlight the importance of HEIs teaching about resilience, and the "cultivation of flexible and adaptive practices to support resiliency" (Creed et al., 2021, p. 69; Bertolotti, 2021, p. 309; Pallant et al., 2020, p. 71; Pascua, 2019, p. 76). In a public survey that asked respondents to choose "10 attributes which they considered important for resilience", the most common (in descending order) included: (1) education and information; (2) preparedness; (3) adaptive capacity; (4) technology; (5) self-organization; (6) cooperation; (7) decentralization; (8) social-collective memory; (9) citizen participation; and (10) availability (Borquez et al., 2017, p. 171). These most common attributes demonstrate how citizens understand resilience. The United Nations' (UN) Sustainable Development Goals (SDGs) draw attention to resilience too. For example,

Goal 9 states, "Build resilient infrastructure, promote inclusive and sustainable industrialization and foster innovation", and Goal 11 asserts, "Make cities and human settlements inclusive, safe, resilient and sustainable" (Shiel et al., 2020, p. 14). In turn, existing research illustrates that resilience is a critical theme inside and outside of HEIs. Furthermore, by promoting resilience in HEIs, individuals and communities can be equipped with the necessary knowledge and skills to prepare, respond, and recover from adverse events, such as climatic shocks (e.g., heatwaves, flooding, hurricanes, earthquakes).

Much literature at the intersection of HEIs, resilience, and sustainability, however, has focused primarily on sustainability in classrooms and living labs. Notably, HEIs "offer significant opportunities to deliver" results on the UN's SDGs, and can establish "living lab[s]", which are defined as "a situation or circumstance where real-world sustainability challenges are formally addressed in stakeholder partnerships" (Purcell et al., 2019, p. 1344). These labs purportedly offer "real-world learning and research opportunities for students and faculty" by drawing on institutional resources and become a "test bed for SDG solutions" (Purcell et al., 2019, p. 1345). Therefore, living labs can produce benefits for "faculty and student scholarship" and assist in the creation of a "more connected university community", but there is a need for leadership (Purcell et al., 2019, p. 1352). Sustainability at a "strategic level" demands that "leaders at all levels" within HEIs act with purpose, harness the power of stakeholders, and inspire them to create a "shared vision of the future" (Purcell et al., 2019, p. 1354). Outside of discussions of living labs and sustainability in classrooms, research has seldom considered students to be the primary stakeholder in HEIs (with faculty and staff playing a facilitatory role) or their potential to be leaders in sustainability and resilience.

Some HEIs have made efforts to integrate the SDGs into different academic programs and integrate students' future career aspirations with sustainability. For example, the Office for Sustainability at Harvard University brought together faculty and students to co-create a "trans-disciplinary climate change learning course" to "investigate solutions to real-world sustainability challenges" (Purcell et al., 2019, p. 1350). At Bournemouth University, faculty were encouraged to "submit case studies of where they incorporate[d] the SDGs" in their academic programs, such as students in the Film Language program being required to "produce a three minute film and consider the environmental sub-plot" (Shiel et al., 2020, p. 19). Allegheny College offers a four-year program that gradually transitions students from a theoretical understanding of sustainability to practicing sustainability, with themes for each academic year: (1) introduction to sustainability ("think sustainability"); (2) environmental problem analysis ("analyze sustainability") and research methods ("research sustainability"); (3) junior seminar in sustainable development ("apply sustainability"); and (4) senior project ("becoming an agent of change") (Pallant et al., 2020, pp. 72–78). These examples show that there have been efforts by HEIs, to some extent, to integrate sustainability and resilience into higher education curricula and student learning outcomes to advance theoretical knowledge, acquire practical experience, and enhance sustainability- and resilience-related outcomes at different scales (e.g., individual, communal, national, global).

Thus, with an understanding of extant literature pertaining to sustainability and resilience and the role played by HEIs in leading society toward resilience and sustainability, this chapter turns to an outline of UD, which later features as part of an integrated assessment of the seven goals.

INTEGRATED CASE STUDY ASSESSMENT: THE UNIVERSITY OF DELAWARE

A case study approach is used for this chapter because of its "usefulness in obtaining an in-depth appreciation of an issue or area of interest in its natural real-life context" (Purcell et al., 2019, p. 1346). As part of this approach, this chapter conducts an integrated assessment of UD with regard to the seven goals for HEIs to lead society toward resilience and sustainability. This chapter draws on observations, experiences, and university documents at the University of Delaware between September 2020 – when the author joined the Graduate Sustainability Committee – and May 2023 – when the author graduated from UD. Drawing on these data, insights are provided as to how UD made progress toward each of the seven goals. This chapter is not designed to provide a comprehensive, quantifiable account of UD's "success" in achieving the seven goals, but to offer an ethnographic, qualitative account of the application of the seven goals in practice and potential gaps in UD's efforts by the end of the observation period. By providing this integrated case study assessment, other HEIs can conduct similar assessments, and develop a stronger understanding of how progress can be made toward each goal and how they can lead society toward a more resilient and sustainable future for all.

UD is a mid-size (23,613 total enrolled students in 2023) land-, sea-, and space-grant university based on the east coast of the US, with its main campus in Newark, and it is the leading university in the state of Delaware. It has a history dating back to 1743, but NewArk College opened as a degree-granting institution in 1834. NewArk College was renamed to Delaware College in 1843 and became UD in 1921. In January 2023, UD established the Office of Sustainability and hired a Director of Sustainable Operations and an Academic Director. The Office was, at the time, home to four undergraduate interns, and one graduate fellow. According to the Office of Sustainability's mission statement, the Office recognizes the social, economic, and environmental value of: interdisciplinary education; operations; holistic wellness; and quality of life. In practice, this means the Office will work across operations, academics, student life, research, and community engagement – a reflection of the intersectional nature of sustainability and resilience, and the need to bring diverse stakeholders together to inform decision-making that will continually improve the university's and community's sustainable practices and resilience.

Additionally, students have played a primary role in the development of the Office of Sustainability, which includes helping to shape the strategies and initiatives that will advance the university's trajectory toward a greener, brighter future. However, to make progress toward the seven goals, UD and other HEIs will need to empower student leaders and recognize the value of faculty and staff as facilitators in this process of empowerment. Further, the UD Office's strategy highlights that it needs to curate existing knowledge and create new knowledge, defend environmental justice principles, coalesce and collaborate with diverse stakeholders to maximize regenerative sustainable outcomes, manage investments, establish powerful initiatives, advance wellness, build narratives and share engaging stories, and implement a principle of no-net ecological harm, steeped in ecological sustainability. To deliver on these action items – which are embedded within and across the seven goals, further showcasing the synergy between the goals – UD and other HEIs must draw on the strengths of its faculty, students, staff, alumni, and community. By utilizing their social capital, HEIs can promote a flourishing campus, and draw on new skills as they emerge to support a resilient and sustainable environment for all.

Empowering Student Leaders, and Faculty and Staff as Facilitators

Stakeholder theory emphasizes the importance of "relationships between an organization and its stakeholders", and stakeholders are, for the purpose of this chapter, understood to be "those groups and individuals who can affect or be affected" by actions relating to sustainability and resilience (Hörisch et al., 2014, p. 329). Thus, this chapter specifically highlights the value of students in sustainability and resilience in HEIs – inside and outside of the classroom – as well as faculty and staff as facilitators, which includes executives, administrators, and facilities' staff. The selection of students, faculty, and staff is based on the previously mentioned "triple-win" – wins for student learning and experiences, wins for faculty and staff development and organizational sustainability, and wins for institutional image and public relations. The triple-win scenario reflects the "mutual sustainability interests" between these stakeholders (Hörisch et al., 2014, p. 337). Additionally, leadership is understood to be crucial in promoting "success" in sustainability- and resiliency-related outcomes, primarily displayed through management of "power imbalances" between stakeholders, establishment of a shared, "bigger picture" vision, and empowerment of stakeholders (Hörisch et al., 2014, pp. 339–340).

Such leadership can be displayed by students in bottom-up approaches (e.g., student groups), but their leadership can also be facilitated and empowered by faculty and staff. These relationships between the primary stakeholders (students) and facilitatory stakeholders (faculty and staff) exist across the seven goals, as illustrated in the subsequent sections of this chapter. The language of primary and facilitatory or secondary stakeholders helps to shed light on the role of students in leading positive change in sustainability and resilience, thereby showcasing their value beyond the narrative of students being passive recipients of educational information (Klein et al., 2021, p. 1728; Richards et al., 2016, pp. 242, 254).

The next seven subsections of this chapter draw attention to existing literature relevant to the seven goals and how HEIs, including UD, have made progress toward these goals, as well as opportunities for improvement.

Interdisciplinary approaches
The first goal is to emphasize interdisciplinary approaches to sustainability and resilience, whereby HEIs promote interdisciplinary approaches in their curricula and research. Sustainability- and resilience-related challenges often require interdisciplinary solutions, and by encouraging collaboration across different fields of study, HEIs can equip students with the skills and knowledge to address these challenges effectively (Creed et al., 2021, p. 80; Pallant et al., 2020, pp. 72–77).

At the institutional level, an interdisciplinary approach also requires that a "whole institution approach is adopted", which ensures that sustainability and resilience concepts and practices are integrated into curricula across various disciplines (Liu & Gao, 2020, p. 338). Thus, not only are sustainability- and resilience-specific courses offered to students, but those with less interest in these courses will encounter related concepts in different courses, be it journalism, engineering, fine art, or fashion. In turn, students across different disciplines will develop a strong understanding of sustainability and resilience and their relevance to their respective disciplines and enable them to become leaders in their respective disciplines (Creed et al., 2021, p. 80). However, despite the calls for integrative, holistic, and interdisciplinary approaches to sustainability, existing research shows that few institutions have "actually found ways to embed education for sustainable development across the entire curriculum" (Shiel et al., 2020, p. 13).

One example of an integrative approach is at Bournemouth University, where an understanding of "sustainable development" was tied to the "future career aspirations" of students, such as Films and Television students learning about the British Academy of Film and Television Arts' (BAFTA) carbon calculator (Shiel et al., 2020, p. 22). Additionally, through interdisciplinary courses, faculty can create opportunities to connect students with external experts in sustainability and resilience (e.g., research projects, guest lectures, networking events, professional development opportunities) (Liu & Gao, 2020, pp. 326–327). At Aalto University, a Master's program on Creative Sustainability unified students from the School of Arts, Design and Architecture, the School of Business, and the School of Engineering to address "environmental challenges" and "increase understanding of different disciplines and enable adapting a holistic approach" (Schröder, 2018, p. 132). Therefore, faculty can play an active role in facilitating student leadership by creating, modifying, and teaching courses that incorporate diverse sustainability and resilience topics, concepts, and tools that are rich with opportunities for growth.

Collaborating with a capstone group from UD's Business and Economics School, the Office of Sustainability built a database of sustainability-related courses. Later, adopting the AASHE STARS language of "sustainability-focused" and "sustainability-inclusive" classes, the Office surveyed faculty across all disciplines to update the database and develop a stronger understanding of the extent to which "sustainability" was integrated across different programs. Students were increasingly presented with new opportunities to engage in sustainability directly, such as the establishment of the Delaware Master Naturalist Program to train people to be ambassadors and stewards of Delaware's natural resources and ecosystems through science-based education and hands-on opportunities. A Graduate Certificate in Sustainability was also established, and a Minor in Sustainability was in the process of being created. Moreover, experiential learning opportunities were available through capstone projects, volunteering and/or interning with the Office of Sustainability, energy audit training, sustainable transportation planning collaboration with the Delaware Department of Transportation, and collaborative research with faculty.

However, for UD to make greater progress toward the first goal, the Office needs a more comprehensive inventory of all the programs that incorporate elements of sustainability to better understand how an interdisciplinary approach to sustainability and resilience can be better integrated and adopted. Additionally, the growing interest in different program, course, and degree offerings means that the Office, as well as other HEIs, will need to adapt by catering to these interests, such as offering certificates in sustainability through asynchronous learning (Creed et al., 2021, p. 80).

Critical thinking and problem-solving
The second goal is to foster critical thinking and problem-solving skills. Resilience requires students, faculty, and staff to have the ability to analyze situations, think critically, and identify solutions. By incorporating experiential learning, case studies, simulations, and real-world problem-solving projects

into academic programs, HEIs can help students develop these skills needed to achieve the triple-win (Creed et al., 2021, p. 78; Liu & Gao, 2020, p. 327; Pallant et al., 2020, pp. 71, 80). For students to become leaders, they need to acquire these skills and this requires developing familiarity with key sustainability and resilience concepts, theories, practices, and how these are tied to potential career opportunities (Pallant et al., 2020, pp. 71–72).

First, by enabling students to acquire the requisite knowledge through interdisciplinary courses and relevant experience, faculty and staff can further facilitate student leadership by establishing co-curricular sustainability programs. Sustainability programs – such as those developed by sustainability offices, committees, or groups – help elevate communal awareness regarding sustainability and resilience and, in turn, engage students in campus programs and initiatives (Pallant et al., 2020, p. 81; Purcell et al., 2019, pp. 1345, 1353). Such programs and initiatives often include events (e.g., Earth Day), workshops (e.g., bicycle/clothing repair), and campaigns (e.g., Campus Race to Zero). Additionally, these initiatives need not only be targeted at students, but they can be led by students as bottom-up projects. For example, students may help "prepare and implement education plans for middle school students around issues of food, gardening, and nutrition" (Pallant et al., 2020, p. 81).

To inspire students and bring together local stakeholders interested in sustainability and resilience, UD held numerous events. These include seminars, workshops, and on-campus fairs for Earth Day, Earth Week, the university President's Climate Symposium, participation in the Campus Race to Zero (waste minimization), and the establishment of new programs like the Graduation Gown Re-Use Program (donate used gowns for students in need), several food security programs for students, UDontNeedIt (donate used furniture), and the Clothing COOP (donate clothes). Looking to the future, the Office of Sustainability began to consider the establishment of an annual Sustainability Symposium, in addition to the integration of sustainability into first-year student activities to bolster awareness.

Allegheny College's four-year sustainability program illustrates how investigating real-world problems, identifying solutions, and gaining experience in the process are combined. In their second year, students draw on "quantitative, qualitative, social science, and natural science methods" placed inside "social, cultural, political and economic contexts", such as an examination of the "use of bottled water on Allegheny's campus" (Pallant et al., 2020, p. 75). Early in their program, students are strongly encouraged to "engage in at least one co-curricular experience of applied learning", and they may elect, for example, to participate in an "internship, conduct research with a faculty member through independent study, participate in a study abroad or experiential learning trip (2–3 weeks in duration) or serve as a regular volunteer in the community" (Pallant et al., 2020, p. 80). The research conducted by students on bottled water consumption was used to inform sustainability operations, such as increasing the "number of filtered, bottle refill stations throughout campus" (Pallant et al., 2020, p. 75). In turn, students' contributions are demonstrably perceived as valuable as they inform decision-making and lead to real-world improvements sustainability and resilience. By valuing student contributions, they can be empowered as leaders (Klein et al., 2021, p. 1753).

Another way to empower student leaders in sustainability and resilience is to offer students the opportunity to obtain firsthand, experiential learning. Experiential learning can be offered through internships in campus sustainability offices, with faculty engaged in relevant research and innovative projects, and with institutional partners (e.g., non-profit organizations, city, county, and state governments, and businesses) (Purcell et al., 2019, p. 1355). Faculty and staff can support these learning opportunities by, first, creating them and, second, broadcasting them to students to raise awareness. Further, they can advise students and provide guidance and resources, and help students develop leadership skills through associated professional development opportunities (Creed et al., 2021, p. 80). Importantly, through the creation and maintenance of these opportunities, faculty and staff demonstrate to students that they are valuable stakeholders in manifesting real-world change. These efforts also demonstrate that faculty and staff have the power to put the tools – such as professional development opportunities – into the hands of students.

Although UD offered numerous experiential learning opportunities, as noted in the preceding subsection, the Office of Sustainability needs to collaborate more with existing groups on campus to deliver transformative opportunities that further empower students. For example, the Office could work with faculty to increase student participation in energy audit training. This also means that the Office needs to collaborate with local businesses and non-profit organizations, the state of Delaware, and the City of Newark for energy audit training to occur. This example of collaborating with diverse stakeholders to improve students' critical thinking and problem-solving skills further exemplifies the synergy between the seven goals. Notably, students can acquire the knowledge regarding the value of energy audits in an interdisciplinary program prior to conducting an energy audit through an experiential learning opportunity.

Justice, diversity, equity, and inclusion

The third goal is to promote justice, diversity, equity, and inclusion, which helps to strengthen sustainability and resilience because different perspectives are considered, including perspectives that have been historically marginalized and excluded, such as indigenous knowledge (Creed et al., 2021, p. 68; Weber & Tascón, 2020, p. 853). These values can be practiced by HEIs by creating inclusive spaces for underrepresented groups, promoting cultural awareness, and developing inclusive teaching and learning environments (Pallant et al., 2020, p. 73; Purcell et al., 2019, p. 1354; Weber & Tascón, 2020, p. 850). Further, diversity should not be limited to the inclusion of diverse perspectives in program curricula, but it should also recognize that students themselves are diverse learners and some may prefer to access sustainability- and resilience-related programs through different means (e.g., in-person, synchronous, asynchronous online) and with varied commitments (e.g., full-time, part-time, self-paced) (Creed et al., 2021, p. 80).

In one assessment of student engagement in sustainability classes, the "development of an inclusive environment" was considered an essential component of "engaged campus action" (Liu & Gao, 2020, p. 327). Additionally, in the previously mentioned survey regarding citizen perception of resilience as a concept, *education-information* was the most voted attribute. This attribute refers to the "opportune, equitable and universal access to information and education", which underscores the key role played by HEIs in leading society toward improved levels of resilience and sustainability vis-à-vis the provision of equitable access to education (Borquez et al., 2017, p. 170). At Nottingham Trent University, the inclusion of students in the design and creation of visual displays was one of the university's "most important" takeaways (Odell et al., 2020, pp. 233, 244). The visual displays were used to communicate the UN SDGs, thereby helping "draw attention to the issues the SDGs are trying to solve" and signaling to students "how they should act to work towards them" (Odell et al., 2020, p. 233). Like Allegheny College, Nottingham Trent University shows that the inclusion of students can help generate improvements in sustainability – in this case, raising student awareness of the SDGs and how they can create real-world change.

Weber and Tascón (2020) argue that organizing "inclusion and sustainability" has become "increasingly relevant for universities" (p. 850). The same authors highlight that "essential approach[es] of Latin American Higher Education sustainability strategies" are to empower "indigenous people", and "to unfold new [educational] possibilities in order to create a harmonic balance between human beings" (p. 853). To achieve inclusion, diversity, and empowerment, the authors further argue that deliberative methods are crucial, which are characterized by four common features: (1) "getting relevant information about the issues considered"; (2) "having ample opportunity for free and open discussion between citizens and researchers", and other stakeholders; (3) "encouragement to discuss information and position"; and (4) "consider each other's views...before finally making decisions or giving recommendations for action" (p. 858).

At UD, justice, diversity, inclusion, and equity are valued through different means. The university's Anti-Racism Initiative (UDARI) aims to take action against systemic racism and contribute to the reduction of racial disparities on campus and in the larger community. UDARI provides a Summer Scholars program for undergraduates to immerse themselves in a creative research project based on race, anti-racism, or racial justice. Students can also learn about environmental justice through a broad range of sustainability-related classes, which draw attention to the intersectionality of diverse identities and the adverse effects of climate change and natural disasters.

Additionally, UD has collaborated with Principal Chief of the Lenape Indian Tribe of Delaware, Chief Coker, in considering sustainable land management practices and the university's relations with the tribe. Moreover, the Office of Sustainability collaborated with the university's Center for Teaching and Assessment of Learning to consider whether to mandate the inclusion of "sustainability" in new syllabi to help foster an interdisciplinary approach. These efforts by UD and other HEIs to be inclusive further illustrate the synergy across the seven goals. For example, the creation of deliberative spaces for diverse perspectives can align with intersectional discussions of sustainability (e.g., land management, indigenous people, racial justice) and, in turn, foster critical thinking and encourage the adoption of an interdisciplinary approach in curricula.

Collaboration

The fourth goal is to collaborate with communities and stakeholders, whereby HEIs build resilience and increase sustainability by actively engaging with stakeholders on- and off-campus (e.g., undergraduate, graduate, and post-doctoral students, faculty, staff, alumni, local city/county, state, regional, and national, international, and global communities). By building partnerships with different stakeholders, including government agencies, non-profit organizations, businesses, and other HEIs, these institutions can contribute to the development of sustainable and resilient solutions (Nam and Lee, 2021, p. 153; Pallant et al., 2020, p. 76; Purcell et al., 2019, p. 1344).

Collaboration, however, should not be understood as exclusively top-down. Students, as primary stakeholders, can also work to build partnerships and collaborative projects with their peers and others (Purcell et al., 2019, p. 1354). Change can be "initiated from the bottom, or else it can be lead from the top", thereby reinforcing the value of students in leading change, as well as faculty and staff in facilitating change (Liu & Gao, 2020, p. 339; Odell et al., 2020, p. 230). A bottom-up approach can empower student leaders by creating a sense of "ownership of joint involvement and action", and valuing student contributions (Nam & Lee, 2021, p. 154). Alternatively, a top-down approach in education can be beneficial because of its "efficiency in decision-making", "ability to mobilize more resources", and ability to "generate widespread awareness", which can help "get things done" (Nam & Lee, 2021, p. 154). In turn, calls have been made to infuse bottom-up and top-down approaches and allow for greater degrees of collaboration between stakeholders to assist in the improvement of sustainability-related outcomes in HEIs (Nam & Lee, 2021, p. 154). HEIs can infuse top-down and bottom-up interactions by promoting "mutual respect, common understanding, and shared responsibility" (Nam & Lee, 2021, p. 168). These calls for infusion have been associated with the calls for deliberative methods to promote diversity and inclusivity, whereby "participatory democracy" can establish engagement opportunities (Nam & Lee, 2021, p. 154). This synergy between two of the seven goals illustrates how the goals can be synergized to enhance sustainability and resilience.

An interdisciplinary approach to educating students about sustainability and resilience can also serve to support collective action. This approach overcomes "disciplinary boundaries to generate interdisciplinary research", and allows for the integration of "multiple forms of knowledge, activism, and experiences", thereby supporting efforts by faculty and staff efforts to boost diversity and inclusivity (Schröder, 2018, p. 133). Further, some sustainability topics are argued to be inherently interdisciplinary and present opportunities for interdisciplinary research. For example, permaculture can involve the "planning of the gardens", "practical courses", learning about the "behavior of specific insects or plants", "design systems", "ethical principles of permaculture", and alternatives to permaculture (Schröder, 2018, pp. 136–137).

Moreover, collaborative efforts have been displayed at UD. Together with undergraduate and graduate students, alumni, staff, faculty, and external stakeholders, the Sustainability Council was created in 2019. The Council operates alongside the Office of Sustainability and collaborated with Ameresco and the City of Newark to jointly apply for a grant by the Delaware Department of Natural Resources and Environmental Control for public electric vehicle chargers. Further, a team of graduate students across different disciplines – the Graduate Sustainability Committee – developed a Sustainability Report to evaluate UD's progress toward reducing its environmental footprint. Spurred by this report in 2021, the Sustainability Council collaboratively worked with them to create an Executive Sustainability Plan in 2022 that laid the foundation for further institutional action on sustainability and resilience.

Other institutional plans and reports have since been collaboratively constructed at UD, including with local and state stakeholders (e.g., city planners, non-profit organizations, Delaware Department of Transportation planners), such as a Bikeshare Action Plan, Transportation Master Plan, Office of Sustainability Strategic Plan, and others remain in development (e.g., Climate Action Plan). The development of these strategies with diverse stakeholders underscores how HEIs lead society's sustainability plans, practices, and performance, as well as the roles played by students, faculty, and staff – all of whom help to inform plans, practices, and performance.

One factor that is likely conducive to the working relationship between UD and the City of Newark is that Newark is a college town. This can foster a symbiotic relationship because both stakeholders are significantly involved in activities at the local scale. For example, university facilities' staff, executives, faculty, and students have collaborated with the city and interested residents to discuss the greening of transportation infrastructure (e.g., promoting cycling and walking, electric vehicles) and energy (e.g., renewable energy, community energy generation, solar city, infrastructure resilience).

By collaborating with different stakeholders, students can obtain real-world experiences, as demonstrated by the bottom-up development of the Sustainability Report. Other examples of students obtaining these experiences at UD include developing social media content for the Sustainability Council, attending City Council sustainability meetings, and supporting efforts to apply for grants or raise funds to support sustainability initiatives, among other things. Collaborative projects can also expose students to diverse perspectives and help them develop soft skills that are essential for leadership, such as teamwork, communication, collaboration, and organizational skills (Bertolotti, 2021, p. 315; Creed et al., 2021, pp. 78–79).

However, to achieve the goals outlined across UD's reports and plans, the Office of Sustainability must do more to harness the power of its enthusiastic students. To this end, the Office had a graduate fellow and four undergraduate interns, with the ambition of expanding fellowship and internship opportunities to allow for greater student input into the university's trajectory regarding action on sustainability. Thus, UD, like other HEIs, can lead society toward heightened levels of resilience and sustainability by empowering students and other stakeholders through collaborative efforts. Drawing on the passion of stakeholders can help to fill gaps in personnel and resources, with the recognition that appropriate compensation is needed (e.g., monetary, course credit, certificates, awards).

Research and innovation
The fifth goal is to promote research and innovation in resilience and sustainability. HEIs can lead society toward a sustainable and resilient future by conducting research that addresses climate change, biodiversity loss, air pollution, and disaster preparedness and response, among other challenges. Innovation can be supported through entrepreneurship initiatives that focus on developing resilient technologies, solutions, and strategies, in addition to the establishment of the aforementioned co-curricular activities (Hörisch et al., 2014, p. 336; Purcell et al., 2019, pp. 1345, 1353).

Innovative projects, such as the establishment of a living lab, provide HEIs the opportunity to connect with "external organizations, such as local government or business" (Purcell et al., 2019, p. 1345; Weber & Tascón,

2020, p. 850). For example, Plymouth University established the "Growth Acceleration and Innovation Network (GAIN) as a regional innovation ecosystem with the City Council bringing $150m worth of innovation assets (regional science park, incubation and innovation centers) under one governance entity" (Purcell et al., 2019, p. 1348). At Harvard University, the Office for Sustainability functioned as a convener and connector of "talented faculty, students and staff" around the university's sustainability plan, and used language that excited "them of research, teaching, discovery, [and] innovation" (Purcell et al., 2019, p. 1353). Other examples of innovation at Harvard University included its Campus Sustainability Innovation Fund and Green Revolving Fund, which co-fund projects (Purcell et al., 2019, p. 1350).

Faculty can encourage students to conduct research on sustainability and resilience topics, and provide mentorship, support, and guidance throughout the research process. Alternatively, faculty can employ students to support faculty-led research through grant-sponsored research. Through student participation or leadership in research and innovation, students can develop the skills needed to succeed in sustainability-related careers, such as critical thinking, problem-solving, teamwork, communication, and research skills (Purcell et al., 2019, p. 1350; Rhodes & Wang, 2021, p. 60).

Mentoring and advising presents opportunities to enhance student development and understanding of interdisciplinary research. For example, it has been found that students may find their experiences of interdisciplinary courses "lack coherence" and, in turn, faculty can help facilitate connections between courses and interactions between experiences through advising (Pallant et al., 2020, p. 82). More specifically, faculty can be facilitators by discussing the "selection of courses and content connections, the sequencing of co-curricular activities and application of knowledge outside of the classroom, and future goals and aspirations" as they relate to sustainability and resilience (Pallant et al., 2020, p. 83).

UD's Office of Sustainability supports research and innovation in sustainability and resilience by funding on-campus projects through its Green Grants program, and it began the process of establishing its own Green Revolving Fund. In 2022, some faculty acquired external funding for undergraduate students to work with the Sustainability Council, and the Office continued this trend of sharing student interns and creating opportunities for interdisciplinary, collaborative, and experiential learning in 2023. From this angle, the Office became a "convener and connector as well as adviser, trainer, mentor and coach to those involved in shared projects" (Purcell et al., 2019, p. 1350). Greater resources, including those available from federal and state governments, must be harnessed in addition to the continued building of collaborative relationships with diverse stakeholders to maximize the positive impact of UD in leading society toward sustainability and resilience.

Mental health and resilience
The sixth goal is to highlight the relationship between mental health, well-being, sustainability, and resilience. By providing resources and support services, promoting self-care practices, and reducing stigma around mental health issues, HEIs can help to build a resilient, sustainable, and support-ive campus community that is prepared to tackle sustainability challenges (Lawrence et al., 2022, p. 474; Purcell et al., 2019, p. 1350).

Faculty and staff, as previously noted, can serve as advisors and mentors to students who are interested in sustainability and resilience. They can provide advice, resources, and connections to help students better understand their own interests, goals, and opportunities to pursue leadership activities. Faculty and staff can also share their own experiences, which can inspire students as faculty and staff themselves may be perceived by students as leaders. The guidance and mentorship offered can extend to discussions about climate anxiety and the relationships between mental health, well-being, sustainability, and resil-ience (Lawrence et al., 2022, p. 477). For Lawrence et al. (2022), effective "climate change communication and education" underscores the importance of diversity by highlighting the need for "an understanding of how people will respond differently" to climate change communication and education (p. 469). The same authors stress that students must be equipped with "opportunities to process their climate-related feelings, learn coping strategies and participate in relevant climate action" (p. 474).

By helping students to become resilient to the "psychological, emotional and social burden of climate change", HEIs must be cognizant of climate change compounding "existing vulnerabilities to poor mental health and wellbeing" (Lawrence et al., 2022, pp. 474, 477). Further, HEIs need to tackle issues that can exacerbate mental health, such as "poor governance, high social and income inequalities, cultures of extractivism and polluting air and eco-systems with fossil fuels", which are "the same societal issues that perpetuate the climate crisis" (Lawrence et al., 2022, p. 476). Thus, it is not sufficient for HEIs to only educate students about the risks posed by climate change, but they must practice what they preach and help students to become resilient in the face of mounting ecological crises. As Hurley et al. (2022) suggest, it is "unfair to ask a generation of young people to develop enhanced psychological stamina to face climate change" as a result of "decades of inaction", and so HEIs must invest in tools to support students' mental well-being (p. 190).

The Academic Director of the UD Office of Sustainability and the Office's graduate fellow attended a UD Wellbeing Event to draw attention to the inter-sectionality of mental health and sustainability. Together, they engaged other stakeholders by using a large roll of paper to encourage visitors to write down what sustainability meant to them and what the university could be doing to help improve sustainability. More collaboration on this front is needed, including a concerted push to feature sustainability across curricula to demonstrate to students what can be done to tackle the environmental crises and, in turn, support their well-being. By bringing more students into the Office through internships, research projects, and volunteering opportunities, students can be better equipped to tackle these crises. It is also critical that the Office and university are both transparent in their sustainability achievements to avoid students falling into a cycle of pessimism regarding perceived inaction.

Sustainability leadership and environmental stewardship

The seventh and final goal is to become and facilitate sustainability leaders and environmental stewards. To create student leaders, HEIs must lead by example in promoting sustainability and environmental stewardship. By adopting practices to enhance organizational sustainability and resilience, integrating sustainability and resilience into curricula, promoting environmental awareness, empowering student leadership, HEIs can contribute to building a more resilient and sustainable future. These actions further illustrate the synergy across the seven goals, and how their interrelatedness can likely strengthen sustainability outcomes and facilitate student leadership.

For students to become leaders, they must be recognized as valued stakeholders. By recognizing student leadership, they are further encouraged to share their "unique and diverse perspectives" (Purcell et al., 2019, p. 1354). One example of valuing student input is Plymouth University's Change Academy and Enabler network, which "included students as partners (rather than customers)", and treated them as "active global citizens fully aware of the need to build and maintain a sustainable society" (Purcell et al., 2019, p. 1348). At Bournemouth University, elected student representatives attend "meetings with academics" to influence curricula and encourage faculty "to pledge to include the SDGs within their teaching, learning, and assessment on their course(s)" (Shiel et al., 2020, p. 20). At UD, the Office of Sustainability operates the Green Hen Awards to recognize the achievements of student, faculty, and staff leaders in advancing sustainability.

However, it is important that the development of student leaders in sustainability and resilience is not reduced to a "neoliberal ideal" in which "students are expected to be self-evaluating, responsible and self-monitoring", without support from faculty and staff or with engagement limited to a checkbox exercise (Szulevicz & Feilberg, 2018, p. 322). Given that student engagement has become "omnipresent" in "mainstream higher education discourses", HEIs must do more than "'wear the clothes' of progressivism" by demonstrating their ability to mobilize students through diverse and inclusive engagement methods (Szulevicz & Feilberg, 2018, p. 322).

Faculty and staff, as facilitators of student leadership, can support students by recognizing and celebrating their achievements through awards, scholar ships, and other forms of recognition (e.g., blogpost on the HEI's website). These forms of recognition can further motivate students to participate in sustainability initiatives, encourage their peers to participate, and present opportunities for improved institutional leadership image (e.g., potential allure for prospective students) (Purcell et al., 2019, p. 1344; Rhodes & Wang, 2021, p. 60). Improving institutional image by facilitating student leadership in sustainability is one key aspect of the triple-win. Other forms of engagement include the involvement of student representatives in faculty-staff-student groups, or to permit the establishment of student groups (e.g., student sustainability group). Through these opportunities, faculty and staff can support students becoming "agents of change" (Bertolotti, 2021, p. 316).

However, recognition must also be given to other stakeholders – such as alumni, staff, faculty, executives, administrators, and local community advocates – who help to advance sustainability and resilience. Students are often time-restricted (e.g., degree requirements, work, volunteering, internships, fellowships), and although they are important players in these processes, they are not the *only* stakeholders that deserve recognition. For example, facilities' staff are often responsible for the execution of sustainability strategies, such as campus landscaping, waste management, and energy management.

At UD, there are numerous opportunities for students to participate in leadership positions and develop skills critical for a career in sustainability, including internships, fellowships, and capstone projects. Beside these, there are student representatives on the university's Sustainability Council, and student groups and positions (e.g., Student Sustainability Alliance, Graduate Sustainability Committee, Undergraduate Sustainability Senator) that help to inform university-wide and Office of Sustainability decision-making. To enhance student leadership and environmental stewardship, the Office needs to raise awareness of these opportunities for participation, and create an integrated leadership program that fosters student leadership and prepares them for careers in sustainability and resilience.

At an institutional level, sustainability leadership and environmental stewardship can be demonstrated by engaging in sustainability reporting and accountability. For HEIs, AASHE STARS is a commonly used benchmarking tool that enables comparative analyses over time and across institutions, creates incentives for improvement, facilitates information-sharing, and builds a sustainability-oriented community (AASHE, n.d.). By employing these tools, HEIs can track their progress toward sustainability goals, evaluate progress, hold themselves accountable, be transparent with different stakeholders (including students), set new targets, and publish sustainability reports that summarize performance. Additionally, leveraging these tools presents opportunities for experiential learning, thereby further illustrating the synergy between the goals. Students can help collect and analyze data, identify solutions and opportunities for improvement, and communicate data in creative ways – all of which can empower them by virtue of learning new skills, developing a stronger understanding of accountability and reporting, and helping prepare them for careers in sustainability (Rhodes & Wang, 2021, p. 54).

UD's Office of Sustainability worked to institutionalize sustainable change by committing itself to different goals and reporting tools, such as the Nature Positive Pledge University, Campus Race to Zero, Second Nature Climate Leadership Commitment, and reported to the University of New Hampshire's SIMAP tool, and AASHE STARS. Previously, in 2020, UD received a Bronze AASHE STARS rating, and is intending to report again in 2023–24, which is a monumental undertaking (e.g., significant data collection, management, and analysis). To satisfy reporting requirements, the Office of Sustainability collaborated with the Sustainability Council and drew on the strength of its undergraduate interns, graduate fellow, and facilities' staff. This ensured data were collected and reported, which bolstered students' experiential learning opportunities and benchmarked the university against peer institutions with the goal of improving organizational sustainability and resilience.

CONCLUSION

Overall, HEIs can do more to lead society toward resilience and sustainability by adopting best practices centered on the seven goals, including a concurrent thematic focus on empowering student leaders, and understanding the facilitatory role played by faculty and staff. By equipping students with the knowledge and experiences needed to address sophisticated societal challenges, such as climate change, ecological collapse, and disaster preparedness, HEIs can – and *must* – play a critical role in building a more sustainable and resilient future. However, it is equally important to acknowledge that executives, staff, faculty, alumni, and local communities also play critical roles in helping or collaborating with HEIs in advancing resilience and sustainability.

Existing literature offers diverse approaches and conceptualizations of sustainability in HEIs. The seven goals match the broad conceptualization of ecological sustainability, which strives to include recognition of the board impacts of climate change and ecological degradation – all of which can be translated to students through an interdisciplinary education, experiential learning, collaborative research, leadership opportunities, and more. By using the integrated assessment of a case study, UD, and drawing on extant literature, there are evidently key stakeholders that HEIs must utilize to enhance sustainability and resilience, and support progress toward the seven goals. Stakeholder theory illuminates these primary and secondary stakeholders – faculty and staff as facilitators, and undergraduate and graduate students as leaders. Although there is "no one-size-fits-all approach or blueprint" to enhancing sustainability and resilience, co-creating solutions with students and empowering student leaders are a vital thread throughout synergistic progress toward the seven goals (Purcell et al., 2019, pp. 1351–1352).

By drawing on student support, time, knowledge, resources, and input, HEIs not only foster student leadership, but student leaders can fill institutional resource gaps (e.g., financial, personnel). These leaders can be facilitated by faculty and staff through mentoring, integrating sustainability across curricula, supporting co-curricular and experiential learning opportunities, recognizing student efforts and achievements, and advocating for greater institutional support and leadership for institution-wide mobilization toward a shared vision and narrative, among other things. These shared visions, as suggested by existing literature, help to coalesce stakeholders around sustainability and these stakeholders can be connected or convened by, for example, an Office of Sustainability (Purcell et al., 2019, p. 1353). Furthermore, these stakeholders from different disciplines can work together to "collectively address real-world sustainability issues" and create future leaders in sustainability and resilience (Purcell et al., 2019, p. 1354). Further, students themselves must recognize that their success does not exclusively derive from opportunities facilitated by faculty and staff, but they can work toward enhancing sustainability and resilience through bottom-up means, such as creating reports, participating in student groups, electing student leaders, and advocating for action.

Thus, evidence has been provided to demonstrate the value of achieving the triple-win for HEIs, how faculty and staff facilitation empowerment of students plays an important role in creating student leaders, and how the goals can be synergized to broaden their impact. For example, students can partake in interdisciplinary classes that present opportunities for professional development and experiential learning, foster critical thinking, and bolster mental well-being. However, to build on the research conducted in this chapter and elsewhere, future studies ought to assess whether a causal relationship exists between student leadership in sustainability and resilience and real-world improvements in sustainability and resilience outcomes.

REFERENCES

Agyeman, J. (2008). Toward a 'Just' Sustainability? *Continuum: Journal of Media & Cultural Studies*, *22*(6), 751–756. https://doi.org/10.1080/10304310802452487

Association of the Advancement of Higher Education Institutions (AASHE). (n.d.). *About STARS.* https://stars.aashe.org/about-stars/

Bertolotti, W. (2021). Empowerment, Resilience, and Stewardship as Learning Outcomes. In R. Iyengar and C.T. Kwauk (Eds.), *Curriculum and Learning for Climate Action: Toward an SDG 4.7 Roadmap for Systems Change* (Ch. 19). Brill.

Borquez, R., Aldunce, P., and Adler, C. (2017). Resilience to Climate Change: From Theory to Practice Through Co-Production of Knowledge in Chile. *Sustainability Science, 12*, 163–176. https://doi.org/10.1007/s11625-016-0400-6

Byrne, J., Glover, L., and Martinez, C. (2002). The Production of Unequal Nature. In J. Byrne, L. Glover, and C. Martinez (Eds.), *Environmental Justice: Discourses in International Political Economy* (pp. 261–291). Routledge.

Byrne, J., and Rich, D. (1992). Towards a Political Economy of Global Change: Energy, Environment and Development in the Greenhouse. In J. Byrne and D. Rich (Eds.), *Energy and Environment: The Policy Challenge* (pp. 269–302). Routledge.

Callicott, J. B., and Mumford, K. (1997). Ecological Sustainability as a Conservation Concept. *Conservation Biology, 11*(1), 32–40. https://doi.org/10.1007/978-94-017-1337-5_3

Chen, A.J.W., Boudreau, M-C., and Watson, R.T. (2008). Information Systems and Ecological Sustainability. *Journal of Systems and Information Technology, 10*(3), 186–201. https://doi.org/10.1108/13287260810916907

Creed, I.F., Ramaswamy, M., Wolsfeld, M., Calvez, S., Fulton, M., Liber, K., Marciniuk, D.D., Ottman, J., Turner, N., Zink, L., Akins, E., Hudson, K., Bell, J., LaRose-Smith, A., and McKay, J. (2021). Radical Transformation of Universities to Prepare the Next Generation of Climate Champions. In R. Iyengar and C.T. Kwauk (Eds.), *Curriculum and Learning for Climate Action: Toward an SDG 4.7 Roadmap for Systems Change* (Ch. 4). Brill.

Hörisch, J., Freeman, E.R., and Schaltegger, S. (2014). Applying Stakeholder Theory in Sustainability Management: Links, Similarities, Dissimilarities, and a Conceptual Framework. *Organization & Environment, 27*(4), 328–346. https://doi.org/10.1177/1086026614535786

Hurley, E.A., Dalglish, S.L., and Sacks, E. (2022). Supporting Young People with Climate Anxiety: Mitigation, Adaptation, and Resilience. *The Lancet Planetary Health, 6*(3), 190. https://doi.org/10.1016/S2542-5196(22)00015-8

Intergovernmental Science-Policy Platform on Biodiversity and Ecosystem Services (IPBES). (2019, May 31). *Chapter 2.3 Status and Trends – Nature's Contributions to People*. https://ipbes.net/sites/default/files/ipbes_global_assessment_chapter_2_3_ncp_unedited_31may.pdf

Klein, S., Watted, S., and Zion, M. (2021). Contribution of an Intergenerational Sustainability Leadership Project to the Development of Students' Environmental Literacy. *Environmental Education Research, 27*(12), 1723–1758. https://doi.org/10.1080/13504622.2021.1968348

Lawrence, E.L., Thompson, R., Le Vay, J.N., Page, L., and Jennings, N. (2022). The Impact of Climate Change on Mental Health and Emotional Wellbeing: A Narrative Review of Current Evidence, and its Implications. *International Review of Psychiatry, 34*(5), 443–498. https://doi.org/10.1080/09540261.2022.2128725

Liu, L., and Gao, L. (2020). Enhancing Student Engagement in a Sustainability Class: A Survey Study. In W.L. Filho, A.L. Salvia, R.W. Pretorius, L.L. Brandli, E. Manolas, F. Alves, U. Azeiteiro, J. Rogers, C. Shiel, and A. Do Paco (Eds.), *Universities as Living Labs for Sustainable Development: Supporting the Implementation of the Sustainable Development Goals* (pp. 323–334). Springer.

Nam, Annie Hyokyong., & Lee, Sueyoon. (2021). "Students as Partners. Implementation of Climate Change Education Within the Harvard Graduate

School of Education." In Fernando M. Reimers (ed), *Education and Climate Change: The Role of Universities*. Springer.

Odell, V., Molthan-Hill, P., Erlandsson, L., and Sexton, E. (2020). Visual Displays of the Sustainable Development Goals in the Curricular and Extra-Curricular Activities at Nottingham Trent University: A Case Study. In W.L. Filho, A.L. Salvia, R.W. Pretorius, L.L. Brandli, E. Manolas, F. Alves, U. Azeiteiro, J. Rogers, C. Shiel, and A. Do Paco (Eds.), *Universities as Living Labs for Sustainable Development: Supporting the Implementation of the Sustainable Development Goals* (pp. 227–246). Springer.

Pallant, E., Choate, B., and Haywood, B. (2020). How Do You Teach Undergraduate University Students to Contribute to UN SDGs 2030? In W.L. Filho, A.L. Salvia, R.W. Pretorius, L.L. Brandli, E. Manolas, F. Alves, U. Azeiteiro, J. Rogers, C. Shiel, and A. Do Paco (Eds.), *Universities as Living Labs for Sustainable Development: Supporting the Implementation of the Sustainable Development Goals* (pp. 69–85). Springer.

Pascua, L. (2019). The Question Of 'Knowledge' About Disaster Risk Reduction in Sustainability Education. In C.-H. Chang, G. Kidman, and A. Wi (Eds.), *Issues in Teaching and Learning of Education for Sustainability: Theory into Practice* (Ch. 6). Taylor & Francis Group.

Purcell, W.M., Henriksen, H., and Spengler, J.D. (2019). Universities as the Engine of Transformational Sustainability Toward Delivering the Sustainable Development Goals: 'Living labs' for Sustainability. *International Journal of Sustainability in Higher Education, 20*(8), 1343–1357. https://doi.org/10.1108/IJSHE-02-2019-0103

Rhodes, D., and Wang, M. (2021). Learn to Lead: Developing Curricula that Foster Climate Change Leaders. In F.M. Reimers (Ed.), *Education and Climate Change: The Role of Universities* (Ch. 2). Springer.

Richards, D., Saddiqui, S., White, F., McGuigan, N., and Homewood, J. (2016). A Theory of Change for Student-Led Academic Integrity. *Quality in Higher Education, 22*(3), 242–259. https://doi.org/10.1080/13538322.2016.1265849

Schröder, A. (2018). Arts-Based Approaches for Environmental Awareness in University Campuses. In W.L. Filho, F. Frankenberger, P. Iglecias, and R.C.K. Mülfarth (Eds.), *Towards Green Campus Operations: Energy, Climate and Sustainable Development Initiatives at Universities* (pp. 127–140). Springer.

Scoones, I. (2007). Sustainability. *Development in Practice, 17*(4–5), 589–596. https://doi.org/10.1080/09614520701469609

Shiel, C., Smith, N., and Cantarello, E. (2020). Aligning Campus Strategy with the SDGs: An Institutional Case Study. In W.L. Filho, A.L. Salvia, R.W. Pretorius, L.L. Brandli, E. Manolas, F. Alves, U. Azeiteiro, J. Rogers, C. Shiel, and A. Do Paco (Eds.), *Universities as Living Labs for Sustainable Development: Supporting the Implementation of the Sustainable Development Goals* (pp. 11–27). Springer.

Somogyi, Z. (2016). A Framework for Quantifying Environmental Sustainability. *Ecological Indicators, 61*, 338–345. https://doi.org/10.1016/j.ecolind.2015.09.034

Starik, M., Schaeffer, T.N., Berman, P., and Hazelwood, A. (2002). Initial Environmental Project Characterizations of Four US Universities. *International Journal of Sustainability in Higher Education, 3*(4), 335–345. https://doi.org/10.1108/14676370210442373

Szulevicz, T., and Feilberg, C. (2018). What Has Happened to Quality? In J. Valsiner, A. Lutsenko, and A. Antoniouk (Eds.), *Sustainable Futures for Higher Education: The Making of Knowledge Makers* (Ch. 26). Springer.

Weber, S.M., and Tascón, M.A. (2020). Pachamama—La Universidad del 'Buen Vivir': A First Nations University in Latin America. In W.L. Filho, A.L. Salvia, R.W. Pretorius, L.L. Brandli, E. Manolas, F. Alves, U. Azeiteiro, J. Rogers, C. Shiel, and A. Do Paco (Eds.), *Universities as Living Labs for Sustainable Development: Supporting the Implementation of the Sustainable Development Goals* (pp. 849–862). Springer.

5. Transition 2026: stakeholder engagement and the co-construction of a climate strategy in a French business school

María Castillo, Susana Esper, Gustavo Birollo and Frank G.A. de Bakker

INTRODUCTION

Higher education institutions (henceforth, HEIs) have a unique position to train graduates and adequately equip them to address the complex sustainability challenges in the next decades (Krizek et al., 2012; Menon and Suresh, 2020; Žalėnienė and Pereira, 2021) and help shape the future of business and society (Purcell et al., 2019). In addition to their teaching, research and knowledge and technology transfer missions, HEIs around the world are currently making sustainability a core reason for their existence (Aversano et al., 2022; Trencher et al., 2014) through different dimensions: implementing sustainability programs and reviewing existing course content, developing sustainability-focused research; and becoming "living labs" for sustainability (Purcell et al., 2019).

Within the universe of HEI, business schools play a relevant role in shaping future business leaders (Figueiró and Raufflet, 2015; Khurana, 2007). As sustainability becomes a strategic imperative for organizations, business schools should ensure they provide the skills, competences, and knowledge necessary to contribute to a sustainable transition and to prepare future managers for this transition (Krizek et al., 2012). This requires new approaches such as the creation of dedicated courses, the integration of sustainability transversally into all business and management disciplines, strong concrete experiences for students to allow them to practice what they learn, supplemented by research to help drive change in organizations.

Furthermore, by adopting sustainable practices on campus, aimed at reducing carbon emissions and increasing energy efficiency, HEIs can serve as role models for sustainable behavior and thus inspire students, faculty, and staff to make sustainable choices in their personal and professional lives. While the impact that HEIs can have by introducing sustainability topics in their curricula and by improving the environmental performance of their campuses has already been explored (e.g., Alshuwaikhat and Abubakar, 2008; Cullen, 2017; Figueiró and Raufflet, 2015; Leal Filho et al., 2019), we argue that to further unleash their "transformative" sustainability role (Starik et al., 2010), these institutions can strategically plan such pedagogical and operational transitions together with their stakeholders – a stakeholder being "any group or individual who is affected or can affect the achievement of an organization's objectives" (Freeman, 1984, p. 46).

The practice of stakeholder engagement (henceforth, SE) is a way to build cooperative and mutually beneficial relations between an organization and its stakeholders by involving the latter in organizational activities (Greenwood, 2007; Noland and Phillips, 2010). This approach moves beyond a "one-sided" approach to stakeholder management, according to which managers interpret and handle external stakeholders' demands (Pedrini and Ferri, 2019). SE comprises practices such as information dissemination, reporting, collaboration, consultation, stakeholder dialogue, and joint-decision-making (Herremans et al., 2016; Mitchell et al., 2022; O'Riordan and Fairbrass, 2014). Developing SE activities can increase the positive environmental impact of HEIs beyond their pedagogic and operational activities. HEIs (and, specifically, Business Schools) are important intermediaries between theory and practice and can gain valuable insights from engaging in dialogue and considering stakeholders' concerns (Greenwood, 2007; O'Riordan and Fairbrass, 2014). HEIs can also appease internal and external resistance towards organizational change related to sustainability transitions. Likewise, when collaborating with industry, governments, and other stakeholders, HEIs can contribute to these actors' better understanding of sustainability challenges, thus multiplying their impact. However, the lack of real examples in the SE literature (Kujala and Sachs, 2019) hampers the potential that tools such as multistakeholder dialogue or collaboration could have to tackle wicked problems that cannot be coordinated by sole organizations, such as climate change or inequality (Roloff, 2008; Rühli et al., 2017; Schneider and Sachs, 2017). While HEI's engagement with external actors in the development of business ideas has received some attention (McAdam et al., 2012), stakeholder engagement in sustainability strategy-making processes has remained understudied.

Additionally, the fast-changing context surrounding sustainability globally, and in higher education in particular, means institutions find themselves constantly adapting to potential disruptions to their traditional way of working, driving engagement, and in their strategic paths (Chiu et al., 2020). Punctuated equilibrium theorists allow us to understand processes of engagement as activities that incrementally lead to agreements between the participants; but during which there are also occasional moments that are disruptive and imply a departure from the pre-established path (True et al., 1999). These disruptions affecting the engagement process present actors with a clear-cut confrontation that requires decision-making on how to move forward (Baumgartner et al., 2018; Hayward, 2020).

Through a case study, this chapter contributes to the literature on sustainability in HEIs and looks to fill this gap by exploring a HEI's stakeholder engagement process that led to the co-construction of a sustainability-oriented strategy to tackle grand challenges.

To do so, we explore the case of *Transition 2026*, a French business school's climate strategy co-constructed through a multistakeholder engagement process. The case study concerns a top-ranked business school in France that offers a variety of programs and currently hosts around 7,500 students and 500 permanent staff in its two campuses. In addition to the efforts made to integrate corporate social responsibility (CSR), sustainability, and ethics in the school programs, hire dedicated researchers, and improve the impact of its operations; the school launched a dedicated SE process to create its first-ever sustainability and climate strategy, *"Transition 2026"*. Between 2019 and 2023, the school developed an elaborate SE process which included both internal stakeholders, such as students and employees, and external ones from the industrial, governmental, and social spheres. When the process was launched, the main objective was exclusively operational, merely focused on establishing a first carbon footprint assessment and setting environmental targets for both campuses and school services. However, the engagement with stakeholders led to a more ambitious strategy that covered all activities of the HEI with a strong focus on the integration of climate change and sustainability into all courses, discussions around research and impact, and the need to upskill all staff and faculty.

This chapter is organized longitudinally, following the four stages through which the SE process took place: (1) issue and stakeholder identification; (2) stakeholder involvement and co-construction; (3) definition of objectives and ambitions; and (4) stakeholder empowerment. We present the main initiatives taken during each stage, and we assess their main challenges and opportunities. We also discuss how stakeholder engagement – different from the optimistic assumption that it will lead to consensus – also sparks disagreement between stakeholders (Arenas et al., 2009; Bridoux and Stoelhorst, 2022; Castelló and Lopez-Berzosa, 2023; Crilly, 2019). Finally, we present the insights and lessons that schools and policy makers could consider when developing a SE process to define a sustainability and climate strategy. By exploring a comprehensive SE process, we aim to provide practical tools for HEIs to be more ambitious in their "transformative" sustainability role (Starik et al., 2010).

CONTEXT: DEVELOPMENTS IN FRANCE

Like other organizations, HEIs develop, adopt, and implement strategies as a way to achieve their goals. Especially in the last decades, higher education has become a global service, and it is delivered by quasi-companies in an increasingly competitive knowledge market (Pucciarelli and Kaplan, 2016). Higher education often faces clear and significant pressures, comparable to those faced by for-profit organizations (Zajac and Kraatz, 1993). Hence, the institutional context is relevant to analyze the development of sustainability strategies as stakeholder pressures appear to have considerably accelerated the integration of sustainability into HEIs activities. Tellingly, in the case of France, a 2019 survey by RESES (the French student network for an eco-logical and solidarity-based society) reported that 78% of students consider institutional engagement in sustainability as a key criterion for their HEIs choices (Revelli and Lagoarde-Segot, 2023). Furthermore, groups of students have increasingly voiced their concerns on what they consider to be a slow adaptation of HEIs to the global sustainability challenges we face today, notably climate change, have boycotted corporate events and have voiced their disagreements in graduation speeches.

Likewise, alumni are now also engaging with their HEIs to collaborate in the transition towards sustainability and to push their HEIs to go further in terms of levels of ambition. This is revealed by the number of sustainability alumni clubs that have been created in the last two years and that actively mobilize their members via meetings with the school's governance, events and conferences (Revelli and Lagoarde-Segot, 2023). These alumni clubs pressure their institutions directly, but also work together to create events and forums that bring together students and alumni from different schools. Alumni movements and increasing mobilization is also illustrated through the creation of the "Alumni for the Planet" association which gathers alumni who want to drive change in their current professional organizations (Alumni for the Planet, 2023).

Additionally, in France, recent governmental guidelines mandate the inclu-sion of climate change and environmental concerns into syllabi and HEIs operations within the next five years. An example of these new mandates is the *Jouzel Report*, based on four main axes: stimulating the evolution of all higher education training to include climate and environmental concerns; providing steering and support by public authorities; accelerating and strengthening the involvement of higher education institutions; and encouraging the mobiliza-tion and (re)training of HEIs staff, students, and alumni networks. Finally, all French HEIs have recently been informed that all HEIs under the responsibility of the French Ministry of Education must submit a roadmap by 2024 on how they intend to address and incorporate sustainability in five areas: strategy and governance, teaching and learning, research and innovation, environmental impact, and social policy.

Interestingly, media scrutiny on HEIs and sustainability has increased and new rankings on sustainable performance of HEIs – such as the *ChangeNow* ranking and the *HappyatSchool* ranking – have appeared. In France, several media outlets publish business school rankings and have begun to include criteria for sustainability performance. While pressures to evolve towards an environmental transition are clear and mounting, tensions emerge as other actors, which are essential components of change, resist them. Tellingly, previous research has shown how universities resist transparency policies and reporting around certain issues related to corporate social responsibility (Aversano et al., 2020; see also Alonso-Almeida et al., 2015). One source of opposition to curricula changes in the French case has been identified to be HEIs faculty (Le Nevé, 2023), some of whom are reluctant to adapt their teaching or to incorporate issues of sustainability into their courses. Such opposition signals that any strategic change towards sustainability requires taking into account diverse stakeholders' claims, rather than planning a one-sided transition.

THE CASE: TRANSITION 2026

To explore how this evolving French context may be used to catalyze change towards sustainability in a HEI, we study the case of a top-ranked business school in France that offers programs at different levels and operates in two campuses.

Since 2016, this school has integrated CSR, sustainability, and ethics courses into its programs, hiring dedicated researchers, and has also worked on improving the impact of its operations. A key challenge HEIs face is ensuring coherence between the content of their courses and the actions they take as an institution. Failing to address both can lead to student discontent and accusations of greenwashing (Christensen et al., 2020; Winkler et al., 2020). To ensure coherence and promote stakeholder participation in sustainability activities of the institution, the school launched a SE process to create its first-ever sustainability strategy and its first-ever climate strategy *"Transition 2026"*. The SE process was led by the Sustainability team, and supported by the school's Sustainability Steering Committee, an organ composed of representatives of different services from the school that meets to discuss matters around CSR and sustainability and to advise the school's board of directors.

To develop *Transition 2026*, this school engaged in a collaboration process with its stakeholders for 39 months (12/2019 to 03/2023), including students, faculty, staff, alumni, partner companies from different industries, other HEIs, student movements, non-governmental organizations, and local authorities.

STARTING THE TRANSITION

Sustainability became an important topic for this school years before the beginning of the SE process that we assess in this chapter. Having signed its membership to the UN Global Compact (UNGC) and the UN Principles of Responsible Management Education (PRME) in 2008 and adhering the Responsible Campus Network in France in 2010, the school was one of the first in France to include a mandatory CSR and ethics course for all its students in 2015, as well as a mandatory consulting project on CSR in 2016. It also founded the Center for Organizational Responsibility in 2014, bringing together professors from different departments within the school with the dual intention of creating and spreading knowledge and practice-oriented tools in the fields of social responsibility, sustainability, and business and society relations, and strengthening research on issues of sustainability and CSR. While the Center had a strong focus on the integration of sustainability into pedagogy and research, less attention and resources were devoted to the operational side of the school activities and, particularly, to the measurement of the impact of its operations on the wider environment. As climate discussions intensified in HEIs, both in France and abroad, the school sought to take a lead among business schools in the integration of climate objectives into its full operations. In 2019, the school therefore decided to move forward with the measurement of this impact with the aim of developing its first-ever climate strategy.

MEASURING THE CARBON FOOTPRINT? NOT ENOUGH!

When the school initially started working on this project, back in 2019, the objective was exclusively operational, focusing on establishing a first carbon footprint assessment and setting environmental targets for both campuses and all services in the school and did not include other dimensions of the school's activities. Initial discussions involved the Sustainability Manager, the Director of Operations, and the General Services team, thus limiting the scope and reach of the project. The school hired an external consultancy firm to help with the carbon footprint assessment and collected the required data.

In parallel to the data collection for the footprint assessment, a group of internal stakeholders (faculty members and administrative staff), raised the importance of going beyond the carbon footprint assessment and having a much clearer view on the different issues that are important to the school's stakeholders regarding sustainability. Indeed, while the school had been integrating sustainability for some time, no formalization of its ambitions existed yet. Discussions around the carbon footprint implications, and the need to have a broader vision of what is important for the school led to a slight deviation from the original objective of meeting some environmental targets, embarking instead on a much broader strategy creation process that covered sustainability more broadly, with a 360-degree view on all activities and stakeholders, before zooming in on the climate strategy.

THE PATH TOWARDS "TRANSITION 2026"

In this section, we revise longitudinally the entire process across its four different stages: (1) issue and stakeholder identification; (2) SE and co-construction; (3) definition of objectives and ambitions; (4) and stakeholder empowerment. While during the first two stages, the SE started to be shaped, it was not until the third and the fourth stage that the climate strategy *Transition 2026* emerged and consolidated. Figure 5.1 summarizes this process.

Stage 1: Issue and Stakeholder Identification (December 2019–August 2020)

The initial phase of this process began in December 2019, triggered by discussions related to carbon footprint assessment and the need to look beyond this footprint and more broadly into the different issues – environmental and social – that surrounded the school. As the school advanced in the institutionalization of sustainability, the need for a sustainability strategy became apparent, and thus the strategy-building process began.

The main objective during this stage was to map the stakeholders of the school and understand their needs, interests, and priorities when it comes to sustainability. A benchmarking process also took place to understand how different HEIs in different parts of the world were addressing sustainability issues and mobilizing their stakeholders. Benchmarking indeed is essential when building a strategy because it provides organizations with relevant insights into their own performance and the performance of their competitors. It allows the identification of best practices, comparison of performance, and identification of potential gaps (Johnson et al., 2020). These two first steps were done by the sustainability team and debriefed with the Sustainability Steering Committee. This benchmarking exercise led to the creation of a long list of sustainability issues that were useful in igniting discussions on the relevance of topics at the school and their prioritization. The debates within this group regarding the relevance of topics signaled a need to implement a materiality analysis to develop a clear understanding of stakeholders and issues.

Conducting a materiality analysis presented advantages to advance the SE process. A materiality analysis is an essential tool for organizations seeking to develop sustainability strategies. It involves identifying and prioritizing the

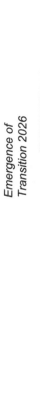
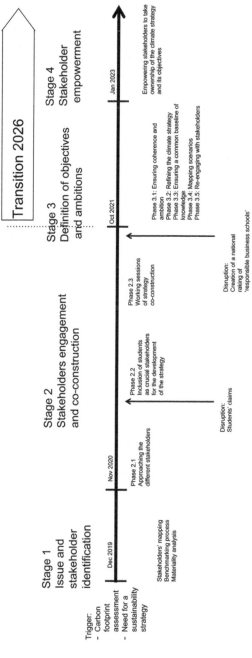

Figure 5.1   Process timeline

most significant environmental, social, and governance issues that are relevant to an organization's operations and to its stakeholders. Then, materiality analysis helps organizations focus on the most relevant issues and to prioritize where they affect their resources. Furthermore, materiality analysis helps organizations engage with their stakeholders, better understanding their needs and priorities, and leading to more open dialogue and collaboration (Beske et al., 2020; Whitehead, 2017). The materiality analysis was discussed in the school's Sustainability Steering Committee. During this meeting, potential objectives of the materiality assessment were defined, including the ambition to formalize a sustainability strategy and the desire to establish a connection with internal and external stakeholders to identify trends and opportunities. The initial long list of issues was reduced to a list of 38 issues, classified in 4 categories (environmental, social, academic, other (including issues related to governance)) and 6 months after the initial discussions began the survey was shared with students, staff, faculty, alumni, parents, and partner companies. The results of the materiality analysis indicated that stakeholders' views of the relevance of environmental issues at the school were quite heterogenous, with climate change and biodiversity being noted as important for stakeholders but less relevant for the school, and sustainable mobility and green buildings appearing among the most material issues. Most importantly, the materiality analysis provided an overview of stakeholders' interests and became the starting point of a much deeper SE process.

Stage 2: Stakeholder Engagement and Co-Construction (November 2020–January 2022)

The results of the materiality analysis were presented and discussed in the Sustainability Steering Committee at the beginning of the Fall 2020 semester and there was a collective decision to further pursue SE to build a comprehensive strategy that was relevant for the activities of the school. Stage 2 of the strategy-building process focused on a thorough and rather long SE process that included three different phases: (2.1) Interviews and group discussions, (2.2) Disruption in planned process; and (2.3) Co-creation via working groups.

Phase 2.1: interviews and group discussions (November 2020–April 2021)

The Sustainability team mapped key people in different administrative services, academic departments and student associations and held 32, one-on-one, in-depth interviews to understand how they – as representatives of their group – viewed their role when it came to the future sustainability strategy of the school, including a potential climate strategy. These different interviews led to some quick wins and became a crucial step to achieve buy-in from different services. For example, the interview with the Head of the Alumni network in February 2021 led to a discussion on the need of creating an alumni club on sustainability to further integrate these stakeholders in the creation of the sustainability and climate strategy of the school. The Head of the Alumni network organized a meeting with alumni, and by June 2021 the alumni club on sustainability had been launched. This alumni club has been a key driving force and ally in the development of the strategy. This first round of strategies also allowed the sustainability team to identify potential barriers such as resistance to change and – to a certain degree – a lack of understanding of the importance of sustainability for business schools.

Within the school a structure of Professional Advisory Boards (PABs) already existed; these boards offer a mechanism to bridge the academic content of its programs with practitioners' experiences. A dedicated PAB on sustainability was organized in March with a group of company representatives to better understand the needs and perceptions of companies in terms of the sustainability skills and knowledge students must acquire by the time they graduate to successfully integrate the job market. This PAB was particularly interesting as the companies present stressed the need for students to be "activists" and "revolutionaries", to have much deeper knowledge on climate issues, to be ready to integrate the climate dimension and sustainability in general to whatever management position they would have in their professional career, and to drive change. As a conclusion, one of the companies participating stated that "the role of a business school is to make 'internal business activists' instead of 'sustainability activists'", hence ensuring students change business from within and disrupt current models while working to make them evolve. Although this strong discourse was encouraging to hear, it also came with some tensions and questioning on how "far" business schools should go in their discourse on sustainability, particularly on whether the school should position their students as "activist" to drive internal change as the word activist can have negative connotations for some managers. This led to interesting and difficult conversations on the positioning of the HEI in this field.

In parallel to the different consultations, the school also engaged in dialogues with local authorities. This was particularly the case in one of the cities for the School is present where a group of 100 local actors, including several HEIs and companies engaged in discussions on defining a collective engagement to reduce CO_2 emissions in the region. These discussions led to the signing of the *Low-Carbon Pact* in June 2021, which tackles six main themes that were collectively selected: water and energy use; low-carbon construction materials and circular economy; biodiversity and urban agriculture; soft-mobility; and citizen well-being. Signing this agreement was a key step in the institutionalization of the climate discussions in the school, as it was the first time it engaged in a formal commitment on climate-related issues.

Finally, numerous exchanges with other HEIs, including engineering schools, took place during this period to share best practices and explore opportunities for collaboration. These conversations are of importance as HEIs share similar challenges and opportunities and many of them are more-or-less in a similar degree of maturity in the integration of climate-related considerations into their strategies.

The results from the various stakeholder dialogues were grouped into four pillars by the sustainability team and became the four pillars of the sustainability strategy: (a) developing sustainability knowledge, competences, and passion; (b) responsible campus; (c) research and partnerships for impact; and (d) diversity, inclusion, and well-being. The climate dimension emerged through conversations as a transversal element, particularly for the first three pillars, meaning that the school identified the need to further integrate attention for climate change into courses, operations, and research. The results of these discussions and the four pillars were presented to the Board of Directors of the HEI in February 2021 with the intention of including Sustainability as a key axis in the new school's strategic plan. While the new axis was accepted, no formal decisions were taken yet on how to move forward with this integration the following months.

Phase 2.2: disrupting a planned process (February–March 2021)
A major disruptor in the strategy-building process occurred when two students contacted the Dean, the Vice-Dean, and the Sustainability Manager to express their concerns about how climate-related issues were being addressed by the school. Indeed, following a rating questionnaire that was shared by the Sustainability team to all students, two master students questioned the school's ambition and asked for the HEI to go much further in the integration of climate issues, both in courses and in the school's operations. In the message, a list of proposals was drafted and the desire to engage in a conversation about this topic was explicitly mentioned.

> More and more students feel a deep gap between higher education and the climate crisis. This can be seen in particular through the demand of (another HEI) students for a new dean aligned with the ecological transition or the latest report of the association Pour Un Réveil Ecologique (For an Ecological Awakening) which highlights the delay of higher education institutions in teaching courses related to sustainable development. We know that our HEI included CSR in its strategy and is fully committed to implement further CSR actions at all levels. Nevertheless, we truly believe that HEI can and has to do more… Therefore, we wish the school to consider our next proposals that aim to help both the school and its students to fully understand what is at stake with global warming and give them the tools to become true changemakers: … (email from students received by Sustainability Manager, Dean, and Vice-Dean on February 3rd, 2021)

This email ignited conversations internally about student expectations and marked the beginning of a much closer dialogue with "engaged" students. Shortly after these conversations, a small group of six students formed to work closely with the Sustainability team and propose initiatives. The group recognized the efforts being done by the school but dreaded the speed at which change was happening. As the next step of the strategy-building and SE process was about to begin with the launch of four working groups, the Sustainability team proposed that some of these students became group leaders to help push the discussions and establish a closer link with these key stakeholders.

Phase 2.3: co-creation via working groups

Working groups round 1 (March–June 2021). In March 2021, four student-led working groups, one per pillar, were launched to collectively set priorities and ambitions for the school in each pillar. These working groups were open to students, staff, faculty, and alumni and mobilized around 50 people. The working groups all had a similar kick-off meeting to explain the objectives and the process and then met on a regular basis for three and a half months to come up with concrete proposals and key performance indicators (KPIs) for the school. The process was very open from the start, meaning participants were given information on what already existed, and then given a blank page to imagine what could (or should) come next. All working groups used the same visual collaboration tool, Miro, to gather their ideas, group them into themes, and then use that to formalize a proposal.

One of the main challenges faced by the working groups was to keep all participants engaged and motivated throughout the entire process as the schedule was demanding. Additionally, each working group had its own dynamic, strongly influenced by the group leader, and participants had different levels of ambition for the topic. This created some tensions and caused a few people to leave the working groups as they were not aligned with what was being proposed.

The proposals from the working group on pillar (a) (developing knowledge, competences, and passion) and the working group on pillar (b) (responsible campus) had a very strong orientation towards climate and carbon-reduction. Pillar (a) contained recommendations such as including a new mandatory course on planetary boundaries, energy, and climate for all first-year students, and integrating a climate dimension into all courses and programs. Proposals from pillar (b) included becoming a zero-waste campus by 2025 and net-zero by 2050. All proposals were presented to the Dean, Vice-Dean, and the Sustainability team in May 2021 to get feedback and discuss their implications. Now it was time to broaden these debates.

Vision seminar 1 (June 2021). A key milestone in the development of the strategy was the Vision Seminar organized in June 2021. This bi-annual seminar includes all staff and faculty and is commonly used to work on the future of the school and present advances in the strategy. While COVID-19-related restrictions existed, the process was able to continue by using digital tools. During this vision seminar, the main focus was on the integration of sustainability as a new strategic axis for the school. Several structured brainstorming sessions were organized to allow the key interests and priorities of the community in terms of sustainability to emerge. Also, the proposals of the working groups were presented here with the objective of opening another space of collective discussion among a larger group of people, allowing them to question and/ or build on the existing proposals. This seminar allowed for further reflection regarding a definition of sustainability at the school, the priorities, and the need to accelerate the process.

Process debrief (July–September 2021). After several intense months, the summer brought a period of reflection on the work done since November 2020. This time was useful for the Sustainability team to reassess all the different ideas and proposals gathered through the different consultation and engagement processes and to start drafting a unique and overarching document, including the definition of sustainability for the school, the level of ambition intended, and the proposals from the different working groups. It also provided time to think about the governance and the role of the Sustainability Steering Committee in all of this. Inspired by those insights, a second series of working group meetings was scheduled.

Working groups: round 2 (October 2021–January 2022). A second round of working groups was launched in October 2021. The intentions of this round were twofold: to provide stakeholders who had not had the chance of previously engaging in these discussions to integrate a group, and to work on better defining the key strategic objectives of each axis following the feedback and work from the Vision Seminar and building on the proposals from the first round of working groups to establish a timeline of actions and priorities and their measurement.

Soon after the launch of the second round of working groups, another disruption occurred. For the first time in France, a ranking on "responsible business schools" appeared, and the school was not in it. This generated frustration from different stakeholders and an alumnus contacted the Dean and Vice-Dean with the following email:

> It is now a risk for our dear school to be outdated on this subject while awareness is growing among students and future students…Here are, in my humble opinion, a few ways for our school to live up to the expectations of its role as a guide for tomorrow's managers, and which must now take into account the concept of planetary limits to enable students to have the right reading keys in an economic world that must reduce its footprint… (email, October 2021)

The publication of this ranking was useful in reframing the priorities and ambitions for the school as it now realized that while its efforts were going in the right direction, the level of ambition needed to be significantly increased, particularly concerning the integration of environmental sustainability – mostly climate change – into its curriculum and its daily operations. This again led to discussions in different groups about the need to educate all students on the challenges of climate change as soon as they joined the school, and the need to set a more ambitious target regarding emission reductions. Among the proposals that emerged following these discussions were the implementation of a serious game called the Climate Fresk and a webinar for all first-year students during their integration week. A new stage began.

Stage 3: Definition of Objectives and Ambition (October 2021–December 2022)

Stage 3 was composed of 5 phases that allowed the school to build on their sustainability strategy to create their Climate Strategy. The phases were the following: (3.1) Ensuring coherence and ambition; (3.2) Refining the climate strategy; (3.3) Ensuring a common baseline of knowledge for all; (3.4) Mapping emission reduction scenarios; and (3.5) Re-engaging with stakeholders.

Phase 3.1: ensuring coherence and ambition (January–March 2022)
The process of active stakeholder consultation extended over almost one year and set the scenario for a third stage of the strategy-building process. This third stage was strongly inspired by the results of discussions with stakeholders following the publication of the ChangeNow ranking and the desire to set more ambitious objectives. This stage focused on the definition of the school's strategic objectives, the level of ambition, and the KPIs used to measure progress. The objective of this stage was also to ensure coherence between the different proposals of working groups and the chosen objectives and priorities. This meant that as the HEI was committing to more ambitious emission reductions, the rest of the school strategic plan had to be aligned with this commitment and that sustainability objectives were integrated transversally through all proposals.

The Sustainability team developed an initial set of objectives and ambitions, based on the ongoing proposals of the working groups, and presented these to the Sustainability Steering Committee by the end of October 2021 to integrate different comments, observations, or suggestions, and ensure that the Steering Committee agreed with the proposals. Once the Steering Committee approved the proposed objectives and ambitions, the Sustainability team went back to the working group leaders to communicate the decisions. All group leaders then presented their proposals to the school's Executive Committee in January 2022. Following those presentations and discussions with the Executive Committee, the Sustainability Strategy was finalized and communicated externally and internally and was integrated into the school's strategy.

Phase 3.2: refining the climate strategy: towards a systemic and comprehensive approach (January 2022–March 2023)

Once the overall sustainability ambitions of the school had been defined and accepted, and based on the results of the carbon footprint, the next step was to deep dive into the emission reduction objectives and work on the development of a stand-alone Climate Strategy that would soon after be called *Transition 2026.* Based on the extensive stakeholder consultation process to first build the overall sustainability strategy, the school's intention now was to develop a climate strategy that touched upon all elements of the sustainability strategy rather than merely incorporating operational impact. The process to finalize the climate strategy required a new round of SE which included three parallel processes: consultations with professors and alumni on integrating sustainability and climate into teaching and programs; a working group to project scenarios for emission reductions; and a third working group focused on international mobility – the highest source of emission for most schools (Shields, 2019). Additionally, in January 2022, the school signed the "Grenoble Agreement" (CTES, 2021), an agreement created by a student network to drive the engagement of HEIs in their environmental transition. By signing this agreement, the school committed to achieving carbon neutrality by 2050 as well as revisiting programs and courses.

Phase 3.3: ensuring a common baseline of knowledge for all (April 2022–March 2023)

The first of these parallel processes focused on establishing the ambition and objectives related to integrating climate into courses, programs, and the overall learning experience for all the school's community. Training all students, but also professors and staff, was identified as a critical success factor for the overall success of the Climate Action Plan. The HEI committed to training all its professors and administrative staff on the basics of climate change and other sustainability dimensions by September 2024. At the same time, all first-year students would go through an introduction to climate change via a serious game called the Climate Fresk. This first-year seminar was launched in September 2022. The mandatory training for staff and professors – which began in February 2023 – should give them the knowledge and competences to be able to draft their own roadmaps by 2024. Additionally, by 2024, professors are expected to integrate climate into the discussions of their different courses, and in some cases into the main course content, and will be required to reflect on this integration in their annual performance evaluations. Furthermore, a review of already existing mandatory sustainability courses in the main program of the HEI took place to ensure they include the most relevant and recent content on climate change, including the science behind climate change, the regulatory context, and how companies are integrating climate and climate risk into their operations. Also, an additional mandatory course on Environmental and Energy Economics was added to the undergraduate program, starting September 2023.

This step was probably one of the most relevant and yet challenging for the HEI as the imposition of mandatory training led to resistance by some professors. The resistance was driven by different factors, including: a lack of time to follow such training, a lack of interest in the topic, the perception of already being knowledgeable enough in the topic, and a degree of questioning on the ideology behind this initiative. Although resistance was expected, more communication with different services before launching the training could have been useful to facilitate the implementation of the initiative.

Phase 3.4: mapping out possible emission reduction scenarios (March 2022–March 2023)

To map different emission reduction scenarios, the HEI engaged with several external stakeholders. Therefore, this stage included consultations within a working group composed of five HEIs in the region which discussed topics related to sustainable impact of the different campuses. Among the members of this group were engineers specialized in the calculation of carbon impact. The HEI worked closely with them to develop three possible scenarios and trajectories for emission reduction. The first scenario, the most ambitious one, required the HEI to set a target of −56% by 2030. The second scenario established a target of −38% by 2030, and finally, the third, and least ambitious, scenario determined a reduction of −31%. Together with one of the engineers of the working group, a dashboard was developed to clearly visualize and measure the impact of different decisions on emission reductions.

Phase 3.5: re-engaging with internal stakeholders to revisit emission reduction goals (September 2022–ongoing)

These three scenarios and the dashboard were very useful in the different consultations with internal stakeholders such as General Services, Corporate Relations, International Relations, and IT, as they allowed to fix a range of potential emission reductions, understand the impact and implication of certain decisions, and then envision what each of those scenarios would represent in terms of actions and implementation for the different internal stakeholders. This helped to develop a shared understanding and responsibility of the plan and its actions and helped to secure the resources needed to achieve the objectives.

A new working group on international mobility was set up in January 2023 bringing together the Research, International Relations, Corporate Relations, and Sustainability teams to work on a common proposal on how to reduce emissions related to international travel of students, professors, and staff. The topic of international mobility is particularly complex as the institutional landscape around business schools highly values internationalization. This means that accreditation bodies such as Equis and AACSB, international and national rankings, and the job market reward international experience such as student exchanges and internships abroad. Meanwhile, research also strongly relies on participation in conferences around the world. An objective to reduce international mobility by −35% by 2030 was fixed and a final action plan is being currently developed by the HEI.

Stage 4: Stakeholder Empowerment (January 2023–to date)

The final but critical step of the strategy process was empowering stakeholders to take ownership of the climate strategy and its objectives. The empowerment process is ongoing (at the time of writing) but has included two main actions: communication and raising awareness on the climate strategy, and launching training sessions for all students, staff, and faculty. These two actions are the stepping stones to the final step of the process which is the co-construction of roadmaps for all services and student associations. Once the training process is over, the sustainability team will work with all internal stakeholders between January and March 2024 to develop actionable roadmaps that detail how each administrative service, academic department, and student associations will contribute to the reduction of emissions by 2026 and beyond. The main objective is that stakeholders develop ownership of the strategy, establish measurement and reporting processes, and create a culture of shared responsibility.

Furthermore, the school has identified that one of the main blocking points for the community is often the complexity of finding relevant and reliable information and resources. To facilitate ownership and empowerment, a resource center will be made available to all to ensure that all members of the HEI community have easy access to reliable information and content on sustainability and climate, course material such as case studies, simulations, videos, and tools to easily measure individual environmental footprints.

Transition 2026 is the final product of this long 39-month SE process. It is based on the comprehensive sustainability strategy of the HEI, reflects the ambitions of different stakeholders, and incorporates all core dimensions of the HEI activities: courses and programs; training of professors and staff; research; operational impact and carbon neutrality (IT, energy, buildings, etc.);

and community engagement. It is important to note that *Transition 2026* is a living strategy, meaning that continuous SE is foreseen to adapt to strategy in time.

The *Transition 2026* process also reveals the challenges a complex SE process faces, mainly the emergence of disagreements and tensions among stakeholders regarding the level of ambition of the process, the priorities, and their own role in the transition.

CONCLUSIONS – LESSONS LEARNED FROM TRANSITION 2026

The case of this school in a context such as France is helpful to better understand how organizations and particularly HEIs are tackling the challenges of sustainability and sustainable transformation. It provides insights on how organizations can mobilize stakeholders to ensure their ambitions and strategy are aligned with the general expectations of their stakeholders.

The HEI landscape, and particularly the business school industry in France is currently undergoing an important transition towards sustainability. Sustainability transitions are deep systemic changes in industries or business models that aim to address the major grand challenges of our times. These transitions lead to innovation, but also spark resistance, changes in practices and expectations from stakeholders, and require solid governance mechanisms (Markard et al., 2020). The transition towards more sustainable business models also faces potential disruptions, making the process more complex, and requiring a higher degree of adaptability and resilience from institutions.

This case is of interest as it spotlights the complexity of SE and the challenges of leading a sustainability transition. It highlights the benefits and challenges of engaging stakeholders and the role of organizations in managing such a process to reach a satisfactory result. It shows how the original vision doesn't always translate into the final product as the process can be "disturbed" by evolving stakeholder expectations or by vocal stakeholder dissatisfaction.

In this case, the starting point in terms of climate strategy was mostly reduced to the measurement of the carbon footprint and then deciding how to reduce it. However, the influence of stakeholders, notably students, alumni, and companies, drove the school towards a much more ambitious journey that broadened the scope of the strategy to become more comprehensive by including the discussions around climate and the environment in the learning experience of students, but also staff and professors. And as time passed, stakeholders were more invested and interested in "doing this right" and setting goals and objectives that demonstrate the ambition and commitment of the school. Of course, the practice of SE has not been without complexities. The case of this school reveals the following key insights:

Solid foundations are essential. When the school performed its first carbon footprint and intended to define objectives and reduction targets, it very quickly realized that it was missing solid foundations as even though sustainability had been around for a long time, there was no formal strategy to guide sustainability at the school. Thus, to be able to build its climate strategy *Transition 2026*, the school first had to build a solid and coherent sustainability strategy, covering all topics including climate. As HEIs set out to develop their climate objectives, ensuring the foundations are there – even if that requires additional time – becomes a key success factor. Often, the building of foundations will happen in parallel to a fast-changing environment. The capacity to adapt and react while building those foundations becomes essential.

Time and more time are important, but also deadlines. Properly engaging with stakeholders regarding sustainability grand challenges to ensure the strategy is aligned with their expectations requires time: it can't be done in just a few months as the topics are complex, and so is the process. When the strategy-building process began for this school, the process had been planned to last a maximum of 12 months. However, as the process advanced, the school realized much more time was needed to build a strategy that made sense, that involved everyone, and that actually had an impact. "Doing it right" becomes the guiding force, and this requires time. However, constantly setting deadlines for processes remains essential to ensure the process keeps moving forward at a steady pace. These deadlines might evolve with the process, but they become checkpoints for accountability.

Adaptability is crucial. As mentioned before, the original objective of the strategy was very simple compared to what the final climate strategy turned out to be. Throughout the 39 months, several disruptions to the process occurred. Students and alumni raising their voice; companies expressing their expectations; and services and individual members of the organization asking the school to be more ambitious. SE processes require the teams driving them to adapt and pivot when needed.

SE can't be successful without constant management of disagreements and tensions. Complex stakeholder engagement processes seek to build consensus and build strategies that respond to the expectations of stakeholders. However, the *Transition 2026* process reveals that disagreements and tensions arise at different moments, and sometimes from unexpected stakeholders. This requires the leaders of the SE process to manage and deal with tensions and disagreements to ensure the process can continue moving forward. This also means that there are moments where the SE leaders need to take decisions in the interest of the organization, even if they might not be supported by all stakeholders.

Setting ambitious targets – an ongoing challenge. This SE process also highlights that setting the right level of ambition is difficult and that it doesn't easily create consensus among stakeholders. All stakeholders have different expectations and ambitions regarding sustainability topics making this a difficult negotiation. Furthermore, given the rapid evolution of the topic and the context, the HEI had to review its ambitions several times during the process as what was considered good enough in the early stages of the SE process, might no longer be enough mid-way through.

SE unlocks unknown possibilities (and surprises). Through the intense SE process, initiatives or actions emerged that would not have been discussed otherwise. When the school began thinking about training all of its community, the SE process led to a broader 18-month program to provide a common framework for all colleagues. Also, the work done with the HEI working group has allowed the creation of useful tools to calculate and simulate the impact of decisions, also beyond the Lille context.

Quick wins and buy-ins go a long way. The creation of a sustainability and or a climate strategy can be a long and complex process. Therefore, quick wins and ensuring buy-in from different stakeholders become essential to keep people engaged and motivated. This could be done through lower impact but high-visibility actions or projects such as plastic reduction initiatives, community-building events, among others – the literature on issue selling offers several ideas here (Wickert and de Bakker, 2018).

FUTURE CHALLENGES

Despite the advancements, a couple of challenges remain for the school. As for many organizations, measuring impact and progress can often be challenging. The school is currently working on establishing more adequate KPIs to track and monitor progress, with the intention of increasing its communication efforts internally, but also externally via an impact report. This will require greater cooperation, collaboration, and communication between services to ensure coherence and to ensure that the latest and most relevant data is reported.

A second major challenge relates to climate/sustainability-fatigue. The long process has also led to a lot of communication on sustainability topics including: SE opportunities; the inclusion of sustainability into the school strategic plan; the energy sobriety; the communication of the *Transition 2026* strategy, including the mandatory training for all. The amount of communication, and the increasingly mandatory actions that have been put in place can lead to a sense of fatigue around the topic. Finding the good balance between setting the right level of ambition and using communication to help create a sense of empowerment and appropriation of the topic can be challenging, as there are risks of over-communicating and potential perceptions of greenwashing.

REFERENCES

Alonso-Almeida, M., Marimon, F., Casani, F., & Rodriguez-Pomeda, J. (2015). Diffusion of sustainability reporting in universities: Current situation and future perspectives. *Journal of Cleaner Production, 106*, 144–54.

Alshuwaikhat, H.M., & Abubakar, I. (2008). An integrated approach to achieving campus sustainability: Assessment of the current campus environmental management practices. *Journal of Cleaner Production, 16*(16), 1777–1785.

Alumni for the Planet (2023). https://alumnifortheplanet.org, accessed 24 April 2023.

Arenas, D., Lozano, J.M., & Albareda, L. (2009). The role of NGOs in CSR: Mutual perceptions among stakeholders. *Journal of Business Ethics, 88*, 175–197.

Aversano, N., Di Carlo, F., Sannino, G., Tartaglia Polcini, P., & Lombardi, R. (2020). Corporate social responsibility, stakeholder engagement, and universities: New evidence from the Italian scenario. *Corporate Social Responsibility and Environmental Management, 27*(4), 1892–1899.

Aversano, N., Nicolò, G., Sannino, G., & Tartaglia Polcini, P. (2022). Corporate social responsibility, stakeholder engagement, and universities. *Administrative Sciences, 12*(3), 79.

Baumgartner, F.R., Jones, B.D., & Mortensen, P.B. (2018). Punctuated equilibrium theory: Explaining stability and change in public policymaking. In C.M. Weible & P.A. Sabatier (Eds.), *Theories of the policy process* (pp. 55–101).

Beske, F., Haustein, E., & Lorson, P.C. (2020). Materiality analysis in sustainability and integrated reports. *Sustainability Accounting, Management and Policy Journal, 11*(1), 162–186.

Bridoux, F., & Stoelhorst, J.W. (2022). Stakeholder governance: Solving the collective action problems in joint value creation. *Academy of Management Review, 47*(2), 214–236.

Castelló, I., & Lopez-Berzosa, D. (2023). Affects in online stakeholder engagement: A dissensus perspective. *Business Ethics Quarterly, 33*(1), 180–215.

Chiu, A.S., Aviso, K.B., Baquillas, J., & Tan, R.R. (2020). Can disruptive events trigger transitions towards sustainable consumption? *Cleaner and Responsible Consumption, 1*, 100001.

Christensen, L.T., Morsing, M., & Thyssen, O. (2020). Timely hypocrisy? Hypocrisy temporalities in CSR communication. *Journal of Business Research, 114*, 327–335.

Crilly, D. (2019). Behavioral stakeholder theory. In J.S. Harrison, J.B. Barney, R.E. Freeman, & R.A. Phillips (Eds.), *The Cambridge handbook of stakeholder theory* (pp. 250–255). Cambridge University Press.

CTES (2021). Accord de Grenoble accesible at https://la-ctes.org/accord-de-grenoble/

Cullen, J.G. (2017). Educating business students about sustainability: A bibliometric review of current trends and research needs. *Journal of Business Ethics, 145*(2), 429–439.

Figueiró, P.S., & Raufflet, E. (2015). Sustainability in higher education: A systematic review with focus on management education. *Journal of Cleaner Production, 106*, 22–33.

Freeman, R.E. (1984). *Strategic management: A stakeholder approach.* Pitman.

Greenwood, M. (2007). Stakeholder engagement: Beyond the myth of corporate responsibility. *Journal of Business Ethics, 74*, 315–327.

Hayward, C.R. (2020). Disruption: What is it good for? *The Journal of Politics, 82*(2), 448–459.

Herremans, I.M., Nazari, J.A., & Mahmoudian, F. (2016). Stakeholder relationships, engagement, and sustainability reporting. *Journal of Business Ethics*, *138*, 417–435.

Johnson, G., Whittington, R., Regnér, P., Angwin, D., & Scholes, K. (2020). *Exploring strategy*. Pearson UK.

Khurana, R. (2007). *From higher aims to hired hands: The social transformation of American business schools and the unfulfilled promise of management as a profession*. Princeton University Press.

Krizek, K.J., Newport, D., White, J., & Townsend, A.R. (2012). Higher education's sustainability imperative: How to practically respond? *International Journal of Sustainability in Higher Education*, *13*(1), 19–33.

Kujala, J., & Sachs, S. (2019). The practice of stakeholder engagement. In J.S. Harrison, J.B. Barney, R.E. Freeman, & R.A. Phillips (Eds.), *The Cambridge handbook of stakeholder theory*. Cambridge University Press (pp. 227–241).

Le Nevé, S. (2023, January 6th). L'urgence écologique se heurte à la culture académique des universités. *Le Monde*. https://www.lemonde.fr/societe/article/2023/01/06/crise-climatique-dans-les-universites-l-urgence-ecologique-se-heurte-a-la-culture-academique_6156904_3224.html

Leal Filho, W., Skouloudis, A., Brandli, L.L., Salvia, A.L., Avila, L.V., & Rayman-Bacchus, L. (2019). Sustainability and procurement practices in higher education institutions: Barriers and drivers. *Journal of Cleaner Production*, *231*, 1267–1280.

Markard, J., Geels, F.W., & Raven, R. (2020). Challenges in the acceleration of sustainability transitions. *Environmental Research Letters*, *15*(8), 081001.

McAdam, R., Miller, K., McAdam, M., & Teague, S. (2012). The development of University Technology Transfer stakeholder relationships at a regional level: Lessons for the future. *Technovation*, *32*(1), 57–67.

Menon, S., & Suresh, M. (2020). Synergizing education, research, campus operations, and community engagements towards sustainability in higher education: A literature review. *International Journal of Sustainability in Higher Education*, *21*(5), 1015–1051.

Mitchell, J.R., Mitchell, R.K., Hunt, R.A., Townsend, D.M., & Lee, J.H. (2022). Stakeholder engagement, knowledge problems and ethical challenges. *Journal of Business Ethics*, *175*, 75–94.

Noland, J., & Phillips, R. (2010). Stakeholder engagement, discourse and strategic management. *International Journal of Management Reviews*, *12*, 39–49.

O'Riordan, L., & Fairbrass, J. (2014). Managing CSR stakeholder engagement: A new conceptual framework. *Journal of Business Ethics*, *125*, 121–145.

Pedrini, M., & Ferri, L.M. (2019). Stakeholder management: A systematic literature review. *Corporate Governance: The International Journal of Business in Society*, *19*, 44–59.

Pucciarelli, F., & Kaplan, A. (2016). Competition and strategy in higher education: Managing complexity and uncertainty. *Business Horizons*, *59*(3), 311–320.

Purcell, W.M., Henriksen, H., & Spengler, J.D. (2019). Universities as the engine of transformational sustainability toward delivering the sustainable development goals: "Living labs" for sustainability. *International Journal of Sustainability in Higher Education*, *20*(8), 1343–1357.

Revelli, C., & Lagoarde-Segot, L. (2023, January 26th). Vers une reconstruction écologique et social. *Les Echos*. https://www.lesechos.fr/idees-debats/cercle/opinion-vers-une-reconstruction-ecologique-et-sociale-1900840

Roloff, J. (2008). Learning from multi-stakeholder networks: Issue-focussed stakeholder management. *Journal of Business Ethics*, *82*, 233–250.

Rühli, E., Sachs, S., Schmitt, R., & Schneider, T. (2017). Innovation in multistakeholder settings: The case of a wicked issue in health care. *Journal of Business Ethics*, *143*, 289–305.

Schneider, T., & Sachs, S. (2017). The impact of stakeholder identities on value creation in issue-based stakeholder networks. *Journal of Business Ethics*, *144*, 41–57.

Shields, R. (2019). The sustainability of international higher education: Student mobility and global climate change. *Journal of Cleaner Production*, *217*, 594–602.

Starik, M., Rands, G., Marcus, A.A., & Clark, T.S. (2010). From the guest editors: In search of sustainability in management education. *Academy of Management Learning & Education*, *9*, 377–383.

Trencher, G., Yarime, M., McCormick, K.B., Doll, C.N., & Kraines, S.B. (2014). Beyond the third mission: Exploring the emerging university function of co-creation for sustainability. *Science and Public Policy*, *41*(2), 151–179.

True, J.L., Jones, B.D., & Baumgartner, F.R. (1999). Punctuated equilibrium theory. In C.M. Weible & P.A. Sabatier (Eds.), *Theories of the policy process* (pp. 175–202).

Whitehead, J. (2017). Prioritizing sustainability indicators: Using materiality analysis to guide sustainability assessment and strategy. *Business Strategy and the Environment*, *26*(3), 399–412.

Wickert, C., & de Bakker, F.G.A. (2018). Pitching for social change: Towards a relational approach to selling and buying social issues. *Academy of Management Discoveries*, *4*(1), 50–73.

Winkler, P., Etter, M., & Castelló, I. (2020). Vicious and virtuous circles of aspirational talk: From self-persuasive to agonistic CSR rhetoric. *Business & Society*, *59*(1), 98–128.

Zajac, E.J., & Kraatz, M.S. (1993). A diametric forces model of strategic change: Assessing the antecedents and consequences of restructuring in the higher education industry. *Strategic Management Journal*, *14*(S1), 83–102.

Žalėnienė, I., & Pereira, P. (2021). Higher education for sustainability: A global perspective. *Geography and Sustainability*, *2*(2), 99–106.

6. Crystallization of a university's sustainability efforts around Laudato Si': a case study of opportunities and challenges

Michael J. Pawlish[1]

INTRODUCTION/BACKGROUND

In the crystallization process, atoms come together through dissolved minerals, melted rock, or vapor, forming unique, beautiful, and natural crystals. Metaphorically, individuals at my university are increasingly uniting around social, economic, and environmental sustainability issues. This has resulted in an organizational culture that is becoming increasingly focused on sustainability, creating a unique, beautiful, and natural university. Despite challenges that may be transformed into opportunities, this chapter investigates the evolution of sustainability at Georgian Court University (GCU), a small private Catholic university situated in the Pine Barrens of New Jersey in the United States of America (USA). GCU was established at the present location by the Sisters of Mercy in 1924. The former grounds and estate of a railroad baron were repurposed as a female college, which transitioned into a coeducational university in 2013. With a declining number of nuns on campus and changing leadership, GCU continues to evolve. However, the university currently faces a crossroads due to lower college enrollment post-COVID and a smaller incoming population of college-age students.

In 2015, Pope Francis issued the encyclical letter *Laudato Si'*, which in Latin translates to "Praised Be." *Laudato Si'* included a challenge for Catholic institutions to prioritize sustainability. GCU embraced this challenge on various organizational levels. As demonstrated throughout this chapter, the commitment to sustainability extends from top administration to faculty and staff, with many individuals personally identifying with the Pope's call. This personal "calling" to sustainability is embedded in the organizational culture at GCU. Despite the challenges involved in implementing sustainable changes, GCU embraced the Pope's call because sustainability is already aligned with the university's values, beliefs, and norms. This chapter will document GCU's journey towards sustainability, recognizing that sustainability is an ongoing process without a final destination, as the journey to a more sustainable future is ongoing (Howard-Grenville et al., 2014).

GCU's sustainability journey is connected to Pope Francis's 2015 letter, *Laudato Si'*, which identifies seven goals for addressing environmental and social crises. These goals include the Cry of the Earth, the Cry of the Poor, Ecological Economics, Simple Lifestyles, Ecological Education, Ecological Spirituality, and Community Involvement and Participation. Pope Francis challenged Catholic institutions to embrace sustainability and strive to achieve these goals. As an example, GCU is currently engaging in stakeholder collaboration to develop initiatives aligned with the Cry of the Earth goal.

- Standardizing collection streams of interior and exterior locations.
- Committing to a culture of food waste diversion.
- Investing in a food composter.

The Pope's challenge has strengthened our existing sustainability efforts and the integration of our mission regarding ecological conversion on campus. Ecological conversion recaptures the interconnectedness among individuals, communities, and the environment, offering a holistic perspective that we strive to embody and impart at GCU.

Pope Francis draws his name from Saint Francis of Assisi, who is recognized as the patron saint of ecology (Francis, 2015). The name Francis was chosen to highlight the inseparable connection between concern for nature, justice for the poor, commitment to society, and peace (Francis, 2015). In his encyclical letter, the Pope encourages the importance of engaging in dialogue with all people about our shared home (Francis, 2015). He appeals for collective effort to pursue sustainable and integral development, acknowledging the potential for change (Francis, 2015). The Pope urges inclusive conversation that includes everyone, as the environmental challenge and its human origins affect us all (Francis, 2015). He emphasizes the importance of personal engagement and transforming the world's challenges into personal concerns (Francis, 2015). The Pope asserts that an ecological approach *should* also encompass a social approach and incorporate justice when discussing environmental issues, to address *both the cry of the earth and the cry of the poor* (Francis, 2015, p. 35).

This chapter investigates our institution's potential as a model sustainability organization, focusing on our operations. Our aim is to help other organizations in learning how to contribute more to sustainability solutions and minimize their impact on sustainability problems. We anticipate future collaborations with other institutions to exchange knowledge and share the results of our respective programs.

Based on the *Laudato Si'* goals, our institution has developed a seven-year action plan encompassing seven broad goals for sustainability and ecological conversion. GCU's Laudato Si' committee collaborated to adapt Pope Francis' *Laudato Si'* goals into the following seven broad goals for our institution: Waste Policy, Pollinator Protection Plan, Restore and Expand the Mercy Garden, Encourage a Culture of Decision-Making Based on Sustainability, Energy Conservation Measures, Academics, and Ecological Spirituality.

The results of this study have practical implications for staff and faculty in leadership and administrative roles within their respective institution's sustainability journey. Additionally, this study can assist other universities in developing knowledge on pressing socio-economic and environmental issues.

METHOD

Following Rubin and Rubin's (2012) method of qualitative interviewing, this chapter conducted interviews with GCU staff and faculty to explore sustainability and ecological conversion issues. The interviews focused on members of the Laudato Si' committee, consisting of approximately eight individuals, as well as other university employees. Unfortunately, due to time constraints, students were not interviewed for this chapter. A total of eight interviews were conducted with two employees not responding to multiple email requests for potential interviews. The interviews, ranging from approximately one hour to a half an hour in duration, were recorded and transcribed using Otter software. The transcriptions were carefully reviewed and checked for accuracy. Subsequently, all interviews were analyzed and coded to identify common themes. The coding process aligned with the goals established by the Laudato Si' committee, along with a few additional terms. For instance, waste policy served as a code term, and all transcribed interviews were examined for discussions related to waste management at the university. The Appendix at the end of the chapter provides a list of the questions asked for all interviewees.

CHALLENGES

The main challenge faced by GCU is the decrease in enrollment caused by COVID-19 and the ongoing trend of declining college-age students in the USA. Consequently, the university is currently experiencing deficit spending. Implementing sustainability solutions is already challenging, but it becomes even more difficult under deficit spending. Under these circumstances, sustainability solutions must generate positive revenue or at very least be revenue neutral. Since the start of the COVID-19 pandemic in the 2019–2020 academic year, GCU has witnessed a 25% decline in enrollment. This, combined with lower retention rates and increased tuition discounts, has contributed to the deficit spending. It is important to note that addressing the financial situation will not be a quick fix. The university will require several years of increased enrollment and cost control measures to overcome the present financial situation.

Despite the present financial challenges, university leaders remain focused on the future. As of the spring semester of 2023, the university leaders are preparing the staff, faculty, and students for transformative organizational change. These changes will undoubtedly present challenges. One area of change stems from the commitment of GCU's president to Pope Francis' *Laudato Si'* challenge. Throughout the 2022 calendar year, the Laudato Si' committee convened and formulated seven university goals and opportunities for sustainability-focused improvement. To present these goals in this book chapter, an internal report prepared by DaPonte (2022) was paraphrased and further developed upon.

UNIVERSITY GOAL 1: WASTE POLICY

The first of the seven broad goals developed by the Laudato Si' committee at GCU focuses on Waste Policy. Currently, there is confusion regarding proper recycling with different color bins. Taking feedback from students and employees into account, the committee has developed a goal to standardize the collection of waste streams across all locations on campus. The university aims to install standardized bins for interior spaces, specifically for plastics and metals, paper, compost, and landfill (for such products as Styrofoam). Additionally, designated collection areas will be conveniently located for materials such as batteries, lightbulbs, ink toner cartridges, aerosol cans and packaging. As for the exterior, the goal is to maintain two standardized bins: one for mixed recycling and another for composting. Notably, both the university and the town exhibit a strong recycling culture, as demonstrated by the following statement:

> Our recycling is picked up by Lakewood (the local town). They are very adamant…they actually look in the dumpster before they pick it up. And if there's non-recyclable materials in there, they give us a call. We got to go in and get them (the non-recyclable materials) out because occasionally people will drive by with their car, and they'll just unload some junk…And then the guys (employees) got to dumpster dive, and you know pull all that out. So, we can recycle. They (the town) are very diligent about that (recycling) because we get the calls when it's not, so I know they're doing it… (administrative staff member)

To achieve the goal of an enhanced waste policy, it will be necessary to invest in different color bins for recycling and make a marketing commitment on campus to better educate individuals about the importance of proper waste recycling.

The university has made several advancements to promote a culture of food waste diversion. During the school year, the dining facilities serve approximately 5,400 meals per month in the main dining hall and about 4,000 meals per month in the cafe, which includes breakfast, lunch, and dinner. In the dining hall, the university has retired the use of tray service and transitioned to smaller-sized plates. While students and staff are allowed to come back for more food as many times as they like, the implementation of this policy has resulted in a decrease in food waste. Additionally, Dining Services has implemented an ongoing educational program to inform university students and employees about food waste reduction.

Two recently added developments in the dining hall are a micro-garden and a SodaStream. The micro-garden is conveniently located behind the check-in register as one enters the dining hall, so students and staff are exposed to it. Dining Services have stated that there have been a lot of questions about the micro-garden, and insight from a staff member is as follows:

> ...Right now, as of yesterday, we had our first harvest (mid-April, 2023). We did butter leaf lettuce, and then a romaine, red leaf, green leaf, and leaf blend.... we used them (lettuce) for the salad bar yesterday. Today we had enough that we were able to carry it over. We are currently growing basil and cilantro. I will turn those into pesto which freezes well. If we don't use it all right away, we'll be able to use it over the next six months...and then it takes about a month to get something from seed to harvest so we'll have another two days' worth of lettuce in about a month...the seeds are growing, they're ready to transplant early next week. And then it's about three weeks until we can harvest...we save water, we save petrochemicals, and fuel just because we are not transporting it (produce). So, it's not a huge impact on the grand scheme, but it's a huge impact on a small local idea and it's not something that we get a ton of out of, but we do save a lot of water and a lot of waste... (dining administration employee)

As for running the micro-garden and insights on the SodaStream, the staff member went on to state the following:

> It (the micro-garden) is all LED lighting. The camera probably cost more than anything else with everything being monitored in Richmond (Virginia). So...all the pH balancer and the plant food are metered out by a computer from Richmond (Virginia). We pay about $300 a month in programming and seeds and then with probably only electric it may cost us about $45 a month...and then we also brought in the SodaStream unit for water and for flavored water. We saved so far this year since December (2022) 7,500 plastic bottles just by using that in our location instead

of giving plastic bottles away for them (students and employees) to drink... (dining administration employee)

While the micro-garden and SodaStream are small steps in the direction of a more sustainable university, they both may contribute to raising the awareness and education of students and employees of the importance of lowering their impact on the environment.

A goal for the dining services is to invest in a food composter. The reason is that food waste ends up in landfills and contributes to global warming. By diverting food waste to a composter, the result is rich soil that can eventually be used around campus and possibly provided to the community. The current challenge is that the local town was collecting food waste for composting but recently stopped. This change in policy has left our university without an outlet for our food waste. Simultaneously, in the following employee statement, the dining services has moved to compostable products that have a premium cost for plant-based compostable silverware and packaging.

> ...So, besides getting the food composting done, we want to be able to start composting all the compostable products that we are using for disposables, and most of that is at the cafe. We do have some that goes in the dining hall, but right now not everything in the cafe is compostable. And a large part of that is cost. And the other part is that we don't have any place to put it (food waste). So, there is a gap. We're using the more expensive container that is compostable, but we have nobody who will compost it for us. So, it's kind of a double-edged sword, we want to get away from plastics, and get into the plant-based plastics, but there's no benefit of the plant-based plastics, if we can't get somebody who will process that for us... The plant-based stuff ranges from about 8% to 14% more. On average, the forks are significantly more than the plastic silverware than the other. That's the highest percentage, and then cups we do it (purchase compostable cups) anyway because they're about the same (price)... (dining administration employee)

Reaching the goal of obtaining a composter would solve the gap with the food waste and could potentially justify the added cost of purchasing compostable plant-based silverware. The dining service staff is currently in the process of investigating the purchase and planning of a food composter.

UNIVERSITY GOAL 2: POLLINATOR PROTECTION PLAN

A recent policy shift is to plant and protect native species and maintain pollinator-friendly habitats. Prior to this development under the leadership of the Sisters of Mercy nuns, the policy was to keep the campus in the model of a traditional English garden. The campus does have several non-native trees that were planted either during the former railroad baron era or during the

Sisters of Mercy era. The current leadership has directed to let, for example, some areas remain wild and not trim the grass. Additionally, there has been a shift to use natural pine mulch provided by the native species on the university grounds for the mulching of gardens. This change in policy for the maintenance of the university's grounds is reflected in the following statement:

> It's nice to not have that obsession that everything has to be the perfect harbored manicured lawn appearance. Like we can mulch with pine needles, and no one says anything. I'm not sure that would be the case under another president. So, I guess you could maybe work that into your chapter that people aren't opposed to things that in other campuses might not meet people's standards of what (a) college campus should look like. And so, part of what we have to do culturally is change people's expectations about what they should be seeing and their landscape and that it's not healthy to have everything manicured and cleaned up. And completely green and the mulch neatly arranged and all black (the mulch) and everything has to be pruned into an unnatural shape and all the gardens have to be carefully manicured in the old European dominate nature style. And that hasn't been the case here recently. That under (the current leadership) they are not focused on that (trimming and maintaining a European style university grounds). Whereas (the previous leadership under the nuns) would drive by something and say that looks messy. Get out there and clean it up. I don't want to see it look like that anymore. And it was like, you must do something about it (tidy and trim up the university grounds). So, that's one way that I feel good about sustainability because we're not that kind of campus at this moment where everything must look the old way. (administration employee)

Other recent university policies include banning the use of neonicotinoid-based pesticides and pre-treated plants on campus grounds. Alongside this policy, there will be an emphasis on the importance of pollinators in the classroom through campus outreach. A future goal is to examine the possibility of establishing a beekeeping colony in partnership with the New Jersey Beekeepers Association.

UNIVERSITY GOAL 3: RESTORE AND EXPAND THE MERCY GARDEN

The Mercy Garden has a long history on the campus and is centrally located. The objective of the Mercy Garden is to grow produce for the dining services and the food pantry. The university maintains a food pantry on campus for students who may have financial issues obtaining food. The challenges faced by the Mercy Garden include deer and other wildlife eating the plants, and varying levels of student support for its upkeep depending on interest. To address the issue of wildlife, a taller fence has been installed to keep deer and other animals out. In terms of student support, some faculty members contribute to the garden's upkeep. However, there has been a challenge in maintaining student interest over time. While there were clubs in the past that actively participated in maintaining the garden, the impact of COVID has resulted in a need for revitalization. Currently, faculty members are reaching out to students and student groups to encourage a more active role in maintaining the Mercy Garden.

Future goals for the Mercy Garden include expanding its footprint and creating educational opportunities for students and employees. One way to align the goal of obtaining a waste food composter with the Mercy Garden is to establish a community outreach program. This program would provide educational opportunities for gardening, resulting in additional produce for the community and rich soil from the food composter. Furthermore, as the Mercy Garden expands, there is a future goal to investigate the installation of rain barrels. The challenges for achieving this overall goal of restoring and expanding the Mercy Garden include time constraints, the need for staff coordination, and maintaining student interest.

UNIVERSITY GOAL 4: ENCOURAGE CULTURE OF DECISION-MAKING BASED ON SUSTAINABILITY, RESILIENCE, AND EMPOWERMENT

The overall objective of this goal is to promote socio-economic and environmental sustainability by making decisions that have a positive impact on the environment, students, employees, the community and beyond. The development of the university's organizational culture for sustainability will be encouraged and introduced using the principles from Pope Francis' *Laudato Si'* during the New Employee Orientation. All new faculty and staff members will not only be introduced to the Mercy Core Values but also to how the Pope's call for sustainability relates to these values and the mission of GCU. In the recruitment of prospective employees, the concept of sustainability will be integrated into the expectations of all GCU community members. Similarly, the Mercy Core Values and sustainability are embedded in the new student orientation, and faculty are encouraged to reinforce these values in the classroom. A recommendation from the Laudato Si' committee to management is to integrate the university's *Laudato Si'* sustainability commitments into yearly performance evaluations of employees.

Decision-making by employees that encourages these values will be used in sustainable investment, purchasing, and management. From a socio-economic focus, a living wage will be benchmarked based on the local economic indicators. One recent development resulting from COVID is the encouragement of remote work options. The university has recently introduced a modified work schedule that allows for flexibility in when staff perform their duties. For example, an employee can now work four, ten-hour days with an extra day off or have the flexibility to work from home on specific days. Additionally, most meetings now have remote access capabilities, which saves on travel time and parking.

In the future, a couple of areas have been identified for improvement from a sustainability perspective. One area is the waste generated when students leave the dormitories in the spring. Extra clothing and discarded student furnishings will be relocated to the expanded pantry for future reuse. Another area being studied is the possibility of providing child daycare for students on campus.

UNIVERSITY GOAL 5: ENERGY CONSERVATION MEASURES

The goals for energy conservation are quite detailed and have been derived from the 2021 Investment Grade Audit, which resulted in the Capital Master Plan Sustainability Report. At a high level, the plan includes a $6.2 million investment that will be funded through a $1.2 million annual cost reduction. Some of the key highlights from the plan include the following: examination of all building envelopes to improve HVAC efficiency, installation of modern and efficient HVAC units, upgrading of heating systems, improvement of HVAC controls for building integration management systems, replacement of lighting fixtures with sensors, installation of high efficient plumbing fixtures, implementation of additional solar photovoltaic systems, including a carport canopy solar PV system at two locations. These initiatives build upon prior investments in solar energy, such as the solar PV system located adjacent to the soccer/lacrosse fields. Furthermore, other areas being explored include the future installation of electric vehicle (EV) charging stations for employees and students, as well as the eventual transition of the campus fleet of vehicles to electric vehicles.

During the COVID-19 pandemic, when the university transitioned to virtual and online learning, several improvements were also made to the campus. For example, water fountains were replaced with more modern water bottle filling stations, significantly reducing the use of plastic bottles. Additionally, new large touch screen monitors were installed to enhance instruction. Overall, the university had the opportunity to paint, repair, and complete many tasks from the deferred maintenance list during the COVID period.

UNIVERSITY GOAL 6: ACADEMICS

On the academic side, GCU has numerous goals and opportunities. All GCU students are required to take a course called GEN 199: The Self in the Big Universe, usually in their first year. This course has multiple sections and instructors. The proposal is to provide flexibility to instructors regarding content, while incorporating a standardized assignment that examines the interconnectedness of all life systems. This sustainability focus will consider both environmental and social-economic factors that connect life systems. Additionally, there has been a recent development in the form of a Sustainability minor. Although minors are currently optional at GCU, the Sustainability minor has not met the anticipated levels of student interest. Consequently, the Sustainability minor is currently being reevaluated and updated by faculty. The Sustainability minor is housed in the School of Arts and Sciences, and a recommendation has been made to open the minor to students from all schools. Furthermore, the School of Business and Digital Media will require all incoming first-year students who declare a Business Administration degree to have a minor for the 2023–2024 academic year. In line with this, the School of Business and Digital Media has recently introduced an undergraduate course on corporate sustainability, which will be part of the Sustainability minor. These changes are aimed at attracting more students to the Sustainability minor.

Other developments are on the horizon at GCU that have emerged from the Laudato Si' committee. One of these is the introduction of new spring break trips that will focus on environmental service, environmental justice, and environmental racism. The goal of these trips is to raise awareness and promote solidarity to vulnerable groups. Additionally, there are plans to provide *Laudato Si'* service-learning opportunities, with a focus on training in leadership in climate and sustainability through the Mulcahy Institute for Social Justice, an on-campus resource.

UNIVERSITY GOAL 7: ECOLOGICAL SPIRITUALITY

The final goal identified by the Laudato Si' committee examines the importance of spirituality from the lens of an ecological perspective. Ecological conversion recaptures that lens, emphasizing the interconnectedness between self, community, and the environment. Through ecological conversion, the university offers a holistic vision that we strive to live by and teach at GCU. Several future goals have been identified by the Laudato Si' committee. The first goal is the development of retreat opportunities for GCU employees and staff. This development would be led by the Mission Integration department, with the establishment of a *Laudato Si'* Day established on 4 October. The day will consist of a celebration with various service opportunities and a liturgy of thanksgiving. Other goals include continuing the creation of paths, as well the installation of benches made from recycled products for sitting and quiet meditation.

DISCUSSION

For the year 2015, three important documents on sustainability were put forth by international agencies and the Catholic church. These documents are: the *United Nations Sustainability Development Goals*, the *Paris Agreement* and Pope Francis' Encyclical letter *Laudato Si'*. All three of these documents address the impact mankind is having on the natural world from economic, social, and environmental perspectives. They also express common societal values and ideas. While the acceptance and response to these values and ideas by different groups will continue to be debated, these documents call for action from individuals, institutions, and governments. This chapter focuses on the individuals that make up the institution of GCU and their specific response to the Pope's *Laudato Si'* letter.

Overall, I believe that the students, faculty, and staff at GCU are making significant efforts to address sustainability issues. However, there is still more work to be done. In comparison to other Catholic institutions, we may not be leading the pack, but I believe we are ahead of many others. For example, according to Homan (2016) he describes the sustainability development of 28 Jesuit colleges and universities in the US to the Pope's challenge. Based on Homan's (2016) review, we are on par with many of the schools mentioned, although we may be a few years behind in certain areas. One area where we have made important advances towards sustainability is eco-friendly landscaping. We have made progress by transitioning to native species, using natural pine mulch, and shifting our overall philosophy towards a more natural state. We are also making progress in some areas such as comprehensive recycling and composting. For example, the dining services staff are currently exploring options to obtain a composting machine. However, one area where we seem to be lagging is the development of a carbon audit for the university. Conducting a carbon audit would enable us to identify long-term goals and areas for improvement. Many organizations have set goals to become carbon neutral or even carbon negative, but GCU has not made advanced progress in this area.

The efforts towards sustainability of the individuals at GCU are commendable, resulting in a unique, beautiful, and more natural university. The results of our Laudato Si' committee allowed us to reflect and establish a seven-year plan with seven broad university goals. However, some individuals I interviewed expressed concern about maintaining momentum towards a more sustainable campus and community. One of the main reasons for this is the current deficit spending and decreased enrollment and retention issues since the start of COVID. As mentioned earlier, sustainability solutions need to be revenue positive or revenue neutral in the future. The current financial situation at the university may affect the ability to take bold, long-term sustainability measures. Another reason that relates to cost reduction under the present financial condition is the elimination of the Sustainability Director position during COVID due to budget cuts. This part-time position allowed a faculty member to have a three-credit course release to focus on grant writing and interact with students, faculty, and staff on sustainability-related issues. The elimination of this position was seen by many as a step backwards and a loss of momentum towards a more sustainable campus. On a positive note, enrollment is up for the fall 2023 semester, which may provide an opportunity to reconsider the decision to cut the Sustainability Director position in the future.

As for courses and student interest in sustainability, there appears to be a growing interest in the topic. However, engaging commuter students in after class activities, such as groups and committees, poses a challenge. Commuter students have other non-university commitments, such as work, caring for family members and other issues. Many courses incorporate the Mercy Core Values of respect, integrity, justice, compassion, and service, along with sustainability into the classroom. All GCU graduates are required to take four Common Intellectual Experience classes. These classes cover religion, ethics, women and gender, and a capstone course in the student's senior year called GEN 400: Visioning a Future. The course description for GEN 400 from the online GCU catalog is provided below to give insight into the course:

GEN 400: Visioning a Future
In line with GCU Mercy core values, this writing intensive capstone course invites students to reflect and analyze how the General Education Program has impacted their understanding of themselves in the world, as well as how their worldview has developed. Through course readings, service learning, and guest speakers, students are encouraged to consider key questions of our time. Students contribute to envisioning the future and recognizing humankind's responsibility in shaping that future. This process involves addressing questions that have emerged from the General Education Program, such as: How can we contribute to a more compassionate and just world for humankind and the Earth itself? How can we cultivate thought about fair, healthy, and sustainable ways of living and working on this planet. (Georgian Court University, 2023)

In this capstone class, all students reflect on environmental and socio-economic aspects of sustainability through the lens of the Mercy Core Values.

Regarding the future of GCU, the university developed a Strategic Compass Plan with input from students, faculty, and staff prior to COVID. One major idea that emerged from the Plan was the construction a new building for the School of Nursing. Members of the university are pressing the administration to construct a Leadership in Energy and Environmental Design (LEED) certified building. The most recent significant construction project on campus was the Wellness Center, which houses the Athletic Department and holds LEED Gold Certification. While the administration is open to constructing a LEED certified School of Nursing building, the controversy lies in the funding. To finance the School of Nursing building and other campus improvements, the university recently agreed to sell part of a wooded section land on campus. The land is currently under contract with a local Jewish University, with plans to build apartments for housing. While some students, faculty, and staff view the land sale as necessary progress for the university, others are upset with the decision made by university leadership to sell the land. As of the fall 2023 semester, the current state of the construction of the nursing building is due to start in the spring of 2024.

This leads to my role at the university, which I perceive as a catalyst for change towards a more sustainable university. Through my role as an educator, researcher, and university employee, I focus on sustainability issues. As an educator, I primarily teach strategy and leadership courses. In addition to important theories and concepts, I incorporate a sustainability focus into all my classes. For instance, in the capstone business strategy course for undergraduate business students, I have added a climate change exercise to the sustainability module. Similarly, in my leadership courses, we explore sustainability topics including the response of major corporations to the Paris Accord on climate change. Looking ahead, the MBA program is being revised to allow for electives. Over the summer of 2023, I began development of a new course on corporate sustainability at the MBA level, which will be offered in 2024. I am very interested to see the student's response and enrollment for this upcoming corporate sustainability course, which will be taught using a case-based method. As for my research, I primarily focus on the areas of organizational culture and corporate sustainability. In my service to the university, I apply for committee positions that have a sustainability focus. For example, I have served on the Laudato Si' committee and I am currently on the Sustainability committee. In all three areas of teaching, research, and service; I find my contributions towards sustainability rewarding.

LIMITATIONS

There are a few limitations to this book chapter. While university faculty and staff were interviewed for this project, I did not have the opportunity to identify and interview students due to time constraints. It would have been interesting to gain insight into the views of *Laudato Si'* and sustainability from a student's perspective. Additionally, I did not have the opportunity to explore the investment of the endowment. I would be interested to understand how the endowment is invested and whether sustainability or any environmental, social and governance (ESG) factors are considered in investing for the university's future. Finally, there were limited published articles on the response to *Laudato Si'* and universities action plans to benchmark to our small regional university. Hopefully this chapter sheds additional light on the Pope's call for greater sustainability at universities and colleges.

CONCLUSION

The efforts of faculty, staff, and students moving towards a more sustainable university and world are commendable; however, there is still much work to be done. Achieving a more sustainable university and world requires systematic change, which is always challenging. The guidance of Pope Francis' *Laudato Si'* framework has provided the university with a clear focus on sustainability and has allowed employees to set ambitious goals. Despite the financial deficit at GCU, and with the Pope's focus, the administration's commitment, and the passion of several employees for sustainability will hopefully position the university as a leader in reaching our sustainability goals. It is important to remember that sustainability is an ongoing journey and does not have a final destination. In closing, I would like to reiterate the Pope's message of hope in *Laudato Si'* and emphasize the importance of recognizing interconnectedness of all people and species. It is through this recognition that individuals and organizations can take bold steps towards finding solutions to pressing social, environmental, and economic challenges worldwide.

NOTE

1.   I would like to express my gratitude to the members of GCU's Laudato Si' Committee for their insightful discussions and the final report that was used to prepare this chapter.

REFERENCES

DaPonte, P. (2022). *Laudato Si'Action Plan.* Georgian Court University.
Francis. (2015). *Laudato Si': On care for our common home.* Libreria Editrice Vaticana.
Georgian Court University. (2023). *Undergraduate catalog 2022–2023.* Available at: https://catalog.georgian.edu/undergraduate/academic-programs/bridge-general-education-program-categories-courses/ (Accessed May 3, 2023).
Homan, K.S.J. (2016). An opportunity for conversion: American Jesuits and the response to *Laudato Si'. Journal of Jesuit Studies, 3,* 645–663.
Howard-Grenville, J., Bertels, S., & Lahneman, B. (2014). Sustainability: How it shapes organizational culture and climate. In B. Schneider & K.M. Barber (Eds.), *The Oxford handbook of organizational climate and culture* (pp. 257–274). Oxford University Press.
Rubin, H.J. & Rubin, I.S. (2012). *Qualitative interviewing: The art of hearing data.* Sage.

APPENDIX

Questions for participants –The following are the general questions asked to all participants that were interviewed. Depending on insight from the participant, clarifying questions were also asked, but are not presented here.

1. Casting a wide net…why do you identify with sustainability?
2. Sustainability is a very broad umbrella. What are the areas that you focus on?
3. How did you get involved with either sustainability or the actions of the Laudato Si' committee?
4. Can you identify any successes with sustainability at Georgian Court University?
5. Can you identify any non-successes with sustainability at Georgian Court University?
6. Can you identify with any opportunities for sustainability action for Georgian Court University?
7. Can you identify with any challenges for sustainability action for Georgian Court University?
8. Have you seen any sustainable stakeholder collaboration in the past or future here at Georgian Court University?
9. How do you feel about the results of the sustainability programs here at Georgian Court University?
10. What are the lessons learned for sustainability and Georgian Court University?
11. Anything that you might want to add concerning sustainability that we did not discuss?

7. A student-driven approach to establishing sustainability programs at colleges and universities: lessons from the Green Office Movement in Europe

Jean Wu

Universities shape the students who attend them. In a reversal of roles, at numerous universities in Europe, students have become the architects shaping the universities they attend. In response to climate change and the challenges of sustainable development, student activists and leaders have successfully advocated for the establishment of sustainability programs and curriculum across Europe. As of August 2023, over 45 sustainability programs called "Green Offices" have been created as the result of student action, relying on the support of a network called the Green Office Movement. Green Offices are not clubs or volunteer programs, but rather, they are offices funded and approved by university management and jointly led by students and staff.

Although there are a handful of Green Offices outside of Europe, the movement is largely geographically limited to a few countries at the moment, primarily the Netherlands, Germany and Belgium. At its core, using the Green Office Model, the Green Office Movement provides training and support to empower students to embed sustainability into their university's programs, campus and curriculum. The resources include a freely available online course on how to design, pitch and lobby for a Green Office, as well as how to identify funding sources and how to convince university management to support the establishment of a sustainability program. Ongoing support from the Green Office Movement includes tools for assessing impact, a resources hub for running a Green Office, regularly held coordinator calls, open-source project plans, conference summits, newsletters and a membership platform that connects various Green Offices within the network.

This chapter explores the history of the Green Office Movement, analyzes the mechanics of the Green Office Model, examines a case study of a recently established Green Office and argues that student-led sustainability programs better prepare students for careers in sustainability fields than curriculum alone, by providing practical skills for tackling sustainability issues, by encouraging innovations to address real-world challenges, and by cultivating an attitude of change-making and leadership. This chapter advocates for the increased adoption of the Green Office Model outside of Europe, to expand the network of student-led sustainability programs globally, in order to drive transformative change at universities that have not yet established sustainability programs.

1. BACKGROUND OF THE GREEN OFFICE MOVEMENT

In 2010, a group of students at Maastricht University in the Netherlands established the first Green Office as a student-run sustainability office. According to Maartje Zaal, former Green Office Movement Coordinator:

> In the face of a climate crisis, students wanted to do something, to have an impact. In their institutions, which weren't sustainable themselves, they learned about the impact of keeping the status quo, as well as the many benefits of transitioning towards a sustainable society. They wanted to put that knowledge in practice and started the Green Office Maastricht. This was the start of our movement. (M. Zaal, email, March 22, 2023)

Two years later, in 2012, the founders of the Maastricht University Green Office started rootAbility, a social enterprise aimed at spreading their Green Office model across Europe (Lehnhof & Nolan, 2016). In the following years, the movement grew rapidly in number and in range of countries. By 2016, there were 23 established Green Offices in six European cities.

The Green Office Movement has continued to grow expansively. As of August 2023, there were more than 100 Green Office members and initiatives, with more than 2,150 students and staff working on 825 projects ((n.d.). Join the Movement. Green Office Movement. Retrieved August 1, 2023, from https://www.greenofficemovement.org/). The students staffing the Green Offices include both undergraduate and graduate students. The expansion of the Green Office Movement reflects the vision of the Green Office, which is to "inspire Green Offices to identify how they can become more impactful [and to] encourage collaboration among Green Offices to learn from each other" (https://www.greenofficemovement.org/vision/. Retrieved August 1, 2023).

The Green Office Model differs from other approaches to sustainability programing, as it allows students to actively contribute to their university's sustainability efforts. In order to register as a member of the Green Office Movement, students need to ensure that six principles are met. One, a Green Office must be comprised of a mix of university students and staff. Two, the university of the Green Office must issue an official mandate to drive sustainability issues at their university. Three, the Green Office must be funded by their university. Four, the Green Office must be part of its university's organizational structure. Five, the Green Office must collaborate with internal and external stakeholders such as student groups, facility services, research institutes, city administration and local civil associations. Six, Green Office members should be trained by rootAbility (https://unesdoc.unesco.org/ark:/48223/pf0000245763).

Student groups are able to join the Green Office Movement as either an established Green Office or a Green Office initiative. Green Office initiatives typically include situations where students are trying to establish a Green Office but have not yet fully met the six principles set out by rootAbility. The Green Office Movement advises that groups wishing to register as an initiative have a committed core team before joining the movement.

Registering as a member of the Green Office Movement requires the payment of a registration fee, which is characterized as a "solidarity-based contribution" (https://www.greenofficemovement.org/join/. Retrieved August 1, 2023). The suggested contribution levels range from €850 to no-cost memberships where a Green Office does not have an annual budget or only a very limited budget. The registration fees go towards paying the administrative costs of supporting, training and expanding the Green Office Movement network.

In 2019, rootAbility was integrated as an organization into Students Organizing for Sustainability International (SOS International), an international organization based in Denmark (prezi.com/view/F SiKQimbAdZ uuSBxerf7/. Retrieved August 1, 2023). As an organization, SOS International supports students and youth groups that are working on sustainability and social justice programs and it is a formal educational partner of the United Nations Environment Programme (https://www.unep.org/explore-topics/education-environment/why-does-education-and-environment-matter/formal-education). The Green Office is one of 21 member organizations under the umbrella of SOS International (https://sos.earth/). Within SOS International, there is a dedicated staff member supporting the Green Office Movement. Other than the change in umbrella organization, there was not a significant change from the model developed by rootAbility (https://www.greenofficemovement.org/sos/).

2.   EXAMINING THE GREEN OFFICE MODEL

The Green Office Model is designed to be scalable and replicable, by educating university students on how to set up a Green Office in a way that is institutionalized and permanent. The model applies to both large universities and smaller colleges. In addition, the Green Office Model aims to strengthen collaboration between universities and provides inspiration for the types of progress a college sustainability office might accomplish and how it might accomplish its goals (Adomßent, Grahl & Spira, 2019).

The open-source online course available through the Green Office Movement's website consists of four interactive modules, which teach students: (1) how to map existing sustainability efforts, (2) design their Green Office, (3) pitch their ideas, and (4) lobby for funding. The course is designed to give clarity on the steps to take and the common mistakes to avoid in establishing a Green Office. There is also an online course module for established Green Offices to learn how to manage their team, gain visibility and run projects (www .greenofficemovement .org/ #course). In addition, the Green Office Movement has developed a guide and toolkit that can be used independently or with the online course. These documents are available in several languages, including English, German, French and Ukrainian (https:// www .greenofficemovement.org/sustainability-resources/#model).

Each Green Office determines the resources required for its operations based on their individual needs and project plans, whether that is financial support or institutional support. The modules, case studies and network access provided by the Green Office Movement provide guidance on how to identify what resources each Green Office might need, in order for them to formulate their funding requests.

For established Green Offices, the Green Office Movement continues to offer support. It leads workshops to address common problems, such as when projects lose impact or progress gets lost when teams change each academic year (https://www.greenofficemovement.org/workshops/). The workshops are offered at additional costs and are meant to save time and money by providing guidance on how to master the complex challenges typically faced by established Green Offices.

The Green Office Movement also provides established Green Offices with project and event ideas, creating roadmaps and case students (https:// www .greenofficemovement .org/ sustainability -resources/). One criticism of the Green Office Movement may be that the Green Office Model focuses primarily on environmental sustainability. The project ideas developed by the Green Office Movement typically center on making university campuses more green, such as through recycling, reducing consumption, or circular economy efforts. In order for sustainable development to be more inclusive, it is crucial that socioeconomic sustainability also be addressed (Hariram, Mekha, Suganthan & Sudhakar, 2023). By incorporating socioeconomic sustainability, future efforts to expand the Green Office Model to other universities would be able to progress further at implementing the United Nations Sustainable Development Goals than focusing on environmental sustainability alone (Stafford-Smith, Griggs, Gaffney et al., 2017).

Students who have worked in a Green Office continue to benefit from the support of the Green Office Movement, as members of the Green Office Alumni Network. The alumni network shares information via quarterly newsletters and alumni gatherings in person and online. In addition, the alumni network also shares professional information via its LinkedIn group, such as job postings and information on employers. For alumni who would like to dedicate even more time to growing the Green Office Movement, there is a GO Movement Ambassador Programme that consists of a four-month-long ambassador track to give participants an opportunity to further build their experience in sustainability leadership. Examples of sustainability career positions that former Green Office students have pursued include sustainability communications, working in sustainability for the public sector, pursuing environmental law careers and becoming sustainability educators.

3.   WHY STUDENT-LED SUSTAINABILITY PROGRAMS BETTER PREPARE STUDENTS FOR CAREERS IN SUSTAINABILITY FIELDS THAN CURRICULUM ALONE

It is recognized that universities and colleges are uniquely placed to play a leading role in the attainment of sustainable development (Tilbury, 2011). Through curriculum and research, sustainability education provides crucially important training for students planning on future careers in sustainability (Jarchow, Formisano, Nordyke & Sayre, 2018). Many universities go beyond the classroom, though, to offer co-curricular or extracurricular programs that provide practical experience and training (Deiaco et al., 2012).

The development of institutionalized sustainability programs is far from universal though. Although many universities have increased their efforts towards sustainable development to reduce their own environmental impacts (Filho, Shiel, do Paço & Brandli, 2015), other universities have yet to develop their own sustainability programs. For those universities without firmly established sustainability programs, there is an opportunity for students to play an active role in advocating and architecting sustainability programs. However, "[s]tudents are oftentimes overlooked and side-lined within a university's sustainability efforts. This is a missed opportunity, given the energy and spirit of students, the learning opportunities that sustainability engagement presents and the sheer size of the student body as largest stakeholder group on campus" (Filho et al., 2015).

In some cases, in order for students to unleash their full potential as sustainability change agents, they require additional support and resources. Although there is a will to effect change, students might lack the tools or knowledge to achieve their goals. By providing practical skills for tackling sustainability issues, by encouraging innovations to address real-world challenges, and by cultivating an attitude of change-making and leadership, the Green Office Movement addresses the gap that might exists between the desire of students to establish sustainability programs at their universities and their ability to actually implement such programs. As Miriam Tereick of UNESCO observed: "Green Offices are an excellent way to integrate education for sustainable development into universities, affecting teaching and learning, the physical campus and student life" (www.greenofficemovement.org).

Once a Green Office is established at a university, it provides the wider student body with opportunities to be involved in sustainability efforts. Experience has shown that it is not only the founders and student employees of a Green Office that benefit from the program, but also the various volunteers who work with the Green Office:

> Students that were involved with the Green Office volunteered because they wanted to make an impact, have social interactions, and have learning and career opportunities. Feeling part of the Green Office gave a feeling of legitimacy and increased their belief in their power to make a change. Also, a safe space for trial and error increased their self-efficacy and made them take on bigger projects. Different student groups had different needs and therefore required different engagement strategies from the Green Office. (Lootens, 2017)

In many ways, the work of establishing a Green Office offers a form of experiential education ("learning by doing with reflection") for students (Ritchie, 2013). In working towards designing a sustainability hub for their universities, students are gaining real-world skills in organization building and administration. Rather than remaining passive actors waiting for a university-led sustainability program to develop, students who establish a Green Office play an active role in transforming their educational institution and become social actors that spark change from below (Drupp et al., 2012).

Furthermore, the process outlined by the Green Office Model requires that students work with the leadership and governance structure of their universities, in order to advocate for funding and institutional support. One of the key elements of the Green Office Model is that the sustainability hub created by the students be a permanent, integrated, staffed and university-funded entity and not merely a student club. The experience of participating in higher educational governance in order to help establish a Green Office promotes civic learning, which in turn prepares students for life as active and responsible citizens (Klemenčič, 2011).

Moreover, the work that goes into structuring and staffing a Green Office can potentially be seen as a form of service learning for students (Weigert, 1998; Eyler, 2000). Getting a university to increase its efforts in sustainability requires significant time and effort, in service of meeting the meaningful goal of institutional transformation. The learning component of employing the Green Office Model can be folded into the "course" objectives underpinning the six principles necessary for membership in the Green Office Movement. Reflection and assessment are built into the ongoing work of the Green Office established, especially when paired with the resources developed by the Green Office Movement on assessing impact (https:// www .greenofficemovement .org/ how -to -measure -your -green -or -sustainability -offices -impact -3 -proven -impact-measurement-methods-explained/).

Even when not seen as fully fledged service learning, the experience of establishing a Green Office impacts students profoundly and can form the basis for a "significant learning experience" resulting in "something that is truly significant in terms of the students' lives" (Fink, 2013). As such, the benefits of a student-led effort to develop a more sustainable university are manifold: their experience is the basis for a meaningful experience during their university years and it equips them with skills and knowledge required for working in sustainable development, all while helping to accelerate a transition towards a more sustainable university (Higgins, Nicol, Somervell & Bownes, 2013).

Even though research has shown that Green Offices are an effective tool in supporting the implementation of sustainability initiatives on campuses (Spira & Baker-Friesen, 2015), in addition to fostering awareness among students and staff on sustainability matters, the use of Green Offices is not as wide as it could be despite their usefulness and proven effectiveness (Filho et al., 2019). The geographical reach of the Green Office Movement has been slow to extend beyond Europe (https://www.google.com/maps/d/u/0/embed ?mid=1gdfVdF_yPkgIr0v0YwBxbkgKD-M & ll=18.510564484299078 , -13 .546818177746346&z=3).

Especially for universities located in the Global South, the resources offered by the Green Office Model may be especially impactful. The Green Office Movement currently has one office in each of the following locations: South America (Green Office Universidade de Passo Fundo in Brazil), Africa (Makerere University Students Sustainability Action Group in Uganda), Central America (University for Peace Green Office in Costa Rica) and Oceania (Otago Polytechnic Auckland Green Office Toitū in New Zealand). There are currently no members of the Green Offices Movement located in North America or Asia.

4.   CASE STUDY – FRANKLIN UNIVERSITY SWITZERLAND

The following case study exemplifies the ways in which the Green Office Movement has supported the establishment of a Green Office, and the impact that the newly established Green Office has had on its campus.

Franklin University Switzerland ("Franklin") was founded in 1969. Although Franklin is physically located in Europe, it offers an American liberal arts education and is the only higher education institution in the world fully accredited in both the US and Switzerland. The Franklin mission is:

> to provide a cross-cultural and multinational learning and living environment that inspires students to engage the world. We challenge students through a curriculum that integrates the liberal arts with professional pathways, and classroom learning with Academic Travel to destinations around the world. A Franklin education produces critical thinkers who are culturally literate, ethically aware and intellectually courageous. We prepare students to become responsible, compassionate, and collaborative leaders in an increasingly complex and interconnected world.

The Franklin Green Office began as the result of a senior Environmental Studies capstone project in the Spring of 2021. Student founders utilized the resources made available by the Green Office Movement and, over the course of two years, worked to establish what would eventually become the first Green Office at an American and a Swiss university.

As part of the students' efforts, they created a checklist of necessary steps to implementing a Green Office. The three most important requirements were: (1) the signing of a mandate between the university and the newly formed Green Office, (2) establishing a budget for the Green Office, and (3) the confirmation of office space and staffing positions. The checklist served to outline the requirements for admission as a member to the Green Office Movement, but more importantly, laid a foundation for the establishment of a campus sustainability hub.

Part of the support from the Green Office Movement was the guidance in formulating a mandate. As part of the mandate, Franklin formally recognized the Green Office as an official student-run university office, with the ability to recommend and ensure policy compliance throughout the university. It was an official acknowledgment that the university supports the mission and vision of the Franklin Green Office and a formal commitment to actively working towards helping the Green Office achieve its goals.

The mandate tasked the Franklin Green Office with, among other things, the following responsibilities:

- Provide a framework to promote, develop, and organize sustainability-related initiatives.
- Serve as a contact point for internal and external parties.
- Provide real-world experience for students, including training, internships and leadership opportunities.
- Work to reduce Franklin's social and ecological impacts.
- Ensure that Franklin meets the criteria for membership to the Green Office Movement.
- Serve as a competency center for sustainability.
- Research and apply for grant funding at the Swiss institutional and business level.

Faculty members acknowledged that the newly established Green Office dovetailed nicely with Franklin's mission "in that it actively engages and empowers students to be agents of change in order to enhance the practice of sustainability in what we do and learn" (https://www.fus.edu/news-events/news/introducing-franklin-green-office). Given its broad mandate, the Green Office developed five areas in which to focus and award Green Office Scholar positions, each heading a branch of work that included: event coordination; external affairs and projects; research and education; marketing and communications; and campus operations.

Over the course of its first year, the Franklin Green Office made significant advancements in each of its branches of work. Event coordination held multiple item and clothing swaps, as well as field trips and neighborhood clean-up days. An Earth Day Summit was organized that included over 30 speakers from academia, NGOs, the business world and local government and focused on transdisciplinary approaches to sustainability. The Green Office became a member of the Association for the Advancement of Sustainability in Higher Education (AASHE), a program partner of the UN's Higher Education Sustainability Initiative and a part of the Right Here, Right Now Education Coalition.

In terms of campus operations, the Green Office worked to make the campus more environmentally sustainable, working with food services to implement plant-based menu options, finding ways to encourage energy conservation in university buildings and starting a compost program within the university's residence halls to support the campus sustainable gardens. The Green Office ran an energy conservation competition and shared energy saving tips with the university community.

One of the most impactful and emblematic programs initiated by the Green Office was a stakeholder carbon market created to offset the carbon emissions generated by the university's Academic Travel Program. As a marque component of the Franklin education, Academic Travel is integral to the student learning experience at Franklin. It is also one of the most significant sources of scope 3 emissions and finding ways to address the impact of Academic Travel involved educating students and faculty about the impact of the travel program. The greenhouse gas emissions were calculated for the entire program, faculty leaders were provided with resources on how to travel more sustainably and carbon credits were offered to support on projects that would reduce or eliminate existing sources of on-campus greenhouse gas emissions.

The success of the Franklin Green Office was the result of many factors, including the institutional support that enabled and empowered the students to take such an active role in building the office. In order to fund the office, Franklin's annual University Day, which includes a fundraising campaign, was dedicated to the Green Office in April 2022, with the goal of raising $50,000 to go towards establishing the Green Office. The accomplishment of the University Day was made possible by the school's advancement department, as well as generous supporters and alumni. A founding director of the Green Office sustainability programs was recruited and outreach to staff, faculty, administration, leadership and students consisted of presentations, articles, office hours and social media.

The Franklin Green Office continued to refer to the resources made available by the Green Office Movement even after developing many of its own programs. The experience of the Franklin Green Office supported the premise that campus sustainability projects contribute to helping students build real-life competencies, while at the same time providing a service to the university in helping it become a more sustainable institution.

One of the challenges identified by the Franklin Green Office in relying on the Green Office Movement was finding resources for expanding their programs and initiatives to include social sustainability. The Green Office Movement historically has emphasized environmental sustainability. In their second year of operation, the Franklin Green Office reached out to other resources, including their university's Diversity, Equity and Inclusion Committee, to ensure their programs centered their efforts in an inclusive manner. That year, the Franklin Green Office also placed greater programmatic emphasis on amplifying the United Nation's Sustainable Development Goals (SDG) that focused on social sustainability. For example, one project explored the role of nuclear weapons, which goes to the heart of SDG 16, whose goal is to promote peaceful and inclusive societies.

The work of the Franklin Green Office has received support from its university staff, administration and faculty. This is in part due to the active role of their steering committee, which includes members from every academic division and staff from every unit of the university. The guidance and feedback from the steering committee ensures that the Franklin Green Office purposefully engages with all university stakeholders.

One student founder expressed that the Franklin Green Office "has allowed me to gain more knowledge about sustainability at higher education institutions", while another added, that "this has been a great real-world experience opportunity, helping me learn how to implement sustainability practices at the university level" (https://www.fus.edu/news-events/news/introducing-franklin -green-office). The student founders of the Franklin Green Office have gone on to continue their educational careers in environmental studies, as well as careers in environmental education.

5.   CONCLUSION

The Green Office Movement is one that is leading society towards resilience. The Green Office Model is designed to be replicable and has a growing record of successes, primarily within Europe. Students at universities beyond Europe can learn from the lessons and resources made available by the Green Office Movement. By facilitating the implementation of sustainability programs in universities where student support for sustainability outpaces an existing institutional framework, the Green Office Movement equips student activists to drive change and shape the way their universities address sustainability. There should be an effort to promote increased adoption of the Green Office Model outside of Europe in order to expand the network of student-led sustainability programs globally. Not only do student-led sustainability efforts translate to institutional change at universities with the support of the Green Office Model, but the students involved gain valuable practical skills and experience in change-making that help equip them for a future in sustainability professions and leadership.

REFERENCES

Adomßent, M., Grahl, A. & Spira, F. (2019). Putting sustainable campuses into force: Empowering students, staff and academics by the self-efficacy Green Office Model. *International Journal of Sustainability in Higher Education, 20*(3), 470–481. https:// doi.org/10.1108/IJSHE-02-2019-0072

Drupp, M.A., Esguerra, A., Keul, L., Low Beer, D., Meisch, S. & Roosen-Runge, F. (2012). Change from below: Student initiatives for universities in sustainable development. In W. Leal Filho (Ed.), *Sustainable development at universities: New horizons* (pp. 733–742). Peter Lang.

Enrico, D., et al. (2012). Universities as strategic actors in the knowledge economy. *Cambridge Journal of Economics*, *36*(3), 525–541. https:// doi .org/ 10 .1093/ cje/ bes024

Eyler, J.S. (2000). What do we most need to know about the impact of service-learning on student learning? *Michigan Journal of Community Service Learning.*

Filho, W.L., Shiel, C., do Paço, A. & Brandli, L. (2015). Brandli, Putting sustainable development in practice: Campus greening as a tool for institutional sustainability efforts. In J.P. Davim (Ed.), *Sustainability in higher education* (pp. 1–19). Chandos Publishing. https://doi.org/10.1016/B978-0-08-100367-1.00001-9.

Filho, W.L., Will, M., Salvia, A.L., Adomßent, M., Grahl, A. & Spira, F. (2019). The role of green and sustainability offices in fostering sustainability efforts at higher education institutions. *Journal of Cleaner Production*, *232*, 1394–1401. https://doi .org/10.1016/j.jclepro.2019.05.273

Fink, L.D. (2013). *Creating significant learning experiences: An integrated approach to designing college courses*. John Wiley & Sons. fus .edu/ news -events/ news/ introducing-franklin-green-office

greenofficemovement.org/

Hariram, N.P., Mekha, K.B., Suganthan, V. & Sudhakar, K. (2023). Sustainalism: An integrated socio-economic-environmental model to address sustainable development and sustainability. *Sustainability*, *15*, 10682. https://doi.org/10.3390/su151310682

Higgins, P., Nicol, R., Somervell, D. & Bownes, M. (2013). The student experience: Campus, curriculum, communities and transition at the University of Edinburgh. In S. Sterling, L. Maxey & H. Luna (Eds.), *The sustainable university: Progress and prospects* (pp. 192–210). Routledge.

Jarchow, M.E., Formisano, P., Nordyke, S. & Sayre, M. (2018). Measuring longitudinal student performance on student learning outcomes in sustainability education. *International Journal of Sustainability in Higher Education*, *19*, 547–565.

Klemenčič, M. (2011). The public role of higher education and student participation in higher education governance. *Higher education and society in changing times: Looking back and looking forward*, 74–83.

Lehnhof, R. & Nolan, C. (2016). Making universities more sustainable. https://unesdoc .unesco.org/ark:/48223/pf0000245763

Lootens, F. (2017). *Student empowerment for sustainability in higher education.* https://edepot.wur.nl/424611

Ritchie, M.A. (2013). Sustainability education, experiential learning, and social justice: designing community based courses in the global south. *Journal of Sustainability Education*, *5*.

Spira, F. & Baker-Friesen, A. (2015). Driving the energy transition at maastricht university? Analysing the transformative potential of the student-driven and staff-supported maastricht university green office. In W. Leal Filho (Ed.), *Transformative approaches to sustainable development at universities: Working across disciplines* (pp. 207–224). Springer. https://doi.org/10.1007/978-3-319-08837-2_15

Stafford-Smith, M., Griggs, D., Gaffney, O. et al. (2017). Integration: The key to implementing the Sustainable Development Goals. *Sustainability Science*, *12*, 911–919. https://doi.org/10.1007/s11625-016-0383-3

Tilbury, D. (2011). Higher education for sustainability: A global overview of commitment and progress. In GUNi (Ed.), *Higher education in the world* (pp. 18–28). Palgrave. https://unesdoc.unesco.org/ark:/48223/pf0000245763

Weigert, K.M. (1998). Academic service learning: Its meaning and relevance. *New Directions for Teaching and Learning*, *73*, 3–10.

8. How universities enable sustainable solutions to persistent social problems in Africa: the case of a Pan African university alliance

Alessia Argiolas and Said Benamar

INTRODUCTION

The concept of sustainable development, which initially emerged from ecology, has evolved into a comprehensive framework encompassing the economy, society, and environment (Purvis, Mao & Robinson, 2019). Today, the United Nations' Sustainable Development Goals (SDGs) serve as a global reference point for sustainability, consisting of 17 interconnected objectives to be achieved by 2030 (Franco et al., 2019). These goals are framed around three Ps: People, Planet and Prosperity, and therefore include aspects such as poverty eradication, climate change mitigation, biodiversity preservation, and institutional strengthening (UN, 2014). Higher education institutions are increasingly recognized for their role in promoting sustainability and actively contributing to sustainable development (Koehn & Uitto, 2017). Universities can shape the future through their core activities: teaching, research, and community service. They educate future decision-makers, generate knowledge and innovative solutions through research, and demonstrate sustainability practices through responsible governance and community engagement. While universities worldwide share similar objectives, their approaches and initiatives may vary due to local challenges and institutional contexts. This chapter focuses on the Pan African University alliance as an example of universities' leadership in promoting sustainability within their local communities, specifically by promoting sustainable entrepreneurship education.

Scholars have defined entrepreneurship education as a process of changing the individual's mindset towards creative thinking and innovation to solve global issues and create positive change in societies (Acs, 2010; Bruton, Ketchen Jr & Ireland, 2013). In entrepreneurship, education is triggered by the low level of entrepreneurship programs and courses in African countries. As a result of qualitative research based on 15 interviews with faculty members and the analysis of multiple secondary data covering over 10 years of program and universities alliance development, we elaborated a model that shows how these universities try to actively promote sustainability through sustainable entrepreneurship education and orchestrate a network that helps perpetuate and sustain sustainable entrepreneurial solutions and outcomes at different levels. Examples of sustainable ventures born from the program include tech-based agribusinesses that enable farmers to improve resiliency to climate change or to introduce organic practices, but also circular economy-based businesses that clean suburban areas and create new affordable products such as roof tiles made of recycled plastic, or business models that include marginalized groups such as women or minorities. In this chapter we identify three overall practices that these universities put in place to promote sustainability by supporting sustainable entrepreneurship in Africa: (1) Harvesting locally relevant sustainability knowledge, (2) sowing sustainability symbols, (3) Sustaining sustainable results.

BACKGROUND AND CONTEXT

The case we present is the E4Impact alliance, a university network of 21 universities representing 21 different African countries. The name "E4Impact" means "*E*ntrepreneurship *F*or *I*mpact". Through the case of E4Impact alliance, this chapter illustrates the challenges and the potential of universities to contribute to sustainability and sustainable development in the African context. A focus on the African continent seems particularly relevant given the scale of the challenges facing the continent in achieving the SDGs (Buckler & Creech, 2014). The political and economic histories of African countries have created an array of environments in which higher education institutions operate (World Bank, 2014). Yet, there are similarities across countries that encourage a Pan African perspective to meet complex and interrelated challenges.

Africa possesses a wealth of natural resources encompassing fertile land, water sources, oil, natural gas, minerals, forests, and wildlife. The continent boasts a significant share of global natural resources, comprising both renewable and non-renewable reserves. Africa stands as the primary custodian of the world's mineral deposits, holding approximately 65% of arable land worldwide and 10% of the planet's internal renewable freshwater sources (African Development Bank Group, 2016). Alongside these valuable resources, Africa possesses a burgeoning human capital, courtesy of its expanding population of young individuals eager to contribute to their nations' progress. With the youngest population on the globe – over 60% of its inhabitants are under the age of 25 – Africa holds great potential for growth, provided it can establish a sustainable, robust, and resilient economy. Such an economy would create opportunities for economic development while prioritizing sustainability. According to Sanda Ojiambo, the CEO and Executive Director of the UN Global Compact, sustainability is sparking the emergence of innovative business ideas on the continent. It fosters innovation and addresses critical challenges, such as combating climate change. However, it is crucial to ensure that future growth and resource exploitation are outcome-driven, climate-resilient, and sustainable. Despite that, Africa is home to numerous impoverished nations with high levels of poverty, unemployment, and inequality, where the consequences of an unsustainable economic system are already evident (Bruton et al., 2013; Rivera-Santos et al., 2015). In the continent's context, the environmental, social, and economic dimensions are intertwined and mutually reinforced. Addressing these interconnected challenges requires an integrated and transformative approach, in which universities can play a unique role.

Previous studies and initiatives place the education sector as an important partner in the myriad of development efforts across the continent (Bloom, Canning & Chan, 2006). Indeed, major international initiatives, such as the United Nations Development Programme's Millennium Development Goals mandate that higher education institutions play a central role in advancing development. Eradicating poverty and hunger, improving maternal health, promoting gender equality, and environmental sustainability can and should be addressed at the university level. "[H]igher education has to assume a critical role in the development possibilities in our globalized and knowledge-driven twenty-first-century society" (Zeleza, 2003, as quoted in Puplampu, 2006, p. 31). On the one hand, African universities have a critical role to play in supporting sustainable development, but on the other hand they face several barriers such as lack of funds, lack of adequately trained human resources, lack of awareness about sustainable development at the institutional level, and inadequate institutional policies on sustainable development (GUNi, IAU and AAU, 2011). Different studies confirm that higher education in Africa suffers from lack of resources to adequately engage higher education in development initiatives, most literature refers to the "crisis" of postsecondary institutions and their impotence in the development process (Johnson, Hirt & Hoba, 2011). This crisis is mostly associated with the neoliberal development agenda implemented in post-colonial Africa, which has been reinforced through aid mechanisms (Okolie, 2003). In this scenario, alternative forms of organizing have been considered to facilitate higher education's contribution to the development process in Africa (Ulmer & Wydra, 2020). One such alternative is partnerships and alliances among universities. Joining efforts and intents enable an active role for the university as an institutional agent able to play in the ecosystem for sustainable development.

For this chapter, an alliance is defined by drawing from the literature in international politics as a formal alignment among institutional actors, to supplement each other capabilities towards a common aim (Keohane, Nye Jr, 1973). The E4Impact alliance is exactly that, a formal alignment among 21 high-profile universities around the common aim of promoting sustainability and sustainable development in Africa through sustainable entrepreneurship.

From the E4Impact case, we identify and propose a set of *practices* that can be used by higher education institutions operating under similar resource constraints, regarding building capacity for sustainable development inside the university institution (among students, faculty, and staff) and outside the institutions (disseminating practices among communities, institutional partners, and stakeholders). Through the analysis of the E4Impact case study, we show how universities in Africa can contribute to sustainability at the community, country, and Pan African levels by means of an example of the creation of an ecosystem which supports sustainable entrepreneurs. In the words of one MBA alumna:

> We (students) came across the ecosystem within sustainable entrepreneurship. I have to say sustainable entrepreneurship is a new thing, still new in Kenya, but Tangaza University being the pioneer of this MBA entrepreneurship training has really helped to create a sense of confidence in entrepreneurs like us, who still don't know we are in sustainable entrepreneurship, but realizing it after going through the training. (Kathleen, Alumni Kenya)

The Main Challenges for African Universities

Every effort to describe and improve the role of universities in promoting sustainability should start by considering the existing challenges and boundaries within which they operate. As anticipated, the key challenge is a general lack of resources, especially financial resources (Johnson et al., 2011). This resource scarcity has a complex origin which can be described as a self-reinforcing effect of high poverty rates in the population and the high levels of national indebtment (Okolie, 2003). On a second note, an important scarce resource is locally relevant knowledge: globalization pressures and colonial history created a shortage of contextualized knowledge, such that available theories and frameworks lack meaning and efficacy in the African context. Consequently, several attempts to improve socioeconomic conditions start from the wrong premises and fail or produce marginal results. Theories developed in the "global north" are not necessarily suitable to the African culture and informal institutions (Slade Shantz, Kistruck & Zietsma, 2018). Connected to that, university networks and partnerships are imbalanced towards European or North American universities, with weak relations between African universities and business schools (Ulmer & Wydra, 2020). Within African regions, universities are disentangled from the respective industrial and business sector (Puplampu, 2006). Other challenges come from the need to strengthen secondary education and the overall relations with governments (Ibid.). Along with those challenges, universities also face internal issues. For example, they suffer a lack of access and equality in education; a low development of teaching and learning skills; governance issues; and the quality of research (Johnson et al., 2011).

The E4Impact alliance case illustrates how some universities navigate and partially respond to these challenges in implementing sustainable entrepreneurship education. These universities do not limit themselves to teaching entrepreneurship, but they also join forces in an alliance to create the conditions necessary so that entrepreneurial activities for sustainability might be effectively stimulated and sustained over time. This resonates with an institutional entrepreneurship view where organizations not only navigate and adapt to the environment where they operate, but actively shape the institution around them through collective action (Battilana, Leca & Boxenbaum, 2009).

Opportunities for Universities to Promote Sustainable Entrepreneurship

Many African countries face economic, environmental and social unsustainability, with a large portion of the population living in extreme poverty (Bruton et al., 2013; Rivera-Santos et al., 2015). Access to basic services like water, energy, healthcare, and education is a struggle, especially for isolated rural communities. Despite decades of intervention by international aid organizations, these challenges persist. The traditional foreign aid model has been questioned and criticized for creating dependency (Easterly, 2006; Moyo, 2008). Instead, a new wave of sustainable entrepreneurs is emerging. The growth of entrepreneurial activity, as well as the training of new entrepreneurs, play a key role in boosting economic development. Yet these enterprises, which try to benefit society and/or the environment, along with being financially viable, face significant challenges (Wangai, Burkhard & Müller, 2016). In fact, the entrepreneurial ecosystem for start-ups willing to create a social or environmental impact is in its infancy (even in the global north). Challenges are present at different institutional levels: from formal institutions, characterized by several voids such as at the regulative and policy level and at the informal level, social entrepreneurs face challenges with their primary stakeholders such as customers and beneficiaries on the one side and financiers on the other. Local populations are less familiar with market-based mechanisms but are rather embedded in long-standing community-based traditions in which community and family members support each other in case of need (Acquaah & Eshun, 2010; Argiolas, Rawhouser & Sydow, 2023). The availability of financial stakeholders on the other hand also influences these enterprises. Operating in such impoverished environments, most enterprises find it difficult to access loans or equity, especially in the early stages of venture development. However, the significant presence of international non-governmental organizations (NGOs) and government aid has fostered an environment where financial stakeholders often offer support through grants (McDade & Spring, 2005). These grants assist enterprises in establishing their businesses, enabling them to access additional forms of credit. Various organizations, such as Seed Stars World, Melinda Gates Foundation, and Schwab Foundation, provide funding and training to entrepreneurs, promoting the concept of sustainable entrepreneurship. In light of this situation, entrepreneurship education should not only focus on teaching entrepreneurial skills and techniques but also on empowering entrepreneurs with the entrepreneurial mindset and the necessary tools to navigate and potentially transform the existing institutional arrangements within their specific contexts.

Education is widely accepted as a leading instrument for promoting economic growth, but it might get stunted and challenged in an environment presenting the issues described above. If the foundational infrastructure for the conduct of business is not sufficient it can hinder the business formation and growth (Khanna & Palepu, 1997). In this context characterized by the absence of basic resources, and industrial and market infrastructure for new venture creations, entrepreneurs need more support than training and education in theoretical content.

METHODOLOGY

We use the case study of the E4Impact Pan African university alliance currently numbering 21 university members across the same number of African countries to document their efforts in leading society towards sustainability.

In the following section, we will describe the case selected and we will give more details about the type of data and the methods used for the analysis.

DATA AND METHODS

In our investigation, we draw on qualitative data from 15 semi-structured interviews with members of the alliance and archival materials. We started with collecting and analyzing previous qualitative and quantitative data that the first author had collected as part of a social impact measurement process of the MBA program. These data include focus groups and interviews about the effectiveness of the program and learning outcomes and 46 surveys inquiring about changes at the individual and business levels after the completion of the MBA program. The interviews lasted one hour on average with Alumni of the MBA, the local faculty, and the staff; we also interviewed the program directors, the business coach, and one professor in Kenya. The data also includes interviews and speeches by the Alumni, available as teaching material in the program or as marketing and communication material. Our investigation does not make a systematic analysis of these documents. Instead, we focus on those we consider relevant to our research aim, understanding the role of universities in leading towards the continent's sustainable development. Through the analysis, we identified different practices.

Our analysis of the interviews began with a thematic analysis, during which we examined the interview transcripts to gain a broad understanding of the data and the most prominent issues. We proceeded with our analysis by using manual coding of the transcripts to identify those segments and statements in which the interviewees discussed our topics of interest. This data reduction (Miles & Huberman, 1994) allowed us to identify three relevant phases of a process and key practices. Overall, our data interpretation (Miles & Huberman, 1994) occurred over several rounds, during which we aimed to make sense of our empirical material through various theoretical references. Eventually, we formed a shared interpretation of the enacted practices, which support sustainable entrepreneurship and create social and environmental sustainability.

ANALYSIS

Case Study Description

E4Impact was born as an initiative launched in 2010 by ALTIS – The Graduate School of Business and Society of the Catholic University of Milan, Italy, with the objective of training impact-oriented entrepreneurs in Africa to support the start-up and growth of businesses with the potential to create value for people and the planet. In 2015, the E4Impact initiative became a private and autonomous Foundation with the support of corporate and private participants.

Today E4Impact's portfolio of activities entails:

1. Entrepreneurship programs such as the global MBA in Impact Entrepreneurship and the International Certificate in Impact Entrepreneurship.
2. The creation of a Pan African university alliance that can teach, research, and foster sustainability across the continent.

The E4I Foundation mission is to build the leading University Alliance for training a new generation of Impact Entrepreneurs. Their vision is to offer 25 Sustainable Entrepreneurship programs in Africa by 2025, leading an ever-greater impact on the continent: a goal of over 2,000 entrepreneurs trained, 1,000 new enterprises, and thousands of new jobs in the formal economy.

BOX 8.1   SUMMARY OF THE E4IMPACT ALLIANCE
GOALS

Goals:

- Train a new generation of entrepreneurs capable of combining economic success with positive social impact.
- Partner with local universities to embed entrepreneurial education in African Management Curricula.
- Facilitate the international development of European and African companies attentive to social and environmental impact.
- Promote impactful academic research and include the voice of African scholars into the international community.

E4Impact goals (Box 8.1) and their impact (Figure 8.1) are summarized in the following pictures. The social impact performance indicators are: number of jobs created, number of new ventures in operation, the financial performance improvement (such as revenues, supply chain growth, access to finance, new branches opened) and the direct contribution to four Sustainable Development Goals (1, 4, 8, 17) and indirect contribution, through the ventures created by the MBA alumni to two additional SDGs (9, 12).

Source: E4Impact Impact Report 2019.

Figure 8.1   Summary of E4Impact alliance indicators and results

The Global MBA in Impact Entrepreneurship

The Global MBA in Impact Entrepreneurship is the core program offered by the E4Impact Foundation through allies' African universities. The program is standardized across universities through a bottom-up approach, where the basic content remains the same and faculty are trained on the teaching content and methods, yet every university has the flexibility and potential to change part of the content and is encouraged to adapt it to the local reality. Figure 8.2 below gives an overview of the structure.

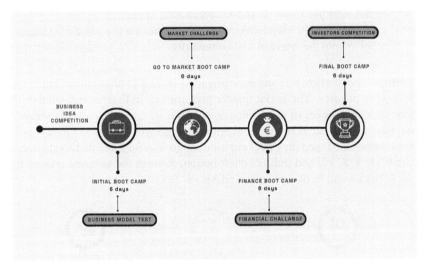

Figure 8.2   Structure of the MBA program

The MBA-level program resembles an entrepreneurship training program for entrepreneurs or aspirants. It is characterized by being both an academic program, as it releases an MBA degree and a practical business acceleration experience. During the program, the participants can develop the business and social skills necessary to start and manage a new social venture or scale an existing one. The MBA program pedagogy leans on a hands-on approach, and the student can utilize tools and solutions for the start-up or scaling (business and social impact) as of a high-growth business.

Faculty and staff members are specifically trained in networking skills, and they have the main goal of supporting the students in developing a personal network of mentors, investors, and peers. Network skills development plays a central role in the program, such that during the MBA students go through four business competitions where they can meet mentors and investors, or the Alumni groups present in each country.

The networking activities aim at establishing links between students and entrepreneurs across Africa and Europe, especially Italy, where the Foundation's headquarters is based. With respect to the program teaching methodology, it is a flexible blend of intensive weeks of in-class lessons, distance learning, long weekends, and competitions. Over a period of 18 months, MBA participants spend a total of 40 days in the classroom and the modules are integrated with online video lessons and exercises. During the program, the entrepreneurs can count on a Business Coach, who provides individual support in refining the enterprise business model. The Coach supports each participant in implementing the Business Plan and developing relationships with the ecosystem. MBA participants also receive experienced mentorship through regular contact with successful local and international businesspeople. The peculiar program structure is designed around the goal of leaving the time to run a business or create one and using the time in class to refine what has been done outside.

One big challenge facing these entrepreneurship students and entrepreneurs is the absence of an established ecosystem and low market familiarity among many stakeholders. Another core of the MBA program pedagogy is the creation of an ambassador's identity inside the students, who are called to become role models outside of the class, in their communities as businesspeople oriented to benefit the planet and the society.

In sum there are three core pillars of the MBA program that enable the university to carve a sustainability path and orientation in their students and their respective communities:

1. *MBA Academic Modules*: to create the appropriate knowledge and entrepreneurial skills. The program includes the following courses among others: Sustainable Business Model Design, Responsible Management & Impact Measurement, Sustainable Business Strategy, Go to Market: Market Analysis, Process & Project Management, Human Resource Management & Leadership.
2. *Networking for growth*: activities including competitions (business idea, business model and business plan competitions), seminars and talks by other entrepreneurs or Alumni, offered to entrepreneurs during the program to give them the opportunity to enlarge their network. Create the conditions to forge their entrepreneurial microcosm.
3. *Peer learning and program legacy*: encouraging local leadership and creation of formal Alumni networks.

Before turning to introducing the second arm of the E4Impact Case study, namely the Pan African university alliance, we introduce below two examples of impact ventures born from the MBA program. We hope this example will help the reader to interpret the subsequent findings as they show the typical hybrid nature of the endeavors pursued through the MBA. They are hybrid as they combine and align business logics to solving social and environmental sustainability goals (Battilana & Dorado, 2010). The two examples selected belong to the agribusiness sector and to the circular economy sector. Table 8.1 below summarizes the main characteristics and relevance of these business sectors in the African continent.

We now present two examples of businesses that were developed during the MBA program in the years 2014. The first example is **Farmdrive**, a female-led enterprise in the agribusiness sector founded in Kenya, while the second example is in the circular economy sector, **Zaacol**, founded in Ghana.

Farmdrive

Farmdrive uses mobile phones' alternative data, and machine learning to close the critical data gap that prevents financial institutions from lending to creditworthy smallholder farmers. Agriculture remains an important source of livelihood for the majority of families and communities in Kenya, but small farmers face continuing challenges in order to secure enough harvest. Small farmers especially struggle to increase productivity and adapt to climate change shocks. One of the main reasons is the lack of access to capital, a barrier to purchasing the critical farming inputs that could increase their yields and revenues. The business promotes financial inclusion by providing innovative tools to extend vital credit. By increasing the efficiency and oper-ational capacity of lenders, it ensures smallholder farmers have easy access to quality, reliable, convenient, transparent and affordable financial services to widen their economic base. By 2021 they had distributed $13 million in loans to small farmers, and are positioned to reach three million smallholder farmers in Kenya in the next five years.

Zaacol

Zaacoal makes charcoal, a source of energy, from coconut and other organic wastes. It is a Social Enterprise based in Accra, Ghana, with a vision to trans-form how Africans access clean fuels. The primary business is to convert ubiq-uitous city waste into clean burning fuels. In the words of the founders "the products are very impactful as they protect the environment, clean the city, protect our forests, reduce indoor air pollution and empower women". Ghana has lost a third of its forests to charcoal and firewood. The forestry commission

Table 8.1   *Key sectors for impact entrepreneurship*

	AGRIBUSINESS	**CIRCULAR ECONOMY**
SECTOR DESCRIPTION	Agribusiness encompasses a wide range of activities that generate economic value;	Circular Economy companies belong to different business sectors: buildings and constructions made of waste or sustainable materials, clean energy production, waste or water management and so on. Companies operating in this sector developed an innovative business solution that gives new value to previously unspoiled value chain resources.
	Agribusiness comprises farming, and many other activities and services that connect farmers to consumers. Agribusiness in its broad definition includes inputs, suppliers, agri food processors, traders, exporters, retailers and many others.	
ISSUES	Low value-added outputs from agriculture;	Polluting sources of energy or lack of access to energy;
	Low contribution towards poverty reduction due to little innovation;	Deforestation and damage to ecosystems to access raw materials;
	Farming input inaccessible and costly for small farmers.	Poor waste management across the Continent.
OPPORTUNI-TIES	Enhance value-added production and rural employment through business mindset development and increased investments;	Circular economy increases diversification in traditional sector like construction, energy or fashion;
	Increase production and processing efficiency through innovation;	Circular economy makes available cheap raw materials reducing production costs;
	Targeting previously excluded small farmers with social-driven business models.	Capitalize on existing skill of recycling and repair and develop new set of skills.
OUTCOMES	New technologies enable higher yields and more revenues for small farmers;	Reducing many causes of environmental damages like deforestation, CO_2 emissions, waste and so on;
	Innovation enhances food security and sustainable agriculture;	
	Social entrepreneurship enables small farmers to access credits and agricultural inputs;	Healthier living conditions, reduced pollution and new job creation. Circular economy has the potential to enable a faster transition from the informal to the formal sector for many workers.
	Value-added production becomes possible and new and specialized employment is created.	

	AGRIBUSINESS	**CIRCULAR ECONOMY**
INTERVENT-IONS	Entrepreneurship and business knowledge to strengthen and define innovative ideas;	Entrepreneurship and business knowledge to strengthen and define innovative ideas and businesses;
	Creating linkages with possible funders;	
	Creating capabilities to obtain funds for the firm;	Creating valuable connections with investors, creating capabilities to obtain funds for the company to create a network of entrepreneurs in the sector fostering synergies and collaborations; create links with Italian experts as mentors and business partners.
	Create a network of entrepreneurs in the sector fostering synergies and collaborations; create links with Italian experts (mentors and business partners).	

estimates that over 91% of all trees cut in Ghana are used for either firewood or charcoal and mainly used as cooking fuel. In addition to that, the World Health Organization estimates that over four million people die annually from indoor air pollution. Estimates say that out of over 2,000 tons of waste generated daily in Accra, only 500 tons are collected daily. Most of these are organic waste. Zaacol founder Sully Amin Abubakar was recognized by *Forbes* magazine as being in the top 30 under 30 in Ghana in 2016. By 2021, the business had reached 25 million customers, created 111 full-time jobs and empowered over 100 vendors around Ghana.

The Pan Africa Alliance Description

The MBA program is delivered through local universities who join an "alliance". In 2019 the Foundation launched the E4Impact African University alliance. The vision of the alliance is "to be the largest internationally recognised pan-African community of universities promoting high-impact social and environmental entrepreneurship on the African Continent and beyond". It currently counts 24 African universities among its member institutions.

The members of the alliance are inspired by the following principles:

1. Entrepreneurship as a driver for inclusive and sustainable growth and job creation.
2. Education, research and innovation as a key factor to assure economic and social empowerment.
3. Academic collaboration as a way of strengthening entrepreneurship across Africa.

4. Partnership between African and International institutions as leverage for mutual growth.

The members' university can take part in the following activities:

1. The teaching: the members of the alliance can offer the E4Impact Global MBA in Impact Entrepreneurship as well as an International Certificate in Entrepreneurship or customized courses for the local executive markets.
2. The research: the alliance convenes a monthly meeting in which members share best practices and plan future research initiatives. These activities foster cross-country collaboration among faculty, staff and impact entrepreneurs. Each year faculty members from the Management and Agribusiness departments of alliance schools can access an international PhD program jointly created by the Uganda Martyrs University and Università Cattolica of Milan.

FINDINGS

In this section, we elaborate on the MBA program and the alliance as an example of how universities can contribute to sustainability and to economic sustainable development, in the face of several challenges and scarcity of resources.

The E4Impact case shows how universities can sustain sustainability across different levels from individuals – by orienting their mindset towards hybrid goals – to businesses – by creating the network and the institutional support – to communities – by effect of ventures externalities.

E4Impact uses entrepreneurship education to leverage individual capacity and knowledge, forge leadership, create networks, and co-create the conditions for their businesses to thrive.

The local level of action is then reinforced by a Pan African level of action enabling the scaling of sustainability results from a local to a much wider scale.

The role of the universities' participation in the alliance is useful to make sure that the efforts and results at the local level are not lost with time but can be continuously reinforced and sustained.

We identify three practices enacted by the alliance members: Harvesting sustainability knowledge, sowing sustainability symbols, and sustaining sustainability results (Table 8.2). Each practice is collocated in a specific operation phase, encompasses a series of specific activities, and aims to create impact at different levels.

These findings are presented in detail in the following paragraphs using quotes and data from the archival analysis.

Table 8.2   *The practices of sustainability knowledge orchestration*

Practices	Operation Phase	Activities	Desired Level of Impact
Harvesting Sustainability Knowledge	MBA program ideation and ongoing design	• Introducing locally meaningful knowledge, • Bridging knowledge from outside, • Determine boundaries of action around sustainability.	Impact at individual level: Student or faculty members
Sowing Sustainability Symbols	MBA operations and running	• Creating enabling conditions and connections, • Fueling sustainability aspirations, • Establishing a legacy of community transformation.	Impact at venture and community level
Sustaining Sustainability Results	University alliance Governance	• Establishing a community of practice with a shared vision, • Improving credibility and legitimization to attract resources, • Maintaining a long-term outlook through research.	Impact at Pan African level

Practice 1: Harvesting Sustainability Knowledge

In the MBA preparation and ongoing design stage, we identified three activities that aim to address two key issues for universities in Africa in terms of leading towards sustainable development, namely the imbalanced power of knowledge creation of outsider theories and the subsequent shortage of knowledge that is locally relevant and meaningful. We categorize these activities under the name of *harvesting* sustainability *knowledge*.

This issue is well described by the words of one Alumni of the MBA program in Rwanda:

> Even if I did Business management and entrepreneurship as my master's degree... it was theories, and it was especially from the western countries which sometimes are not applicable in the "low market" here in Africa. For example, the first time I sent a check to my supplier, he told me he wanted the money, saying that it was only a piece of paper. (Herve, Alumni Rwanda)

Introducing locally meaningful knowledge

According to the E4Impact program director, "the risk of replicating this top-down schema is high", this is why the program design explicitly tries to overcome this limitation by delivering the program through local universities that are conceived as partners and by adopting an agnostic approach to the development of sustainable solutions from the innovative thinking of local entrepreneurs and aspirants.

> (to help leading toward sustainability) on the one side, what we do is to enable local ideas. (…) We don't propose any solution to students, but we connect them to mentors and offer training. So, we enable the development of solutions by the entrepreneurs themselves. And that's a very powerful tool, because, of course, they know better what their communities need, and they also know better, what is doable, and what is not doable in a given community. (Program Director)

Bridging existing knowledge from outside

This bottom-up approach is combined with a "thoughtful contamination of knowledge" (Professor, Uganda). If on the one side, there is the problem of colonial influence in learning and education and a lack of locally relevant knowledge, on the other side there is a **problematic gap between African universities, and especially business schools, and their industrial and business sector**. This is why it becomes particularly important, according to the E4Impact Foundation and the partner universities, to stimulate practical entrepreneurial solutions. The teaching tool developed for this aim is an innovation manual and a digital peer-to-peer platform that includes sustainability innovations that have worked in Africa and worldwide offered to the students as a source of inspiration:

> We have realized over the years, that sometimes, for stimulating native solutions, you need to inspire students with something that already works. So, we've put together innovation manuals, which give access to innovations which have been already deployed in Europe rather than in the African Countries. We see ourselves as collectors and rational analysts of existing knowledge. (…) So it's a kind of, we are guiding them into the wealth of knowledge around let's say, upcycling plastic waste, right. (Program director)

An important element of this teaching tool, that makes it effective in the African context, is the practical nature of the solution proposed. The manuals are very specific as they do not deal with general solutions with respect to broad economic sectors (i.e., circular economy), yet they are based on value chains within single business sectors. As an example, the mango value chain manual, the coffee manual etc., not the agribusiness sector manual. The creation of these tools and the accompanied digital platform is possible thanks to

the alliance form of the E4Impact initiative, which can benefit from entrepreneurial experiences from several African and European countries together.

Determine boundaries of action around sustainability
Additional efforts are dedicated to narrowing the focus of the teaching and
practice of sustainability. One pillar is the establishment of boundaries of
sustainability that the E4Impact alliance addresses. The logic adopted by the
E4Impact alliance revolves around a "materiality approach" (Nicholls, 2018),
whereby areas of sustainability intervention are bounded based on the areas
that seem to have more impact in terms of employability. In line with the
Foundation and alliance's vision of alleviating poverty in Africa through the
development of SMEs able to create decent jobs.

> In our onboarding of students and in the teaching, we are focusing on industries,
> which we believe are particularly impactful on the African continent in terms of the
> number of people who are employed in those sectors and the severity of the issues
> according to the SDGs: 1. civil works, 2. agribusiness, 3. fashion, and 4. circular
> economy. (Program director)

This approach is also visible in the students' efforts.

> I positioned my business in the coffee sector instead of any other due to its scala-
> bility and significant impact. Allow me to elaborate … When considering coffee,
> the cultivation and harvesting process involves numerous individuals. Our local
> community lacks strong organization in this regard, which results in creating ample
> employment opportunities. Coffee undergoes multiple stages before reaching the
> final cup. I perceive both the potential for broad impact and business growth in this
> aspect. The impact is evident among the majority of young people in Kenya, as
> they are not inclined towards farming. However, we believe that by engaging them
> in agribusiness through the coffee value chain, we can pique their interest. Coffee
> presents various opportunities where they can participate, such as sales, without
> necessarily engaging in digging or harvesting. The scalability of coffee extends
> to both its impact and business potential, enabling the involvement of everyone
> throughout the value chain. (Rosbella, Kenya)

Practice 2: Sowing Sustainability Symbols

In the process of running the MBA, we identify some key activities put in place
to respond to a specific challenge in African countries: an early stage, and
immature ecosystem for sustainable entrepreneurship. This issue has different
consequences in terms of entrepreneurial social capital development, with
a lack of connection to market institutions and other peers. Second, this issue
hinders the market growth of the sustainable enterprise specifically because of
a lack of familiarity with the market among key stakeholders such as customers and beneficiaries. The activities put in place by the E4Impact Foundation

and the partner university in this realm can be grouped under the category of *sowing sustainability symbols*.

Creating enabling conditions and social capital around sustainable businesses

There are several activities through which the E4Impact program tries to ensure that the students' business ideas can be implemented and run on their own wheels once the program is finished. The main challenge students face after finishing the program is an entrepreneurial ecosystem that is immature. Few institutional players operate in the environment that are able to support nascent enterprises, even if incubators and accelerators are starting to bloom in the main capital cities, there are still many steps to be taken. This is a particularly early stage in the context of sustainable entrepreneurship. For this reason, the program design has a strong, hands-on component along with the theoretical background. The program "is not just theoretical, it is more practical, and apprentice driven; what you're learning in class is what you really should do" (Benjamin, Alumni Kenya). One of the measures that enable this result-oriented program structure is the presence of a business coach – an experienced mentor who gives practical advice to the students and is a point of reference during the 18 months of the program. "The business coach was very useful and just helping me do my business in a more structured way and like in Kenya we just all over the place we see this works. Most entrepreneurs in Kenya run several businesses at one time as opposed to doing one thing well that becomes successful. We learned how to avoid this" (Edwin, Alumni Uganda).

Key actions are specifically driven by the objective of creating a network of potential investors for the students after the MBA, thanks to the three competitions when several business leaders and investors are invited. According to the social impact measurement report (2019) on the Kenyan MBA, 70% of the Alumni reported

> an improvement in their pitching skills. Increased confidence to communicate with stakeholders and higher exposure to networking opportunities. Thanks to those opportunities 30% of the Alumni had access to some source of finance and could improve their business performances in terms of revenues. After three years from the completion of the program, 30% of the Alumni have increased their financial independence and attribute this result mostly to the MBA program.

The dissemination of knowledge about impact and sustainable entrepreneurship is very challenging "we're looking at 21 universities, which is 21 countries, each country means a different ecosystem with different players. So, it is really complicated to be able to, orchestrate an ecosystem, which is so much diverse" (Program director). They try to do that through three disseminating actions: "at the country level, we are supporting universities, to develop some key relations, with a few investors, with a few incubators, with a few banks, with a few consulting firms. And we try to make sure that organizations stay close to the MBA program, we invite them to competitions, maybe to give some teaching, some assignments etc. This is not easy because of the contextual challenges that we have described "University is by culture, by nature, and by the way they operate, they, they are not too inclined to get out of the campus and keep this kind of relations".

The program director continues "Where we have local offices, we are the ones who try to develop the ecosystem (i.e. by opening our own accelerator hubs such as in Nairobi, Kenya) and keep the relations with the ecosystem, and we try to use this as a role model for the universities themselves. But more importantly, maybe, we embed in our program the ecosystem orchestration skills that are necessary for entrepreneurs operating in the vibrant yet harsh African environment".

The program puts at the center the creation of **peer networks** as a safety net and source of information and opportunity sharing after the end of the program. One explicit action is the creation of Alumni groups.

The first of this group was founded by the students themselves in Kenya, and is called Sesok (social entrepreneurship society of Kenya) and it is currently one of the largest networks for sustainable entrepreneurship in Kenya. Later joiners greatly value their participation to this network.

> The MBA program is also very useful because it brings to us opportunities for founding partnership. Those who came after my class started the Social Enterprise Society of Kenya. We benefit through that membership, being members of the Kenya private sector alliance and because of that you get funding opportunities, you get opportunities for Partnerships. So, I've continued to engage, I would say it's like the program continues to coach the people who went through it even after they have graduated, which is very good. (Justin, Alumni founder of Sesok)

Thanks to these Alumni networking activities a policy draft about social entrepreneurship has been brought to the attention of the Kenyan Government in 2021. The foundation and the alliance put the alumni at the center to reach this ecosystem enabling role, as a force to spread the knowledge and awareness about impact entrepreneurship "sometimes what is lacking (in the environment) is a knowledge of what sustainability really means or what are the differences on a global level or the country level or other regional level" and continues

> The alumni are our deliverable. (…) In every country where we operate, we support the creation of business networks, or alumni groups. Ideally, in a few years, we will have an alumni chapter in every country where we operate. Meanwhile, we are

using newsletters, of course, but also we are using the new b2b platform, designed to establish matches among businesses across the continent and with Italian companies. (Program director)

Fueling sustainability aspirations

One important dissemination strategy consists of fueling sustainability aspirations in the students by means of entrepreneurial aspirations. "I experienced one main transformation in my mindset, something changed" (Johanna, Ghana). Encouraging the development of hybrid goals through several actions such as embedding specific modules in the MBA program: leadership, ethics, social impact measurement and leveraging the advantage of a sustainability strategy in the local environments.

> Honestly, I started the MBA because our country is very competitive and having a bachelor's degree is not sufficient to get a good job. I just wanted to get a better perspective in terms of employment, but the activities that we did during the MBA were so inspiring and made me think about entrepreneurship. I started looking at being an entrepreneur differently ... to create value for society not only for oneself and I'm still of the same opinion. (Karen, Alumni Kenya)

According to the social impact meaurement report in Kenya by going through the MBA, 90% of the Alumni increased their awareness about business ethics and responsible production, consequently increasing their interest in creating social impact besides profit. The study found that most of the Alumni declare they run their ventures not only for themselves (as before the program) but with a prosocial orientation. Eighty percent of the Alumni feel accomplished for being able to help their communities to prosper while doing business.

> Before I used to look just at the profit, how much money I could gain from the business. Now I have another mindset orientation whereby I'm looking at business with three different lenses: profit is important, but I'm also looking at how is that impacting positively on people, positively on the environment. So, my business model has changed because I'm looking at other non-cash returns on investment. (Frank, Alumni Uganda)

The sustainability aspirations are also visible in the group of alumni who did not start a business after completing the MBA but are in employment. From the words of Bernard, we learned that he is still bringing his sustainability knowledge and strives in his workplace to exploit opportunities:

> (After the MBA) I continued to be employed but the skills I got during the MBA I used them in my work, I was working for Kenya Airlines and I developed internal projects and CSR projects for the company I actually got a promotion for them (…) I got many new skills: project management, stakeholder management…I used them

a lot even recently when I applied for a scholarship in Oxford I used the same sustainable project I developed during the MBA 7 years ago. (Bernard, Alumni Kenya)

Establishing legacy towards community transformation

Finally, sustainability knowledge dissemination culminates in the transfer of sustainability knowledge from the student entrepreneurs in the classroom to their respective communities. Several Alumni in their interviews reveal how the knowledge they obtained during the program not only had results at their individual and business level but enabled them to help several others in their entrepreneurial journey of change.

> I also helped my mother to change business: she stopped planting maize, which is really popular in my country, but not very profitable, here people just like to replicate what seems to work for others, but actually this thing of maize is not profitable... I also helped my wife as well to start an entrepreneurship career ... (Getsun, Alumni Kenya).
>
> Yes, some of them don't have the right techniques and skills, so they start farming carelessly wasting a lot of money, they do things just because they saw a neighbour was doing it. I try to teach them what I'm learned because I feel there's a big gap in terms of knowledge and skill set. I like touching so many lives, so I continue in this direction. I have also funded a network so they can advise each other. (Alice, Alumni Rwanda)

The legacy is visible in a new pervasive mindset that the MBA Alumni bring along the value chains where they operate. They become "symbols" of a different – sustainable – way of doing things. On the one hand the Alumni can push their suppliers to become more aware of social and environmental issues. And on the other hand, they provide customers with products that reduce their negative environmental impact, such as in the case of Zarcool. At the same time, this impacts their livelihoods enabling an increase of their own income, thereby being able to "send children to school", "get out of poverty" and change their behavior in terms of sustainability practices.

The MBA did not have only positive outcomes, some of the Alumni report poorer family relationships and poorer mental health. This happens as a drawback of the entrepreneurship journey. According to the focus group results conducted for the social impact measurement, a minority of the Alumni faced family challenges. In some cases when they improved their financial conditions thanks to the business success, the family members of the extended family expect to be given part of their money and be helped; some of the Alumni felt obligation towards the family and try to help as they can, but sometimes it ended up in fights and the family relationships have worsened. On the other hand, if the alumnus's business did not go well an increase in the level of indebtedness could be experienced. Not being able to provide for their families as before, family relationships have worsened.

Practice 3: Sustaining Sustainability Results

In the alliance governance, the actions can be assimilated to protecting and scaling up the fragile results through efforts dedicated to knowledge and action perpetuation:

* establishing a community of practice with a shared vision;
* improving credibility and legitimization to attract resources;
* maintaining a long-term outlook through research.

If the MBA program – with its hands-on teaching methods, the ecosystem orchestration goals, and its transformative pedagogy – enables the creation and dissemination of new knowledge from the individual student to the local communities, the impact on university faculty and staff plays a crucial role to protecting and perpetuating this knowledge circle to a wider Pan African level.

Through the alliance governance, sustainability knowledge is scaled, and reinforced.

Establishing and running a university alliance across 21 African countries can be a complex and challenging endeavor. While such alliances can offer numerous benefits, including the pooling of resources and expertise, promoting regional cooperation, and enhancing educational opportunities, they also face several significant challenges and struggles. Some of these challenges are related to the diversity of the education systems, the political and economic instability, the scarcity of funding and resources and regulatory issues.

To overcome these challenges, the alliance can benefit from careful planning, clear governance structures, strong leadership, and ongoing communication among member institutions. Up to the time of writing this chapter, the alliance is showing some evidence that it is handling these challenges in a positive way. Six African universities – Nile University, Spiritan University Nneochi (SUN) and Agri-business of Nigeria, CENSIL University College of Liberia, Cheikh Anta Diop University of Senegal, and Honoris University of Mauritius have joined the network. Additionally, some universities have volunteered to lead some meaningful initiatives including, among others, launching short courses on agrifood, building women entrepreneurship programs, and organizing a continental annual conference about social entrepreneurship.

While running a university alliance in Africa involving multiple institutions is undoubtedly challenging, the alliance is so far showing example of careful planning, effective leadership, and a commitment to collaboration and shared goals, which can also be a transformative force for higher education and regional development.

Engaging scholarship with a shared vision on sustainability
Increasingly, universities are expected to play a role in sustainable development. In fact, university community engagement is recognized to shape the new mission of academia in its attempt to adapt to the changing environment. Research (Gunasekara, 2004; Wakkee, Sijde, Vaupell, Ghuman 2019; Peterson, 2009; Budowle, Krszjzaniek & Taylor, 2021; Peterson & Kruss, 2021) revealed that community-oriented activities have been used by universities as drivers of change to help regional actors innovate and sustain development. Therefore, education has been adapting its processes, undertaking new initiatives, and incorporating various learning environments to support sustainable change and champion their engagement to serve communities. Scholars argued that universities' missions have undergone a shift from a focus on research and teaching to service and community engagement. They stated that while this shift of paradigm has been acknowledged in the literature, little has been produced about the instrumental pillars and tools used by universities to conduct into effect their transformative community agendas (Gunasekara, 2004; Budowle et al., 2021).

In our case study, we outline how the E4 alliance has formalized its strategic commitment to sustainable development through the adoption of significant levers of scale. The co-author of this chapter is a member of the alliance and has witnessed with all Pan African members the process of its reinforcement and outreach. Launched in 2010, the alliance totaled 21 and will grow to 25 African universities by the end of 2025.

Over the last three years, there has been a strong commitment from the E4Impact leadership to create a shared vision and commitment among members. Members demonstrated regular participation in webinar alliance universities' meetings to discuss issues related to E4Impact MBA development and training workshops on topics in relation to faculty development and research methodology.

We also consider the change that took place in the structures and mode of governance of the alliance, which may be regarded as assuring the importance of focus on Pan African and community engagement. This was underpinned by the shift from the "alliance meeting" status to the establishment of the alliance council seeking to institutionalize a legal commitment to sustainable Pan African development. The alliance council role is to strengthen collaboration with African universities, recognize the role of African universities and raise funds in the US. Importantly, the voice of the African continent has been formally represented in the alliance council through the election of two representatives of universities and three others from alumni in the strategic board of the alliance.

Improving credibility and legitimization to attract resources

No one knows the African context and challenges better than Africans themselves. So, the participation of African universities in the formal governance body will contribute to better inform the E4Impact strategic plan and attract donors and investors.

Interviews with the alliance manager and academic staff revealed that a key challenge to embracing a focus on scale impact entrepreneurship in Africa was to remain relevant to universities by providing them with new initiatives likely to tighten the relation among the members. Therefore, the alliance pursued three actions to strengthen the engagement of universities. The first was to improve the MBA programs to make sure they are sustainable and profitable to universities. They did so by designing new learning manuals and providing entrepreneurs with digital platforms that offer a technological space for experiential learning (Gunasekara, 2004). This continuous improvement on the quality of the curriculum has and will contribute to the increase of the number of candidates enrolled in the MBA programs in African universities following the direction of the managers of the alliance.

The second action was to expand the portfolio of academic programs. The alliance designed two programs, one for corporate innovation and the other for family businesses. These programs are featured with the specificities of the local contexts where learners could innovate and feel capable of driving positive change. (Wakkee et al., 2019). These programs have been offered in Kenya, Tunisia, Cameroon, and Ghana, and soon might be spread to other universities of the alliance. These "… [programs] offer a way to engage with local and global social, environmental, economic, political, and cultural problems in a way that is sustainable and truly enable [entrepreneurs] to think globally and act locally" (Peterson, 2009, p. 550).

The third initiative was to start using the alliances as a fund raiser. Research (Gunasekara, 2004) revealed that one of the challenges facing universities seeking to institutionalize sustainable development is pressure to raise funding specifically from private sectors. African economies are dominated by SMEs that might be reluctant to engage their scarce resources into research projects. Therefore, the alliance believes that "…there is nothing like these 21 universities in Africa working all together on entrepreneurship, and a big opportunity to raise funds, namely in the US, that will expand the activities of the alliance" (Director of the program).

The social value behind this kind of academic entrepreneurship consists in the establishment of channels of communication and exchange of ideas between the social market, the universities, and the alliance, which illustrate the collective action of the alliance to achieve sustainable development (Wakkee et al., 2019). Similarly, the creation of innovative ventures will contribute to job creation and socioeconomic development of the community

leading to sustainable and scalable social transformation in African communities (Mars & Metcalfe, 2009).

Maintaining a long-term outlook through research

The E4Impact Ph.D has been a valuable subject of substantial collaboration
among the members of the alliance. Its aim is to contribute to enhancing African
university research and allow graduates to join an international network of
scholars and publish in top journals about the global issues facing the African
continent. The Ph.D is offered by the University of Cattolica in Milan, Uganda
Martyrs University from Uganda and the E4Impact Foundation. The program
offers two tracks: Innovation management and Agribusiness systems. As
a result, the alliance has granted a scholarship to two Ph.D. cohorts of 30
African scholars representing the universities' members of the alliance.

The Ph.D. aims to integrate sustainable-based research projects into the
teaching curriculum of universities to enhance the qualities of their faculties
and as sources of innovation drivers for African economies.

The aims of the alliance's Ph.D are to:

* offer lecturers a career development opportunity through a quality program
  funded by international donors;
* meet the highest standards for faculty qualifications set by national and Pan
  African authorities; and
* develop opportunities for Pan African collaborations and research projects.

This kind of engaged scholarship provides an opportunity for faculty and
researchers to scale up an intellectual link between local and continental community engagement. This will contribute to recognizing African scholars to
have an impact through local activism in producing knowledge that yields to
address the sustainable issues of African communities (Peterson, 2009).

CONCLUSION

While an important body of literature has covered university linkage to sustainability issues in Africa, the E4Impact experience is a unique experience
that leverages an activist ecosystem composed of 21 Pan African universities,
international academic institutions, companies, and funding agencies. This
case study of the Pan African university alliance has been successful in
developing a sustainability vision and modeling a changed behavior among
the actors of the ecosystem to become drivers of social change in Africa. The
extensive network of the alliance might be considered a solution to the issue
of the smallness of campuses in creating significant sustainable local impacts.

As the director of the programs put it:

There is nothing like these alliances of 21 universities in Africa working all together on sustainable entrepreneurship…There is a certain degree of excitement because we really are doing something nobody did before … something that could bring substantial impact. We want to turn universities from houses of theoretical knowledge into hubs of practice where entrepreneurs can develop their solutions that have positive impact on society and the environment. (Program Director)

That said, the alliance will face several challenges in embracing a focus on extensive sustainable entrepreneurship in Africa. Because of the multicultural identities of its members, the E4 alliance should increase its attention to the development and use of specific skills including relationship and people management to upgrade its efforts to serve its strategic mission. While the strategic plans and governance are essential for the effective work of the alliance, these could be but half of the battle for the sustainability of the business model. Members should make great effort to know each other, tighten relationships and foster trust. Rethinking the alliance's practices and considering how to promote cooperative behavior among its members is far more fruitful. For this purpose, we could summarize the following recommendations to help this strategic alliance achieve its goals:

- Prioritize collaboration on matters that commit to the alliance's vision and drive value for all stakeholders.
- Ensure that the alliance is an emotional and cultural experience where members collaborate and trust each other.
- Design the strategy and governance as much for effectiveness as for adaptability to the African context.
- Invest time to define a roadmap, performance metrics and research-oriented tools for effectiveness assessment.

REFERENCES

Acquaah, M., & Eshun, J.P. (2010). A longitudinal analysis of the moderated effects of networking relationships on organizational performance in a sub-Saharan African economy. *Human Relations, 63,* 667–700. https:// doi .org/ 10 .1177/ 0018726709342928

Acs, Z.J. (2010). High-impact entrepreneurship. In Z.J. Acs & D.B. Audretsch (Eds.), *Handbook of entrepreneurship research: An interdisciplinary survey and introduction* (pp. 165–182). Springer.

African Development Bank Group. (2016). African Natural Resources Center catalyzing growth and development through effective natural resources management.

Argiolas, A., Rawhouser, H., & Sydow, A., (2023). Social entrepreneurs concerned about impact drift. Evidence from contexts of persistent and pervasive need. *Journal of Business Venturing, 39*(1), 106342.

Battilana, J., Leca, B., & Boxenbaum, E. (2009). How actors change institutions: Towards a theory of institutional entrepreneurship. *The Academy of Management Annals*, *3*(1), 65–107.

Battilana, J., & Dorado, S., (2010). Building sustainable hybrid organizations: The case of commercial microfinance organizations. *Academy of Management Journal*, *53*, 1419–1440.

Bloom, D.E., Canning, D., & Chan, K. (2006). *Higher education and economic development in Africa* (Vol. 102). World Bank.

Bruton, G.D., Ketchen Jr, D.J., & Ireland, R.D. (2013). Entrepreneurship as a solution to poverty. *Journal of Business Venturing*, *28*(6), 683–689.

Buckler, C., & Creech, H. (2014). *Shaping the future we want: UN Decade of Education for Sustainable Development*; final report. UNESCO.

Budowle, R., Krszjzaniek, E., & Taylor, C. (2021). Students as change agents for community–university sustainability transition partnerships. *Sustainability*, *13*(11), 6036.

Easterly, W. (2006). The white man's burden. *The Lancet*, *367*(9528), 2060.

Franco, I., Saito, O., Vaughter, P., Whereat, J., Kanie, N., & Takemoto, K. (2019). Higher education for sustainable development: Actioning the global goals in policy, curriculum and practice. *Sustainability Science*, *14*, 1621–1642. https://doi.org/10.1007/s11625-018-0628-4

Gunasekara, C. (2004). Universities and communities: A case study of change in the management of a university. *Prometheus*, *22*(2), 201–211.

GUNi, IAU, & AAU. (2011). The promotion of sustainable development by higher education institutions in Sub-Saharan Africa: A survey report.

Johnson, A.T., Hirt, J.B., & Hoba, P. (2011). Higher education, policy networks, and policy entrepreneurship in Africa: The case of the association of African universities. *High Education Policy*, *24*, 85–102. https://doi.org/10.1057/hep.2010.26

Khanna, T., & Palepu, K. (1997). Why focused strategies? *Harvard Business Review*, *75*(4), 41–51.

Koehn, P.H., & Uitto, J.I. (2017). *Universities and the sustainable development future: evaluating higher-education contributions to the 2030 Agenda*. Taylor & Francis.

Liska, G. (1962). *Nations in alliance: The limits of interdependence*. Johns Hopkins Press.

Mars, M., & Metcalfe, A. (2009). Contemporary issues in the entrepreneurial academy. *ASHE Higher Education Report*, *34*(5), 37–61.

McDade, B.E., & Spring, A. (2005). The 'new generation of African entrepreneurs': Networking to change the climate for business and private sector-led development. *Entrepreneurship & Regional Development*, *17*(1), 17–42.

Miles, M.B., & Huberman, A.M. (1994). *Qualitative data analysis: An expanded sourcebook*. Sage.

Moyo, D. (2008). *Dead aid: Destroying the biggest global myth of our time*. Allen Lane.

Nicholls, A. (2018). A general theory of social impact accounting: Materiality, uncertainty and empowerment. *Journal of Social Entrepreneurship*, *9*(2), 132–153.

Okolie, A. (2003). 'Producing knowledge for sustainable development in Africa: Implications for higher education'. *Higher Education*, *46*(2), 235–260.

Peterson, H.T. (2009). Engaged scholarship: Reflections and research on the pedagogy of social change. *Teaching in Higher Education*, *14*(5), 541–552.

Peterson, I., & Kruss, G. (2021). Universities as change agents in resource-poor local settings: An empirically grounded typology of engagement models. *Technological Forecasting & Social Change, 167*, 120693.

Puplampu, K. (2006). Critical perspectives on higher education and globalization in Africa. In A. Abdi, K. Puplampu & G. Sefa Dei (Eds.), *African education and globalization: Critical perspectives* (pp. 31–52). Lexington.

Purvis, B., Mao, Y., & Robinson, D. (2019). Three pillars of sustainability: In search of conceptual origins. *Sustainability Science, 14*, 681–695.

Rivera-Santos, M., Holt, D., Littlewood, D., & Kolk, A. (2015). Social entrepreneurship in sub-Saharan Africa. *Academy of Management Perspectives, 29*(1), 72–91.

Slade Shantz, A., Kistruck, G., & Zietsma, C. (2018). The opportunity not taken: The occupational identity of entrepreneurs in contexts of poverty. *Journal of Business Venturing, 33*, 416–437.

Ulmer, N. & Wydra, K. (2020). Sustainability in African higher education institutions (HEIs): Shifting the focus from researching the gaps to existing activities. *International Journal of Sustainability in Higher Education, 21*(1), 18–33. https://doi.org/10.1108/IJSHE-03-2019-0106

United Nations (UN) Global Compact. (2014). The role of business and finance in supporting the Post-2015 Agenda. https://www.unglobalcompact.org/docs/news

Wakkee, I., Sijde, P., Vaupell, C., & Ghuman, K. (2019) The university's role in sustainable development: Activating entrepreneurial scholars as agents of change. *Technological Forecasting and Social Change.* https://doi.org/10.1016/j.techfore.2018.10.013

Wangai, P.W., Burkhard, B., & Müller, F. (2016). A review of studies on ecosystem services in Africa. *International Journal of Sustainable Built Environment, 5*(2), 225–245.

World Bank. (2014). Higher education for development. An evaluation of the World Bank Group's support. https:// documents1 .worldbank .org/ curated/ en/ 729101493052924041/pdf/Higher-education-for-development-an-evaluation-of-the -World-Bank-Group-s-support.pdf

9. Schools of management making an impact: operationalization mechanisms and methods for contributing to organizational change

Bart van Hoof and Sjors Witjes

1. INTRODUCTION

Schools of management play a special role in the development of solutions to societal challenges (GBSN, 2013), preparing future decision-makers and generating knowledge to guide decision-making in organizations and institutions (Snelson-Powell et al., 2016) in the face of pressing societal challenges, such as climate change, biodiversity loss, and resource scarcity. Schools of management have been criticized for their failure to address complex societal problems (Hoffman, 2016; Blanchard et al., 2009), focusing instead on isolated disciplinary knowledge delivery (Slater & Dixon-Fowler, 2010) for limited practical learning in teaching and research (Gröschl & Gabaldon, 2018; Jackson et al., 2021; Khurana & Spender, 2012). This has created a reductionist approach to problem-solving in these institutions (Findler, 2021; Gröschl & Gabaldon, 2018), which could result in the ineffective or counter-productive management of organizations in the future (Datar et al., 2010; Sorge & van Witteloostuijn, 2004).

External stakeholders have called upon schools of management to contribute to solutions. In 2007, the United Nations (UN) Global Compact launched the Principles for Responsible Management Education (UN PRME), requiring schools of management to make tangible contributions to the Sustainable Development Goals and train engaged managers who take part in public and political discourses (Gröschl & Gabaldon, 2018; Hoffman, 2016). In addition, accreditation schemes from renowned international associations, such as the Association to Advance Collegiate Schools of Business (AACSB), European Quality Improvement System (European schools assessment program EQUIS), and Association of Master of Business Administration (AMBA), require the scientific output of schools of management to be published in high-impact academic journals, as well as to foster high-quality, locally relevant management education and to influence the development of local business communities and public institutions (Miles et al., 2010; Urgel, 2007).

Responsible management learning (RML) research has elucidated how schools of management have responded to the growing demand for societal impact (Gullen, 2020; Laasch et al., 2020). So far, most of the studies have focused on professional responsible management education and emphasize the role of the individual manager. Laasch et al. (2020) argued that ethical principles of sustainability and responsibility in organizational practice are missing and identified platforms for responsible management education (such as UN PRME and other certification schemes) as fundamental mechanisms for academic reform. Recent debates on RML call for schools of management impacting non-educational organizations and businesses using organizational change literature and longitudinal research to determine the impact of responsibly oriented management (Schaltegger et al., 2020; Schaltegger et al., 2013; Cullen, 2019; Laasch et al., 2020).

The research presented in this chapter aims to enhance the understanding of operationalization principles for schools of management striving to actively contribute to organizational change. Based on a transdisciplinary approach to RML, section 2 presents a framework of operationalization mechanisms and methods underpinning the analysis of the impact of responsible-oriented management research and education. Section 3 explains and supports the longitudinal case of the network of sustainable companies (RedES; according to its abbreviation in Spanish), developed by the School of Management of the Universidad de los Andes (UASM; according to its abbreviation in Spanish) in Bogotá, Colombia. Moreover, section 3 presents the case study data based on the framework presented in section 2. Section 4 discusses the lessons learned from the RedES case analysis, and proposes operationalization mechanisms and methods for schools of management impacting organizational change. The conclusions can be found in section 5.

2.   TRANSDISCIPLINARITY FOR RML

The RML literature comprises research into the ways in which management educators can promote progressive environmental, social, and cultural values among students, faculty colleagues, and stakeholders (Cullen, 2019). This research was bolstered by the 2007 initiation of the PRME component of the UN Global Compact. The RML literature critically reflects on management education in encouraging sustainable development in general and the business–society interface in particular (Moratis & Melissen, 2022).

With RML still a new field of knowledge, Cullen (2019) identifies four different ways in which schools of management can have an impact by collaborating with organizations in practice: (i) understanding the engaged scholar as a provider of diverse pedagogical approaches and RML content (see also Van de Ven, 2007); (ii) understanding the individual manager and their capacity for responsibility (see also e.g., Schaltegger, et al., 2020); (iii) understanding of institutional guidelines for organizing responsible management education (see also UN PRME); and (iv) understanding how organizations advance responsible performance (see also Laasch et al., 2020).

Figure 9.1 presents these four impact categories in two complementary dimensions: individual (students) and organizational, and supply (faculty and universities) and demand (organizations and practitioners).

Figure 9.1   Categories of RML Literature

Based on their review of the RML literature, Cullen (2019) and Laasch et al. (2020) highlighted the need for research into the ways in which schools of management can actively contribute to organizational change. This focus entails the exploration of the stories and theories of RML and learners in the context of non-academic organizations and businesses (Schaltegger et al., 2020). Such research practices are also ideally intersectoral when collaborating with managers to tackle the challenges of RML, indicating the research is deeply immersed at the managerial level, with managers co-shaping it (Laasch et al., 2020).

Transdisciplinarity (TD) is proposed as an academic approach by which schools of management can actively contribute to organizational change beyond traditional education (i.e., bachelors and masters degrees) and research (Schaltegger et al., 2020; Cunliffe & Pavlovich, 2021). The application of a TD approach in RML research is particularly promising as it creates a richer, more realistic analysis of the existing challenges and support for transformative change toward responsible management (Beckman & Schaltegger, 2020; Laasch et al., 2020). The TD approach enables the continuous translation between academic and business sectors (Ren & Bartunek, 2020), and a shared problematization of managerial and academic sector practices (Stutz & Schrempf-Stirling, 2020).

With TD understood as "a community-based, interactive, and participatory research approach" (Lang et al., 2012; Sellberg et al., 2021), these approaches involve knowledge development as a social, interactive process that comprises embodied, experienced, and emotional aspects used to make sense of rational information (Servaes et al., 1996). TD approaches integrate two pathways for addressing societal challenges (Lang et al., 2012): the path of societal problem-solving and the path of scientific knowledge production. TD has advantages over multidisciplinarity because TD is based on the collaboration between disciplines, and over interdisciplinarity because TD entails the integration of knowledge from different disciplinary backgrounds into one knowledge base which is reflected upon while developing societal interventions.

While TD is, on the one hand, a scholarly approach addressing the societal impact of academic institutions (Laasch, 2020; Miles et al., 2010), from a research perspective, TD is grounded in a pluralist epistemology (Söderbaum, 2009; Vildåsen et al., 2017). In addition, taking a TD approach stresses the role of arbitrage in knowledge creation (Hessels & van Lente, 2008) while promoting the co-production of knowledge between academics and non-academics (Pohl et al., 2010). In so doing, TD enables schools of management to actively contribute to solving organizational change problems while still influencing knowledge development and capacity building (Lang et al., 2012). Schools of management applying a TD approach while aiming for a contribution to organizational change will achieve the following academic outcomes (Miles et al., 2010):

(i)   knowledge, measured in publications and other media;
(ii)   innovation, measured in terms of tangible contributions to complex societal problems;
(iii) capacity, measured in the quality and outreach of training programs.

In short, schools of management aiming to impact society through organizational change are expected to focus on the tangible triple-pronged impacts of knowledge development in collaborations between academics and non-academics, and the capacity building of current and future managers based on active participation in innovations in the organizational change processes. These academic outcome categories align with solution-driven TD, as identified by Vermeulen and Witjes (2021). TD reflects a combination of diverse methods familiar to the practices of schools of management, such as abductive logic for the generation of knowledge providing legitimacy, consultancy for stimulating resource supply for innovation, and experience-based learning for capacity building.

2.1   Abductive Logic

Abductive logic, as a scientific approach to the generation of knowledge, legitimizes the interactions of schools of management from a societal-responsibility perspective (as emphasized by Snelson-Powell et al., 2016). Abductive logic draws on matching empirical data with existing literature by seeking knowledge-based explanations for intuitive ideas (Mantere & Ketokivi, 2013). Emerging results are data-driven and consistent with the existing literature as a result of iterations between data and theory (Dalhmann & Grosvold, 2017), and therefore start from prior knowledge (Strauss, 1987).

Abductive logic is the logic of hunches – a mechanism of making connections between topics based on intuitive reasoning despite the fallible insights of the researcher. This intuition is nurtured by practical experience (Gummesson, 2003; Kovács et al., 2005), but can also derive from theoretical prior knowledge (Strauss, 1987). Abductive logic research approaches comprise simultaneous data collection and theory building, implying a learning loop (i.e., the collaboration between practice and theory). Within TD, abductive logic is identified to operationalize theory building on societal-change processes and enables active contribution. The final result of abductive logic is the development of a framework that combines related theories (Olsson & Olander Roese, 2005). Abductive logic, as part of TD, is highly suitable for use in complex social contexts and encourages researchers to connect practical experience to theory, rather than relying on the formal laws of deductive and inductive logic (Reichertz, 2009).

2.2   Consultancy

Consultancy is a professional service that supports decision-making in organizations by providing an external perspective; consultants furnish information, specialized skills, and strategic tools that drive innovation and change in organizations, thus creating value (Kubr, 2002). Ordinarily, a professional consultant directs the process in a single organization, but the method can be applied with groups of organizations in workshops (Gomez et al., 2018). Management consulting plays a vital role in generating organizational change by disseminating innovations and best practices (Casartelli, 2010), and enables schools of management to participate in the process of decision-making in organizations. As such, the consultancy practice part of TD involves a collaborative process aimed at understanding the situation at hand; moreover, it supports the application of knowledge created in a process of innovation, developing interventions to solve problems (Vermeulen & Witjes, 2021).

2.3   Experience-Based Learning

Experience-based learning involves apprenticeships with the phenomenon being studied (for instance, an organizational challenge) rather than merely thinking about the problem (Keeton & Tate, 1978). A key element of experience-based learning is that learners analyze their experience by reflecting, evaluating, and reconstructing the experience (sometimes individually, sometimes collectively, sometimes both), in order to draw meaning from it in the light of prior experience. This review of their experience may lead to further action (Andresen & Boud, 2000).

Experience-based learning is a common capacity-building method applied in schools of management, consultancy practices, training students, simulations, and case-based methods (Ramos et al., 2015). According to Kolb and Kolb (2009), experience-based learning helps students become aware of their transformation and learning through an iterative process of: (a) planning an active experiment, (b) having concrete experience, (c) reflecting on the experience, and (d) concluding from the experiment. The educator designs the start of the learning process by planning an active experiment, through which the learner gains concrete experience through observation and reflection. By reflecting on their experience, the learners make sense of what happens and see the consequences of their actions. This can aid management consultancy as a high-impact knowledge-generating capacity-building mechanism (Raffo et al., 2002) through deep-learning based on experience.

2.4   Framework for Operationalizing TD in Schools of Management

Figure 9.2 presents the framework combining the methods of experience-based learning, abductive logic, and consultancy to operationalize TD approaches in schools of management.

The framework presents mutually reinforcing mechanisms through synergies among the methods, which generate complementary outcomes. The consultancy method generates innovation and supplies financial and information resources for research activities based on abductive mechanisms, resulting in knowledge generation. Abductive logic for knowledge generation, as an outcome, contributes to legitimacy and credibility, and is therefore an added value for the consultancy method. Experience-based learning is a method using knowledge for its pedagogical process for upscaling organizational change through capacity-building mechanisms. Together the mutual reinforcement of these mechanisms represents the operationalization framework for schools of management, with triple-pronged outcomes coming from the interplay between the methods.

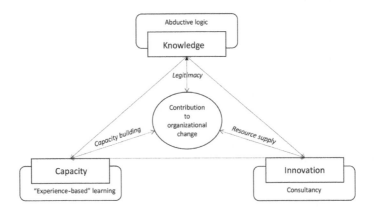

Figure 9.2   The framework for operationalization of TD for schools of management contributing to societal challenges

3.   METHOD

Case study research is a valid method for understanding the long-term impact of the responsible-oriented management and business research and education underpinning theory building (Eisenhardt & Graebner, 2007; McCutcheon & Meredith, 1993). The outcomes of the case study in the present research serve as a self-reinforcing approach to analyze its societal impacts in terms of knowledge development, engaged scholarship, and innovation, as well as enhancing the understanding of operationalization principles for schools of management striving to actively contribute to societal challenges. The framework, developed based on the literature review in section 2, was tested through its application in the longitudinal case. Whereas the output of this research cannot be considered generally applicable, its intention is to provide a theoretical perspective for the examination of the contributions of schools of management to organizational change (as emphasized by Yin, 2009).

The documentation of the case was based on academic and non-academic publications about RedES, including doctoral theses, peer-reviewed publications, and two books documenting RedES experiences. While documenting the case study data, theoretical sampling allowed the collection of new data based on the continuous application of theoretical knowledge to the case study data (Chun Tie et al., 2019). One of the authors of this chapter was involved in both the research and practical application of the initiative since it began, resulting in additional insights included in the case description and analysis. As an experienced action researcher, the other author of this chapter assured a critical research view and detailed discussions and analysis (Eisenhardt & Graebner, 2007).

3.1   The RedES Case

RedES emerged as an academic initiative developed by full-time faculty staff of the School of Management of UASM in Bogotá, Colombia, which was designed to craft a cost-effective, scalable approach for improving the environmental performance of small- and medium-sized enterprises (SMEs) in Mexico and Colombia. Enhancing the performance of these firms represents a major societal challenge, as most of them are unaware of their environmental impact, or think that reducing this impact would require investments beyond what they can afford. Also, SMEs in the emerging market context seem to be invisible to the environmental authorities who would enforce the legal require- ments for environmental regulation (Blackman, 2010). Moreover, reviews of dissemination programs for cleaner production (CP) initiatives based on technical assistance consultancy services reveal modest outcomes: Sakr and Abo Sena (2017) found implementation rates of 53% for CP uptake in Egypt, Dieleman (2007) found that less than 40% of firms receiving CP technical assistance improved their performance, while Stone (2006a) reported low success rates in terms of organization change in New Zealand.

The initial idea of the RedES model builds on the experience of a newly appointed faculty member. First, the experience of acting as a consultant pro- viding technical assistance in CP to SMEs of diverse industries in Colombia gives the faculty member insights into the organizational dynamics related to decision-making on the implementation of CP. Second, experience gained as a part-time instructor at the School of Engineering of the Universidad de los Andes gave initial insights into the uptake of CP by students. Moreover, the need for academic inquiry motivated the idea to search for external finances to support data gathering.

The RedES model was designed to attract a variety of stakeholders by addressing the diverse interests of environmental authorities, large firms, and SMEs, and potential multiplication centers interested in the described societal problem. To ameliorate the environmental performance of SMEs, CP was selected as the main focus for improving resource efficiency (Luken et al., 2016). The RedES model followed a sustainable supply model as the driving force for the dissemination of CP, as proposed by Seuring and Müller (2008). For support, the environmental authority, together with UASM as program manager, invited anchor companies to urge their SME suppliers to partici- pate in CP dissemination. UASM proposed training experienced consultants and academics to be representatives of the RedES model, working in their service centers to strengthen their outreach to business practices, generate remuneration for services, and enhance their academic reputation in business development.

In Mexico, an agency of the North American Free Trade Association (NAFTA) called the Commission for Environmental Cooperation launched RedES in 2005 as the Environmental Leadership for Competitiveness Program (PLAC) in the Federal District and the state of Queretaro. In 2009, the Secretary of Environment and Natural Resources (SEMARNAT) and the Federal Attorney for Environment (PROFEPA) expanded the program nationally, enlisting over 6,000 companies by 2015, assisted by 25 service centers (universities and consultancy firms) in 23 states (Van Hoof et al., 2018).

In Colombia, the regional environmental authority of Cundinamarca (CAR) initiated RedES in 2013, inviting four anchor companies and 40 supply firms to pioneer the process of improving the environmental performance of their businesses. Over the following years, the diverse group of actors expanded the RedES community to include 35 anchor companies, 529 suppliers, and five universities as service centers (Van Hoof et al., 2018).

Figure 9.3 shows the operational structure of the RedES model, including the roles of various stakeholders.

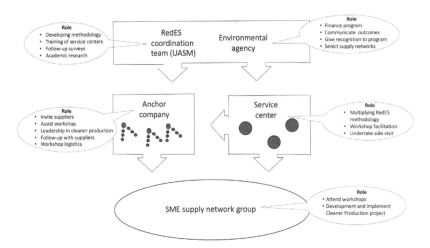

Figure 9.3   *RedES operating structure indicating the roles of various stakeholders*

The RedES model offered consultancy services, including capacity building and technical assistance, to improve the performance of firms. Both the environmental authority and the firms were willing to pay for the service, which included a CP assessment. The CP assessment resulted in the presentation of innovative initiatives which aimed to provide significant economic, environmental, and social benefits. The overall expenses of the operational costs of RedES in Colombia totaled around USD 3.5 million during the period of its operation between September 2013 and December 2019, which was financed by the environmental authority. In Mexico, diverse public funds financed the operation of RedES, and costs and payments were compared in terms of the average per participating firm. As of December 2019, the economic benefits of the RedES model in Colombia are estimated at USD 12 million, with an average payback period of 14 months. The environmental benefits include 1,500,000 m^3 in water savings, 13,000,000 kWh in energy, and 29,000 tons of waste reduction, with an estimated 67,000-ton annual reduction of greenhouse gases (Van Hoof & Duque, 2020; Van Hoof et al., 2018).

Within the RedES model, capacity building occurred in an experience-based learning setting, where academic consultants guided SME managers and staff to apply CP tools while designing their respective projects. To scale RedES, a "train-the-trainer" method was deployed as part of the systemic model. Service centers with SME consultancy experience were invited to join RedES as multipliers of the model. Selected consultants were first trained in the RedES intervention cycle, comprised of ten three-hour workshops teaching participants about CP, tools, and the project design procedure. Once trainees were certified as facilitators, they visited 10–15 supply chain firms to assist with project adjustments and implementation.

Besides the training of managers of the firms participating in RedES, teaching materials and case studies were applied in various formal educational programs in UASM and the affiliated universities: six Mexican universities and five Colombian universities are affiliated with RedES. Since 2012, the RedES experience has led to a course on sustainable supply in an executive education program, and to modules in courses of both undergraduate and MBA programs. Over the years, as part of RedES, approximately 17,000 students have been trained in diverse programs at the affiliated universities in Colombia and Mexico. Formal education courses motivated graduate and undergraduate students to join RedES as teaching assistants, developers of research projects, and/or interns as part of the operational team.

From its start, RedES was conceived as a problem-based research opportunity to study the topic of environmental management by SMEs. Research questions centered on the study of differential performances in adopting environmental management practices. Subsequent topics of study included organizational learning, collaboration, governance structures, sustainable supply systems, social and environmental impacts, and industrial ecology – all subfields of management research that enhance the understanding of organizational dynamics. Moreover, the lack of knowledge on SMEs in emerging markets highlights the importance of our research on the RedES case (Blackman, 2010; Van Hoof & Lyon, 2013).

The RedES databases were developed to hold quantitative and qualitative data, including the multi-level and longitudinal technical and organizational characteristics of the participating SMEs as suppliers, anchor firms, cooperating universities, and environmental authorities in Mexico and Colombia. Different inquiries and research protocols were developed over the years to fill the databases. Additionally, the RedES research team was able to improve data collection and database maintenance throughout the research. The research website (www .redescar .org) provided a knowledge platform about the program outline and results. A database containing a search engine provides public access to information about all the CP projects designed by the participating companies.

Since 2007, research based on the RedES project has yielded significant academic knowledge, resulting in nine articles in peer-reviewed academic journals, three book chapters, four books for practitioners, and numerous professional publications (Park et al., 2018; Van Hoof et al., 2018; Van Hoof et al., 2016; Van Hoof & Medina, 2022; Van Hoof & Duque, 2020; Van Hoof, 2013; Van Hoof et al., 2023; Van Hoof & Thiell, 2014a, 2014b; Van Hoof, 2014; Van Hoof & Lyon, 2013). The research capacity was generated by students, professionals, and faculty to advance our understanding of the dynamics occurring in RedES. Two facilitators advanced doctoral studies using RedES as their research topic, five master theses were developed by professionals of the RedES team, and over 30 undergraduate students who learned about the RedES case in undergraduate courses on environmental management ended up using it as their study case in their final-year research project. Annual seminars involved academics, representatives of public institutions, anchor firms, suppliers, and business associations, who discussed the RedES methodology and outcomes. Over 30 events were organized in both Mexico and Colombia, serving about 10,000 participants in total.

RedES operational expenses included payments to service centers (mostly universities) to facilitate the capacity-building cycle of the workshops on CP project formulation, but also to provide technical assistance, including site visits of consultants to firms, costs for program coordination and knowledge management, and the organization of annual events. UASM, as a founding organization, also received payments for material development and methodological design.

The impact of RedES on organizational change was evaluated in several studies. A quantitative analysis covering 189 companies (12 different leading companies plus 177 SME suppliers) participating in the RedES program in Mexico revealed a CP project adoption rate of 70% (Van Hoof, 2014). The same evaluation shows how some participating firms (23%) confirmed their design of additional CP projects following their RedES participation. Both indicators illustrate organizational change toward the improvement of environmental performance. In the Colombian application of the RedES model, 56% of a group of 490 companies implemented CP projects, and 40% developed additional projects (Van Hoof et al., 2023).

4. OPERATIONALIZATION MECHANISMS AND METHODS FOR SOCIETAL IMPACT BY SCHOOLS OF MANAGEMENT

The RedES case stresses problem-solving and the implementation of support for environmental management practices in SMEs. The RedES case uses incremental improvements at the company scale, coming from multi-actor collaboration, demonstrating that sharing experiences within a broader societal network of diverse stakeholders over time can support schools of management to contribute to the transformation of governance and transition management at regional and national levels (as underlined by Vermeulen & Witjes, 2021). Applying the TD approach to RedES highlights innovation, capacity, and knowledge as societal contributions of schools of management while contributing to organizational change.

Following Schaltegger and colleagues (2020), RedES' contribution to innovation moves beyond the role of the individual manager and includes non-educational organizations and businesses. Firms that were part of the supply networks in RedES improved their environmental and competitive performance simultaneously (Battat et al., 1996) through the formulation and implementation of CP projects. This coincides with the diversity of stakeholders within the setting of a TD community necessary to generate mutually reinforcing innovations around a shared vision (Lang et al., 2012; Furr & Shipilov, 2018). CP projects involve managerial decision-making on innovations such as best practices to adjust operational procedures, technological innovations, and/or new business model development (Van Hoof & Lyon, 2013; Stone, 2006b). For environmental agencies such as CAR in Colombia, and CEC, SEMARNAT, and Profepa in Mexico, innovation consists of developing public policy mechanisms, such as the voluntary improvement company behaviors, which is complementary to reinforcement mechanisms such as regulation (Blackman, 2010; Lyon & Maxwell, 2008).

Another societal contribution of RedES includes capacity building, which is aligned with the principles of RML when taking a TD approach. RedES highlights the ability of schools of management in formal institutionalized education to support the capacity for organizational change (Laasch et al., 2020), particularly in combination with the informal process of capacity building and empowerment of practitioners, as emphasized by TD (Cullen, 2019).

RedES capacity building includes the training of managers of companies to improve the environmental performance of the productive process (Van Hoof, 2014), as well as the collaboration capacity among firms to connect to networks (Van Hoof & Thiell, 2014b). Environmental agencies participating in RedES acquired explicit knowledge of CP concepts and tools, and additional tacit experience in managing voluntary environmental policy instruments, confirming similar outcomes by Lyon and Maxwell (2008). The train-the-trainer method, as part of RedES, motivated the faculty of universities, participating as service centers, to multiply capacity building in both executive-education programs and in undergraduate and graduate courses.

RedES' focus on building capacity creates competencies and explicit knowledge of management decision-making, similar to the creation of competences and explicit knowledge found by Lam (2000). The RedES program included capacity building for individuals from different educational contexts: in the participating companies, universities, and environmental authorities. This resonates with schools of management aiming to equip future managers with knowledge of societal issues and intervention competencies through applied cases (Datar et al., 2010), and contributes to their goal of educating individuals at different starting levels and from different backgrounds.

An additional contribution of RedES consists of diverse types of knowledge generation, as emphasized in the definition of TD (Lang et al., 2012; Sellberg et al., 2021). Within RedES, the integration of knowledge from different academic and non-academic actors results in co-production of knowledge and solutions for complex societal problems, such as the improvement of the environmental performance of SMEs. Explicit knowledge produced by the academic partners of RedES includes formal research, such as academic articles, books, and other knowledge content, as well as illustrations of outcomes that enable hypothetic-deductive theory testing (Eastwood et al., 2016). This explicit academic peer-reviewed knowledge production underpins the reputation and legitimacy of the RedES model (Kampf et al., 2023), contributes to management literature, and aligns with the debate on the contribution of academic research from schools of management, as demanded by international accreditation schemes such as AACSB, EQUIS, and AMBA (Miles et al., 2010; Urgel, 2007). The tacit knowledge contribution (Lam, 2000) of RedES consists of the development of trust (Meqdadi et al., 2017) among supply networks, environmental agencies, and universities that are part of the RedES as a TD community. Trust relations among stakeholders result from a shared vision and concrete interactions as key elements of communities of practice (Muller, 2006).

Academic research on the RedES model supports reinforcing mechanisms enabling the triple-pronged outcomes of schools of management applying a TD approach, while also aiming for an active contribution to organizational change. First, knowledge production as an outcome of academic research contributes to legitimatizing RedES' innovation resulting from the consultancy methods (as highlighted by Sorge & van Witteloostuijn, 2004). Second, the RedES intervention method was found to provide a framework to assess the consultancy methods applied. Third, knowledge production outcomes of the RedES model generated inputs to improve educational materials (e.g., study books and simulation games) for capacity building among practitioners, as well as for graduate and undergraduate students in schools of management. Planning the research process entails an abductive research strategy with a mid- and long-term timespan (5–15 years), which is required for database development and academic writing and involves a variety of research projects, such as graduation projects, master theses, and doctoral dissertations.

Overall, the RedES case presents empirical evidence for the operationalization of TD as an approach for enabling schools of management to contribute to organizational change. The case emphasizes operation principles for the planning, alignment, and multiple reinforcement of knowledge production, consultancy, and capacity-building methods. Well-balanced TD, as shown by RedES, creates systemic structures among communities of organizations, resulting in virtuous cycles that accumulate outcomes on diverse levels and for a variety of academic and non-academic stakeholders. The systemic reinforcing mechanisms of RedES include empowerment and collaboration over a longer period of time within a broader societal network (the importance of which was also highlighted as important by Escobar, 2018; Goodman et al., 2017), supporting societal innovation (Midgley & Reynolds, 2004), and therefore show that a TD approach can enable a school of management to contribute to societal change by means of the triple-pronged impacts of education, research, and interventions as called for by RML.

As part of the operationalization framework for schools of management to enhance their societal impact by contributing to organizational change (see Figure 9.2), the RedES case analysis above leads to the following:

- The **consultancy method** multiplies value for academic and non-academic stakeholders in terms of financial resources to support the operation of TD processes, as well as data resources for academic research to generate explicit knowledge to impact organizational change with innovative concepts and tools.
- **Experience-based learning** enhances the organizational capacity for change through the dissemination of new information, empowering managers to make decisions in terms of planning, action-taking, evaluating, and revising, in order to best effect the desired organizational change.

- **Abductive reasoning** connects empirical evidence and intuition with the production of new knowledge to advance the literature, legitimizing consultancy models and learning methods for scaling organizational change.

5.   CONCLUSIONS

This chapter presents research to enhance the understanding of operationalization principles for schools of management striving to make an active contribution to societal challenges. By taking a TD approach to RML, a framework of operationalization mechanisms and methods was presented and used to explain the impact of the longitudinal case of RedES. The case data illustrate a self-reinforcing approach to realize triple-pronged impacts on knowledge development, engaged scholarship, and innovation in society. The research outcomes invite schools of management to reposition their academic output in order to actively contribute to organizational change. The approach aligns with the requirements of the main accreditation schemes of academic quality in management.

This research on the RedES case answers "what" and "how" questions about the strategy and coordination of resources required for advancing the triple-pronged impact of schools of management. To address the "what" question, this research identifies complex, structural, and societal challenges as opportunities to position innovation, capacity, and knowledge, and highlights this process as an important objective of schools of management. The "how" questions are addressed by the alignment of methods such as abductive logic, consultancy, and experience-based learning. Reinforcing mechanisms for making a societal impact include capacity building, resource supply, and legitimacy. The process of advancing the triple-pronged impact of schools of management entails: (i) identifying structural societal challenges, including mid- and long-term timespans of planning (5–15 years); (ii) experience-based learning in a triple-helix setting among public, private, and academic organizations; and (iii) the empowerment and organization of a growing community of practice.

The contribution of this research is the clarification of the operationalization of the process schools of management must undertake if they want to make positive societal impacts by contributing to organizational change. This study emphasizes a systemic approach for a TD approach on RML that offers tangible ways to counteract societal challenges, resulting in the framework presented in Figure 9.2. The analysis of the RedES model using this framework elucidates how to integrate formal, informal, and non-formal education and training processes using TD approaches to enable schools of management to actively contribute to organizational change. Moreover, it offers longitudinal empirical evidence as a reference for operational principles, as well as methods for reinforcing the triple-pronged outcomes. This puts schools of management and management approaches at the heart of societal development.

Despite the longitudinal development and geographic impact (i.e., Mexico and Colombia) of the RedES case and the thorough reflection on the wider debates in literature, this research is limited due to the empirical data coming from a single-case analysis. More empirical research is recommended to gain insights into what schools of management do and should do to enhance their impact on society. Future research should address the role of the diversity of actors, the capacities needed to advance TD within multi-actor communities, and the dynamic process of advancing learning in these communities using a TD approach. Moreover, developments in the field of RML in combination with engaged scholarship seem to align with the proposed framework in this chapter. Consequently, we recommend merging the contributions of TD with the engaged scholarship literature on RML.

BIBLIOGRAPHY

Andresen, L., & Boud, D. (2000). Experience-based learning: Contemporary issues. In G. Foley (Ed.), *Understanding adult education and training* (2nd ed., pp. 225–239). Allen & Unwin.

Aram, J.D., & Salipante, P.F.J (2003). Bridging scholarship in management: Epistemological reflections. *British Journal of Management, 14*(3), 189–205. https://doi.org/10.1111/1467-8551.00374

Arthur, L. (2005). *Reflections on the form and content of participatory action research and implications for social innovation research* (D.M. Frank Moulaert, A. Mehmood & A. Hamdouch, Eds.). Edward Elgar Publishing Limited.

Baas, L. (2007). To make zero emissions technologies and strategies become a reality, the lessons learned of cleaner production dissemination have to be known. *Journal of Cleaner production, 15*(13-14), 1205–1216.

Balsiger, J. (2015). Transdisciplinarity in the class room? Simulating the co-production of sustainability knowledge. *Futures, 65*, 185–194. https://doi.org/10.1016/j.futures.2014.08.005

Battat, J. Y., Frank, I., & Shen, X. (1996). Suppliers to multinationals: Linkage programs to strenghten local companies in developing countries (Vol. 6). World Bank Publications.

Beckmann, M., Schaltegger, S., & Landrum, N.E. (2020). Sustainability management from a responsible management perspective. In *Research handbook of responsible management* (pp. 122–137). Edward Elgar Publishing.

Benn, S., Edwards, M., & Angus-Leppan, T. (2013). Organizational learning and the sustainability community of practice. *Organization & Environment, 26*(2), 184–202.

Berg, B.L., Lune, H., & Lune, H. (2004). *Qualitative research methods for the social sciences* (Vol. 5). Pearson.

Blackman, A. (2010). *Small firms and the environment in developing countries: Collective impacts, collective action.* Routledge.

Blanchard, L.W., Belliard, J.C., Krichbaum, K., Waters, E., & Seifer, S.D. (2009). Models for faculty development: What does it take to be a community-engaged scholar? *Metropolitan Universities, 20*(2), 47–65.

Boons, F. (2009). *Creating ecological value: An evolutionary approach to business strategies and the natural environment*. Edward Elgar Publishing.

Bradbury-Huang, H. (2010). What is good action research? *Action Research, 8*(1), 93–109. https://doi.org/10.1177/1476750310362435

Brown, J.S., & Duguid, P. (1991). Organizational Learning and Communities-of-Practice: Toward a Unified View of Working, Learning, and Innovation. *Organization Science, 2*(1), 40–57. https://doi.org/10.1287/orsc.2.1.40

Carayannis, E.G., Campbell, D.F.J., & Rehman, S.S. (2016). Mode 3 knowledge production: systems and systems theory, clusters and networks. *Journal of Innovation and Entrepreneurship, 5*(1). https://doi.org/10.1186/s13731-016-0045-9

Casartelli, G.E. (2010). Desarrollo de la Industria Consultora de México: Direcciones Estratégicas, Agenda de Acciones y Política. *Inter-American Development Bank,* 1–65.

Cassell, C., & Lee, B. (2012). Driving, Steering, Leading, and Defending. *The Journal of Applied Behavioral Science, 48*(2), 248–271. https://doi.org/10.1177/0021886312438861

Chun Tie, Y., Birks, M., & Francis, K. (2019). Grounded theory research: A design framework for novice researchers. *SAGE Open Medicine, 7*, 2050312118822927.

Cope, J., & Watts, G. (2000). Learning by doing–an exploration of experience, critical incidents and reflection in entrepreneurial learning. *International Journal of Entrepreneurial Behavior & Research, 6*(3), 104–124.

Cullen, J.G. (2019). Varieties of responsible management learning: A review, typology and research agenda. *Journal of Business Ethics, 162*(4), 759–773.

Cunliffe, A.L., & Pavlovich, K. (2021). Making our work matter: From spectator to engagement through a public organization and management studies. *Academy of Management Perspectives.*

Dahlmann, F., & Grosvold, J. (2017). Environmental managers and institutional work: Reconciling tensions of competing institutional logics. *Business Ethics Quarterly, 27*(2), 263–291.

Datar, S.M., Garvin, D.A., & P. Cullen, P. (2010). *Rethinking the MBA: Business education at a crossroads*. Harvard Business Press.

Dieleman, H. (2007). Cleaner production and innovation theory: Social experiments as a new model to engage in cleaner production. *Revista internacional de contaminación ambiental, 23*(2), 79–94.

Dubois, A., & Gadde, L.E. (2002). Systematic combining: An abductive approach to case research. *Journal of Business Research, 55*, 553–560.

Dudin, M., Frolova, E., Gryzunova, N., & Shuvalova, E. (2015). The Deming Cycle (PDCA) concept as an efficient tool for continuous quality improvement in the agribusiness. *Asian Social Science, 11*(1), 239–246.

Eastwood, J.G., Kemp, L.A., & Jalaludin, B.B. (2016). Realist theory construction for a mixed method multilevel study of neighbourhood context and postnatal depression. *Springerplus, 5*(1), 1081. https://doi.org/10.1186/s40064-016-2729-9

Eisenhardt, K.M., & Graebner, M.E. (2007). Theory building from cases: Opportunities and challenges. *The Academy of Management Journal, 50*(1), 25–32.

Epple, D., Argote, L., & Devadas, R. (1991). Organizational learning curves: A method for investigating intra-plant transfer of knowledge acquired through learning by doing. *Organization science, 2*(1), 58–70.

EQUIS. (2019). 2019 Equis Standards & Criteria. In Brussels, Belgium: EFMD.

Escobar, A. (2018). *Designs for the pluriverse: Radical interdependence, autonomy, and the making of worlds*. Duke University Press.

Fahy, F., & Rau, H. (2013). *Methods of Sustainability Research in the Social Sciences* (F. Fahy & H. Rau, Eds.). SAGE Publications.

Farnsworth, V., Kleanthous, I., & Wenger-Trayner, E. (2016). Communities of Practice as a Social Theory of Learning: a Conversation with Etienne Wenger. *British Journal of Educational Studies*, *64*(2), 139–160. https://doi.org/10.1080/00071005 .2015.1133799

Feola, G. (2015). Societal transformation in response to global environmental change: A review of emerging concepts. *Ambio*, *44*(5), 376–390. https://doi.org/10.1007/ s13280-014-0582-z

Findler, F. (2021). Toward a sustainability assessment framework of research impacts: Contributions of a business school. *Sustainable Development*. https://doi.org/10 .1002/sd.2218

Freire, P. (1970). *Pedagogy of the Oppressed* (Vol. 68).

Furr, N., & Shipilov, A. (2018). Building the right ecosystem for innovation. *MIT Sloan Management Review*, *59*(4), 59–64.

GBSN (2013). *Cutting a path to prosperity: how education pioneers are building better business schools for the developing world and why*. Global Business School Network.

Geels, F.W. (2012). A socio-technical analysis of low-carbon transitions: introducing the multi-level perspective into transport studies. *Journal of transport geography*, *24*, 471–482. https://doi.org/10.1016/j.jtrangeo.2012.01.021

Ghoshal, S. (2005). Bad management theories are destroying good management practices. *Academy of Management Learning & Education*, *4*(1), 75–91. https://doi.org/ 10.5465/Amle.2005.16132558

Gibbons, M., Limoges, C., Nowotny, H., Schwartzman, S., Scott, P., Trow, M., Schwarzman, H., & Scott, S. (1994). *The New Production of Knowledge: The Dynamics of Science and Research in Contemporary Societies* (Vol. 31). SAGE Publications.

Glaser, B.G., & Strauss, A.L. (2017). *Discovery of Grounded Theory: Strategies for Qualitative Research*. Taylor & Francis.

Gomez, H., Servantie, V., & Hoof, B.V. (2018). Management consulting in Latin America: research opportunities. *ARLA Academia Revista Latinoamericana de Administración*.

Goodman, J., Korsunova, A., & Halme, M. (2017). Our Collaborative Future: Activities and Roles of Stakeholders in Sustainability-Oriented Innovation. *Business Strategy and the Environment*, *26*(6), 731–753. https://doi.org/10.1002/bse.1941

Gröschl, S., & Gabaldon, P. (2018). Business Schools and the Development of Responsible Leaders: A Proposition of Edgar Morin's Transdisciplinarity. *Journal of Business Ethics*, *153*(1), 185–195. https://doi.org/10.1007/s10551-016-3349-6

Gummesson, E. (2003). All research is interpretive! *Journal of Business & Industrial Marketing*, *18*(6/7), 482–492. https://doi.org/10.1108/08858620310492365

Hahn, T., Figge, F., Aragon-Correa, J. A., & Sharma, S. (2017). Advancing Research on Corporate Sustainability: Off to Pastures New or Back to the Roots? *Business & Society*, *56*(2), 155–185. https://doi.org/10.1177/0007650315576152

Hessels, L.K., & van Lente, H. (2008). Re-thinking new knowledge production: A literature review and a research agenda. *Research Policy*, *37*(4), 740–760. https://doi .org/10.1016/j.respol.2008.01.008

Hoffman, A.J. (2016). Reflections: Academia's emerging crisis of relevance and the consequent role of the engaged scholar. *Journal of Change Management*, *16*(2), 77–96.

Jackson, D., Shan, H., & Meek, S. (2021). Enhancing graduates' enterprise capabilities through work-integrated learning in co-working spaces. *Higher Education*, 1–20. https://doi.org/10.1007/s10734-021-00756-x

Jantsch, E. (1972). Inter- and transdisciplinary university; a systems approach to education and innovation. *Higher education*, 403–428.

Jiménez-Jiménez, D., & Sanz-Valle, R. (2011). Innovation, organizational learning, and performance. *Journal of business research*, *64*(4), 408–417.

Jonsson, L., Baraldi, E., Larsson, L.E., Forsberg, P., & Severinsson, K. (2015). Targeting Academic Engagement in Open Innovation: Tools, Effects and Challenges for University Management. *Journal of the Knowledge Economy*, *6*(3), 522–550. https://doi.org/10.1007/s13132-015-0254-7

Kampf, C.E., Brandt, C.J., & Kampf, C.G. (2023). Using action research in innovation project management: Building legitimacy and organizational learning in an SME during a merger process. *International Journal of Managing Projects in Business*, *16*(1), 92–118.

Kaplan, A. (2014). European management and European business schools: Insights from the history of business schools. *European Management Journal*, *32*(4), 529–534. https://doi.org/10.1016/j.emj.2014.03.006

Kaplan, A. (2018). A school is "a building that has four walls…with tomorrow inside": Toward the reinvention of the business school. *Business Horizons*, *61*(4), 599–608. https://doi.org/10.1016/j.bushor.2018.03.010

Keeton, M., & Tate, P. (1978). Editor's notes: "The boom in experiential learning". In M. Keeton & P. Tate (Eds.), *Learning by experience – what, why, how* (pp. 1–8). Jossey- Bass.

Kemp, R., Loorbach, D., & Rotmans, J. (2007). Transition management as a model for managing processes of co-evolution towards sustainable development. *International Journal of Sustainable Development and World Ecology*, *14*(1), 78–91. https://doi.org/10.1080/13504500709469709

Khurana, R., & Spender, J.C. (2012). Herbert A. Simon on What Ails Business Schools: More than "A Problem in Organizational Design". *Journal of Management Studies*, *49*(3), 619–639. https://doi.org/10.1111/j.1467-6486.2011.01040.x

Koehn, P.H., & Uitto, J.I. (2013). Evaluating sustainability education: lessons from international development experience. *Higher education*, *67*(5), 621–635. https://doi.org/10.1007/s10734-013-9669-x

Kolb, A.Y., & Kolb, D.A. (2009). The learning way: Meta-cognitive aspects of experiential learning. *Simulation & Gaming*, *40*(3), 297–327. https://doi.org/10.1177/1046878108325713

Kovács, G., van Hoek, R., & Spens, K.M. (2005). Abductive reasoning in logistics research. *International Journal of Physical Distribution & Logistics Management*, *35*(2), 132–144. https://doi.org/10.1108/09600030510590318

Kubr, M. (2002). *Management consulting: A guide to the profession*. International Labour Organization.

Laasch, O., Moosmayer, D., Antonacopoulou, E., & Schaltegger, S. (2020). Constellations of transdisciplinary practices: A map and research agenda for the responsible management learning field. *Journal of Business Ethics*, *162*(4), 735–757. https://doi.org/10.1007/s10551-020-04440-5

Lam, A. (2000). Tacit knowledge, organizational learning and societal institutions: An integrated framework. *Organization Studies*, *21*(3), 487–513.

Lang, D.J., Wiek, A., Bergmann, M., Stauffacher, M., Martens, P., Moll, P., Swilling, M., & Thomas, C.J. (2012). Transdisciplinary research in sustainability science:

Practice, principles, and challenges. *Sustainability Science, 7*(S1), 25–43. https://doi .org/10.1007/s11625-011-0149-x

Lederman, D., Messina, J., Pienknagura, S., & Rigolini, J. (2014). *El emprendimiento en América Latina: muchas empresas y poca innovación.* The World Bank.

Levitt, B., & March, J.G. (1988). Organizational learning. *Annual review of sociology, 14*(1), 319–338.

Li, L. C., Grimshaw, J.M., Nielsen, C., Judd, M., Coyte, P.C., & Graham, I.D. (2009). Evolution of Wenger's concept of community of practice. *Implementation science, 4,* 1–8.

Luken, R.A., Van Berkel, R., Leuenberger, H., & Schwager, P. (2016). A 20-year retrospective of the National Cleaner Production Centres programme. *Journal of Cleaner Production, 112,* 1165–1174. https://doi.org/10.1016/j.jclepro.2015.07.142

Lyon, T.P., & Maxwell, J.W. (2008) Corporate social responsibility and the environment: A theoretical perspective. *Review of Environmental Economics and Policy, 1,* 1–22.

Mantere, S., & Ketokivi, M. (2013). Reasoning in organization science. *Academy of Management Review, 38,* 70–89.

Max-Neef, M.A. (2005). Foundations of transdisciplinarity. *Ecological Economics, 53*(1), 5–16. https://doi.org/10.1016/j.ecolecon.2005.01.014

McCutcheon, D.M., & Meredith, J.R. (1993). Conducting case study research in operations management. *Journal of Operations Management, 11*(3), 239–256.

Meqdadi, O., Johnsen, T.E., & Johnsen, R.E. (2017). The role of power and trust in spreading sustainability initiatives across supply networks: A case study in the bio-chemical industry. *Industrial Marketing Management, 62,* 61–76.

Midgley, G., & Reynolds, M. (2004). Systems/operational research and sustainable development: Towards a new agenda. *Sustainable Development, 12*(1), 56–64. https://doi.org/10.1002/sd.218

Miles, R.E., Snow, C.C., Fjeldstad, O.D., Miles, G., & Lettl, C. (2010). Designing organizations to meet 21st-century opportunities and challenges. *Organizational Dynamics, 39*(2), 93–103. https://doi.org/10.1016/j.orgdyn.2010.01.009

Mintzberg, H. (1989). *Mintzberg on Management: Inside Our Strange World of Organizations.* Free Press/

Moratis, L., & Melissen, F. (2022). Bolstering responsible management education through the sustainable development goals: Three perspectives. *Management Learning, 53*(2), 212–222.

Morin, E. (1994). *La complexité humaine.* Flammarion.

Muller, P. (2006). Reputation, trust and the dynamics of leadership in communities of practice. *Journal of Management & Governance, 10*(4), 381–400.

Nicolescu, B. (2014). Methodology of Transdisciplinarity. *World Futures, 70*(3-4), 186–199. https://doi.org/10.1080/02604027.2014.934631

OECD, America & Caribbean (2012). *Latin American Economic Outlook 2013.* https:// doi.org/10.1787/leo-2013-en

Olsson, A., & Olander Roese, M. (2005). *Multi theoretical perspectives in an abductive action research study.* In Conference Proceedings Lund University, Sweden.

Park, J., Duque-Hernández, J., & Díaz-Posada, N. (2018). Facilitating business collaborations for industrial symbiosis: The pilot experience of the sustainable industrial network program in Colombia. *Sustainability, 10*(10), 3637.

Pesqueira Fernandez, L.d.L. (2014). *Friendly Outsider or Critical Insider?: An Action Research Account of Oxfam's Private Sector Engagement.* Utrecht University.

Pfeffer, J., & Fong, C.T. (2002). The end of business schools? Less success than meets the eye. *Academy of Management Learning & Education, 1*(1), 78–95.

Pohl, C., & Hirsch Hadorn, G. (2008). Methodological challenges of transdisciplinary research. *Natures Sciences Sociétés, 16*(2), 111–121. https://doi.org/10.1051/nss:2008035

Pohl, C., Rist, S., Zimmermann, A., Fry, P., Gurung, G.S., Schneider, F., Speranza, C.I., Kiteme, B., Boillat, S., Serrano, E., Hadorn, G.H., & Wiesmann, U. (2010). Researchers' roles in knowledge co-production: experience from sustainability research in Kenya, Switzerland, Bolivia and Nepal. *Science and Public Policy, 37*(4), 267–281. https://doi.org/10.3152/030234210x496628

Quist, J., & Vergragt, P. (2006). Past and future of backcasting: The shift to stakeholder participation and a proposal for a methodological framework. *Futures, 38*(9), 1027–1045. https://doi.org/10.1016/j.futures.2006.02.010

Raffo, D.M., Harrison, W., & Vandeville, J. (2002). *Software process decision support: making process tradeoffs using a hybrid metrics, modeling and utility framework.* Proceedings of the 14th international conference on Software engineering and knowledge engineering.

Ramos, T.B., Caeiro, S., van Hoof, B., Lozano, R., Huisingh, D., & Ceulemans, K. (2015). Experiences from the implementation of sustainable development in higher education institutions: Environmental Management for Sustainable Universities. *Journal of Cleaner Production, 106*, 3–10. https://doi.org/10.1016/j.jclepro.2015.05.110

Reason, P., & Bradbury, H. (2006). *Handbook of Action Research.*

Reed, M.G., Godmaire, H., Abernethy, P., & Guertin, M.A. (2014). Building a community of practice for sustainability: Strengthening learning and collective action of Canadian biosphere reserves through a national partnership. *Journal of environmental management, 145*, 230–239.

Reichertz, J. (2009). Abduction: The Logic of Discovery of Grounded Theory [grounded theory methodology; Strauss; abduction; deduction; induction; methodology; Peirce; qualitative social research; construction of knowledge]. 2009, *11*(1). https://doi.org/10.17169/fqs-11.1.1412

Ren, I.Y., & Bartunek, J.M. (2020). Creating standards for responsible translation of management research for practitioners. In *Research handbook of responsible management* (pp. 729–744). Edward Elgar Publishing.

Rotmans, J. (1998). Methods for IA: The challenges and opportunities ahead. *Environmental Modeling & Assessment, 3*(3), 155–179.

Sakr, D., & Sena, A.A. (2017). Cleaner production status in the Middle East and North Africa region with special focus on Egypt. *Journal of Cleaner Production, 141*, 1074–1086.

Schaltegger, S., Beckmann, M., & Hansen, E.G. (2013). Transdisciplinarity in corporate sustainability: Mapping the field. *Business Strategy and the Environment, 22*(4), 219–229.

Schaltegger, S., Horisch, J., & Loorbach, D. (2020). Corporate and entrepreneurial contributions to sustainability transitions. *Business Strategy and the Environment, 29*(3), 1617–1618.

Scholz, R.W., & Tietje, O. (2002). *Embedded Case Study Methods: Integrating Quantitative and Qualitative Knowledge.* SAGE Publications.

Sellberg, M.M., Cockburn, J., Holden, P.B., & Lam, D.P.M. (2021). Towards a caring transdisciplinary research practice: Navigating science, society and self. *Ecosystems and People, 17*(1), 292–305. https://doi.org/10.1080/26395916.2021.1931452

Servaes, J., Jacobson, T.L., & White, S.A. (1996). *Participatory Communication for Social Change*. SAGE Publications.

Seuring, S., & Müller, M. (2008). From a literature review to a conceptual framework for sustainable supply chain management. *Journal of Cleaner Production, 16*(15), 1699–1710. https://doi.org/10.1016/j.jclepro.2008.04.020

Slater, D.J., & Dixon-Fowler, H.R. (2010). The future of the planet in the hands of MBAs: An examination of CEO MBA Education and Corporate Environmental Performance. *Academy of Management Learning & Education, 9*(3), 429–441. https://doi.org/10.5465/Amle.2010.53791825

Smith, A., Stirling, A., & Berkhout, F. (2005). The governance of sustainable socio-technical transitions. *Research Policy, 34*(10), 1491–1510. https://doi.org/10.1016/j.respol.2005.07.005

Snelson-Powell, A., Grosvold, J., & Millington, A. (2016). Business school legitimacy and the challenge of sustainability: A fuzzy set analysis of institutional decoupling. *Academy of Management Learning & Education, 15*(4), 703–723. https://doi.org/10.5465/amle.2015.0307

Söderbaum, P. (2009). Making actors, paradigms and ideologies visible in governance for sustainability. *Sustainable Development, 17*(2), 70–81. https://doi.org/10.1002/sd.404

Sorge, A., & van Witteloostuijn, A. (2004). The (non)sense of organizational change: An essay about universal management hypes, sick consultancy metaphors, and healthy organization theories. *Organization Studies, 25*(7), 1205–1231. https://doi.org/10.1177/0170840604046360

Spender, J.C., & Grant, R.M. (1996). Knowledge and the firm: Overview. *Strategic Management Journal, 17*(S2), 5–9.

Stone, L.J. (2006a). Limitations of cleaner production programmes as organisational change agents. II. Leadership, support, communication, involvement and programme design. *Journal of Cleaner Production, 14*(1), 15–30.

Stone, L.J. (2006b). Limitations of cleaner production programmes as organisational change agents I. Achieving commitment and on-going improvement. *Journal of Cleaner Production, 14*(1), 1–14.

Strauss, A.L. (1987) *Qualitative analysis for social scientists*. Cambridge University Press. http://dx.doi.org/10.1017/CBO9780511557842

Stutz, C., & Schrempf-Stirling, J. (2020). Using the past responsibly: What responsible managers and management academics can learn from historians' professional ethics. In *Research handbook of responsible management* (pp. 745–758). Edward Elgar Publishing.

Urgel, J. (2007). EQUIS accreditation: Value and benefits for international business schools. *Journal of Management Development, 26*(1), 73–+. https://doi.org/10.1108/02621710710721698

Van Breda, J., & Swilling, M. (2019). The guiding logics and principles for designing emergent transdisciplinary research processes: learning experiences and reflections from a transdisciplinary urban case study in Enkanini informal settlement, South Africa. *Sustainability Science, 14*(3), 823–841.

Van Capelleveen, G., Amrit, C., & Yazan, D.M. (2018). A Literature Survey of Information Systems Facilitating the Identification of Industrial Symbiosis. *From Science to Society: New Trends in Environmental Informatics*, 155–169. https://doi.org/10.1007/978-3-319-65687-8_14

Van de Ven, A.H. (2007). *Engaged scholarship: A guide for organizational and social research*. Oxford University Press on Demand.

Van de Ven, A.H., & Johnson, P.E. (2006). Knowledge for theory and practice. *Academy of Management Review, 31*(4), 802–821.

Van Hoof, B. (2013). *Supply networks for cleaner production: Framework for improvement of environmental performance of SMEs in emerging markets, doctoral thesis* (p. 190). Erasmus University.

Van Hoof, B. (2014). Organizational learning in cleaner production among Mexican supply networks. *Journal of Cleaner Production, 64*, 115–124. https://doi.org/10.1016/j.jclepro.2013.07.041

Van Hoof, B., & Duque, J. (2020). *Supply Chain Management for Circular Economy in Latin America: RedES-CAR in Colombia. Industrial Symbiosis for the Circular Economy Operational Experiences, Best Practices and Obstacles to a Collaborative Business Approach* (pp. 103–118). Springer Nature.

Van Hoof, B., Duque, J., Gómez, H., & Saer, A. (2018). *Liderazgo Ambiental para la transformación productiva: lecciones de América Latina* (p. 211). Alfaomega-Universidad de los Andes, Facultad de Administración, Bogotá.

Van Hoof, B., & Gomez, H. (2015). *Advanced Small and Medium Sized Enterprises, motors for development in Latin America.* Uniandes-ECLAC.

Van Hoof, B., Gómez, H., Saer, A., & Duque, J. (2016). *Red de empresas sostenibles (RedES-CAR); encadenamiento para la transformacion productive [Networks of sustainable entreprises for industrial transformation]* (p. 65). Centro de Estrategia y Competitividad, Facultad de Administración Universidad de los Andes, Bogotá, Colombia.

Van Hoof, B., & Lyon, T.P. (2013). Cleaner production in small firms taking part in Mexico's Sustainable Supplier Program. *Journal of Cleaner Production, 41*, 270–282. https://doi.org/10.1016/j.jclepro.2012.09.023

Van Hoof, B., & Medina, A. (2022). Dissemination of circular water practices in Colombia. In A. Alvarez-Risco, M.A. Rosen, & S. Del-Aguila-Arcentales (Eds.), *Towards a circular economy: Transdisciplinary approach for business* (Ch. 13, pp. 301–317). Springer Nature.

Van Hoof, B., & Thiell, M. (2014a). Anchor company contribution to cleaner production dissemination: Experience from a Mexican sustainable supply programme. *Journal of Cleaner Production.* https://doi.org/10.1016/j.jclepro.2014.08.021

Van Hoof, B., & Thiell, M. (2014b). Collaboration capacity for sustainable supply chain management: Small and medium-sized enterprises in Mexico. *Journal of Cleaner Production, 67*, 239–248.

Van Hoof, B., Thiell, M., & Mejia, S. (2023). 'Shrinking effects' in cleaner production dissemination: An analysis of the Colombian RedES-CAR programme. *Journal of Cleaner Production, 405*, 137012.

Vermeulen, W.J.V., & Witjes, S. (2021). History and mapping of transdisciplinary research on sustainable development issues: Dealing with complex problems in times of urgency. In W.J.V. Vermeulen & M. Keitsch (Eds.), *Transdisciplinarity for sustainability: Connecting diverse practices.* Routledge.

Vildåsen, S.S., Keitsch, M., & Fet, A.M. (2017). Clarifying the epistemology of corporate sustainability. *Ecological Economics, 138*, 40–46. https://doi.org/10.1016/j.ecolecon.2017.03.029

Vives, A., Corral, A., & Isusi, I. (2005). *Responsabilidad social de la empresa en las PYMEs de Latinoamerica.* Banco Interamericano de Desarrollo.

Wegner, P.M. (2011). *The relationship between employee engagement and employee retention in an acute healthcare hospital.* Proquest, Umi Dissertation Publishing.

Wenger, E. (1998). *Communities of practice: Learning, meaning, and identity.* Cambridge University Press.

Wenger, E., Trayner, B., & De Laat, M. (2011). Promoting and assessing value creation in communities and networks: A conceptual framework. *Ecological Economics, 20,* 2010-2011. https://doi.org/10.1016/j.ecolecon.2017.03.029

Witjes, S., & Vermeulen, W.J.V. (2021). Transdisciplinary research: Approaches and methodological principles. In W.J.V. Vermeulen & M. Keitsch (Eds.), *Transdisciplinarity for sustainability: Connecting diverse practices* (pp. 27–52). Routledge.

Yin, R.K. (2009). *Case study research: Design and methods* (4th ed.). SAGE Publications.

10. Sustainable transformation in business and management higher education: an analysis of global and European collaborative initiatives for positive impact

Julia Wolny

INTRODUCTION

The purpose of this chapter is to identify and analyse five global and European initiatives that promote the integration of sustainability and responsibility into business and management higher education (HE). The initiatives, such as the Globally Responsible Leadership Initiative, UN Principles for Responsible Management Education, and Positive Impact Rating are all centred around the imperative of promoting collaboration for sustainable transformation.

As the number and variety of actors in the higher education sustainability ecosystem grows, it is important to take stock of the existing initiatives which help universities and business schools towards positive environmental and social impact. Many universities find themselves at a transition stage seeking guidelines, models and inspiration for this necessary and important shift. The initiatives explored here provide a wealth of activities, communities and resources for this purpose.

Little has been written about the nature of the initiatives that promote sustainable transformation in HE. Haddock-Fraser (2023) in her chapter entitled "Sustainability Member Associations for Universities" explores "the role and impact of mission-led organisations, with a clear mandate to enhance, improve and expand interest and action in sustainability in higher education institutions (HEIs) and among their staff and students" (p. 199). While she mentions several global sustainability associations, and includes a valuable case study, a systematic analysis or comparison of those initiatives is lacking.

This chapter conversely compares the key elements of every initiative, including their: (1) history and goals, (2) governance structure, (3) stakeholders, (4) signatories and membership, (5) scope of activities, and (6) leadership for collaboration. The goal is to benchmark these initiatives and provide distilled recommendations for universities and business schools to follow in their journey towards sustainability and positive impact.

Sample and Approach

The initiatives that are included in the analysis have been selected based on the following predetermined criteria:

- The initiatives support sustainable transformation in HE.
- The initiatives are focused on business and management disciplines.
- The initiatives must have a collaborative element, that is, not only encouraging membership but also providing opportunities for collaborations among HEIs.
- The initiatives are currently active (2023).
- The initiatives' geographical scope is Europe OR it has a major footprint in Europe.

These supra-HEI organisations and initiatives (defined as such due to the overarching nature that congregate many HEIs), analysed in this chapter are:

1. HESI – Higher Education Sustainability Initiative.
2. UN PRME – United Nations Principles for Responsible Management Education.
3. GRLI – Globally Responsible Leadership Initiative.
4. PIR – Positive Impact Rating.
5. BSIS – Business School Impact System.

For the purpose of this chapter, organisations such as AMBA, AACSB or Global Business School Network that are actively supporting environmental and social focus in education but have a much broader remit, are not included in the analysis; nor are student institutions such as oikos International that are focused on students specifically, and not schools per se.

In terms of data collection, secondary sources were used to gather information about each supra-HEI initiative. Following a textual analysis from organisational websites and reports published by the initiatives, it was deemed imperative to interview a sample of strategic representatives of these organisations. Strategic representatives of three out of the five organisations were available to be interviewed at this time. Their names feature in Table 10.1 below, along with their initials used in text to refer to their quotes, their organisational titles and dates of interviews.

Table 10.1   Names and roles of interviewees

Organisation	Name of interviewee	Initials for in-text citations	Title	Date of interview
UN PRME	Gutavo Loiola	GL	Manager, Leadership Education	06/09/2023
GRLI	John North	JN	Executive Director	22/09/2023
PIR	Thomas Dyllick	TD	Founder	21/09/2023

Objectives

This chapter aims to address the following questions:

- What have the initiatives accomplished in responsible business and management education? Where are they heading?
- What activities and strategies have they used for advancing responsible management education, research and stakeholder impact?
- How do they collaborate and foster dialogue and partnership with other stakeholders towards creating positive societal impact?
- How can the initiatives be helpful to universities and colleges transitioning to sustainability?

ROLE OF BUSINESS AND MANAGEMENT EDUCATION IN SUSTAINABLE TRANSFORMATION

Over two decades ago, during the 2002 World Summit on Sustainable Development (WSSD), a notable emphasis was placed on the importance of adhering to a universal set of guiding principles for sustainable development partnerships. These principles revolved around the concepts of local engagement, global relevance, alignment with globally agreed-upon goals, tangible results, transparency, accountability, and embracing the integrated and multi-disciplinary approaches (Goodall & Ivanova, 2023).

These principles underscore that such partnerships should be voluntary and mutually respectful and have been adopted by the multi-stakeholder initiatives for sustainability in HE, leading to generation of organisations such as PRME and GRLI. These organisations have become a key participation mechanism for business schools and universities to collaborate and engage in activities towards sustainable and responsible business, management and leadership. While the nature and context of HEIs vary dramatically, regional and international university sustainability networks are emerging with the shared purposes of information exchange and common solutions. The United Nations Global Compact (UNGC) is an example of evolving complex multilateralism on a global level, based on global multi-stakeholder governance and corporate citizenship values (Gonzalez-Perez & Leonard, 2015).

It has long been recognised that business and management education institutions are key actors and stakeholders towards positive impact within the economic and societal system. What renders HEIs, especially business schools, essential to the cause of sustainable transformation is their role in shaping a new generation of responsible citizens and professionals. Nevertheless, universities face challenges in shifting their focus and their systemic understanding to align with this mission (Goodall & Ivanova, 2023).

As indicated from the outset, this shift reflects a global movement. Yet, the readiness of leaders and the variety of circumstances in different regions can lead to variations in the understanding of terms like "global leadership" or "sustainable transformation" over time and space (Purvis & Grainger, 2004). For instance, in Europe, historical factors such as colonial history of specific countries, post-World War II economic policies, and more recent legal structures such as EU directives on sustainable business have ALL shaped the meaning and practice of sustainable development education. On a global scale, the United Nations has played a leading role in crystallising key principles and guidelines of positive impact, such as transparency and accountability, which should guide future initiatives in higher education and its institutions. Nevertheless, there are several commonalities among HEIs that make them fertile grounds for spreading and amplifying responsible and sustainable leadership within broader social and economic ecosystems.

To begin, HEIs serve as producers of high-quality research on contemporary and emerging grand challenges. Thus, they serve as knowledge brokers, innovation catalysts, and pioneers, bringing together various elements to significantly magnify their impact. Second, these institutions are responsible for preparing the next generation of professionals and leaders across all segments of society and governance levels (Arevalo & Mitchell, 2017). Third, due to their not-for-profit orientation, HEIs can experiment with emerging systems and processes with less financial risk compared to businesses. Lastly, many universities can act as neutral forums for dialogue and exploration, helping to transcend political tensions. In the realm of leading collaborations, few entities are better suited to drive transformative change (Edwards, Benn & Starik, 2017). They can operate across various scales, influencing local, regional, and international initiatives, and often partnering with the private sector and NGOs. Their expertise, leadership, capacity, and connectivity render them ideal for implementing multilevel programs (Goodall & Ivanova, 2023).

The following pages will explore how the supra-HEI initiatives facilitate the integration and collaboration between HEIs, by understanding their: (1)

history and goals, (2) governance structure, (3) stakeholders, (4) signatories and membership, (5) scope of activities, and (6) the leadership for collaboration of each initiative.

1.   HESI – Higher Education Sustainability Initiative

The Higher Education Sustainability Initiative (HESI) is a macro-level partnership that gathers over two dozen UN agency members and Higher Education Sustainability Networks. The Higher Education Sustainability Initiative (HESI) is a partnership between the United Nations Department of Economic and Social Affairs (UNDESA), United Nations Environment Programme (UNEP), United Nations Global Compact (UNGC), UNESCO, and other international organisations. HESI aims to promote sustainability in higher education institutions (HEIs) and encourage them to become agents of change for sustainable development (UN DESA, 2023).

The initiative tackles the most crucial challenges of our time by redesigning higher education to provide leadership on education for sustainable development, spearheading efforts for "green" campuses, and supporting sustainable efforts in communities, while also ensuring the quality of education, equity, and gender equality. It was an outcome of the Rio+20 conference, signed by over 300 universities. In 2012 the Commission on Sustainable Development (CSD) recognised it as the document with the highest number of signatories coming out of the Rio conference (UN DESA, 2023).

Goals

HESI's stated purpose is to "provide higher education institutions with a unique interface between higher education, science, and policy making" (UN DESA, 2021). The main goal of HESI is to encourage HEIs to contribute to the United Nations' Sustainable Development Goals (SDGs) by integrating sustainability principles into their teaching, research, and operations. The initiative also aims to facilitate collaboration among HEIs and other stakeholders, such as governments, civil society organisations, and the private sector, to promote sustainability (UN DESA, 2023).

HESI provides higher education institutions with a vibrant confluence of higher education, science, and policymaking by enhancing awareness of higher education's role in supporting sustainable development, facilitating multi-stakeholder discussions and action, and sharing best practices. The initiative emphasises the crucial role that higher education plays in educating the current and next generation of leaders, propelling the research agenda for public and private sectors, and helping to shape the path of national economies. HESI also aims to directly address the problem of aligning research programs and outcomes in scholarly publications (UN DESA, 2023).

Governance

HESI is currently chaired by the United Nations Department of Economic and Social Affairs (UN DESA) and the Sulitest Association – a non-profit organisation and online platform aimed at improving sustainability literacy for all. HESI is governed by a steering committee, that provides guidance on the initiative's strategic direction, policies, and activities. It is supported by a secretariat, which is responsible for coordinating the initiative's activities and promoting its objectives (UN DESA, 2023).

Stakeholders

HESI engages with a broad range of stakeholders, including HEIs, governments, civil society organisations, the private sector, and international organisations. The initiative aims to create a platform for collaboration among these stakeholders to promote sustainability in higher education.

Membership

It has 659 members that are global HEI institutions. Higher education institutions can become signatories to HESI by submitting a letter of commitment to the initiative's principles and goals (UN DESA, 2023).

Activities

HESI designates Action Groups to tackle topics related to higher education for sustainable development. Action Groups draw upon the full HESI community to carry out its work and are often composed of several organisations and contributors. Results are published on the HESI website and promoted by the network. Current Action groups include:

1. HESI Partner programme – a community of shared learning in support of SDG integration into curricula, research, programmes and campus practices to facilitate transfer of knowledge;
2. Rankings, ratings and assessment – guidelines on performance of higher education institutions to contribute to SDGs;
3. Education for Green Jobs – supporting curricula updates to build the workforce we need for a sustainable and inclusive future;
4. SDG Publishers Compact – promotes SDG-alignment and action from the wider publishing sector.

One of the most tangible outputs of HESI was the Sulitest – a test of sustainability literacy, to "ensure that all learners acquire the knowledge and skills necessary to promote sustainable development" (Sulitest, 2023). The Sulitest movement was recognised in 2016 as one of the remarkable initiatives in the United Nations partnership for the Sustainable Development Goals and the association now has three UN accreditations and a very strong international recognition. Since 2021 Sulitest is a separate social and solidarity economy company (SAS of the ESUS type) and since 2022 receives external financing (Sulitest, 2023).

Leading on collaboration

Each year, HESI organises a global forum as a special event to the High-level Political Forum on Sustainable Development (HLPF) – UN's main platform for the follow-up and review of the 2030 Agenda for Sustainable Development at the global level – to highlight the critical role of higher education in achieving sustainable development (UN DESA, 2023).

HESI organises various activities to promote sustainability in HEIs, including workshops, webinars, and publications. The initiative also provides guidance and tools to help HEIs integrate sustainability into their teaching, research, and operations. Importantly, it facilitates collaboration among HEIs and other stakeholders to promote sustainability. It organises Green Gown Awards that recognise the exceptional sustainability initiatives being undertaken by universities and colleges across the world (UN DESA, 2023).

2.   UN PRME – United Nations Principles for Responsible Management Education

The Principles for Responsible Management Education (PRME) is a United Nations-supported initiative founded in 2007 by an international task force of 60 deans, university presidents and official representatives of leading business schools, academic institutions and UN Global Compact. The idea was officially introduced by the Global Compact Office at the Global Forum "Business as an Agent of World Benefit" at Case Western Reserve University in October 2006 (Araç & Madran, 2014). It was driven by the desire to change the role of business – "The idea at the start was driven by the need for global responsible leaders in industry, in the private sector" (GL interview, 2023)

PRME is perhaps the most visible initiative for promoting sustainability in Business and Management education, it has become a signature that many universities antibusiness schools include on their websites and corporate materials. It has gained visibility through the annual conference as well as publicly available biannual SIP (Sharing Information on Progress) reports that each member organisation must submit, with indicators of progress on specific criteria aligned with the UN PRME priorities (UN PRME, 2023).

Goals

Working through Six Principles – Purpose, Values, Method, Research, Partnership, Dialogue – PRME engages business and management schools to ensure they provide future leaders with the skills needed to balance economic and sustainability goals, while drawing attention to the Sustainable Development Goals (SDGs) and aligning academic institutions with the work of the UN Global Compact. The principles seek to establish a process of continuous improvement among management-related academic institutions to develop a new generation of business leaders capable of managing the complex challenges faced by business and society. Its mission is to transform management education and develop the responsible decision-makers of tomorrow to advance sustainable development (UN PRME, 2023), as "PRME plays an inspirational and aspirational role for its members" (GL interview, 2023).

Governance
Until 2020, the governance of PRME was structured in the following way – the PRME Steering Committee (PRME SC) was the main governing and decision-making body, with the PRME Secretariat executing the day-to-day operations and the PRME Advisory Committee (PRME AC) providing strategic and governance recommendations to the PRME SC and PRME Secretariat. In 2020, an Interim Management Council developed a new governance structure with one unitary PRME Board comprised of members representing a mix of PRME Signatories, students, business, the United Nations and other key stakeholders, with the majority of seats reserved for signatories (PRME, 2017).

Stakeholders
PRME identifies direct stakeholders – Signatory members, and country chapters and indirect ones – Business and Management students, leadership, administration (UN PRME, 2023). PRME's Steering Committee includes AACSB International, EFMD, AMBA, GMAC, the Association of African Business Schools and Association of Asia-Pacific Business Schools, CEEMAN, Latin American Council of Management Schools, EABIS, GRLI, and Net Impact (UN PRME, 2023).

Membership
Membership includes over 880 plus higher education institutions (according to the PRME website, 2023), with access to an ever-evolving network of around three million students and 200,000 faculty (Morsing, 2021).

Signatories to PRME are divided into two categories: basic and advanced. Basic signatories are compliant with the SIP Policy, and have limited engagement with the PRME community. Advanced signatories are compliant with the SIP Policy, but also make a nominal contribution to the Annual Service Fee. This contribution entitles a signatory to advanced engagement and leadership opportunities within the PRME community (UN PRME, 2023).

Activites

PRME engages with business school deans, faculty, and students to take action on a range of issues – from poverty, inequality and climate change to sustainable finance and human rights. "As a network we offer opportunities for learning and sharing different experiences" (GL interview, 2023).

The only requirement for signatories to PRME is the submission of a Sharing Information on Progress (SIP) report once every two years. As its name suggests, the report is a communication to stakeholders – faculty, staff, students, partners, and the public – of the progress made implementing the Six Principles in teaching, research, and thought leadership.

PRME facilitates thoughtful research and collaboration through thematic Working Groups exploring issues like poverty, anti-corruption, climate change, gender equality, peace, human rights, and sustainability.

PRME Chapters are regional platforms that advance the Six Principles of PRME within a particular geographic context, performing an important role underscoring the diverse global network of different national, regional, cultural and linguistic academics.

Involving students and youth will be crucial for achieving the Sustainable Development Goals. Today's business and management students will be the leaders of tomorrow, and their role will be pivotal in tackling the challenges of the 21st century. The recently launched PRME SDG Student Engagement Platform empowers students to support and advance the SDGs by proactively identifying, analysing, and sharing the sustainability achievements of companies' activities and business operations (UN PRME, 2023).

Two current developmental projects are the i5 project – "pedagogical training on how to develop different skillset for positive impact on society" (GL interview, 2023); and the SIP 2.0 project, aiming to "create a community and allow members to measure and track impact beyond the qualitative information from signatories and chapters, thus creating PRME commons" (GL interview, 2023).

Leading on collaboration

"Everything we do is community based, we don't have a service – the secretariat is there to support the network" (GL interview, 2023).

PRME, as part of the UN Global Compact, can inspire the world by setting a new tone for collaboration between business and business schools (Ojiambo, 2023). It has three fundamental roles to play in advancing the broader view of business as a force for good. These include:

- Advocacy for business as a force for good.
- Collaboration with the UN Global Compact and its network of over 10,000 companies.

- Knowledge exchange (Mihov, 2023).

3.   GRLI – Globally Responsible Leadership Initiative

The Globally Responsible Leadership Initiative (GRLI) aims to develop a new vision for management education and business leadership that integrates sustainability and social responsibility. The Globally Responsible Leadership Initiative is a worldwide partnership of over 74 companies, business schools and learning organisations working together to develop a generation of globally responsible leaders (GRLI, 2023).

In 2002, the EFMD (European Foundation for Management Development) held its annual meeting. The theme was "Global Responsibility" and there was a consensus, especially in the wake of 9/11, that EFMD could and should take action on this vital issue. In 2004, UNGC and EFMD invited 21 companies and business schools to hands-on address the question of how to develop a generation of globally responsible leaders. This resulted in the 2005 founding call of the GRLI, which is also the first organised relationship between the United Nations and business schools (GRLI, 2023).

Subsequently the GRLI played a central role in the development of Principles for Responsible Management Education (PRME) (2006–2007). In 2012, following the impact of the 50+20 vision and GRLI's pioneering work on Whole Person Learning, AACSB International and EFMD entered into a strategic partnership agreement with the GRLI in terms of which "GRLI will serve as a primary operational arm of AACSB and EFMD in the arena of responsible leadership and sustainability" (Muff et al., 2014). The Strategic Partnership agreement with AACSB and EFMD was reset in 2016 to include UNGC and in terms of which GRLI hosts a "collaboratory" on Responsible Management Education which includes co-facilitation of the PRME Champions (Muff et al., 2014).

Goals
The GRLI's vision is – global responsibility embedded in leadership and practice of organisations and societies worldwide.

"GRLI exists to tell the story of how global responsibility develops and how it evolves. In doing so, we are following not a strategic plan but a strategic direction, and that strategic direction has a number of pathways through which we work – such as Ecosystem facilitation: stewarding the landscape" (JN interview, 2023). Other pathways include: (a) Governance: Taking care of the vehicle, (b) Essential purpose: Telling the story of Global Responsibility, (c) Engagement: Developing the relationships needed to sustain transformative change and (d) Exploration: Exploring the edges of Global Responsibility and new areas of inquiry.

Since its initiation, the GRLI has advocated for exploration beyond sustainability and CSR by placing an emphasis on global responsibility. The GRLI started and continues to exist as an inquiry which asks "what is global responsibility and how might it be developed?". The inquiry is held by a deeply engaged international, multi-sector community of partners and associates comprising companies, universities, business schools, transnational networks and NGOs (GRLI, 2023).

Governance
The GRLI is not a member-serving organisation but rather an inquiry that is held and driven by its partners and associates. Since its foundation, its work has relied on a relational and partnership approach which is also reflected in its unique governance model. Two living documents, the Governance Framework and Guardian Group Terms of Reference, are meant to assist the Board and Guardian group (as Council representatives) in their governing role. As an entity advocating that leaders everywhere should behave in a globally responsible way, it is important that the GRLI practises appropriate transparency and accountability in its dealings with a wide range of stakeholders (GRLI, 2023). All its principles, current actions and how they contribute to outcomes are publicly available on its website. This not only is evidence of its transparency but also its ongoing activism in the positive impact ecosystem.

Stakeholders
Today, the GRLI is both a formal partnership of 42 organisations (4 companies, 33 learning institutions and 3 global organisations) and a less formal global community comprising a number of organisations involved informally in communities of responsible action. The GRLI has important strategic partnerships with EFMD and AACSB International and oikos International, as well as the UNGC. It also has a total of 71 alumni organisations that have been involved in the GRLI at one time or and are considered as alumnus of the initiative (GRLI, 2023).

Membership
The GRLI is not a membership organisation but engagement as Partner or Associate is open to companies, universities, business schools, transnational networks, NGOs and independent individual actors. It remains a community driven by the energy, ambitions, dreams and dedication of active participants globally. Joining GRLI opens new possibilities to:

• Build reputation through association with and visible engagement in the key global issues of our times.

- Invest in personal development of individuals by engaging with a global community of peers in hands-on delivery of impact projects.
- Accelerate and leverage organisational change through access to the GRLI's global partnership network and knowledge resources.
- Drive systemic transformation by developing new knowledge and driving initiatives focused on key lever points in global systems.
- Engage with a worldwide group of learning organisations committed to collaborative initiatives and sharing learning on global responsibility.

Activites

> The GRLI has remained a very small partnership and collaborative inquiry, which, in the process of holding these questions the global responsibility has sparked new ideas and initiatives. We started working in 2009 on something called Blue Sky Business School, which was a blueprint of what would a business school would look like if people and planet mattered. That eventually became the 50+20 vision, a blueprint of what the management education that strives to be the best FOR rather than the best IN the world might look like. That vision acted as a catalyst and gave momentum for a number of things, including the formation UN HESI and the advancement of Sulitest. (JN interview, 2023)

Through visible advocacy, thought-and-action leadership, and hands-on prototyping and experimentation the GRLI community works to:

- Convene, facilitate and foster collaboration amongst actors and actions that hold a shared interest in promoting and developing responsible leadership.
- Pioneer and prototype new methods for learning and community building.
- Incubate ideas and initiatives that create impact and that accelerate progress and transformation towards global responsibility.
- Contribute systemic and integrative thinking to the discourse on responsible leadership in education, research and practice.

Current activities include:

1. The Deans & Directors Cohort, formed in 2017, has grown into a Collaboratory comprising 100+ deans, directors, and learning partners acting as catalysts of change. The Cohort brings committed, senior-level individuals with skin in the game together in a participant-driven peer-learning initiative that involves and mobilises their institutions and ultimately strives to create systemic change. "In joining the cohort, the participants actually get to build deep and meaningful relationships that engender trust, and that sets up the conditions for collaboration beyond the logo or the ego" (JN interview, 2023).

2. GRLI collective action initiatives focus on transforming the role of higher education. One example is involvement in holding business school rankings to account. The conversation was initiated in 2017 asking "Can Business School rankings measure the positive impact of management education instead?" working closely with the Higher Education Sustainable Initiative where UN entities, sustainability networks and mainstream ranking agencies collaborate to address the incorporation of sustainability into ranking processes and criteria (GRLI, 2023).

3. The GRLI convenes, incubates and supports initiatives within and beyond their network, aimed at making global responsibility real. Examples include helping establish and steer UN PRME (2006), the 50+20 Agenda (2012), the Responsible Research for Business and Management (RRBM) initiative, the Sustainability Literacy Test, AIM2Flourish and the Positive Impact Rating among others (GRLI, 2023).

Leading on collaboration

The GRLI holds and facilitates an inclusive and collective call for deep systemic change across three domains: how we live and make a living, how we learn, and how we lead. Being consciously connected to one's own self, to others in meaningful relationships and to the whole is a prerequisite for making that change a reality. This emergent paradigm represents a shift in consciousness from "I" to "We" to "All of Us" and is illustrated in the GRLI logo.

The systemic change ambition of GRLI is at the core of their collaborative activities. "The driving question for its future work is 'how can we better align the landscape so that schools and institutions that need to collaborate can make sense of what's going on and figure out where to put their efforts – where should they be engaging?'" (JN interview, 2023)

One of the most recent collaborative efforts is to host conversations about questions for which there are no easy answers, named Courageous Conversations – which are publicly available online, thus "inviting voices that are not typically heard" (JN interview, 2023).

4.   PIR – Positive Impact Rating

The Positive Impact Rating (PIR) is a Swiss Association, governing the first rating of business school sustainability conducted by students for students. The PIR annual survey is the first time that students around the world assess their business schools on their positive impact. The rating survey asks students 20 questions in seven relevant impact dimensions. The Positive Impact Rating is inspired by the 50+20 Vision, which invites and challenges management education institutions to make a paradigm shift: seeking to be best for the world instead of best in the world (PIR, 2023).

> PIR is really very much a student oriented organization, it is student run – they collect the data and are the main stakeholder who is interested in the results. We have a student collaboration with oikos International, with PRME, GSBN and many further links. (TD interview, 2023)

Goals

PIR from the start had a clear goal to generate an alternative rating to the established rankings, such as the Economist or FT rankings, that are mostly based on economic, research and employability performance measures.

> The established rankings created differences between schools where there could sometimes be very little difference, we decided from the start to create a rating with 5 different ratings – like in the Michelin stars. We present schools alphabetically within the levels, and we only publish the top 3 levels because we don't want to play the shaming game, we want to be a positive force and help schools to develop. (TD interview, 2023)

PIR is capturing the voice of students to:

- Define the positive impacts of schools.
- Move from competition to collaboration.
- Provide a tool for change.

"Our intention was to be transformative of the business schools, we were convinced that business schools had to be more adaptive and contributing to (addressing) societal problems" (TD interview, 2023).

Governance

The PIR is formally organised as an independent, not-for-profit association under Swiss law. The organisational structure includes a president, a managing director, supervisory board and advisory board. It openly publishes its statutes on the website (PIR, 2023). The financial support initially was by external sponsorship, but quickly it was changed into a fee-based model. Discounts to participation fees are offered to schools from the Global South (TD interview, 2023).

Stakeholders

The PIR was created by concerned business school experts together with global NGOs – WWF, Oxfam, UN Global Compact – representing the environmental, social and economic perspectives respectively – as well as international student associations. It was supported by VIVA Idea and The Institute for Business Sustainability (IBS) (PIR, 2023).

Membership

In this fourth PIR edition in 2023, students from 71 business schools (69 rated) located in five continents and 25 countries participated in the survey. The number of student responses collected increased significantly from 8,802 in 2021, to 8,141 in 2022 and to 12,836 responses in 2023. This represents a 58% increase in 2023 compared to 2022 (PIR, 2023a).

One of the most interesting learnings from the PIR results relates to the difference between Global North and Global South schools. Based on the results published in the PIR ratings, schools from the Global South perform significantly better than schools from the Global North on the impact scale (PIR, 2023a).

Activities

PIR is involved in the collection and dissemination of ratings and best practices in the following ways:

1. Case studies provide real-life examples of positive impact in different business school settings from around the globe. They trace the individual stories and learning curves experienced by innovative business schools, faculty and students.
2. PIR provides schools with an international benchmark of progress on sustainable and positive impact, and the intelligence and data to drive internal change. The schools have used the results for social impact evidence, an annual KPI and to stimulate a student-led curriculum review.
3. While rankings position business schools typically in a highly differentiated league table, the PIR reduces the potential for competitiveness by grouping the schools on five different levels ("quintiles") according to their overall impact scores. In addition, the schools are listed alphabetically on these levels not by position. And only schools on the three highest levels are published.
4. PIR is being made useful to participating schools as a learning and developmental tool by integrating add-on questions that can be used for reporting to AACSB (student voice) and for the 2023/2024 rating cycle it will include PRME-related assessments. This clearly allows for more integrated effort on the reporting side among the various initiatives (TD interview, 2023).

Leading on collaboration

"The Positive Impact Rating aims to foster collaboration, inspire deep change and remove the competition and pressure of a traditional rating" (Katrin Muff, President, Positive Impact Rating Association).

The benchmarking capability of the PIR reflects in the PIR dashboard which allows participating schools to view and track their own performance but also compare their results against the overall average of schools participating. "There are plans to extend the comparison to within-level schools – e.g. comparing results against other schools on level 4" (TD interview, 2023).

During Global Deans' summits, deans from PIR schools jointly explore what impact means to them, in their regions and how they can learn from peer schools and global experiences. Cooperation and collaboration has been integrated into the PIR from the beginning, though efforts are being made to develop it further.

5.   BSIS – Business School Impact System

BSIS (Business School Impact System) initially created by FNEGE (French Foundation for Business Management Education) and internationalised by EFMD (European Foundation for Management Development) since 2012 is the first comprehensive impact assessment tool for business schools (Kalika, 2022).

The BSIS framework helps to create a global view of impact based on seven structured dimensions: financial, educational, business development, intellectual, ecosystem, societal and image impact (Kalika, 2022). It aims to communicate to business schools' stakeholders the real impact of the academic institution and help the institution understand its role and importance in its impact zone(s).

Goals

The main goal of the initiative is to demonstrate the impact of business schools to internal and external stakeholders. At a time when organisations are being held accountable for the externalities of their activities, the assessment provides evidence of their impact (EFMD, 2023).

Governance

Since its launch in 2012, BSIS is run as a joint venture between EFMD Global and FNEGE. Michel Kalika is the founder of BSIS and was the director for a decade. BSIS established a Steering Committee of 26 members worldwide to strengthen, guide and oversee the fast-growing BSIS (EFMD, 2023).

Stakeholders
The stakeholders within the process are the business schools, the governing organisations and the local or regional impact zones (EFMD, 2023).

Membership
Currently there are over 60 business schools that have been successfully accredited, the majority of them in France (EFMD, 2023). An EFMD member school can apply to use the assessment, it can be applied at a level of a business school, faculty or a whole university.

Activities
There are 3 main stages in the BSIS process:

- Stage 1 – Application: definition of the impact zone (city or region) and of the scope of the business school; submission of documents.
- Stage 2 – Data collection: preparation of documentation needed before the on-site visit with the help of the BSIS team.
- Stage 3 – On-site visit: a team of BSIS experts interviews a carefully selected group of key players within the School and a range of external stakeholders, after which a post-visit report by the experts is produced.

The BSIS team has an online data collection system to facilitate a simpler, streamlined and more efficient data collection process. Once the application process has been completed, schools will be given access to the system to begin the input of the assessment data. The data required is of two kinds:

- quantifiable data relating to measurable impact indicators (such as the number of jobs created in the impact zone or the money spent by out-of-zone students on board and lodging);
- qualitative data that can only be measured through judgement, corroborated with factual evidence (such as the School's contribution to the image of the city or region).

The expert report is written in two parts, the first part assesses the impact of the business school while the second part provides recommendations on how to improve impact.

The data collection should be finalised one month before the date of the on-site visit. The BSIS team will produce the pre-visit report directly from the BSIS online data collection system.

Subsequently, BSIS experts conduct a two-day, on-site visit. Their role during the interviews is to verify the accuracy of the information given, to challenge the conclusions in a constructive manner, to raise awareness both inside and outside the institution of the value of the school's regional impact and finally to make recommendations for more effective management of the relationship with its local environment.

After the school receives the BSIS label for a period of three years, they must commit to providing an annual progress report as an ongoing engagement to the process. They also have the option to renew the BSIS label after the three-year period (EFMD, 2023).

Leading on collaboration

While the assessment is applied on an individual school basis and the report on progress is not public, BSIS provide best practice cases and guidelines through public webinars and conferences. Though BSIS does not seem to create collaborative impact activities, it creates an impact in three ways: (1) on the communication of schools; (2) on their strategy, positioning and branding; and (3) ultimately on the culture of impact in HEIs (EFMD, 2023).

ANALYSIS OF SUPRA-HE INITIATIVES FOR POSITIVE IMPACT

What have the Initiatives Accomplished in Responsible Business and Management Education? Where are they Heading?

The initiatives described in this chapter have collectively, and separately, raised the expectations of business schools to be agents of change. The geographic reach and thematic scope of the initiatives, though not exhaustive, provides a snapshot in time of where the sustainable transition is taking place.

Interestingly an organisation such as GRLI has a sunset plan, meaning they hope that their positive impact will render their presence unnecessary and indeed have been set up with the vision to cease operations in some years (JN interview, 2023). Others have ambitions for increasing its membership – through expanding its geographic scope (BSIS) or types of organisations that contribute to responsible leadership beyond traditional business school (PRME).

What Activities and Strategies have been Used for Advancing Responsible Management Education, Research and Stakeholder Impact?

Although the majority of the initiatives adopted a membership association status – the variety and frequency of their activities vary significantly. From a survey to understand students needs and perceptions of their schools and universities (PIR) to impact reports publicly communicating Status on Progress (PRME), and internal impact assessment (BSIS) to shaping a community inquiring into global responsibility (GRLI) and developing a test of sustainability literacy (Sulitest /HESI). It is fair to say that most of the activities of those associations are not focused on promoting academic sustainability research, but rather on education and internal/external impact on stakeholders. In terms of research, a relatively new organisation (and beyond the scope of this chapter) called B Academics, associated with B Labs globally, aims to foster research on business as a force for good.

How do they Collaborate and Foster Dialogue and Partnership with other Stakeholders Towards Creating Positive Societal Impact?

"Collaboration (...) means creating the value together with a common purpose to bring the impact to society" (Pascual, 2021, p. 54).

It is evident from the research conducted here that collaboration is the underlying motivation of the great majority of those initiatives, as they recognise this is how they can multiply their impact. The environmental, social and economic state of the world demands deep change in many domains. The origins of many of those initiatives, such as the 50+20 movement, offers a vision of how management education can contribute to a world worth living in.

To achieve this, business and management schools must educate and develop globally responsible leaders; enable business organisations to serve the common good; and engage in the transformation of business and the economy. Within the ecosystem there is potential for several initiatives working together as they evidently have been – e.g., through meta structures such as HESI and shadow networks such as GRLI.

At each initiative level, they foster dialogue through creating spaces for different stakeholder groups within and outside business schools – Deans and students (GRLI), students and administrators (PIR), private industry sector and UN (PRME), an creating a multi-stakeholder fora (HESI).

How can the Initiatives be Helpful to Universities and Colleges Transitioning to Sustainability?

The challenge of transitioning established business schools into a positive impact space requires taking on a responsibility for educating a new generation of sustainable and responsible leaders. While many business schools adopt this responsibility, the route to achieve this transformation is not entirely clear and certainly not easy. Various layers of cultural and legacy systems permeate their internal structures, faculty knowledge and internal/external communications. Therefore, by engaging with the supra-HEI initiatives, schools and universities can find both inspiration and aspiration.

Inspiration can come from even passive engagement with these initiatives – understanding their foundational principles, following their webinars, reading case studies of achievement of highlighted member organisations, researching their many publicly available resources. Naturally joining as a member allows for additional benefits. Once a critical evaluation of the benefits is undertaken, it is advisable to create a roadmap, with specific goals that the HEI aims to achieve and select the right membership and participation person(s) within the organisation. For example – if internal assessment of the school's impact is the most urgent, the Business School Impact Assessment (BSIS) can be a very useful tool. If, on the other hand, there is a strategic need to engage the students' body and understand their needs – getting involved in the Positive Impacts Rating (PIR) and administering a survey to own students can be advantageous. In the case of learning from peers, there are many options – at a Dean Level, GRLI organises the Dean's summit and Courageous Conversations, and PRME hosts an annual high-level conference. Gradating into more active involvement within the initiatives themselves, equally, the options are extensive – from working and action groups (GRLI, PRME, HESI) to award self-nomination (HESI Green Gown Awards).

In the end the number and level of involvement in supra-HEI initiatives will be determined by each business school and university, aligning with their strategic goals and current status.

CONCLUSIONS

In conclusion, the initiatives in responsible business and management education have made remarkable progress in reshaping the landscape, emphasising sustainability and responsible management practices. Their achievements and activities reflect a shared commitment to promoting positive societal impact and fostering a transformative mindset within business schools. Nevertheless, it is important to recognise the complexity of these challenges. Sustainable development is a multifaceted issue that requires not only research and education but also substantial changes in policy, industry practices, and societal behaviour. HEIs play a role, but they are just one part of the puzzle.

The supra-HEI initiatives have raised the bar for business schools, encouraging them to become agents of change in a rapidly evolving world. They have demonstrated their geographic reach and thematic diversity, offering a comprehensive snapshot of where the sustainable transition is taking place.

There seems to be a consensus among the interviewees that what is needed is responsible leadership, which goes beyond business management and assessments. This is reflected in the names of several of the initiatives (e.g., GRLI) and if not in name, then certainly in remit (e.g., PRME). One reflection therefore is that we should talk about business and leadership education, rather than business and management education as has been customary, when it comes to sustainable transformation.

These supra-HEI initiatives, which bring together higher education institutions for collaborative efforts, are instrumental in advancing sustainability and responsible business education. Each has its own history, goals, governance structure, stakeholders, signatories, and scope of activities, but they all provide a framework for universities and business schools to align with common principles set out by HESI. On a single-school level, however, the gap between shared purpose and practical application can be substantial, which raises questions about how effectively HEIs can bridge this divide. Indeed, it is heartening to see how activities and tools are being updated to allow for a more practical application of the activities offered by supra-HEI initiatives. Projects such as the SIP 2.0 report dashboard from PRME leading to the development of PRME commons or the new functionalities in the PIR dashboard allowing for comparison against average on key student-led metrics or even the GRLI Courageous Conversations tackling conceptually difficult questions – are exemplars of the progress made.

One notable aspect of these initiatives is their forward-thinking approach, with some organisations, like GRLI, having a sunset plan that envisions a future where their presence is no longer required due to the positive impact of the whole ecosystem. Others, such as BSIS and PRME, aim to expand their membership and scope, further diversifying their influence. In either case it is imperative to assess the actual impact of these initiatives. Are they effectively catalysing change, or are they primarily symbolic in nature? A critical analysis would delve into the concrete outcomes and challenges faced by these initiatives. Here, apart from case studies and shared community knowledge, a stronger focus on data-led impact measures can be useful. This would also provide discernment on how best to allocate the membership fees that most initiatives require, at a time when the resources in business schools are scarce and could be put to more on-the-ground projects.

Collaboration and dialogue are central to these initiatives, with a strong emphasis on working together with various stakeholders to create a positive societal impact. They create spaces for dialogue among different stakeholder groups, both within and outside business schools. They may however face pressures from various stakeholders and may need to navigate complex political landscapes, potentially limiting their ability to remain entirely neutral.

For universities and colleges looking to transition to sustainability, these initiatives offer a wealth of inspiration, guidance, and resources. They provide a roadmap offering tools for assessment, engagement, and learning from peers. The level of involvement in these initiatives can be tailored to each institution's strategic goals and current status.

In summary, the role of HEIs in addressing global challenges and fostering sustainable transformation cannot be overstated. This overview sets the stage for a deeper exploration of how supra-HEI initiatives can facilitate collaboration, not competition, among HEIs guiding them towards the common goal of sustainability and responsible leadership.

LIMITATIONS AND RECOMMENDATIONS FOR FURTHER RESEARCH

This analysis sets the stage for further reflection on guiding schools towards sustainable transformation. It is based on secondary research through published reports and websites as well as structured interviews with three strategic representatives of those initiatives. Further research could contribute through conducting a field survey with a randomised sample of business schools shedding more light on the realities of engaging with these initiatives and their perceived strengths and weaknesses.

Furthermore, due to the scope of this inquiry limited to the business and management education sector, it is important to recognise there is much to be learned from other disciplines in sciences and arts that are also working towards positive impact (Shrivastava et al., 2020). It is crucial to be outward facing to benchmark not just within but also outside our own communities.

Finally, knowing how organisations with broad remits in higher education accreditation such as AACSB and AMBA are adopting sustainability leadership can provide an important extension to the existing research in future.

REFERENCES

Araç, S.K., & Madran, C. (2014). Business school as an initiator of the transformation to sustainability: A content analysis for business schools in PRME. *Social Business, 4*(2), 137–152, https://doi:10.1362/204440814X14024779688115

Arevalo, J.A., & Mitchell, S.F. (Eds.). (2017). *Handbook of sustainability in management education: In search of a multidisciplinary, innovative and integrated approach.* Edward Elgar Publishing.

Edwards, M., Benn, S., & Starik, M. (2017). Business cases for sustainability-integrated management education. In J.A. Arevalo & S.F. Mitchell (Eds.), *Handbook of sustainability in management education: In search of a multidisciplinary, innovative and integrated approach* (pp. 45–66). Edward Elgar Publishing.

EFMD (2023). EFMD Global website, https:// www .efmdglobal .org/ assessments/ business-schools/bsis/

Gonzalez-Perez, M.A., & Leonard, L. (2015). The Global Compact: Corporate sustainability. In M.A. Gonzalez-Perez & L. Lenard (Eds.), *The Post 2015 world in beyond the UN Global Compact: Institutions and regulations.* Emerald Publishing.

Goodall, M.B., & Ivanova, M. (2023). Collective ambition for global action: Role for the knowledge sector. In W. Purcel & J. Haddock-Fraser (Eds.), *The Bloomsbury handbook of sustainability in higher education: An agenda for transformational change.* Bloomsbury Publishing.

GRLI (2017). Global Responsibility Now manifesto, GRLI, https://grli.org/wp-content/uploads/2017/12/GRN_manifesto_2017-yr-logo.pdf

Haddock-Fraser, J. (2023). Sustainability member associations for universities. In W. Purcel & J. Haddock-Fraser (Eds.), *The Bloomsbury handbook of sustainability in higher education: An agenda for transformational change.* Bloomsbury Publishing.

Kalika, M. (2022). BSIS: A decade of impact, Edition EMS. Retrieved from https://www.perlego.com/book/3740447/bsis-a-decade-of-impact-pdf (Original work published 2022).

Mihov, I. (2023). *PRME's Role In Advancing The Broad View Of Business As A Force For Good, in Responsible Management Education The PRME Global Movement.* Routledge.

Morsing, M. (2021). *PRME – Principles For Responsible Management Education Towards transforming leadership education, in Responsible Management Education The PRME Global Movement.* Routledge.

Muff, K., Dyllick, T., Drewell, M., North, J., Shrivastava, P., & Haertle J. (2014). *The 50+20 origin of the collaboratory 1.* Routledge.

Ojiambo, S. (2023). *PRME – An initiative of the UN Global Compact, in Responsible Management Education The PRME Global Movement.* Routledge.

Pascual, J. (2021). *Innovation and collaboration in the digital era.* De Gruyter.

PIR (2023). Positive Impact Rating. www.positiveimpactrating.org/

PIR (2023a). PIR Report 2023: Accelerating the societal impact of business schools.

PRME (2017). PRME Impact Report: Impact A Decade of Principles for Responsible Management Education.

Purvis, M., & Grainger, A. (2004). *Sustainable development: Geographical perspectives.* Earthscan.

Shrivastava, P., Smith, M.S., O'Brien, K., & Zsolnai, L. (2020). Transforming sustainability science to generate positive social and environmental change globally. *One Earth, 2*(4), 329–340.

Sulitest (2023). Sulitest governance website, en.sulitest.org/gouvernance.

UN DESA (2023). UN Department of Economic and Social Affairs: Sustainability website, https://www.sdgs.un.org

UN PRME (2023). PRME website, https://www.unprme.org/

11. Disrupting the business curriculum for sustainability and the common good: the Glasgow Caledonian New York College experiment

Jacqueline LeBlanc and Gastón de los Reyes

1. INTRODUCTION

With inspiration from its then-Chancellor, Nobel Peace Prize laureate Muhammad Yunus, Glasgow Caledonian University (GCU) launched its newest campus in 2017 in New York City to promote its common good mission and commitment to the United Nations Sustainable Development Goals. The resulting experiment, Glasgow Caledonian New York College (GCNYC), is a graduate institution offering master's programs in sustainability and social impact. In 2020, it launched the only master's program in Sustainable Fashion in the US, complementing its business degree. As a new player in higher education still on a journey to accreditation and approval for Title IV, GCNYC focused on business relationships with fashion industry employers willing to sponsor employees and partnered with these employers to bring impactful change to business practice. Those who have graduated from our programs have in turn become directors of sustainability efforts at major fashion companies or have launched their own social ventures. Perpetuating a symbiotic relationship between education and business, these alumni, together with practitioner faculty, infuse the GCNYC education with impact projects to redesign business for social and environmental improvement.

In this chapter, we show that GCNYC has radically reimagined sustainable business education from the ground up. We argue that GCNYC's success in doing so is the product of two important strategic commitments. The first is that the College sees itself fundamentally existing to respond to the needs and aspirations of professionals who have come face-to-face with the devastating limitations of business-as-usual and urgently want to contribute to transformative business practices. Second, the College made the strategic decision to embrace the teaching potential of faculty who are themselves leading professionals at the cutting edge of sustainability practice. This combination of commitments has yielded a curriculum and institution that meet the moment in real time, transforming education into the practice of politics, allyship, and the co-creation of innovative solutions to the 21st century's most pressing challenges. The result of this co-creative exercise is a mode of education that is hypersensitive to the needs of the professionals coming to GCNYC and their aspirations to become disruptors for sustainability.

In the institution's short life, the GCNYC community has experienced the virtuous circle of mission encouragement that we label the Sustainability Impact Loop (Figure 11.1), providing an education that responds to, influences, and is influenced by business practice. GCNYC recruits professionals who aspire to answer the increasing demand for sustainable innovation, and these students learn from more seasoned professionals who are actively meeting that demand, graduating to become activist practitioners themselves, redoubling GCNYC's educational impact.

As crucial as the College's strategy has been to its success delivering student-professionals the sustainable business education they are looking for, we argue that GCNYC's capacity to enact this strategy has depended on unique governance features that are rare in higher education. As an institution chartered by New York State, GCNYC exists entirely outside the faculty governance forms of its parent university in Scotland. Moreover, the College is governed through an executive, the Vice-President & Provost, who is accountable to a Board of Trustees and yet not slowed down or held back by traditional forms of faculty governance. This has allowed GCNYC to move nimbly and boldly in transforming its curriculum and creating new programs unbounded by faculty factions and outmoded routines and ideas. In doing so, the relationship between GCU and GCNYC has exemplified the message of Clayton Christensen's classic studies in disruptive innovation: "Place responsibility for building a disruptive technology business in an independent organization" (Bower & Christensen, 1995, p. 52). Indeed, as will be discussed, the gravest threats to the College's positioning as a disruptor in sustainable education result from the ways that Bower and Christensen's admonitions to incumbents committed to disruption *have not* been heeded (see de los Reyes & Scholz, 2019).

Through our case study of GCNYC, we seek to make two contributions. First, we describe what we consider an inspiring experiment in sustainable business education to show leaders in higher education and student-professionals what is possible today. Second, we contribute to the literature on disruptive governance in higher education by demonstrating opportunities and limitations for governance innovations to yield pedagogical innovations that drive towards sustainability. In concrete terms, we would like to elucidate the governance strategies that higher education boards of trustees, presidents, and deans might undertake to stimulate bottom-up experimentation geared to prepare today's professionals for tomorrow's sustainable business practices. In suggesting to GCNYC's competitors in higher education how to promote sustainable business education successfully, we share the sentiment of Allbirds cofounder, Tim Brown, who justified his company's partnership with Adidas (see Brandenburger & Nalebuff, 2011) this way: "When it comes to sustainability, we don't see ourselves competing with one another, but competing for the future" (Alger, 2021). "If we don't bring about change quickly, there won't be a future to speak of."

To frame the governance and strategy puzzle implicated by GCNYC's founding mission to provide professional education *for the common good*, the chapter begins with a review of the literature on sustainable governance in higher education as applied to the history of business ethics. Next, the case study begins with a brief history of GCNYC that sets the stage for the key strategic commitments that give rise to what we have labeled the Sustainability Impact Loop. After reviewing the key dimensions of this loop and the nature of its virtuous circle, we identify key challenges and limitations that face GCNYC itself – organizationally and as a function of increasingly competitive market conditions in higher education – as well as the general opportunity in higher education for disruptive governance that experiments with ways to respond to the needs of today's business professionals who demand no less than an authentic and effective commitment to sustainable business.

2.   DISRUPTIVE GOVERNANCE IN HIGHER EDUCATION

The core thesis of the classical literature on disruptive innovation is that the "resource allocation process" (Bower, 1970; Bower & Gilbert, 2005) of the large, publicly traded corporation – from the answerability of top management to capital markets to the evaluation and incentive structures that influence middle managers responsible for business units – systematically undermines the proclivity of these organizations to invest for the long term in exploratory ways that might create value for customers and address social needs not well served by the status quo (Bower & Christensen, 1995; Christensen & Bower, 1996; Christensen, 2013). Christensen extended the theory of disruptive innovation to the contemporary university, elucidating the resource allocation process in higher education by virtue of its genesis and genetics:

> Much as the identity of a living organism is reflected in its every cell, the identity of a university can be found in the structure of departments and in the relationships among faculty and administrators. University DNA is not only similar across institutions, it is also highly stable, having evolved over hundreds of years … . The

way things are done is determined not by individual preference but by institutional procedure written into the genetic code. (Christensen & Eyring, 2011, pp.2–3)

This institutional legacy manifests in myriad ways that conspire to frustrate universities' capacity to radically innovate whenever faculty or alumni are not convinced they will benefit from the experiment.

We are especially concerned with the hindrance the typical university's resource allocation process creates for radical changes to the curriculum, even when those curriculum changes are required to address serious deficiencies in the status quo learning objectives of business education. To explain the ideological orientation and limitations of the curriculum that still prevails today, Sharma and Hart (2014) also, like Christensen, look to the past with appeal to the values dominant in business and law at the end of the 19th century and the start of the 20th when business schools first came on the scene (see Stinchcombe, 1965). In 1886, they observe, the Supreme Court reversed earlier precedent that put the state's interest in corporations ahead of corporations' private interests, holding instead that "a corporation is a natural person under the U.S. Constitution and is entitled to protection under the Bill of Rights, and its rights to free speech and due process of law cannot be taken away by the state" (Sharma & Hart, 2014, p. 11). Not surprisingly, the resulting curriculum aligned with the burgeoning views of neoclassical economics that privileged the autonomy of private power over accountability to public interests (see also Khurana, 2010).

Ever since, whenever public criticism of business has put pressure on business schools to change, change has generally come, if at all, at the margins and consequently joins the standing curriculum cacophonously:

> In response to societal criticisms, during the 1960s and 1970s, business schools began to gradually add courses in business ethics and CSR. However, these courses were either solitary electives or, if required, were overwhelmed by the often-contradictory messages contained in the "core" curriculum. (Sharma & Hart, 2014, p. 12)

The case of business ethics illustrates just how difficult it is to transform the business curriculum from the ground up. The University of Pennsylvania's Wharton School is renowned today for its influential business ethics faculty and outsized influence on the subject. Much of that success owes to the vision of Thomas Dunfee, who among other feats transformed the "Business Law" department, dating back to the school's founding in 1881, into the "Legal Studies and Business Ethics" department for the 21st century, launching the first Ph.D. program in business ethics. Decades earlier (and sponsored by the

Exxon Education Foundation) Dunfee anticipated Sharma and Hart's concerns by arguing for the integration of business ethics in *every course*:

> There are many reasons why ethics typically takes a back seat in a business curriculum. In our ever more complex economic world, there are many topics that are important for future managers to understand. New technologies, internationalization, and new techniques in marketing, management, and finance all compete for limited openings in the required curriculum. Many schools find it difficult to obtain qualified faculty to teach ethics courses. When a school such as Wharton creates a new core course required of all students, it is necessary to hire or reallocate five or six faculty to teach the many sections required for the course. But a required separate course in business ethics may not be the most effective way to teach the subject. A separate course may imply that the topic is somehow exogenous to functional business school courses such as finance and marketing. When there is a separate course, ethics may tend to be discussed in that course and deemphasized in the "real" business courses. (Dunfee, 1986, p. 5)

Notwithstanding the capacity of the Wharton School to attract corporate funds for an in-depth study of curriculum change, the proposal never took. The Legal Studies and Business Ethics department continues to serve as the purveyor of a stand-alone business ethics course that invariably has to contend with the challenge of helping students question the premise that the purpose of the corporation is to maximize shareholder profits, which is what their finance professor still teaches them.

How, then, should universities try to catch up to meet today's crisis in planetary sustainability? Given the similarity in the reasons why universities and large corporations as institutions each struggle to innovate transformatively (see de los Reyes & Scholz, 2019; Christensen & Eyring, 2011), the pathway towards disruptive innovation in higher education may parallel those that have been identified for business: "forming small teams into skunk-works projects to isolate them from the stifling demands of mainstream organizations" (Bower & Christensen, 1995, p. 52). If "[c]reating a separate organization is necessary ... when the disruptive technology has a lower profit margin than the mainstream business and must serve the unique needs of a new set of customers" (p. 52), what this means for graduate education is that a new academic organization may well be necessary when the innovative program under development will draw fewer students at the start precisely because the program is serving the unique needs of a new set of student-professionals.

Whereas at the turn of the 21st century, public concerns drove attention to business ethics (even if at the margins), public concerns today express themselves in the language of "sustainability" and for good reason (Wright & Bennett, 2011). As much as the fraudulence of management at companies like Enron and the greed of bankers on Wall Street undermined public confidence in business, the gravity and palpability of imminent ecological collapse has created an existential imperative for professionals worldwide who are personally committed to learning how to engage in business with a positive impact on people and the planet. The fact that universities appear, as Christensen would predict, hamstrung to adequately answer the educational needs of these new students means that, as educators, we are each moved by the imperative of finding ways to deliver what these professionals seek from a graduate professional degree. Consequently, we were each drawn by the unique circumstances that, as we will now review, (intentionally or not) endowed GCNYC with the exact conditions Bower and Christensen advise incumbent parent organizations to create if they genuinely wish to foster disruptive innovation.

3.   GCNYC'S ORIGINS AND STRATEGIC COMMITMENTS

As we noted, GCNYC's innovative curriculum benefits from a simplified and nimble governance structure. The initial curricula for the master's programs at GCNYC were modeled on those developed by faculty of similar master's programs offered at Glasgow Caledonian University. While the courses within these curricula provided a strong foundation in building an innovative curriculum that featured sustainability at its core, GCNYC has since had the opportunity to reshape the courses from a practitioner lens, a disruption that was made possible by our independence from the parent university's faculty governance structure. The syllabi for these courses were not subject to approval by the long-established curriculum committee within the School of Business & Society at GCU. Rather, they were approved by a newly created GCNYC Academic Board constituted by a panel of practitioner faculty led by the Provost, an academic with a humanities background and a long career of working with non-traditional practitioner faculty. In addition to ensuring a level of challenge and learning appropriate for graduate-level education, the main objective of the GCNYC Academic Board was to shape a curriculum that would transcend long-held assumptions about business strategy. To achieve this, inviting professionals who were active in the field to teach was clearly imperative and achievable because the tenure structure and accompanying scholarship expectations of the parent university did not apply to this new campus. The faculty members of the Board understood the challenges of creating sustainable business practice from the front lines and sought to support the Provost's effort to formulate solutions in real time, a perspective that was weaved into the coursework and refreshed each trimester. GCNYC's curricula have remained current through faculty who practice at the cutting edge. GCNYC's faculty has included the head of sustainable finance solutions for Bloomberg, a strategist for the voting rights activist organization Future Now, the leader who spearheaded Unilever's legendary ESG efforts, and the program director for impact investments and social entrepreneurship at the Pershing Square Foundation.

In addition to instituting a professionally driven Academic Board and faculty, GCNYC has formed close ties to business. At its launch in 2017, GCNYC took advantage of a growing demand within businesses for sustainability professionals in the fashion industry. Led by its founding Vice President, a veteran fashion executive, the College very intentionally addressed the mounting pressures felt by fashion companies to stem their destructive environmental impact (Bick et al., 2018). This included creating the Fair Fashion Center, which convened fashion CEOs to strategize a new path towards sustainable practice. GCNYC's direct connection to employers proved fertile ground for initial recruitment to a program that sought to challenge the standard business trope of shareholder primacy, and the first cohorts of students came from the fashion firms participating in the events of the Fair Fashion Center. These companies sponsored employees to complete the master's programs and tapped them to bring their education to bear on what they hoped would be new business strategies to balance a concern for people and planet with profit. GCNYC's first classes of students were overwhelmingly comprised of mid-level leaders in the fashion industry, personally disillusioned with the environmentally and socially destructive practices of the business and passionate for change. With this kind of experience and personal commitment, GCNYC's professional students and its practitioner faculty pushed each other forward to contemplate new frontiers of sustainability in business.

GCNYC's effort to directly meet an industry's needs and demands translated into career outcomes for these first cohorts that positioned them to make a real impact on sustainability practice. Over 40% of these first alumni moved into positions within business directly related to sustainability. Alumni positions have included Sustainability Lead at Macy's, Vice President for Materials and Sustainability at PVH, Director of Sustainability at Ralph Lauren, and Sustainability Manager at Theory. Other alumni advanced in their careers as fashion designers and worked from those positions to institute more sustainable practices. Still others left the fashion industry to work for consultancies and non-profits such as Forum for the Future and the Savory Institute that push for change throughout the supply chain.

As sustainability strategy took firmer hold in the fashion industry, subsequent cohorts of students came through more traditional recruitment channels such as referral or digital search. They enrolled in the master's programs to upskill for careers that would match their values. While not sponsored by employers, they came with a desire to fix the social and environmental damage they witnessed on the job, and their work for change would often come at the grassroots level – through their own imagination and initiative. One discouraged student, Emily, was a designer of children's apparel frustrated that her company demonstrated little-to-no interest in changing their practices to reduce the company's damaging impacts. Within six months after graduation, however, Emily reported the good news that her company had begun to listen to her pleas and had approached her to design their first-ever sustainability strategy, awarding her the additional title of Sustainability Manager. Emily was positioned and prepared by her GCNYC education to see and seize the opportunity for change created by a gradual evolution in management's values coupled with the demands of retailers for evidence of sustainable sourcing.

The increasingly widespread call to act responsibly throughout the supply chain resulted in more positions for GCNYC graduates to fill, within companies and also within the growing number of consultancies hired by businesses to develop sustainability strategy. By 2022, over 60% of GCNYC alumni were in positions specific to sustainability and/or social justice, and the positions included a range of fields outside of fashion. Graduates achieved titles such as Sustainability Consultant for Anthesis Group, Training Coordinator for Social & Labor Convergence Program, and ESG Lead for Private Equity at Blackstone. The career trajectories of alumni, particularly within positions poised to make positive impact, represent GCNYC's key metric in measuring the success of our programming. The importance of our alumni for the realization of GCNYC's common good mission means that we follow our alumni closely and learn from their on-the-job experiences to make sure our curriculum continues to deliver what our students and future changemaker alumni require.

Sustainability through Responsiveness to Professionals Personally Committed to Sustainability

The foundations and trajectory of GCNYC have spurred innovation at rates unusual in higher education at all levels – from revising curricula to launching new programs and adapting to the preferences of professionals who are personally pushing the frontiers of diversity and inclusiveness in business. Four years after the College's launch, the Provost and Faculty Chair spearheaded a comprehensive curriculum review and revision with a process grounded in input from alumni and other industry professionals (Tables 11.1 and 11.2). Recent graduates and practitioner focus groups advised GCNYC to add even more practical information to the curriculum, recommending a roadmap of learning objectives mirroring the demands of a sustainability manager. Practitioner faculty noted the increasing policy-driven demands on ESG strategists to measure environmental and social impact and report the outcomes to external authorities. If the curriculum, they said, can anticipate the needs of sustainable business strategy, graduates will be poised to meet demand as soon as it arises.

The curriculum revision's response to these recommendations is exemplified in the development of two key courses: The Chief Sustainability Officer and Sustainability Policy & Metrics. Taught by the former global sustainability lead for Unilever, the former takes students through the key responsibilities of a CSO and the design of a comprehensive sustainability initiative. The Policy & Metrics course introduces students to the methods, challenges, and potential of impact measurement and how policymakers translate such metrics into the practice of sustainability. This course has been taught by the Head of Corporations and Supply Chains at CDP, the non-profit whose carbon-footprinting methodology is now required of major suppliers to the federal government (CDP, 2022), and also by one of the founding members of the Investment Advisory group of SASB (Sustainability Accounting Standards Board), the leading purveyor of sustainability standards and metrics for investors. Sustainable Fashion coursework was further strengthened by the introduction of courses that home in on sustainable materials and labor practices in the fashion supply chain. The hands-on nature of this curriculum is also enhanced by a sustainable fashion proseminar that features guest speakers from the field. Driven by faculty and an Academic Board whose priority was the immediate needs of business to drive social change, the curricula revision process was conducted and approved in under nine months. Just introduced in fall 2022, the new curriculum is already showing positive outcomes among graduates, one of whom has been hired by CDP, reportedly impressed with her up-to-date knowledge of sustainability measurement and reporting practice.

The introduction of new programs has been similarly responsive to the current and anticipated needs of business, and GCNYC has been able to move swiftly from conception to approval and implementation. In the wake of the George Floyd murder and Black Lives Matter protests, projections for job openings in diversity managers increased dramatically, and GCNYC saw an opportunity to fulfill this projected demand and social need. A Master of Science in Diversity, Equity, and Inclusion Leadership was thus included in the College's Strategic Enrollment Plan, and a consultant was hired to design the curriculum. A master's in Data Analytics for Sustainability was also conceived and designed to fulfill the growing need for data scientists specializing in the analysis of environmental and social impact. Both of these programs were co-created by academics and practitioners from organizations such as B-Lab to ensure the up-to-date relevance of the curricula. Benefitting from GCNYC's distinctive governance structure, each of the programs was designed and approved within six months.

Table 11.1   GCNYC curricula revisions for M.S. business for social impact & sustainability

M.S. Business for Social Impact & Sustainability

Original	Credits	Revised	Credits
Navigating Global Change	4	Navigating Global Change	3
Business Strategy for the Common Good	4	Business Strategy for the Common Good	3
Values-Based Leadership	4	Values-Based Leadership	3
Global Political Economy	4	Introduction to Quantitative Analysis	1.5
Money as a Force for Social Good	4	Economic Concepts & Policy	1.5
Impact through Social Entrepreneurship	4	Sustainability Policy & Metrics	3
Research Methods/Thesis	12	The Chief Sustainability Officer	3
		Money as a Force for Social Good	3
		Impact through Social Entrepreneurship	3
		Research Methods/Thesis	12
Total	36	Total	36

4.   THE DISRUPTIVENESS OF THE SUSTAINABILITY IMPACT LOOP

We have shown that the strategic commitments available to GCNYC and embraced on account of its mission for the common good have allowed GCNYC to break the business school mold for a curriculum conceived from the ground up from *today's* needs. In this section, we describe the virtuous circle of reinforcement that has resulted, as depicted in Figure 11.1, and the disruptiveness this loop has stimulated. We will discuss how GCNYC has spurred: (i) political activism from students militating for the New York Sustainable Fashion Act, (ii) allyship between alumni and students that continues to cross-fertilize their education with the state of the art, and (iii) the co-creation of real-world solutions by GCNYC and its students with industry. GCNYC carefully tracks the work of alumni to understand the success and challenges they face in their drive to apply what they learned in the classroom to be truly transformative leaders of business.

Table 11.2   Curriculum revision for M.S. in sustainable fashion

M.S. Sustainable Fashion			
Original	Credits	Revised	Credits
Navigating Global Change	4	Navigating Global Change	3
Business Strategy for the Common Good	4	Business Strategy for the Common Good	3
Values-Based Leadership	4	Values-Based Leadership	3
Sustainable Fashion Strategy	4	Sustainable Fashion Strategy	3
Fashion as Culture/Culture as Fashion	4	Fashion as Culture/Culture as Fashion	3
Purpose-Driven Marketing and Communications	4	Sustainability Policy & Metrics	3
Research Methods/Thesis	12	Material Considerations in the Fashion System	1.5
		Social Considerations in the Fashion System	1.5
		Introduction to Quantitative Analysis	1.5
		Sustainable Fashion Proseminar	1.5
		Research Methods/Thesis	12
Total	36	Total	36

Alumni Action

Alumni well placed in leadership roles in sustainability have presented opportunities to infuse the GCNYC curriculum with practitioner faculty and impactful practice. An alumna, Michelle, who worked in sustainability strategy for fashion company Mara Hoffman, pivoted to an academic career, embarking on a Ph.D. dissertation in sustainable fashion and helping GCNYC to design and then lead its unique M.S. in Sustainable Fashion. Another alumna, Lorenza, launched both a sustainable farming venture and a career in teaching sustainable textiles after a long career in product development at Ralph Lauren. A third alumna became Senior Sustainability Strategist at Forum for the Future and partnered with a student writing her thesis whose research supported Forum's projects. These alumni are emerging scholar professionals who mentor GCNYC students and collaborate with them on both scholarly and professional projects. Shanley, an alumna deeply involved in GCNYC's work, brought to the college her research work related to workers' rights in the fashion supply chain. A project born out of her master's thesis at GCNYC, the project created a system for tracking the experiences of factory workers in

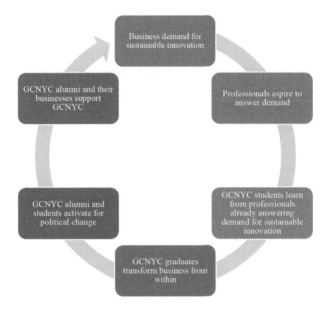

Figure 11.1   Sustainability Impact Loop

the fashion supply chain in Rwanda. To expand the project, Shanley worked with two GCNYC international students who decided to use the holiday break to conduct interviews with factory workers in their home countries of Peru and India. Alumni connections have also brought relationships to local small businesses and organizations working in circularity. These include Fabscrap, where students volunteer to sort and organize textile waste for repurposing and Anybag, which has benefitted from student contribution to strategies supporting its re-use of plastic bag waste in its manufacturing.

Another graduate, Sharon, demonstrates the progression of the Sustainability Impact Loop in her own trajectory to GCNYC and as alumna. Coming from a family tradition in fashion, Sharon came to GCNYC with a passion for circular approaches to sustainability and wrote her thesis, "Building a Profitable Domestic Textile Waste Recycling and Innovation Industry in New York City in a Covid-19 Impacted Economy", as an applied public policy exercise, partnering with a variety of New York City government officials for her applied research. As a graduate, Sharon brings what she learned at GCNYC to her contributions as Textile Waste Committee Chair of the Manhattan Solid Waste Advisory Board (MSWAB).

The ideal expression of this approach at GCNYC creates a virtuous circle (Figure 11.1), with alumni educated in sustainable practice at GCNYC obtaining positions of impact that bring projects to our students that continue this impact. A strong example of this is a collaborative proposal for Calvin Klein, where GCNYC alumna Elizabeth is now VP for Innovation and Sustainable Business Transformation. Elizabeth brought to the College two research projects, one evaluating the impact of natural and imitation leathers and the other measuring the lifecycle impacts of garments before and after updated manufacturing practices. Our goal is to make these ongoing research projects for GCNYC's Center for Social Impact and Innovation pursued by multiple students over several cohorts.

Maintaining close connections with alumni who are working on the front lines of nascent sustainability efforts has helped keep GCNYC curricula current and impactful. Many alumni report applying what they learned in classes to the strategies they put in place at work. Conversations with alumni, however, have also made us acutely aware of a discouragingly intractable gap between the practices they are taught in the classroom and what happens in the workplace. Alumni who are sustainability managers, report they have to assume defensive postures, intent on promoting genuine change but finding themselves instead frequently fighting against greenwashing practices within corporations whose persistent focus is still the bottom line. As one alumna put it, "I am an anti-capitalist in a capitalist framework. Who is really listening to me?" GCNYC's courses bring these themes into the classroom to prepare our graduates psychologically with the resilience they will need. They are reminded, for example, that John Elkington, who popularized the triple bottom line (people, planet, and profit) has abandoned his own concept in favor of a radical redesign of capitalism (Elkington, 2020).

Any business program deeply committed to sustainability must also recognize that achieving social and environmental goals will not come simply from changing business one company at a time. Government policy must be considered central to the effort, a reality that has entered the GCNYC curriculum through the new course Sustainability Policy & Metrics. Indeed, with the new environmental protection laws passed in 2022 by the Biden administration, sustainability managers have reported that federal regulations following this new law coming in 2023 will give them the clout they need to push forward their strategies. To address human rights and environmental concerns in fashion, GCNYC created the Fashion Policy Initiative co-led by the Program Director of the M.S. in Sustainable Fashion and two GCNYC alumni. This initiative puts GCNYC students and alumni in contact with other fashion sustainability leaders as well as environmental activists to develop and support public policy that protects natural resources and ensures fair labor practices. Through the Fashion Policy Initiative, GCNYC students and alumni have become actively involved in lobbying for the New York State Fashion Act which, if passed, will require mandatory social and environmental due diligence from fashion companies operating in the state. Students speak at rallies for the Fashion Act, travel together to Albany to meet with state legislators, and host these legislators on campus to promote the bill. The Fashion Act has become an important focal point of students' extracurricular activity and educates them firsthand on the role of policy in bringing about just and sustainable business practice.

Disruptive Outcomes of the Sustainability Impact Loop

GCNYC's unique approach to governance and teaching has connected with its distinctive cadre of students to transform business education, leading over 60% of GCNYC graduates to enter sustainability or social impact fields. We will continue to track career outcomes annually and interview alumni working in the field. Identifying metrics beyond alumni career outcomes is a next important step. Do alumni professionals make a difference in their companies' impact? Can key company metrics be used as a secondary metric for GCNYC? Our alumni as well as practitioner faculty will be engaged to guide the assessment's design.

5.   CHALLENGES FOR DISRUPTIVE GOVERNANCE IN HIGHER EDUCATION AND WAYS FORWARD

The independence from faculty governance and the resource allocation processes of its parent that GCNYC has enjoyed are in large degree the happy consequences of GCU's unique initiative to open a campus in New York City. In contrast with companies that have intentionally followed Bower and Christensen's (1995) seminal advice to create independent units that are "isolate[d] from the stifling demands of mainstream organizations" (p. 52), GCU did not impose upon itself a long-term horizon for GCNYC to explore and grow, as for example, Volkswagen has done with its own experiment in skunk works, Moia (Volkswagen, 2022). Consequently, GCNYC has become subject to the short-term pressures imposed by GCU's governance board.

Naturally, GCU's board is keen to see enrollment growth from its investment in New York. Unfortunately, for reasons that are well understood by scholars of innovation, this pressure and the demands imposed upon GCNYC's VP & Provost have steered resources towards efforts to achieve short-term enrollment growth and away from the project of building a curriculum for the future. Regardless, GCNYC's curricular experimentation has already borne fruit that can be harvested for new growth at home in Glasgow.

Table 11.3   Recommendations to leaders in higher education

Policy Principles	Actionable Recommendations	Examples in Practice
1. Free the experimental program / college to experiment	• Executive authority for the experiment not limited by vested interests in the status quo, i.e., faculty governance	• GCNYC's governance is not subject to GCU's faculty governance
2. Reconceive faculty roles to accommodate and privilege professional expertise	• Reconceive faculty roles to include lines practitioners with an evaluation structure that honors professional in addition to scholarly contributions	• Courses taught in the evenings or weekends, sometimes with hybrid and asynchronous formats • Grow ranks of professors of practice and teaching professors
3. Incorporate cutting-edge practice into the curriculum and student experience through industry and NGO partnerships	• Connect to businesses and organizations that will involve students in their sustainability work and embed this work in curricular and co-curricular activities	• Connect to organizations like the B Lab to facilitate applied student research and internships
4. Crowd out the status quo with the success of the growing experiment	• Once the experiment is getting traction "titrate" students from the status quo to the experiment	• The future of GCNYC?

6.   RECOMMENDATIONS FOR A DISRUPTIVE MODEL FOR COLLEGES AND UNIVERSITIES

GCNYC's model for disruptive change is highly unique, and the financial challenges of creating a separate start-up in an increasingly competitive higher education landscape make this particular model difficult to replicate. How, then, can more established institutions foster education geared towards transformative impact? First, those institutions should consider implementing a governance structure for curriculum development that puts decision-making in the hands of leadership that does not have a vested interest in maintaining the status quo. Include practitioners as well as scholars external to the institution in the decision-making process; create an advisory board of practitioners who have meaningful and ongoing influence. Second, rethink the make-up of your faculty. Create faculty lines specifically for practitioners with an evaluation structure that honors professional in addition to scholarly contributions. This could include lecturer roles but also non-tenure-track professors of practice and teaching professors. A corollary of this recommendation highlights the importance of flexibility in course delivery to accommodate the schedules of active professionals. Third, connect to businesses and organizations that will involve students in their sustainability work and embed this work in curricular and co-curricular activities. B-Lab offers B-Academics as a specific way for schools to engage in this work, but GCNYC found connecting directly to the professionals who do the work of sustainability assessment at B-Lab to be particularly valuable.[1] In addition to maintaining practical professional networks, schools should offer students opportunities to engage in the social and political activism aligned with the goals of environmental sustainability. These connections will breed career opportunities for graduates who will give back to the school's efforts. Finally, while the development of independent curricula specific to sustainability management remains important, developing these programs as niche opportunities running outside the "standard" management programs will not result in the impact needed for real transformation in business practice. The ultimate goal is the revision of the core business curriculum itself to shift its perspective to prioritize the social good and the protection of the environment alongside profit. The idea is to crowd out the old ways with the new, and we believe this means that university leadership should find way to "titrate" enrollment patterns away from the incumbent programs to the growing experiment. Embracing a bold governance approach and partnering with professional allies in a Sustainability Impact Loop can bring about transformation that can reverberate from education to business practice in generations to come.

7. CONCLUSION

GCNYC has pioneered cutting-edge graduate programs that respond to industry needs today and, therefore, the curricular needs of student-professionals committed to joining business to contribute positively to sustainability in business. GCNYC's success, we have argued, resulted from the confluence of strategic commitments enabled by a unique governance structure in higher education. Freed from the conservatism of faculty governance, GCNYC has leapfrogged over MBA programs, even at universities that have invested in sustainability by, first of all, embracing the needs of student-professionals in everything the school does, as best illustrated by the curricula currently offered to students (Tables 11.1 and 11.2). Second, by tapping into practitioner experts to teach its new courses, GCNYC has enacted the conditions for the powerful Sustainability Impact Loop that picks up on its students' and alumni's enthusiasm for sustainability to enrich curricular and extracurricular opportunities. We are especially proud of GCNYC's contributions to political discourse surrounding New York's Sustainable Fashion Act, representing everything the GCNYC community cares about.

The framework for action by higher education leaders that we have set forth in Table 11.3 will only succeed in universities that are open and attentive to the inevitable frictions involved in genuine transformation. Short-term demands are ever present on the dashboard of higher education leaders, and it is difficult to keep these demands from seeping through in ways that hinder innovation, for example, when launching a new educational venture in an unfavorable market. The risk of closure haunts these experiments in hope, and leaders committed to transformative innovation are unlikely to succeed if they deny these facts. By analyzing the significance of the parent university's governance choices and reviewing GCNYC's successes and challenges, we aim to provide higher education boards, presidents, and deans a framework for disruptive innovation poised to close the gap between aspirations for sustainable business and the education students receive today.

NOTES

1.   GCNYC hosted members of the B Lab in a webinar titled, B Lab and the Purpose of the Corporation, available at https://youtu.be/HhDpz88tisI

REFERENCES

Alger, K. (2021). Allbirds and Adidas have made the world's lowest carbon footprint running shoe. *Wired*. https:// www .wired .co .uk/ article/ adidas -allbirds -futurecraft -footprint

Bick, R., Halsey, E., & Ekenga, C.C. (2018). The global environmental injustice of fast fashion. *Environmental Health, 17*, 1–4.

Bower, J.L. (1970). *Managing the resource allocation process*. Harvard Business School Press.

Bower, J.L., & Christensen, C.M. (1995). Disruptive technologies: Catching the wave. *Harvard Business Review, 73*(1), 43–53.

Bower, J.L., & Gilbert, C.G. (2005). A revised model of the resource allocation process. In J.L. Bower & C.G. Gilbert (Eds.), *From resource allocation to strategy* (pp. 439–456). Oxford University Press.

Brandenburger, A.M., & Nalebuff, B.J. (2011). *Co-opetition*. Currency.

CDP. (2022). *In bold new move, Biden Administration makes CDP's model the law*. https://www.cdp.net/en/articles/media/in-bold-new-move-biden-administration -makes-cdps-model-the-law

Christensen, C.M. (2013). *The innovator's dilemma: When new technologies cause great firms to fail*. Harvard Business Review Press.

Christensen, C.M., & Bower, J.L. (1996). Customer power, strategic investment, and the failure of leading firms. *Strategic Management Journal, 17*(3), 197–218.

Christensen, C.M., & Eyring, H.J. (2011). How disruptive innovation is remaking the university. *Harvard Business School Newsletter, 25*.

de los Reyes Jr, G., & Scholz, M. (2019). The limits of the business case for sustainability: Don't count on Creating Shared Value to extinguish corporate destruction. *Journal of Cleaner Production, 221,* 785–794.

Dunfee, T.W. (1986). *Integrating ethics into the MBA Core Curriculum.* Trustees of the University of Pennsylvania.

Elkington, J. (2020). *Green swans: The coming boom in regenerative capitalism.* Greenleaf Book Group.

Khurana, R. (2010). *From higher aims to hired hands: The social transformation of American business schools and the unfulfilled promise of management as a profession.* Princeton University Press.

Sharma, S., & Hart, S.L. (2014). Beyond "saddle bag" sustainability for business education. *Organization & Environment, 27*(1), 10–15.

Stinchcombe, A.L. (1965). Social structure and organizations. In J.G. March (Ed.), *Handbook of organizations* (pp. 142–192). Rand McNally.

Volkswagen. (2022). *MOIA.* https:// www .volkswagenag .com/ en/ group/ brands -and -models/moia.html

Wright, N.S., & Bennett, H. (2011). Business ethics, CSR, sustainability and the MBA. *Journal of Management & Organization, 17*(5), 641–655.

12. Education for climate change: an andragogical approach with a transdisciplinary framework

Younsung Kim

1. INTRODUCTION

Climate change is a core global challenge requiring significant societal changes. Our society demands more climate education as extreme weather patterns and the physical impacts of climate change become more severe. Climate change education has expanded dramatically over the past decade (Monroe et al., 2019), and universities and colleges have been at the forefront of climate change education. The expansion reflects the increased funding for climate education (Anderson, 2012) and growing concerns over human livelihoods, such as disrupted food systems by droughts, floods, or wildfires (McNeill & Engelke, 2014; Moorhead, 2009; Wheeler & von Braun, 2013). Society will thus need more climate education, including not only basic climate science but the understanding of how to build solutions to the complex challenges posed by climate change.

Prior scholars admit that climate education is a complex curricular and pedagogical endeavor (Holtuis et al., 2015; Monroe et al., 2019). An apparent reason for the complexity is that climate change education requires contributions from various fields, including climate science, science education, social sciences, and curriculum education. Relying on such multidisciplinary aspects, students can identify problems and employ methodologies shared by multiple disciplines (Kim et al., 2022; McCright et al., 2013; Wickson et al., 2006). It is further argued that climate change, the most complicated environmental science subject, could be understood and researched well with a transdisciplinary approach (Kim et al., 2022; OECD, 2020), as the issue features complexity, diverse knowledge systems, contestation amongst diverse stakeholders, power imbalance, and disagreement on the need for transformative change (Kim et al., 2022).

Likewise, the subject itself and the approach to climate change education beyond disciplinary domains raise a critical question of how to teach it for knowledge transfer as well as perception and behavioral changes. It is known that when education helps students develop a strong *personal* connection to climate solutions and a sense of personal empowerment, it can have a consequential impact on students' daily behaviors and decision-making that lower their carbon emissions (Istance & Paniagua, 2019). However, little is known about how to design learning modules that effectively educate climate scientific facts and create personal connections to climate solutions, including personal support for climate policy formation that could affect their welfare.

This chapter fills this research gap and aims to explain an andragogical approach taken to teaching climate change in an environmental policy course at a public university in Virginia, US. As compared to pedagogy used for K-12 education, andragogy for adult education recognizes that learners have sufficient developmental maturity to explore the perspectives of others and cope with their own shifts in paradigm (Hampton & Rich-Tolsma, 2015).

There are two research questions asked in this study: (1) To what extent does the modular approach from climate science to management and policy increase students' understanding of core climate scientific information, and (2) whether the modular approach would beget students' support for regulatory climate policies. To answer the questions, this study employed a pretest-posttest experimental design approach with the climate change learning modules, ranging from science to international governance. The findings reveal that students enhanced their scientific knowledge of climate change and supported climate regulations that would require economy-wide carbon emissions cuts, not limited to emissions reductions from specific industrial sectors.

2.   CHALLENGES FOR EDUCATION ABOUT CLIMATE CHANGE

Climate change has become political, particularly in the US, and views on climate change are often aligned with political allegiances. Conservative belief-held people tend to ignore or contest scientific evidence on climate change (Cutter-Mackenzie & Rousell, 2018). People with liberal political orientations are more likely to accept climate change as a catastrophic crisis. They are then concerned about the disastrous impacts of climate change (Colebrook, 2014; Lowe et al., 2006; Stokols et al., 2009) and argue for concrete climate actions with serious concerns for the pessimistic future (Tucci et al., 2007). The competing perspectives illustrate that teaching climate change needs to aim for shifting students' attitudes toward climate change that would possibly contribute to their environmental behavior changes.

In discussing climate change education, several challenges should be laid out to understand why strategic approaches would merit climate education (Monroe et al., 2019). The first challenge is misconceptions about the cause and effect of climate change. For instance, despite the sixth assessment report by the Intergovernmental Panel on Climate Change (IPCC) (IPCC, 2023; Plumer, 2023), climate misinformation still thrives, leaving educators to think about how to change peoples' strong perception of climate change (Chen, 2011; Cutter-Mackenzie & Rousell, 2018; Sterman, 2011). Another challenge is that many teachers and faculty think they are not qualified to teach climate change and need more training and resources that could allow them to instruct climate science and actionable projects (Kwauk & Winthrop, 2021; Leiserowitz et al., 2011; Shepardson et al., 2009; Taber & Taylor, 2009).

Linked with the second challenge, the third challenge is that climate education has still been taught in a fragmented way, confined to disciplinary domains. For instance, science teachers focus on the carbon cycle and climate change-driven ecosystem changes. Teachers who value active learning underpin climate change as a local issue and focus on resilience projects. Still, others weigh in on teaching the topic with the international, evolutionary, and ethical aspects of climate change and climate injustice (Brownlee et al., 2013; Grady-Benson & Sarathy, 2015; Harris, 2009; Selin & VanDeveer, 2022). Nothing is wrong with each individual approach, but it is questionable how a transdisciplinary approach could be introduced to teach climate change to inform climate science and elicit voices and actions toward climate change (Rousell & Cutter-Mackenzie-Knowles, 2020). Further, the approach could offer insight and practical guidance for ethical living, having people be mindful of the preservation of all forms of life and practice self-control, restraint, simplicity, and guidelines respectful of the sanctity of all life (Millais, 2006; Posas, 2007).

Lastly, cognitive bias is problematic, creating a setback for climate change education. Unlike other environmental issues like biodiversity, cognitive bias diverges or affirms peoples' opinions about climate change and policies to address climate change. As a cognitive bias, confirmation bias is a tendency to seek and recall information that reinforces one's initial judgment. The bias creates cultural cognition, enabling people to protect their cultural identity and discounting information that conflicts with their group's position (Kahan, 2009). Therefore, designing and implementing programs about climate change may require a balancing act of increasing knowledge of climate change and shifting perception. To do so, educators acknowledge how cultural ideology plays a role in perception and learning (Guy et al., 2014; Hoffman, 2015; Monroe et al., 2019).

Climate change education in universities and colleges seems to address such challenges compared to primary and secondary education (Rousell

& Cutter-Mackenzie-Knowles, 2020). Open-source and web-based climate change education resources have been used (Haslett & Wallen, 2011). Cross-disciplinary consortiums between universities and communities have been created to develop pedagogy for climate education (Davison et al., 2014; Pharo et al., 2014). To create university students' energy-reducing actions, social media has been employed. While not linked with environmental and behavioral changes, climate change documentaries helped change students' attitudes toward climate change (Lowe et al., 2006; Leiserowitz, 2004; Howell, 2014). These examples indicate a trend toward interdisciplinary teaching, learning, and research, which employs diverse resources to teach climate change in universities and colleges.

Interestingly, some studies argue that climate change education should be associated with public policy (Hill, 2010), along with critical analyses of the implications of international climate policy for remote agricultural communities (Rai, 2010). This chapter in part responds to this call, highlighting the need to teach more climate policies to young voters who need to shape their future for carbon neutrality and to avoid climate-induced disturbances and hazards.

3.   METHODS

3.1   Climate Change Learning Modules

This research employs a one-group pretest-posttest design to examine students' climate science-related knowledge increase and their support for regulatory climate policy. The four climate change modules, from science and management to climate policy, were created in an environmental policy course and delivered to a public university in the mid-Atlantic region of the US. The university has a diverse student body and culture from highly engaged and vibrant student communities. The university is committed to impactful, transformative experiences for community engagement and civic learning so that students learn to be passionate about working to generate social change, whether in a small community, the nation, or the world.

The course is required for students majoring in environmental science and environmental and sustainability studies. With the rapidly rising interest in climate change and sustainability, recently, the course has drawn students from diverse academic disciplines, including communication, engineering, management, etc. It overviews various environmental policy and sustainability issues, covering natural resource management, biodiversity loss, industrial pollution control, climate change, energy transition, environmental justice, etc.

Climate change is taught in the second half of the semester, with four sequential modules. The sequential learning mode and formative assessment were taken in designing the learning modules. Sequential learning is when students go through a course in a specific order set by a teacher, frequently favored in online classes (Kim & Olesova, 2022). One part of the course should be thus taken before moving on to the next. Bypassing the contents may result in poor understanding and knowledge retention. To achieve sequential learning, instructors must first understand the logical order in which a skill can be mastered (Conway, 2012). For example, before teaching algae bloom, students first learn about protozoa, nitrogen and phosphorus loads, and agricultural runoffs. This way, when students are introduced to the concept of eutrophication, students will be familiarized with the major factors involved in it and how to address eutrophication by disentangling the driving forces.

On the other hand, the formative learning approach or formative assessment[1] aims to monitor student learning and helps students take ownership of their learning (Trumbull & Lash, 2013). It relies on various learning tools used to shape students' learning experiences, like students assessing themselves or peers through writing, quizzes, conversation, and more low-stakes assignments (Theall & Franklin, 2010). Also, instructors provide ongoing feedback to improve their teaching and to support students' learning (Nicol & Macfarlane-Dick, 2006).

Sequential learning stimulates student learning by introducing concepts and knowledge and then building on them. It prioritizes the logical order in which assignments move from conceptual knowledge to progressively more complex tasks like analysis, application, and synthesis. It thus focuses on an instructional designing process that requires mapping out learning materials and assessment tools (Angelo & Cross, 1993; Conway, 2012; Trumbull & Lash, 2013). In contrast, the formative learning approach focuses on building students' learning more flexibly through student feedback and low-stakes assessments, enabling instructors to respond to learning challenges immediately. As such, sequential learning results in fixed structural modularity, and formative learning helps check if the learning approach works (Marshuetz, 2005).

Following the sequential learning and formative assessment approaches, the four learning modules were created. Table 12.1 below presents topic, learning tools, main points, and assessment of the climate modules.

3.2   Study Design: One-Group Pretest-Posttest Design

A one-group pretest-posttest design is used when it can determine the effect of a treatment or intervention on a given sample. Two features characterize this research design. The first feature uses a single group of participants, indicating that all participants are exposed to the same treatments. The second feature is a linear ordering that requires the assessment of dependent variables before and after treatment is implemented. Within a pretest-posttest research design, the effect of a treatment is determined by calculating the difference in assessment

Table 12.1   Climate change learning modules from climate science to policy

Module	Topic	Learning Tools	Main Points	Assessment
1	Documentary Film. *Coal: Burning the Future*	Film, reflective essay	• Climate change as the greatest market failure	Reflective essay after film watch
2	Climate Science and the Physical Impacts of Climate Change	Lectures, videos, readings including IPCC (Intergovern-mental Panel on Climate Change) summary reports	• Causes and effects of climate change • Major ecosystem changes due to climate change	Assessment quiz
3	International Climate Governance	Lectures, videos, readings, open web-resources	• UNFCCC (United Nations Framework Convention on Climate Change) • Kyoto Protocol • Paris Climate Agreement • Emissions Trading Scheme and Carbon Markets	Assessment quiz
4	Climate Mitigation and Adaptation Policies	Lectures, videos, readings, open web-resources	• Climate actions • Adaptation meas-ures, including nature-based adaptation mechanisms	Research-based assignment for real-world-based climate adapt-ation and mitigation policies

taken before and after the treatment. Despite its simple design characteristic, the research design is criticized due to an internal validity concern. However, it is a pragmatic approach since random assignment to treatment and control groups is challenging for practical and ethical reasons, as seen in clinical experimentation research (Knapp, 2016).

The linear research design is presented in Figure 12.1.

3.3   Sample and Assessments

The environmental policy course was offered in the fall 2022, and there were 57 students in total. Among them, 36 students took part in the assessments before and after learning about climate change modules. Fifty-eight percent of

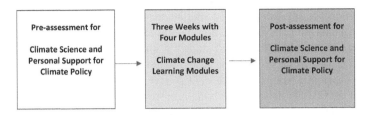

Figure 12.1   One-group pretest-posttest design for the impact of four climate change modules on student knowledge increase and personal support for climate policy

the class was female and 42% was male. Sophomores accounted for 24% of the class, while Juniors (41%) and Seniors (35%) were most of the class. The climate lessons were offered for the three weeks of the semester in October 2022. The assessments were given virtually, and students who took both assessments earned small participation credits, and 36 students participated in both pre-assessment and post-assessment.

Climate science knowledge is a dependent variable, being measured using National Aeronautics and Space Administration (NASA)'s quiz on Global Warming.[2] The quiz tests knowledge about global temperature change and its impact on Earth's climate. The eight questions were randomly selected from the Global Warming quiz questions, and students were asked to answer the same set of questions.

The personal support for climate policy formation is another dependent variable. It was measured using the 5-point Likert scale from strongly supportive to strongly unsupportive. The term "support" indicates a student's explicit favor for a policy. "Neutral" then describes the absence of support or opposition, which would be no active support or opposition against a given policy. In terms of climate policies, regulating carbon pollution from power plants, nationwide carbon taxes, national greenhouse cap-and-trade program, increase of corporate average fuel efficiency standards, increase of energy efficiency in building infrastructure, and subsidies for renewable energy industries were asked to rate students' support level.

4.   RESULTS

4.1   Climate Science Knowledge Enhancement

The study found that students' understanding of climate science was generally improved. Among the eight questions, students showed the largest increase of global warming knowledge in Question 3 as 23.20 percentage points. The question asked if students understand that changes in ocean and atmospheric circulation patterns have created small-scale temperature decreases in a few local regions. In contrast, Question 5 showed no changes in climate science knowledge. The question tested students' knowledge about global warming potentials of various greenhouse gases. Water vapor or other industrial greenhouse gases like Sulfur Fluorides (SF_6) have more heat-trapping power than carbon dioxide, while carbon dioxide is more abundant.

Question 2 also tested students' understanding of greenhouse gases. Water vapor was the only incorrect answer students chose instead of Nitrogen, illustrating that some students may not have clarity on the impact of water vapor to warm the planet.

Table 12.2 presents differences in students' climate science knowledge before and after climate change learning modules were instructed.

4.2   Climate Policy Support

With respect to personal support for climate policies, this study found modest increases compared to changes in climate science knowledge before and after the assessments. Students' support for nationwide carbon taxes had shown as the lowest with 30.56 percentage points in the first assessment, but it increased 55.57 percentage points, nearly an 82% increase. The support for national emissions trading schemes also increased. Students who marked "strongly supportive" increased from 50.00 percentage points to 61.11 percentage points, around 22% increase. However, interestingly, students' support for renewable energy industry subsidies dwindled from 72.22 percentage points to 61.11 percentage points, around 15.4% decrease. The changes might be attributed to students' enhanced understanding of carbon taxes or emissions trading schemes that could create carbon pricing schemes more visibly, through which all economic sectors could be more incentivized to reduce carbon emissions (Kim, 2023).

Students' support for regulating carbon pollution from power plants was not changed after the lesson modules. The increase of energy efficiency standards in building infrastructure was supported strongly regardless of students' learning with the climate modules, ranking as the highest support category among all climate policy measures suggested (Table 12.3). The sustainable design for green buildings seemed to be inarguably favored as they could lower carbon emissions and reduce energy costs cost-effectively.

5.   DISCUSSION

There are several points the study highlights. First, it is interesting to find that even students majoring in environmental science or environmental

Table 12.2 Pre-assessment and post-assessment of students'
understanding of global warming

Questions	Pre-assessment Students who answered correctly (%)	Post-assessment Students who answered correctly (%)	Percentage Changes
1. The six hottest years on record occurred during the last a. 100 years b. 50 years c. 10 years. (Answer: c. 10 years)	72.22	84.21	11.99
2. Which of the following gases does not trap heat/ a. Carbon dioxide b. Nitrogen c. Water vapor d. Methane. (Answer: b. Nitrogen)	69.44	84.21	14.77
3. No place on Earth is colder today than it was 100 years ago. (Answer: False)	41.66	64.86	23.20
4. Where have some of the strongest and earliest impacts of global warming occurred a. In the tropics b. In northern latitudes c. Impacts of global warming are distributed equally all over the planet. (Answer: b. In northern latitudes)	50.00	71.05	21.05
5. Compared to other green-house gases, carbon dioxide is the most effective at trapping heat near the Earth's surface. (Answer: False)	47.22	47.22	0
6. Some kinds of pollution in the atmosphere can act to cool the planet by reducing the amount of solar radiation that reaches Earth's surface. (Answer: True)	77.78	86.11	8.33

Questions	Pre-assessment Students who answered correctly (%)	Post-assessment Students who answered correctly (%)	Percentage Changes
7. Earth has been warmer in the past than it is today. (Answer: True)	58.33	72.22	13.89
8. If you removed the atmosphere's natural greenhouse effect, and everything else stayed the same, Earth's temperature would be a. 10 to 20°F (6 to 11°C) warmer b. 30 to 40°F (17 to 22°C) warmer c. 10 to 20°F (6 to 11°C) cooler d. 50 to 60°F (28 to 33°C) cooler. (Answer: 50 to 60°F (28 to 33°C) cooler	41.67	58.33	16.66

sustainability studies did not show high-level competency in climate change science-related information. Scientific evidence continues to show that human activities, primarily burning fossil fuels, have warmed Earth's surface and ocean basins, which in turn have continued to impact Earth's climate. This is based on over a century of scientific evidence endorsed by leading scientific organizations like IPCC and NASA (National Aeronautics and Space Administration). The scientific uncertainty of human causes for climate change is greatly diminished with greater than 99% consensus within the scientific community (IPCC, 2023, Lynas et al., 2021, Meyers et al., 2021).

In the climate science module in this study, students' learning was reinforced with graphs and key evidence supported by IPCC assessment reports such as carbon dioxide concentration changes in different periods (for the past 80,000, 2,000 years, and 270 years), and isotope evidence for climate change, as isotopes are used to measure past climatic properties. Students were also taught about the rigorous peer-review process that could dismiss subjective, biased, or politicized scientific information. Students acknowledged independent, evidence-based scientific information advances climate-related knowledge and laid out the contextual background for societal discussion about how to solve climate change. This approach could be expanded beyond disciplines in academia. University graduates of any discipline are expected to possess a reasonable level of environmental awareness to participate as responsible citizens in this critically important debate (Meyers et al., 2021).

Table 12.3   Pre-assessment and post-assessment of students' understanding of global policy

	Strongly Supportive		Moderately Supportive		Neutral		Strongly Unsupportive		Moderately Unsupportive	
	Pre (%)	Post (%)	Pre (%)	Post (%)	Pre (%)	Post (%)	Pre (%)	Post (%)	Pre (%)	Post (%)
Regulating carbon pollution from power plants	66.66	69.44	27.78	27.78	5.56	2.78	0	0	0	0
Nationwide carbon taxes	30.56	55.57	44.44	36.11	19.44	5.56	2.78	0	2.78	2.78
Nationwide greenhouse gases cap-and-trade program	50.00	61.11	33.33	19.44	13.89	1.67	2.78	0	0	2.78
Increase of Corporate Average Fuel Efficiency Standards	69.94	55.56	19.45	25.00	11.11	16.67	0	0	0	2.78
Increase of Energy Efficiency Standards in Building Infrastructure	77.78	80.56	16.66	16.67	5.56	2.78	0	0	0	0
Subsidies for renewable energy industries	72.22	61.11	19.44	25.00	8.34	13.89	0	0	0	0

It would be thus imperative to strengthen efforts to teach scientific consensus on climate change, focusing on greenhouse gas effects, greenhouse gases, global warming potentials by greenhouse gases, natural climate cycles, and the difference between global warming and climate change, etc. Such scientific knowledge can narrow the persistent gap between expert consensus on anthropogenic global warming and public understanding, providing the context for young voters to make non-politicized, informed decisions about stabilizing our climate (Abbot et al., 2023; Lynas et al., 2021).

Second, this study found increased personal support for economy-wide carbon pricing mechanisms. Nationwide carbon taxes or emissions trading programs are incentive-based climate policies that put prices on reduced carbon emissions (Kim, 2023). Carbon taxes are the least favored climate policy options, and public support is reported to be the lowest among various regulatory policy options (Levi, 2021; Rhodes et al., 2017), due to citizens' concerns regarding the use of revenues from carbon taxes (Hsu et al., 2008; Kallbekken & Sælen, 2011).

However, students' support for carbon taxes was greatly improved as they could understand that taxes are a direct pricing mechanism in which carbon pollution would be visibly revealed in market prices and governmental revenues could be used to promote equity for the socio-economically disadvantaged groups that bore inequitable environmental and health costs. That means personal support for carbon taxes grew when the benefit of carbon price visibility and the potential ways to increase equitable climate-resilient development by taxes were underscored. In contrast, students' strong support for renewable subsidies was reduced, as students understood the need to adopt carbon pricing schemes in tandem with subsidies for the renewable energy industry and clean technologies.

Third, students' high and unwavering support for emissions cuts from power plants and energy efficiency increases in the building sector indicate that students know that sectoral approaches can mitigate climate change effectively and the building and utility sectors are of high concern by college and university students. Particularly, students were very responsive to the documentary film *Coal: Burning the Future*,[3] which focuses on the impacts of mountaintop mining in the Appalachians and various environmental problems associated with coal mining, including disfigured mountain ranges, extinct plant and animal species, toxic groundwater, and increased flooding. Residents' suffering from water and floods was also highlighted. This film was used to provide students an insight into climate change as a market failure and negative externality, and the formative learning technique was a reflective essay. Students shared their lesson points, including understanding the lifecycle of coal from mining to combustion, along with their opposing sentiment toward fire-based power generation. Students also could tie a local environmental problem, mountaintop removal in West Virginia, and global climate mitigation, which strengthened their understanding of complexity and climate change intricately linked with justice and community development. This affirms coal mining discussion is effective in drawing a transdisciplinary approach to energy transition (Kim et al., 2014), for which explicit societal goals (Klein, 2004), collaborations between researchers and stakeholders (Norström et al., 2020), and stakeholder inputs (Wiek et al., 2014) are required.

With respect to the role of sequencing learning modules and formative assessment, this study found some modest increases in both climate science and personal support for climate change. Prior studies failed to prove the correlation between cognitive increases in knowledge about climate change and pro-environmental attitudes or behavior (Kempton, 1997; Dijkstra & Goedhart, 2012). This study highlights the need to educate about climate change to induce behavior changes, including both knowledge increase and situational or effective influences (Devine-Wright et al., 2004). Whether climate science knowledge increase is directly associated with personal support for regulatory change is beyond the scope of this study. Evidently, it is good to see the lesson modules modestly affected both knowledge increase and personal support for climate regulation, but it appeared that the climate lesson modules did not lead to radical changes in terms of personal support.

Related to the climate politics discussion, when students learned about climate treaties and the challenges of implementing climate adaptation and mitigation measures under COVID-19, energy insecurity, and potential economic losses (Bhutto, 2020; Mazzei, 2021; Selin & VanDeveer, 2022), students developed a nuanced understanding of the tradeoff between economic security and environmental sustainability. Noteworthy is that students' reactions were more analytic than advocating, as they were asked to break down economic, political, financial, and technological challenges related to climate adaptation and mitigation measures. For instance, in discussing the Miami city government's tough choices over how to cope with sea-level rises, students were divided toward creating any defensive mechanisms at the expense of the tourism industry. That resonates with students' learning about the complexity of climate solutions and the cost concerns for climate adaptation, which was translated into a reason for adopting climate mitigation policy mechanisms to curb carbon emissions.

6.   STRATEGIES TO EXPAND CLIMATE EDUCATION

Expanding climate education in universities and colleges must be andragogically strategic (Monroe et al., 2019). The first approach is to teach climate science with a focus on the cause and effect of climate science. Without scientific background or an accurate understanding of global warming and climate change, young people's voices and actions could not result in solutions that address the root causes of the climate issue. For instance, knowledge of Kyoto-based greenhouse gases, their sources, and contributions to climate change could support crafting policy actions to reduce greenhouse emissions more efficiently. Different levels of emissions reductions and regulatory types could be applied for each of the different anthropogenic GHGs, which has not been well understood by the policy community (Kamarck, 2019). The key is to start with climate science education and to get students to realize the connections between greenhouse gases emitted in one part of the world and climate impacts like sea-level rise in another. Realizing the inherently complex, not-straightforward cause and effect of climate change can help students modify their carbon footprints and consider how to support the systematic changes against carbon-intensive production and consumption in our society.

The second approach is underpinning the risk of not actioning toward climate mitigation. William Nordhaus (2015), a Nobel Laureate economist, argued that climate change profoundly alters our world in ways that pose major risks to human societies and natural systems. Using a metaphor of a Climate Casino in which humankind is rolling the global-warming dice, he argued that we should walk back out of the casino. The risk can be hedged if the uncertainty of climate science is dismissed with a precautionary principle. The crucial idea of the principle is that technologies or processes with the potential to harm human health and the environment should be regulated, even if the nature and likelihood of the potential harm that may result are uncertain (Balint et al., 2011). The least-costly carbon-reducing mechanisms should also be emphasized (Nordhaus, 2015). Adults could be more motivated to change their attitude toward and support for climate policy as they find climate measures economically appealing (Albeck-Ripka & Penn, 2020).

Third, various climate policy options and implications must be explained in response to the call for more climate policy education (Hill, 2010; Rai, 2010). Regulatory and self-regulatory approaches are different, and regulatory policies are divided into command-and-control approaches and flexible mechanisms, including carbon taxes and GHG cap-and-trade programs. The deeper discussions of different policy approaches could create the needed public understanding of the carbon cost burden to be ultimately shared by all carbon emitters in society. At the same time, certain industrial actors' responsible reductions correspond to their historical and current emissions contributions. This way could shift climate action discussion from politics to policy level.

Lastly, partnerships with different social actors, such as non-profit organizations, for extracurricular activities and hands-on climate projects can enhance climate education courses or program opportunities in universities and colleges. Climate mitigation aims to reduce the human impacts contributing to climate change, and adaptation intends to reduce the physical impacts of the climate system (Anderson, 2012). Mitigation and adaptation approaches can be mobilized to build adaptive capacity and reduce carbon emissions from communities in climate education courses or programs. These participatory and collaborative approaches can empower students to understand local community carbon reduction needs, developing a sense of how to reduce greenhouse gases at the societal level as well as increasing supportive attitudes toward climate policy actions.

The last point emphasizes the need to advance climate action in and through education. Transformative action is increasingly urgent across all sectors, systems and scales to avert dangerous climate change (Shi & Moser, 2021; Vogel & O'Brien, 2021). It is thus suggested that climate education must aim to make students capable of using knowledge to change unsustainable environmental behaviors or learn new adaptive behaviors, going beyond to understand the causes of climate change (Senbel et al., 2014; Vaugher, 2016). The goal admits that knowledge is not automatically transmitted to actions (Eilam & Trop, 2012). Accordingly, learning outcomes should focus on action competences so that students design climate solutions and carry them out (Negev et al., 2008; Vaugher, 2016). Connecting local actions and initiatives to global climate change processes would make it easier to nurture action competence skills, as engagement must be context specific (Shrivastava et al., 2020). In this regard, universities and colleges could be used as living labs to practice developing and implementing climate action plans (Cohen & Lovell, 2015; Vaugher, 2016). In working for campus gardens, assisting in university or college facility managers' energy auditing, and creating and running small-scale funds to support students' climate action-based research and community services, students would be more likely to be trained as agents for broader social changes to address climate change.

In this vein, climate activism should be considered a form of education alongside its unique role in catalyzing social change. If one is serious about tapping into education's potential to help us achieve a more sustainable future, we need to help build bridges between environmental activism and universities and colleges. For policymakers, this means funding educational efforts that could cultivate action competencies and incorporating activist-inspired pedagogy into climate education programs. For climate-action-oriented organizations, it means highlighting their contributions toward educating young people on environmental solutions and sharing their best practices (Sutoris, 2022).

7.   HIGHER EDUCATION INSTITUTION'S RESPONSIBILITY FOR SOCIAL CHANGE TOWARD SUSTAINABILITY

As much as education for climate change in universities and colleges is valued, our society can advance toward sustainable development. Among many social actors, universities and colleges are uniquely poised to advance the important values of their respective societies, and they have shown a long tradition of embracing eccentric values in organizations (Starik et al., 2002; Newman, 2012). Despite their frontier spirit and efforts, currently, businesses, cities, and local communities appear to be more proactive in experimenting and networking toward addressing sustainability challenges, including climate change.

However, universities and colleges can step up more aggressively as a gateway to advance a sustainable world and sustainability (sciences) that would, in turn, generate positive social and environmental changes globally (Shrivastava et al., 2020). While climate change has been the main focus of this chapter, any grand social and environmental challenges requiring systems change need to be taught using a transdisciplinary framework (Kim et al., 2022). The framework can be composed of promoting scientific or technical understanding about a complex social issue, shifting the economic logic of valuation that has been distorted in free market capitalism, and practicing policy and practical approaches to overhauling existing institutional norms and culture rooted in the social issue. This science-management-policy-ethics approach can work for such complex, controversial social and environmental problems (e.g., how to approach and regulate artificial intelligence) as it is being demonstrated by education for climate change in this study. Figure 12.2 describes the transdisciplinary framework that can enhance personal attitudes and behavioral changes with more holistic learning. The accumulated individualized changes can push society toward transformative change toward sustainability. The transition could be incremental but, at some point, drastically radical (Schumpeter, 1947).

Research activities at universities and colleges need to support weaving the transdisciplinary approach into disciplinary curriculum and research more powerfully and urgently (Bauer et al., 2021; Price et al., 2021; Shrivastava et al., 2020). Many universities' centers for teaching and learning can be instrumental in that type of curriculum development and teaching. The latest survey of representatives of universities engaged in sustainability networks indicated that less than half of universities strategize the notion of sustainable development embedded in their curricula, which implies universities and college administrators' limited attention to sustainable development and to the

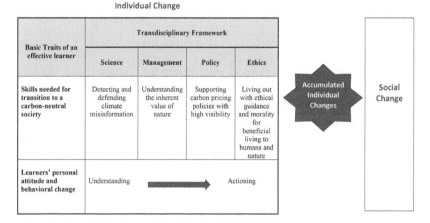

Figure 12.2   An application of a transdisciplinary framework

transdisciplinary approach for teaching sustainable development (Filho et al., 2019).

It is worth noting that embracing sustainability learning in certain disciplines and academic units is not straightforward. For instance, curriculum development in linguistics or mathematics disciplines would be more challenging than in global affairs or communication fields. The setback could be addressed by employing effective andragogical approaches and trainings to help faculty understand how to discover the connections and relevance between their chosen fields and sustainability. As an example, a study in a Swiss university found that a learner-centered approach and professional development courses or certificates for instructors were useful to develop learning outcomes like action competence skills to promote societal change (Trechsel et al., 2018). In this light, universities and colleges can involve a broad range of disciplines and disseminate sustainability concepts and practices on a large scale.

Universities and colleges must address sustainability with the whole institution approach, transmitting sustainability principles and values to teaching, research, and operations (Ferrer-Balas et al., 2008; Bauer et al., 2021). The implementation of operational sustainability seems to be disregarded compared to teaching and research, but without reducing the environmental impacts of operational functions, universities and colleges cannot function as an intensifying force to pressure social changes and connectors to meet social demands for sustainability (Ferrer-Balas et al., 2008). More co-evolutionary relationships between higher education institutions and society could be developed if operational sustainability is more actively pursued and exploited as a new way of learning to connect with various stakeholders for experimenting and scaling sustainability (Purcell et al., 2019).

8.   CONCLUSION

This chapter attempts to explore to what extent the climate lesson modules could be conducive to increasing students' more profound understanding of climate change and personal support for climate policies. A sequencing learning technique with formative assessment and a transdisciplinary approach from climate science and management to policy was utilized in creating learning modules. Findings suggest students' modestly improved understanding of climate science as well as their support for regulatory policy approaches, particularly incentive-based policy mechanisms such as carbon tax and greenhouse gases cap-and-trade programs.

Despite the value of the study outcomes, several future research paths exist. With a small sample size in an environmental and sustainability studies-focused program, future research can include larger groups in different disciplines to examine whether and to what extent climate change learning modules can shape students' understanding about climate science and promote personal support for regulatory policies. Such knowledge could help design a more innovative climate lesson module to drive radical departure to a carbon-neutral society.

In addition, it would also be interesting to undertake a different form of pre/post assessment to understand how individual learners' idiosyncratic contexts relate to their misconceptions about climate issues and whether the misconception could be alleviated or removed due to the transdisciplinary approach-based climate education. In this way, one could gauge how the andragogical approach changed their personal connection to climate change and developed a sense of urgency for climate solutions and regulatory support (Istance & Paniagua, 2019).

When universities and colleges adopt new learning methods about education for sustainability challenges such as climate change, university graduates of any discipline are expected to possess a reasonable level of environmental awareness to participate as responsible citizens. They can also become young voters supporting the needed transformative social change toward sustainability. Universities and colleges should not forgo opportunities to step up as a society's sustainability role model. Integrating sustainability in all dimensions of universities, including research, education, and operations, is vital to that pathway. In doing so, universities and colleges prepare student citizens, including the leaders of their generations, to live low-carbon lifestyles and steer society toward the transformation of a climate-resilient future.

NOTES

1. Summative assessment is contrasted with formative assessment, taking place after the learning has been completed, and provides information and feedback that sums up the teaching and learning process (Hanna & Dettmer, 2004; Trumbull & Lash, 2013).
2. NASA Climate Change website, 2023. Quiz: Global Warming. https:// climate.nasa.gov/climate_resources/16/quiz-global-warming/
3. The film was produced in 2008 by David Novack, and a shorter updated version was released in 2012.

REFERENCES

Abbot, D., Bikfalvi, A., BleskeRechek, A.L., Bodmer, W., Boghossian, P., Carvalho, C.M., Ciccolini, J., Coyne, J.A., Gauss, J., Gill, P.M.W., Jitomirskaya, S., Jussim, L., Krylov, A.I., Loury, G.C., Maroja, L., McWhorter, J.H., Moosavi, S., Nayana Schwerdtle, P., Pearl, J., QuintanillaTornel, M.A., Schaefer, H.F., III, Schreiner, P.R., Schwerdtfeger, P., Shechtman, D., Shifman, M., Tanzman, J., Trout, B.L., Warshel, A., & West, J.D. (2023). In defense of merit in science. *Journal of Controversial Ideas, 3*(1), https://doi:10.35995/jci03010001.

Albeck-Ripka, L., & Penn, I. (2020). How coal-loving became the leader in rooftop solar. *The New York Times.* https://www.nytimes.com/2020/09/29/business/energy -environment/australia-rooftop-solar-coal.html

Anderson, A. (2012). Climate change education for mitigation and adaptation. *Journal of Education for Sustainable Development, 6*(2), 191–206.

Angelo, T.A., & Cross, K.P. (1993). *Classroom Assessment Techniques: A Handbook for College Teachers* (2nd ed.). Jossey-Bass.

Balint, P.J., Stewart, R.E., Desai, A., & Walters, L.C. (2011). The precautionary principle. In P.J. Balint, R.E. Stewart, A. Desai, & L.C. Walters (Eds.), *Wicked Environmental Problems* (pp. 103–127). Island Press.

Bauer, M., Rieckmann, M., Niedlich, S., & Bormann, I. (2021). Sustainability governance at higher education institutions: Equipped to transform? *Frontiers in Sustainability, 2,* 640458. doi:10.3389/frsus.2021.640458

Bhutto, F. (2020). Pakistan's most terrifying adversary is climate change. *The New York Times.* https://www.nytimes.com/2020/09/27/opinion/pakistan-climate-change .html#:~:text=Pakistan%20is%20the%20fifth%20most,weather%20events%20in %20that%20period

Brownlee, M.T.J., Powell, R.B., & Hallo, J.C. (2013). A review of the foundational processes that influence beliefs in climate change: Opportunities for environmental education research. *Environmental Education Research, 19*(1), 1–20. https://doi:10 .1080/13504622.2012.683389

Chen, X. (2011). Why do people misunderstand climate change? Heuristics, mental models, and ontological assumptions. *Climatic Change, 108*(1–2), 31–46. https:// doi:10.1007/s10584-010-0013-5

Cohen, T., & Lovell, B. (2015). The Campus as a living laboratory: Using the built environment to revitalize college education (AACC SEED Center). http://www .igencc.org/wp-content/uploads/2015/07/campus-as-aliving-lab.pdf

Colebrook, C. (2014). *Death of the Post Human: Essays on Extinction* (vol. 1). Open Humanities Press.

Conway, C.M. (2012). Sequential learning. In N.M. Seel (Ed.), *Encyclopedia of the Sciences of Learning.* Springer. https://doi.org/10.1007/978-1-4419-1428-6_72

Cutter-Mackenzie, A., & Rousell, D. (2018). The mesh of playing and researching in the reality of climate change: Children's research play spaces. In A. Cutter-Mackenzie, K. Malone, & E. Barrett-Hacking (Eds.), *International Research Handbook on Childhood Nature*. Springer.

Davison, A., Brown, P., Pharo, E., Warr, K., McGregor, H., Terkes, S., Boyd, D., & Abuodha, P. (2014). Distributed leadership: Building capacity for interdisciplinary climate change teaching at four universities. *International Journal of Sustainability in Higher Education, 15*(1), 98–110.

Devine-Wright, P., Devine-Wright, H., & Fleming, P. (2004). Situational influences upon children's beliefs about global warming and energy. *Environmental Education Research, 10*(4), 493–506.

Dijkstra, E.M., & Goedhart, M.J. (2012). Development and validation of the ACSI: Measuring students' science attitudes, pro-environmental behavior, climate change attitudes and knowledge. *Environmental Education Research, 18*(6), 733–749.

Eilam, E., & Trop, T. (2012). Environmental attitudes and environmental behavior: Which is the horse and which is the cart? *Sustainability, 4*(9), 2210–2246.

Ferrer-Balas, D., Adachi, J., Banas, S., Davidson, C.I., Hoshikoshi, A., Mishra, A., Motodoa, Y, Onga, M., & Ostwald, M. (2008). An international comparative analysis of sustainability transformation across seven universities. *International Journal of Sustainability in Higher Education, 9*, 295–316. https:// doi: 10.1108/14676370810885907

Filho, L.W., Emblen-Perry, K., Molthan-Hill, P., Mifsud, M., Verhoef, L., Azeiteiro, U., Bacelar-Nicolau, P., de Sousa, L., Castro, P., Beynaghi, A., Boddy, J., Lange Salvia, A., Frankenberger, F., & Price, E. (2019). Implementing innovation and sustainability at universities around the world. *Sustainability, 11*, 3807.

Grady-Benson, J., & Sarathy, B. (2015). Fossil fuel divestment in US higher education: Student-led organizing for climate justice. *Local Environment, 21*(6), 661–681.

Guy, S., Yoshihisa, K., Walker, I., & O'Neill, S. (2014). Investigating the effects of knowledge and ideology on climate change beliefs. *European Journal of Social Psychology, 44*(5), 421–429. https://doi:10.1002/ejsp.2039

Hampton, G.P., & Rich-Tolsma, M. (2015). Transformative learning for climate change engagement: Regenerating perspectives, principles, and practice. *Integral Review, 11*(3), 171–190.

Hanna, G.S., & Dettmer, P.A. (2004). *Assessment for Effective Teaching: Using Context-adaptive Planning.* Pearson A&B.

Harris, P.G. (2009). *World Ethics and Climate Change: From International and Global Justice.* Edinburgh University Press.

Haslett, S.K., & Wallen, J. (2011). A component-based approach to open educational resources in climate change education. *Planet,* (24), 89–92.

Hill, J. (2010). Science education must inform and influence climate change policy. *ChemEd NZ, 118*, 9–13.

Hoffman, A. (2015). *How Culture Shapes the Climate Change Debate.* Stanford Press.

Holtuis, N., Lotan, R., Mastrandrea, M., & Saltzman, J. (2015). Why and how we teach about climate change. In E.J. Fretz (Ed.), *Climate Change across the Curriculum,* 183–196. Lexington Books.

Howell, R. A. (2014). Investigating the Long-Term Impacts of Climate Change Communications on Individuals' Attitudes and Behavior. *Environment and Behavior*, 46(1), 70-101. https://doi.org/10.1177/0013916512452428

Hsu, S.L., Walters, J., & Purgas, A., (2008). Pollution tax heuristics: An empirical study of willingness to pay higher gasoline taxes. *Energy Policy*, *36*, 3612–3619. http://dx.doi.org/10.1016/j.enpol.2008.06.010

Intergovernmental Panel on Climate Change. (2023). Assessment Report (AR) 6 Synthesis Report: Climate Change 2023. https://www.ipcc.ch/report/ar6/syr/

Istance, D., & Paniagua, A. (2019). *Learning to Leapfrog: Innovative Pedagogies to Transform Education.* https://www.brookings.edu/wp-content/uploads/2019/09/Learning-to-Leapfrog-InnovativePedagogiestoTransformEducation-Web.pdf

Kahan, D. (2009). "Ideology in" or "cultural cognition of" judging: What difference does it make? Faculty Scholarship Series. Paper 4689. Ttps://digitalcommons.law.yale.edu/fss_papers/4689

Kallbekken, S., & Sælen, H. (2011). Public acceptance for environmental taxes: Self-interest, environmental and distributional concerns. *Energy Policy*, *39*(5), 2966–2973. https://doi.org/10.1016/j.enpol.2011.03.006

Kamarck, E. (2019). The challenging politics of climate change. Washington, DC: Brookings Institute. https://www.brookings.edu/research/the-challenging-politics-of-climate-change/#footnote-22

Kempton, W. (1997). How the public views climate change. *Environment*, *39*(9), 12–21.

Kim, K.M., Douglas, M.M., Pannell, D., Setterfield, S.A., Hill, R., Laborde, S., Perrott, L., Álvarez-Romero, J.G., Beesley, L., Canham, C., & Brecknell, A. (2022). When to use transdisciplinary approaches for environmental research. *Frontiers in Environmental Science*, *10*. https://www.frontiersin.org/articles/10.3389/fenvs.2022.840569

Kim, Y. (2023). *Carbon Markets: Principles and Current Practices*. EBSCO Pathways to Research: Sustainability.

Kim, Y., & Olesova, L.A. (2022). Expanding online professional learning in the Post-COVID era: The potential of the universal design for learning framework, *Journal of Applied Instruction Design*, *11*(2). https://doi.org/10.51869/112/yklo

Klein, T.J. (2004). Prospects for transdisciplinarity. *Futures*, *36*(4), 515–526. https://doi:10.1016/j.futures.2003.10.007.

Knapp, T.R. (2016). Why is the one-group pretest-posttest design still used? *Clinical Nursing Research*, 25(5), 467–472.

Kwauk, C., & Winthrop, R. (2021). Unleashing the creativity of teachers and students to combat climate change: An opportunity for global leadership. Center for Universal Education, The Brookings Institution. https://www.brookings.edu/research

Leiserowitz, A., Smith, N., & Marlon, J.R. (2011). American teens' knowledge of climate change. New Haven, CT: Yale Project on Climate Change Communication. https:// climatecommunication .yale .edu/ wp -content/ uploads/ 2016/ 02/ 2011 _04 _American-Teens'-Knowledge-of-Climate-Change.pdf

Levi, S. (2021). Why hate carbon taxes? Machine learning evidence on the roles of personal responsibility, trust, revenue recycling, and other factors across 23 European countries. *Energy Research & Social Science*, *73*. https://doi.org/10.1016/j.erss.2020.101883.

Leiserowitz A. (2004). Before and after the day after tomorrow: A U.S. study of climate change risk perception. *Environment*, 46, 22–37.

Lowe, T., Brown, K., Dessai, S., de Franca Doria, M., Haynes, K., & Vincent, K. (2006). Does tomorrow ever come? Disaster narrative and public perceptions of climate change. *Public Understanding of Science*, *15*, 435–457.

Lynas, M., Houston, B.Z., & Perry, S. (2021). Greater than 99% consensus on human caused climate change in the peer-reviewed scientific literature. *Environmental Research Letters*, *16*(11). https://doi:10.1088/1748-9326/ac2966

Marshuetz, C. (2005). Order information in working memory: An integrative review of evidence from brain and behavior. *Psychological Bulletin*, *131*, 323–339.

Mazzei, P. (2021, June 2). A 20-foot sea wall? Miami faces the hard choices of climate change. *The New York Times*. https://www.nytimes.com/2021/06/02/us/miami-fl-seawall-hurricanes.html

McCright, A., O'Shea, B., Sweeder, R., Urquhart, G.R., & Zeleke, A. (2013). Promoting interdisciplinarity through climate change education. *Nature Climate Change*, *3*, 713–716. https://doi.org/10.1038/nclimate1844

McNeill, J.R., & Engelke, P. (2014). *The Great Acceleration: An Environmental History of the Anthropocene since 1945*. Harvard University Press.

Meyers, K.F., Doran, P.T., Cook, J., Kotcher, J.E., & Meyers, T.A. (2021). Consensus revisited: Quantifying scientific agreement on climate change and climate expertise among Earth scientists 10 years later. *Environmental Research Letters*, *16*(10). https://doi:10.1088/1748-9326/ac2774

Millais, C. (Ed.) (2006). Common belief: Australia's faith communities on climate change. Climate Institute, Sydney.

Monroe, M.C., Plate, R.R., Oxarart, A., Bowers, A., & Chaves, W.A. (2019). Identifying effective climate change education strategies: A systematic review of the research, *Environmental Education Research*. https://doi: 10.1080/13504622.2017.1360842

Moorhead, A. (2009). *Climate Change, Agriculture and Food Security: A Strategy for Change*. Alliance of the CGIAR Centers. https://cgspace.cgiar.org/handle/10568/33395

Negev, M., Sagy, G., Garb, Y., Salzberg, A., & Tal, A. (2008). Evaluating the environmental literacy of Israeli elementary and high school students. *Journal of Environmental Education*, *39*(2), 3−20.

Newman, J. (2012). An organizational change management framework for sustainability. *Greener Management International*, *57*, 65–75.

Nicol, D.J., & Macfarlane-Dick, D. (2006). Formative assessment and self-regulated learning: A model and seven principles of good feedback practice. *Studies in Higher Education*, *31*(2), 2–19.

Nordhaus, W. (2015). *The Climate Casino: Risk, Uncertainty, and Economics for a Warming World*. Yale University Press.

Norström, A.V., Cvitanovic, C., Löf, M.F., Wyborn, C., Balvanera, P., Bednarek, A.T., Bennett, E.M., Biggs, R., de Bremond, A., et al. (2020). Principles for knowledge co-production in sustainability research. *Nature Sustainability*, *3*, 182–190. https://doi.org/10.1038/s41893-019-0448-2

OECD. (2020). Addressing special challenges using transdisciplinary research. OECD Science, Technology, and Industry Policy Papers. No. 88.

Pharo, E., Davison, A., McGregor, H., Warr, K., & Brown, P. (2014). Using communities of practice to enhance interdisciplinary teaching: Lessons from four Australian institutions. *Higher Education Research & Development*, *33*(2), 341–354.

Plumer, B. (2023). Climate change is speeding toward catastrophe. The next decade is crucial, U.N. Panel says. *The New York Times*. https://www.nytimes.com/2023/03/20/climate/global-warming-ipcc-earth.html

Posas, P. (2007). Roles of religion and ethics in addressing climate change. *Ethics in Science and Environmental Politics*. https://doi: 10.3354/esep00080

Price, E.A.C., White, R.M., Mori, K., Longhurst, J., Baughan, P., Hayles, C.S., Gough, G., & Priest, C. (2021). Supporting the role of universities in leading individual and societal transformation through education for sustainable development. *Discovery Sustainability*, 2, 49. https://doi.org/10.1007/s43621-021-00058-3

Purcell, W.M., Henriksen, H., & Spengler, J.D. (2019). Universities as the engine of transformational sustainability toward delivering the sustainable development goals: "Living labs" for sustainability. *International Journal of Sustainability in Higher Education*, 20, 1343–1357. http://doi: 10.1108/IJSHE-02-2019-0103

Rai, J.K. (2010). Global and local discourses on climate change: A perspective from the concept of embeddedness. *Dhaulagiri Journal of Sociology and Anthropology*, 4, 143–180.

Rhodes, E., Axsen, J., & Jaccard, M. (2017). Exploring citizen support for different types of climate policy. *Ecological Economics*, 137, 56–69. https://doi.org/10.1016/j. ecolecon.2017.02.027

Rousell, D., & Cutter-Mackenzie-Knowles, A. (2020). A systematic review of climate change education: Giving children and young people a "voice" and a "hand" in redressing climate change. *Children's Geographies*, 18(2), 191–208.

Schumpeter, J.A. (1947). The creative response in economic history. *Journal of Economic History*, 7(2), 149–159.

Selin, H., & VanDeveer, S.D. (2022). Global climate change governance: Can the promise of Paris be realized? In N.J. Vig, M.E. Kraft, & B.G. Rabe (Eds.), *Environmental Policy: New Directions for the Twenty-first Century*, 275–299. CQ Press.

Senbel, M., Ngo, V.D., & Blair, E. (2014). Social mobilization of climate change: University students conserving energy through multiple pathways for peer engagement. *Journal of Environmental Psychology*, 38, 84–93.

Shepardson, D.P., Niyogi, D., Choi, S., & Charusombat, U. (2009). Seventh grade students' conceptions of global warming and climate change. *Environmental Education Research*, 15(5), 549–570. https://doi:10.1080/13504622.2 012.696859

Shi, L., & Moser, S. (2021). Transformative climate adaptation in the United States: Trends and prospects. *Science*, 372(6549). https://doi:10.1126/science. abc8054

Shrivastava, P., Smith, M.S., O'Brien, K., & Zsolnai, L. (2020). Transforming sustainability science to generate positive social and environmental change globally. *One Earth*, 2. https://www.cell.com/one-earth/pdf/S2590-3322(20)30161-5 .pdf?_returnURL=https%3A%2F%2Flinkinghub.elsevier.com%2Fretrieve%2Fpii %2FS2590332220301615%3Fshowall%3Dtrue

Starik, M., Schaeffer, T., Berrnan, P., & Hazelwood, A. (2002). Initial environmental project characterizations of four U.S. universities. *International Journal of Sustainability in Higher Education*, 3(4), 335–345.

Sterman, J.D. (2011). Communicating climate change risks in a skeptical world. *Climatic Change*, 108(4), 811.

Stokols, D., Misra, S., Runnerstrom, M.G., & Hipp, J.A. (2009). Psychology in an age of ecological crisis: From personal angst to collective action. *American Psychologist*, 64(3), 181–193.

Sutoris, P. (2022). *Educating for the Anthropocene: Schooling and Activism in the Face of Slow Violence*. MIT Press.

Taber, F., & Taylor, N. (2009). Climate of concern: A search for effective strategies for teaching children about global warming. *International Journal of Environmental and Science Education, 4*(2), 97–116.

Theall, M., & Franklin, J.L. (2010). Assessing teaching practices and effectiveness for formative purposes. In K.J. Gillespie & D.L. Robertson (Eds.), *A Guide to Faculty Development,* 151–168. Jossey-Bass.

Trechsel, L.J., Zimmermann, A.B., Graf, D., Herweg, K., Lundsgaard-Hansen, L., Rufer, L., Tribelhorn, T., & Wastl-Water, D. (2018). Mainstreaming education for sustainable development at a Swiss university: Navigating the traps of institutionalization. *Higher Education Policy, 31,* 471–490. https://doi.org/10.1057/s41307-018-0102-z

Trumbull, E., & Lash, A. (2013). *Understanding Formative Assessment: Insights from Learning Theory and Measurement Theory.* WestEd.

Tucci, J., Mitchell, J., & Goddard, C. (2007). *Children's Fears, Hopes And Heroes: Modern Childhood in Australia.* Australian Childhood Foundation. https://doi:10.1890/140261.

Vaugher, P. (2016). *Climate Change Education: From Critical Thinking to Critical Action.* UNU-IAS Policy Brief (4).

Vogel, C., & O'Brien, K. (2021). Getting to the heart of transformation. *Sustainability Science.* https://doi:10.1007/s11625-021-01016-8

Wheeler, T., & von Braun, J. (2013). Climate change impacts on global food security. *Science, 341*(6145), 508–513. https://doi:10.1126/science.1239402

Wickson, F., Carew, A.L., & Russell, A.W. (2006). Transdisciplinary research: Characteristics, quandaries and quality. *Futures, 38*(9), 1046–1059. https://doi:10.1016/j.futures.2006.02.011

Wiek, A., Talwar, S., O'Shea, M., & Robinson, J. (2014). Toward a methodological scheme for capturing societal effects of participatory sustainability research. *Research Evaluation, 23*(2), 117–132. https://doi:10.1093/reseval/rvt031

13. Enlightened education: advancing the sustainability of schools, colleges, and universities by deployment of solar photovoltaic infrastructure

Kenneth A. Walz[1]

THE OPPORTUNITY FOR EDUCATIONAL INVESTMENT IN SOLAR INFRASTRUCTURE

Over the past two decades, renewable energy has experienced massive growth, while aging and obsolete fossil fuel fired electrical power plants have been retired. This trend is exemplified by the increase in global installed solar photovoltaic (PV) capacity, which has surged from 1.4 GW in 2000 to over 1,185 GW in 2022 (Solar Power Europe, 2022). In just a few years, solar power will eclipse electricity obtained from coal and natural gas. And by 2027, worldwide solar PV capacity is expected to exceed 3,500 GW as the world's largest source of electrical generation (IEA, 2023). This trend is mirrored in the workforce, and solar PV installation has been one of the fastest growing occupations in recent years (DOL, 2023). This growth is driven by dramatic reductions in the cost of solar technology (Nemet, 2019), and solar PV installations today cost less than 10% of what they cost 20 years ago (Ramasamy et al., 2022).

The transformation of the solar industry has created an exciting new opportunity for schools to pursue solar developments for their facilities. At a time when many students have been involved in environmental activism and climate strikes, installing solar is a way for schools to demonstrate a commitment to the students that they serve and fulfill a moral obligation to future generations. Solar PV systems also help to lower ongoing operational costs for schools by reducing utility bills. Moreover, solar facilitates cost hedging by providing budgeting certainty for future electric costs. It is not uncommon for schools to have significant restrictions on their annual operating budgets. Thus, there is an opportunity to use capital expenditures for solar PV systems to reduce energy-related operational costs and address budget gaps. Today, for many parts of the US, solar photovoltaic systems can provide energy at a levelized cost of electricity that is well below the retail rate charged by electric utilities. As a result, schools pursuing solar PV systems can achieve both financial and environmental sustainability.

Schools are long-term public investments, and school buildings often last 50 to 100 or more years. As such, decision-makers at schools have much longer time horizons than owners of residential homes or commercial buildings, who may be reluctant to invest in solar if they are uncertain about how long they will continue to occupy a given structure. Typically, a school's electrical load is largest during the day, at times when electricity rates are at their highest. This synchronizes well with the daily solar cycle, and thus makes solar an ideal energy source for schools. Investing in solar PV systems also represents good stewardship of taxpayer dollars, since the reduction of electrical costs allows for the money saved to be reallocated to things that directly impact student learning (e.g., more teachers, smaller class sizes, new instructional materials, and technology investments). All of these factors have led to the concept of what one solar designer and engineer has called "The Inevitable Solar School" (Hanson, 2019).

Harvard University was founded in Massachusetts in the year 1636. One hundred and forty years later, in 1776 at the signing of the American Declaration of Independence, there were still fewer than 20 colleges in the US (Lynch, 2022). Today there are over 4,000 degree-granting institutions of higher education (NSF, 2022). The vast majority of these schools were founded after 1890 following the Morill Land Grant Acts (NEA, 2022), and thus these schools were built in an era of growing and seemingly limitless fossil fuel abundance. Furthermore, for the wave of schools built in the post-World War II expansion of higher education, many are still operating with legacy energy systems that have exceeded their planned operational lifetimes and are now prime candidates for energy overhauls. As a result, colleges and universities now find themselves at a historically unprecedented tipping point, as they navigate a once-in-a-century transformation in the Energy Sector.

MADISON COLLEGE'S SOLAR EXPERIENCE

In 2019, Madison College commissioned the largest rooftop solar PV system in Wisconsin at its Truax Campus (see Figure 13.1). Comprised of over eight acres of solar panels, the system is rated at 1.9 MWdc. When skies are clear, the system is capable of providing all of the electricity needed to operate the one million square foot facility for several hours throughout the day. After factoring in cloudy days and night-time building operations, when averaged over the entire year the system offsets about 25% of the building's electric bill. The Truax solar PV system was a culmination of effort that spanned several years. The college installed its first solar PV system in 2002. By comparison,

Note: Most of the white colored roof surface has been overlaid with solar panels, with the exception of those sections that have mechanical structures, roof penetrations, or insufficient strength to handle the additional weight load. The system includes over 5,800 Solar PV panels each with a rated capacity of 325 Watts. Most of the panels face south at a fixed tilt angle of 10 degrees. Two roof sections have east–west facing panels at similar angles to allow students to compare the effect of orientation on electrical output.
Source: Photo Credit – Chris Collins, SunVest Solar.

Figure 13.1   *View of the 1.85 MW solar PV system at Madison College's Truax Campus*

that system was only 1.2-kW in size, and the installed cost per Watt was nearly ten times greater than it is today. The college has had a Renewable Energy academic program in place since 2005 and over 600 students have completed coursework through the program. In 2017, the college formed a team to create a Solar Roadmap that examined each of its campuses and buildings for their solar potential. These potential projects were then evaluated for inclusion in the college's future facilities plan. The college worked with the Midwest Renewable Energy Association to develop the roadmap, prioritizing projects based both on their potential energy savings and the educational benefit to students. The effort was funded by the Department of Energy Solar Energy Technologies Office and engaged colleges and universities from across the US in an online course providing direct technical assistance to advance large-scale solar PV projects.

Since the Truax building is the largest energy consumer in the college's portfolio and this facility serves the largest number of college students, the Truax rooftop solar PV system received the highest priority in the college Solar Roadmap. Portions of the Truax building are over 30 years old, so the solar installation was executed in coordination with a roof replacement project.

Planning for the project took place in the latter half of 2017, and construction initiated following the final exam week in spring of 2018. Construction proceeded throughout the following 12 months with some interruptions due to complications in the roof replacement and inclement weather. The solar installation has been fully operational since June 2019, and in the past four years has generated over 7,300,000-kWh of electricity for the school.

ENGINEERING DESIGN CONSIDERATIONS FOR SOLAR INFRASTRUCTURE

Solar developers will design a solar PV system for their client. If a school's solar team can complete some preliminary design work internally, this may reduce costs by focusing the scope of the developer's work. In addition, assembling a knowledgeable solar team for the school provides more confidence in the recommendations provided by a solar developer.

The ideal time to consider a solar installation is during the construction of a new building. In this case the solar PV system can be included in the upfront design of the building and can be most easily integrated into the electrical system. However, most general contractors are not very knowledgeable in solar energy. It may be desirable to contact a solar specialist ahead of time to assist with the preparation of calls for bids for new construction, and to incorporate solar energy into the request in the beginning stages.

If the planned solar installation is intended for an existing building, then there are several initial site assessment screening considerations that will determine if the location is suitable for solar. The site assessment should begin with an examination of the building's structure to determine the type and design of the roof and possible weight and wind load limitations. The age and condition of the roof should also be considered. Ideally, solar installation on existing buildings should be aimed at roofs that are less than five years old. Thoughtful planning can also be used to schedule a targeted solar project to coincide with the replacement of an old roof. If obstacles are discovered in the roof analysis, then it might be prudent to instead consider a ground mounted solar array.

An analysis of the "solar window" should also be conducted to determine the amount of shade (if any) that falls on the planned solar installation location. Cutting down trees to eliminate shade is usually not advised, since trees benefit the atmosphere, and the shade helps to reduce building air conditioning loads. However, tree removal may be warranted in cases where a tree is already compromised due to disease or structural issues, and in the case of undesirable invasive or nuisance tree species.

When designing a solar PV system for energy production, it is also advisable to assess the building's energy use and load profile/patterns. Schools are very different from residential homes in that they are primarily used during the day. They also tend to have peak loads that coincide with daytime hours when solar energy production is at its maximum. However, schools can vary considerably. For example, universities, colleges, and high schools typically have much higher night-time energy consumption than elementary schools. This is especially true for technical and community colleges that frequently offer night classes for working adult students. Seasonal differences in energy consumption should also be examined. Colleges and universities that offer summer terms may have high energy consumption during this time of year, whereas most K-12 schools are out of session and have reduced electric loads compared with the academic year. A trend among many newer buildings is to provide heating and cooling using geothermal ground source heat exchange systems. Schools with geothermal systems are different from those that heat with fossil fuels. With geothermal heat pumps, electricity is used to provide space heat, which greatly increases the winter electric load.

In addition to understanding the building's electric load, it is also necessary to understand how the school is billed for electricity. Electric billing for a commercial building such as a school is considerably more complex than that for a typical residential home. In the US, most residential homes are billed a "flat rate" for the energy consumed. The national average for 2021 was \$0.111/kWh. When considering the average rate for each of the 50 states, the lowest rate was in Idaho at \$0.082/kWh and the highest rate was in Hawaii at \$0.303/kWh. Even within a given state, rates can differ significantly between electric providers (EIA, 2021).

By comparison, commercial buildings typically have lower baseline rates for the energy they consume (measured in kWh). However, they may be subject to Time of Use charges that increase the cost of energy during times when the electric grid has the highest load, which is typically during the day. There may also be seasonal charges to adjust for times when the electric grid has the largest electrical demand. For example, summer air conditioning or winter heating, depending on the regional patterns of climate and predominant HVAC practices.

Commercial buildings such as schools usually have a demand charge, which is determined by the peak power consumption of the building, measured in kW (Dieziger, 2000). Demand charges are typically assessed for the highest average power measured over a 15-minute interval. For large buildings such as schools, there frequently is a demand charge issued for that month, as well as an additional demand charge issued based on the maximum 15-minute demand observed over the prior 12 months. It is not unusual for the demand charges for a school to account for as much as 40% of the monthly bill. Understanding these calculations is key to modeling the financial benefit of a proposed solar PV system.

Teams developing solar projects for a university, college, or K-12 school will benefit from using multiple models to predict the solar performance of the system. There are a variety of tools and calculators available to determine the maximum possible size of a solar array for a given roof or ground surface area. These tools also adjust for panel tilt angle (slope) and for panel orientation (azimuth) relative to due south. The models predict system output based on local historical weather patterns, account for electrical efficiency, shading, soiling, and snow cover losses, and approximate the effects of equipment degradation over time. Many of these tools are available online for free including PV Watts (DOE, 2023a) and the System Advisor Model (Blair et al., 2017), both of which were developed by the National Renewable Energy Lab. Using multiple models to estimate system performance can allow a team to explore the effects of different input parameters. Furthermore, if multiple models yield results that are in agreement, this lends confidence to the analysis.

When using models, it is important to understand the primary benefit of a solar PV system is energy (kWh) reduction. Although a solar PV system can also provide some reduction in a building's peak power (kW) consumption (DOE, 2017), it is wise to be conservative when estimating the benefit on utility demand charges. Because demand is usually billed based on 15-minute intervals, a single cloud event, happening at the wrong moment, might account for the peak demand for that entire month – or depending on the rate structure, possibly for the entire next year. For this reason, the decision to pursue solar energy at Madison College was made solely based on energy (kWh) production, and the resulting electric bill savings. Hence, any reductions in peak demand (kW) that might result simply provide additional financial benefits above and beyond what was included in the solar PV project budget.

When estimating the financial benefit of a solar PV system it is also critical to understand the utility policies toward net-metering of the solar generation, and to know the buyback rates paid for any solar electricity that exceeds the building's consumption. In many parts of the US, buyback rates for solar electricity have been reduced in recent years. If a school is trying to maximize the financial benefits of a solar PV system, it may be desirable to size the system so it meets the building's daytime load, and rely on the utility for energy supplied at night. Schools may also wish to make use of the free SolarProjectBuilder (MREA, 2023) financial modeling tool developed by the Midwest Renewable Energy Association. The tool models installation, operations, maintenance, and decommissioning costs, to visualize the cash flow for the life of a project. The tool also determines financial metrics such as the simple payback period, net present value, internal rate of return, and levelized cost of electricity for the lifetime of the solar PV system.

Alternatively, if the goal of the school is to strive for net-zero carbon emissions from electricity, then it will likely need to overproduce solar energy

Table 13.1   *Useful solar and energy modeling software resources for schools seeking to implement solar PV projects*

PVWatts	Estimates the energy production of grid-connected photovoltaic energy systems.	https://pvwatts.nrel.gov/
ReOPT	Optimizes energy systems for buildings, campuses, communities, and microgrids, recommending the optimal mix of renewable energy, conventional generation, and energy storage.	https://reopt.nrel.gov/
System Advisor Model	Techno-economic modeling software for solar electric, battery storage, wind power, fuel cells, and other renewable technologies.	https://sam.nrel.gov/
Solar Project Builder	A tool for universities, hospitals, municipalities, and businesses to simulate long-term financial forecasting for solar photovoltaic (PV) investment.	https://www.solarprojectbuilder.org/
Helioscope	Commercial software to support the design and analysis of solar photovoltaic systems. A free trial license is available to teachers and students.	https://helioscope.aurorasolar.com/

during the day to offset night-time electrical consumption. In these more ambitious cases, battery systems can be considered to store the excess daytime electrical energy. However, battery systems add significant cost to a solar project. Batteries also require more complex system designs, sophisticated controls systems, and a more detailed understanding of the building's electrical load to extract the maximum benefit from the storage system. Schools considering solar + storage systems and those pursuing net-zero buildings should allow for extra time to plan, design, and install these systems. Even if the upfront cost prohibits inclusion of energy storage in the initial project, it may be of interest to design the solar PV system to be "storage ready" so that battery storage can be added in the future if economic conditions become more favorable. The National Renewable Energy Lab offers the free Re-Opt Lite software tool for sizing a solar + storage system, along with a more robust paid version intended for more complex projects (DOE, 2023b).

If a school is also educating students to be solar professionals, they may wish to engage them at this stage of the project, and to teach students to use some of the commercial software packages that are available for solar project design, financial analysis, visualization, presentation, and reporting. Helioscope software has been incorporated into the curriculum at Madison College, and Aurora Solar offers a free trial license for this product to teachers and students. The various software tools used by Madison College for both system design and student instruction are shown in Table 13.1.

SOLAR ENGINEERING DESIGN FOR EDUCATIONAL PURPOSES

Colleges and universities have a special opportunity to leverage investments in solar infrastructure to enhance the instruction of students. By using campus facilities as "living labs" students can study college buildings and energy systems to gather and analyze data (Walz et al., 2020). Students in Science, Technology, Engineering and Math might also be involved in the design and engineering of energy systems, and more technically inclined students might even be engaged in the installation of the equipment. However, most solar developers and contractors do not have extensive experience designing for, or working in, school environments. For that reason, schools must be prepared for additional work on engineering design and be ready to advocate for what they need to get the best educational benefit from the installation. Finding the right solar developer to partner with can greatly facilitate this process. With planning, schools can strategically design requests for proposals for solar construction projects to ensure that all of their interests are accounted for in the bidding and procurement process.

Schools – A Special Subcategory of the Commercial Solar Building Sector

There are several aspects to solar development at school locations that make these projects different from conventional commercial and industrial solar projects. The decision-making process for educational institutions is usually much longer and more involved than typical businesses. Projects usually pass through several stages of review before various faculty, staff and administrative committees. Budgeting for school-based solar projects is also more involved and will likely require significant financial review to ensure good stewardship of taxpayer dollars. Most large colleges and universities operate with some type of shared governance system, so decisions to proceed with solar development may need to pass through various committees overseen by faculty and staff. They then proceed to a fiscal team for financial analysis, followed by approval at the executive level, and may ultimately require the consent of a governing board. Furthermore, most schools have specific procurement policies for large construction projects that require public notice, solicitation of bids, and competitive award of contracts. These processes lengthen the time to complete the solar project and may create frustration or friction with solar developers who are not accustomed to working with schools.

The solar construction and installation process at school-based sites can also differ from other commercial and industrial locations. Unless the proposed location is a new construction site, it is likely that the solar installation will happen while the building is occupied and in use. Projects of this nature can be quite disruptive to the school learning environment, so thoughtful planning with the school, the solar developer, and any subcontractors will be necessary. If the students are not in attendance during the summer months, it may be desirable to schedule the bulk of the installation work during that time. This can minimize or eliminate the impact on student instruction, restricting the disruption to faculty and year-round staff. If solar construction must be done while school is in session, modifications to work practices can help to minimize the impact on students. Rooftop construction can be noisy, so impacts will largely be concentrated on those occupying the uppermost floor of the building. Class scheduling to move operations away from areas under construction can help. Strategic timing of various installation job tasks can also provide benefit. For example, restricting the use of various types of rooftop power tools to early morning, afternoon, or weekend hours when classes are not in session. Since parking and transportation can be limited at school campuses, scheduling of deliveries and of rooftop crane access will also likely require special considerations to minimize the disruption to students and school personnel. For this reason, the role of project manager for school-based solar installations takes on a heightened importance. When considering prospective solar developers, schools may wish to tailor their procurement processes to seek out and retain developers who have prior experience in this arena.

Designing Solar PV Systems for Educational Benefit

In most commercial and industrial solar installations, systems are designed to operate "invisibly" once the installation is complete. The owners of the building are not expected to interact with the system. In most cases the only information that they seek is the financial impact of the solar PV system on their monthly utility bill.

The situation for schools is different from other commercial and industrial solar customers. Almost all schools will want to have some type of educational activity integrated with the solar PV system. This may take the form of public awareness campaigns, museum-like interpretive displays, open house events and tours, classroom instruction on solar principles, or even hands-on learning for STEM students in aspects of solar installation, operations, and maintenance. For this reason, it is critical that schools plan ahead to design a solar system for educational access. Educational access will likely require design considerations and expenses beyond that of a conventional commercial solar installation. Educational access may also require additional technical experts or subcontractors to work on the design and installation of the system. Engagement of the school's facility managers and faculty members early in the process is essential. Dialogue between these parties and the solar developer can maximize the educational benefits of a solar installation.

Potential Educational Audiences

When designing solar PV systems for educational use, the first step is to consider who the intended educational audience(s) might be. A possible list of educational activities organized from the most general to the most specific includes tours for the general public, open houses for prospective students, field trips for students from other educational institutions, outdoor classroom instruction for students in science courses, system performance and data analysis for students in engineering and mathematical programs, and hands-on installation work for students enrolled in renewable energy or solar-specific programs. Each of these activities requires different levels of access to the solar PV system. Thus, it is necessary to make design considerations to accommodate these users and to minimize the risk of injury to any students or staff who intend to use the solar PV system for educational purposes.

Public Access to the Solar PV System

The first consideration to make regarding public access is whether the planned system will be roof or ground mounted. If the system is ground mounted, it likely will require perimeter fencing to protect individuals from walking unaccompanied into the area of operating electrical equipment. The size and type of fence will need to be considered. In some cases, it may be desirable to also exclude wildlife from the solar array. And in urban locations, it may be desirable to have solid fencing that blocks visual views of the system to discourage potential vandalism.

If the array is mounted on the rooftop, fall hazards and roof safety are of concern. Flat roofs are more conducive to educational use, whereas sloped roofs are very difficult for hands-on instruction. If the solar PV system is going on a new construction site, designs that incorporate flat roofs with taller parapet walls can add significant safety advantages. Strategic placement of the solar array with larger setback distances from the building walls and inclusion of guard rails to restrict student access help define the outdoor workspace to a safe limit. The structural capacity of the roof must also be considered. The size of potential user groups, and the combined weight load of people plus solar equipment must be accounted for in the design.

Whether the system is ground or roof mounted, it is also important to consider the accessibility of the solar PV system for all types of users and to comply with local guidelines for emergency exits and fire safety, as well as requirements specified by the Americans with Disabilities Act (DOJ, 2010).

This will impact design specifications for things like the sizing of doors and gates, placement of wheelchair accessible ramps and thresholds, and the selection of ground or roof surfaces. For ground mounted systems, it may be desirable to have poured concrete or asphalt surfaces within the array rather than the more customary gravel, crushed rock, or grass ground cover. For roof mounted systems, this likely will guide the installation of abrasive grit or raised ridge walkway treads to provide traction on what can otherwise be slippery footings of Ethylene Propylene Diene Monomer (EPDM) rubber or Thermoplastic PolyOlefin (TPO) polymer roof surfaces.

For both ground and roof mounted installations, it is likely desirable to provide some type of marked walkways to guide visitors to certain areas of the installation that are deemed to be safe, and to restrict activity from areas of greater risk such as roof edges or high voltage connection points. Another key difference from commercial and industrial installations is the consideration of space allocation for educational solar PV systems. In most solar installations the solar modules and associated hardware are closely spaced to contain the installation in as small of an area as possible. For educational uses, it is desirable to space this out over a much larger footprint. This is especially true if the school plans to use the system to host tours or field trips, since it will be necessary to provide sufficient space to accommodate larger groups.

The solar PV system at Madison College was designed with these considerations in mind. The building at Madison College consists of over a dozen different roof sections and elevations. One of these was specifically selected to host a 10-kW solar sub-array intended for educational use. The chosen roof section is at a lower elevation relative to the surrounding sections, eliminating any roof edge hazards on three sides (see Figure 13.2). To contain users on the fourth south facing side of the roof section, a guardrail was installed to restrict users to a safe area. As shown in the photo, this location was also designed with ample space outside of the solar array and the roof surface was outfitted with gray anti-slip walkway treads. The roof structure of this section is formed by six inches of reinforced concrete decking overlaid with sheathing, insulation and TPO membrane, and the space can easily accommodate groups of over 100 individuals for tours and open house events. An ADA-compliant doorway and ramp were also installed to provide access to the roof.

Education for the General Student Body

School personnel will likely want to consider several additional methods to enhance the educational value of the solar installation. The simplest of these is creation of a fact sheet or brochure to profile the solar PV system. These are helpful in educating the public, and also help to prepare college students and personnel to lead public tours and open house events. The solar developer

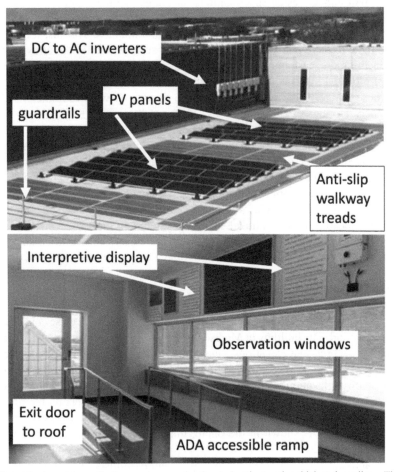

Note: The two strings of solar panels comprise the student instructional lab at the college. The leftmost DC to AC inverter shown in the photo can be de-energized and locked out to isolate this sub-system from the building and from the rest of the solar PV system. This allows teachers and students to work on the solar equipment safely during lab instructional activities. The solar panels located farthest to the left in this photo are partially shaded for a few hours in late afternoon by the taller building section to the west. This allows students to model and understand the impacts of shade on electrical output.
Source: Photo Credit – Ken Walz, Madison College.

Figure 13.2   The 10-kW instructional sub-array for the Madison College solar PV system (top), and the associated ADA-compliant doorway and ramp (bottom)

can help in the creation of the fact sheet, providing important specifications and details to help explain the system design and performance. In many cases, schools will also want to create a museum-like interpretive display. Figure 13.2 shows the interpretive display that was created at Madison College. The large windows provide a viewing area for users to observe the outdoor solar system from inside during times of inclement winter weather. The exhibit includes examples of the hardware components, descriptions of their function, photos of the installation taken during and after construction and additional signage explaining the function and performance of the solar PV system. A smart screen kiosk is also included that presents a monitoring dashboard showing the daily, monthly and lifetime energy production, revenue, CO_2 emissions saved, and the real-time instantaneous power output of the solar installation. The solar PV system has been used by students in classes including Environmental Science, Weather and Climate, and various Mathematics and Statistics courses. The students can see the working system, access the energy production and weather data sets, and use the data to learn skills such as spreadsheet manipulation, data visualization, trend analysis, and fundamental statistics.

Education for Renewable Energy Students

Additional considerations will be necessary if the solar PV system is intended to teach students in renewable energy programs. Students in the Madison College Renewable Energy Program complete several courses that make use of the new solar PV system. Students learn to design, specify, and model performance for various types of solar installations. They also learn to estimate the effects of shading, module soiling, and snow cover. Most importantly, they learn hands-on installation skills that include basic construction, workplace safety, solar assembly and wiring, electrical safety, code compliance, system commissioning and verification practices.

The college's PV system is comprised of several sub-arrays, each of which is connected to one of 17 DC to AC inverters. The sub-arrays include ballast mounted panels in both south facing, and east–west facing rack designs. This includes panels placed on a conventional black Ethylene Propylene Diene Monomer (EPDM) rubber roof, as well as panels placed on a white Thermoplastic PolyOlefin (TPO) membrane roof, and students can compare the thermal profiles of these two roof surfaces and quantify the impact on solar energy production. The system also includes a sub-array composed of modules fastened to a standing seam metal roof deck, which provides yet another thermal environment for solar panel operation. Schools that are installing ground mounted systems might want to consider different types of ground cover for the same reason. For example, comparing panels mounted over a black asphalt parking area, those mounted over white crushed rock, and those located over a grass covered surface. For the system at Madison College, module level power electronics are incorporated in the system that allow for detailed monitoring of the system's performance. Each panel in the system has its own unique hardware ID number, and DC optimizers located on the back of the modules allow for the independent operation and metering of each individual solar panel. The optimizers send a communication signal back to the DC to AC inverters which is then uploaded to the cloud via an Ethernet connection in real time. This allows for large data analytics to compare panels installed in various locations and racking orientations. It also allows students to learn about advanced Supervisory Controls and Data Acquisition (SCADA) systems, which can be programmed to provide alerts when system performance deviates from expectations. This type of SCADA monitoring can detect early indicators of component degradation, allowing for better scheduling of system maintenance, and reduction of system downtime in the event of necessary repairs (DOE, 2015).

Solar electric systems can produce dangerous electric potential and current. If the system is intended for hands-on educational use, it is recommended to locate power disconnect devices near the system array so that it can be de-energized and taken offline for instruction with students. The system at Madison College was designed with a separate inverter and DC disconnect for the 10-kW instructional sub-array. This is used by faculty and students for teaching lock-out tag-out procedures for safe electrical work. The 10-kW instructional sub-array can be taken offline for teaching. Meanwhile, the rest of the system can continue to function, providing uninterrupted power to the campus. The sub-array is also located close to classrooms and a storage area that is used for STEM classes, so there is easy access to tools and equipment. The ADA accessible ramp and roof access point also facilitate transport of rolling carts to haul tools and equipment out to the roof for lab classes. An outdoor Wi-Fi access point was installed so that instructors and students can access the real-time data of the system while outside on the roof.

The bulk of Madison College's 1.9-MW system has an open "solar window", so the panels do not experience any shading throughout the year. However, shade analysis is one of the key concepts that solar students must learn. For this reason, the college intentionally positioned the panels for the 10-kW instructional array in a location that receives a couple of hours of shade in the late afternoon. Students can use shade analysis tools to measure the expected shade of the location and then predict the resulting power reduction over the course of a year. Students also have access to the historical data archive, so they can apply data analytics to confirm if the actual power production is consistent with the shade modeling predictions. The system also includes two weather stations that monitor ambient temperature, wind speed and direction, rainfall, and irradiance in the plane of the solar array. Students can apply data analytics to compare performance on sunny versus overcast days, to quantify the effects of snow cover, and to explore the relationship between solar panel soiling and the frequency of rainfall events.

Engaging Students in Hands-on Installation Work

Many schools are interested in the idea of engaging students in the installation of solar PV systems. In practice however, there are several potential issues that may preclude this. Safety is a primary concern considering that the installers will be working with potentially lethal voltages/currents. In most states or municipalities there are also regulatory restrictions that specify who can conduct electrical work, usually requiring specialized training to earn an electrical license. At Madison College, the solar foreman was a graduate of the college's electrical program, and several members of the crew were current electrical apprenticeship students.

For schools that do not have electrical training programs, this likely precludes students from being involved in much (if any) of the electrical work. Depending on the local regulatory status, it may be possible for students to be involved in the layout and racking of solar panels, if there are workplace restrictions that isolate them from the electrical installation. If this is a goal of the solar project, then it should be included within the request for solar proposals/bids and be negotiated up front with the solar contractor. Solar installations usually come with a workmanship warranty, which may require additional consideration if students are to be involved in the project. Another opportunity to involve students might be in the commissioning and verification of the solar installation, engaging students in analysis of the system power output to see if it meets manufacturer specifications, and matches energy modeling predictions. Few solar contractors will be accustomed to working with students on a job site. Thus, it is imperative for the school and developer to have these discussions early in the planning process, and to negotiate and document any special educational accommodations that are agreed to. After the installation is complete, students could also be involved in the ongoing operations and maintenance (O&M) activities such as performing annual system inspections and diagnosing production issues using infrared cameras and PV string analyzers. If the school intends to sign a maintenance contract with the solar developer, then student-based O&M activities should also be discussed and negotiated ahead of time.

A TEN-STEP GUIDE TO CREATING A SOLAR ROADMAP FOR EDUCATIONAL INSTITUTIONS

Madison College has provided many tours to visitors from other schools, colleges and universities interested in the Madison PV system. The most common questions that are asked are some variations of "How did you manage to do this?", and "What can I do to encourage my school to consider a solar project at my campus?" To address this, we created a ten-step guide to help other schools create a Solar Roadmap. The steps are not necessarily sequential, and in practice many of these activities may take place simultaneously as a given project is executed. The ten steps have been organized to illustrate a logical progression that will facilitate potential projects from conception to implementation.

1.   Assemble Team and Articulate Purpose

Assemble a team of individuals that represent key groups, including a facilities operations manager, renewable energy faculty, institutional financial officer, and students. It is important to have representation from each of these parts of the institution, because they will all be affected by the roadmap. Equal representation on the team ensures valuable input from multiple perspectives. It is also helpful to define the scope of the roadmap planning process at this stage, so that everyone agrees on the goals and understands the intended outcome. Student representation is especially important, since serving students is the core mission of an educational institution. Furthermore, public media and members of the community will be interested in hearing the student perspective, so having an effective student representative as a spokesperson is a key ingredient for the team.

It is also necessary to address the foremost question, "Why do we need a Solar Roadmap?" The most straightforward response is that most school districts, colleges, and universities operate more than one campus location and more than one building facility. Educational institutions also have multiple other potential projects besides solar infrastructure to consider, all of which require investment of both money and staff time. It is likely not feasible to engage in multiple solar construction projects simultaneously, so it is necessary to prioritize. Creating a Solar Roadmap facilitates the planning process and ensures sound use of limited school resources.

2.   Identify Motivating Objectives

Once the team is assembled, use a method to identify what the institution's primary reason(s) are to pursue solar energy. Objectives may include ambi-

Table 13.2   *Madison College's solar roadmap team rankings of motivations for solar energy*

What do you feel are the most important reasons for Madison College to "go solar"	Rank	Rank	Rank	Rank	Rank	Average Rank
cost savings	2	1	2	4	4	2.6
learning opportunities for students	1	4	3	2	3	2.6
energy budget certainty (cost hedging)	3	2	4	1	5	3.0
social and environmental goals	4	5	1	6	1	3.4
energy resilience for critical electrical loads	6	6	6	3	2	4.6
"green" visibility	5	3	5	5	6	4.8

Note: Each member of the roadmap team ranked priorities and a weighted average was calculated. The result was a statistical tie between cost savings and learning opportunities for students. This result was then validated by subsequent interest surveys of students and faculty.

tions such as cost savings, energy budget certainty (cost hedging), learning opportunities for students, social and environmental goals, energy resilience for critical electrical loads, and "green" visibility. Objectives should be ranked or weighted to assess potential solar projects. The team may wish to have individual members rank priorities to capture the point of view of various constituents, and then use some method of averaging to arrive at a consensus (see Table 13.2).

3.   Identify Stakeholders

Create a table listing who will be impacted by the solar plan (students, faculty, staff, different offices from the institution, utilities, community, etc.). This table will help guide the process, identifying who to work with and when their input will be needed. The stakeholder table will also facilitate communications when executing the plan to make sure that everyone is informed (see Table 13.3). Stakeholder roles will vary throughout the sequencing of project execution. In the case of Madison College, initial prioritization, development of projects, and pursuit of grant funding is led by the solar roadmap team, and then project engineering, procurement and implementation is handed off to the college's facilities team. The stakeholder table will also be dictated by internal processes for securing various approvals and authorizations necessary for capital expenditures and construction projects (e.g., working with the College Board, Legal and Procurement Offices, State Agencies, etc.). The most typical activities for direct student engagement would be in the early stages of solar site prioritization where students can assess the roof conditions and shade at given locations and model expected solar energy production for a given site. Schools that teach students in engineering, skilled trades and related technical fields, may also wish to engage students in the project design and/or physical installation of the solar PV system.

4.   Quantify Energy Usage and Costs

At this stage, the team begins to gather information on the school's energy consumption and the associated costs. If the institution has multiple campuses and buildings, the data collection and analysis will be more complex. Some organizations may also wish to consider external costs (e.g., costs to the community's health due to power plant emissions), although these are much harder to quantify.

5.   Document Energy Management Practices and Pursue Energy Efficiency

Quantifying the potential to reduce energy use is an important part of a sound Solar Roadmap. It is usually most cost-effective to first make a strong commitment to energy efficiency and energy management before implementing solar projects. If the total amount of energy required by a facility is reduced, then a solar PV system of a given size can offset a larger portion of the building's energy needs.

6.   Assess Sites for Solar

The team must identify possible locations and structures where solar can be installed. It is necessary to explore the available solar resource, to identify landscape features such as trees that might cause shading, and to research building factors such as orientation and the age and structure of the roof. Local permitting and regulations may also be considered (e.g., interconnection rules, zoning restrictions, airport restrictions, etc.). If the institution has more than one electrical meter, it will be desirable to compare electrical loads and electrical rate structures for each potential solar location.

Table 13.3   Stakeholder table for Madison College's solar roadmap

START <------------------------------- Phases of Development------------------------------> FINISH

	Develop Solar Roadmap	Prioritize SolarSites	Explore Funding Sources	Proposal and Approval of Projects	Legal and Contractual	Project Design	Project Execution	Operations and Maintenance
Internal Stakeholders	*PV Roadmap Team*	*PV Roadmap Team*	*PV Roadmap Team*	*PV Roadmap Team*	Facilities Team	Facilities Team	Facilities Team	Facilities Team
	Admin Faculty and Student Leaders	Campus Managers	CFO & Fiscal Team	President's Office	Legal & Contractual Office	Faculty?	Faculty?	Faculty?
		Students?	Grants Office & Foundation	College Board	Procurement Office	Students?	Students?	Students?
External Stakeholders	Midwest Renewable Energy Association	PV Developers	Federal agencies	State Agencies	PV Contractors	RE Industry Advisory Board	PV Contractors	PV Contractors
		National Renewable Energy Lab	Electric Providers	Electric Providers	Engineering Consultants	Regulatory and Permitting Bodies	Electric Providers	Industry partners and alumni

Source: The table identifies both internal and external stakeholders and indicates the phases of development during which they are engaged. The phases will be similar for other schools, although the stakeholders will likely be different depending on the institution and the specific project.

7. Identify Funding Sources

Funding is another important part of the Solar Roadmap process. Internal sources might include capital or operational dollars, and in some cases could include money from an endowment fund or charitable education foundation. The team may explore financing options such as bonding and tax equity financing. Pursuit of grants and other incentives can also help to improve project economic benefits. Project value can be assessed using several metrics such as the simple payback period, the internal rate of return, the net present value, or the levelized cost of electricity which can be compared to the current retail rate paid to the utility.

8. Model and Prioritize Projects

The team will want to use tools such as NREL's PV Watts, System Advisor Model, and/or ReOpt to model the energy and economic performance of potential projects. The energy generation potential for each of the candidate solar sites should be modeled, and economic parameters estimated. After these steps have been completed, the team formulates a priority list for the Solar Roadmap. Projects should be ranked based on the motivating objectives that were established in Step 2 of the Solar Roadmap process.

9. Share the Plan

Once the roadmap is finalized, team members work to disseminate the plan, sharing it with the various stakeholders identified in Step 3. The roadmap provides a guide for college leadership, and it will likely influence the institution's Facilities Plan, Academic Plan and Sustainability Plan. It also serves as a document for communicating the institution's goals and objectives to potential partners and community supporters who might be able to assist with future solar projects.

10. Implement Projects

The prioritized projects are then executed by the various stakeholders that were identified in the Roadmap. Implementation will require several other steps, some of which are like those of other large campus infrastructure projects, and others are more unique to solar projects. Typically, this involves a competitive contracting process that involves a request for proposals or bids. To develop the request for proposals, it will be necessary to specify equipment and workmanship standards, along with any special considerations for the educational institution. If criteria in addition to the bottom-line cost are to be considered,

Table 13.4   Ten steps to complete a solar roadmap strategic plan

1. Assemble Team and Articulate Purpose
2. Identify and Rank Motivating Objectives
3. Identify Stakeholders
4. Quantify Energy Usage and Costs
5. Document Energy Management Practices and Pursue Energy Efficiency
6. Assess Sites for Solar
7. Identify Funding Sources
8. Model and Prioritize Projects
9. Share the Plan
10. Implement Projects

a methodology will be required to evaluate solar proposals, and a review committee will be needed for scoring. Solar construction projects typically have some additional requirements for zoning and permitting. They may also require an environmental impact review, and an interconnection agreement with the local electric utility will be required. Monitoring and documentation of the construction process is important to provide context for teaching future students about the solar installation. Groundbreaking and ribbon cutting ceremonies can provide great public education and outreach opportunities. When executing projects, the team will want to plan for future operations and maintenance. Solar panels are typically warrantied for 20–30 years, but there will be O&M costs that occur during that timeframe. Ideally, the roadmap can be published as a "living document" so that it can be updated as projects are completed, and priorities can be adjusted as situations change. For example if a roof is replaced on a building, or if a special source of funds becomes available, that might bump a given project up in the rankings.

COLLEGES AND UNIVERSITIES AS TRANSFORMATIONAL SOLAR INSTITUTIONS

Today's education leaders are presented with a once in a generation opportunity to transform the way schools operate their buildings. Some states, counties, municipalities, and school districts are now adopting resolutions that all new construction must incorporate solar power. This trend is very likely to grow in the years ahead. Higher Educational facilities are unique because they can be leveraged to provide learning opportunities for students. College buildings and their operational systems can be used to teach students studying in the STEM fields about energy efficiency, energy management, and on-site solar energy generation. This makes college facilities particularly valuable assets among the portfolio of publicly owned buildings, but also requires some special considerations to facilitate their use for student instruction.

Unlike private citizens and privately owned businesses, colleges and universities have the potential to be transformational institutions in the solar energy sector. Colleges have much longer time horizons – they construct buildings and then own and operate them for 100 years or more. This makes colleges more amenable to long-term investments in high performance building technology, because unlike a home or business owner, they will not be relocating or selling their property to someone else before they can recover the financial return on their investment.

Furthermore, most colleges and universities have separate budgets for annual operating expenses vs long-term capital investments. Electric utility bills are part of the operating budget, whereas building construction projects – including solar PV installations – are capital investments. Most schools are challenged by operational deficits from one year to the next if costs such as staff salaries, health insurance, or utility bills exceed budget estimates, or if revenues from tuition, state, or federal sources do not meet expectations. Managing operational deficits can be very challenging, and this may be a cause of anxiety for faculty and staff. On the other hand, capital budgeting is much easier, since the upfront costs are known and incurred when the construction project is implemented, and those costs are then paid off through regular fixed payments made over a long time horizon (10–30 years). Thus, solar PV technology offers schools the opportunity to remove some (or all) of their electrical costs from the variable and transient operational budget, and reallocate this cost to the predictable and more readily managed capital budget.

Unlike other large institutions (state and local governments, hospitals, libraries, etc.) colleges are by their academic nature more inclined to be aware of new technology and are more likely to be early adopters. This means that colleges are more likely to employ staff who can navigate the learning curve necessary to pursue, plan, engineer, and procure clean energy projects, and college leadership is more likely to embrace adoption of new clean energy technology. Madison College was one of the first in the state of Wisconsin to introduce bifacial solar panels, rapid shutdown safety devices, and lithium ion-storage batteries on publicly owned solar projects. College students have also been involved in undergraduate research to quantify the energy gains provided by bifacial solar panels, to characterize the snow shedding benefits of seasonally adjustable solar racking, and to assess the effectiveness of anti-soiling and self-cleaning thin film coatings for solar panels (Walz and Christian, 2017; Walz et al., 2018, and Walz et al., 2023). In this way, colleges and universities are uniquely well suited to be leaders in the areas of solar photovoltaics, and high performing sustainable buildings.

With funding from the US Department of Energy, the Midwest Renewable Energy Association has supported several college and university teams creating roadmaps for large (>1-MW) solar investments, including the Madison College case study. Based on these activities it was observed that institutions that successfully implemented large-scale solar PV investments shared the following characteristics:

- The school has a Sustainability Director or similar staff person with support from and access to key decision-makers.
- The school has a sustainability plan that includes goals related to energy consumption and carbon footprint.
- The school has academic programs with educational objectives related to sustainability and/or renewable energy.
- The school has an electric service provider that supports school-based solar investments.
- The school has made previous small-scale investments in solar PV on their campus.
- The school has relationships with peer institutions that have made large-scale solar PV investments and have shared their results and recommendations for future projects.

In recent years faculty have been working to incorporate clean energy technology into traditional STEM courses (Walz and Shoemaker, 2017) and educators across the nation have recognized the ascendance of solar photovoltaics as a critical technology (Walz et al., 2022). There is a strong incentive for college and university leaders and renewable energy advocates to become familiar with the principles of solar design and engineering so that they can formulate plans for their facilities and make informed decisions about how solar is deployed on their campuses. Since Madison College commissioned its large solar PV system in 2019, several hundred educators from other colleges and universities have toured the campus to learn more about the college's experience, in hopes of executing similar projects at their own institutions. These individuals and others who champion solar infrastructure projects for their schools can be confident that their efforts will provide enormous benefit for education and the environment, while also delivering great economic value to the schools and communities that they serve. At the same time, these educators and their schools will provide examples for others outside of academia to emulate, as solar photovoltaic technology becomes increasingly common on other public buildings, businesses, and homes across the nation and worldwide.

NOTE

1.   This contribution is based upon work originally shared at the ASEE Annual
       Conference Proceedings, June 2020 Virtual Conference, Paper ID# 30133.
       © American Society for Engineering Education. This work was supported in
       part by the National Science Foundation under DUE Grant Awards #2000714
       and #2201631. The Madison College Solar Roadmap was created with assis-
       tance from the Midwest Renewable Energy Association and funding from
       the US Department of Energy Solar Energy Technologies Office Award
       Numbers DE-EE0006910 and DE-EE0008573. Joel Shoemaker, Nick Hylla,
       and Adam Gusse contributed to the development of this work. Tom Helbig,
       Wes Marquardt, Mark Thomas, and Steven Ansorge were key contributors
       to the Madison College Solar Roadmap. Fred Brechlin, Chris Collins, Greg
       Janke, Kevin Marzalek, Khary Penebaker, and Dave Toso were integral
       members of the Madison College solar project implementation team. Dean
       of Arts and Sciences, Todd Stebbins, and President, Jack E. Daniels III,
       provided invaluable leadership to make the Madison College solar project
       a reality. This work is dedicated to the current and future Madison College
       students, who will continue to learn and benefit from solar energy long after
       those of us involved with the project have departed from the college.

REFERENCES

Blair, N., DiOrio, N., Freeman, J., Gilman, P., Janzou, S., Neises, T., and Wagner, M.
      (2017). System Advisor Model (SAM) General Description. National Renewable
      Energy Laboratory, U.S. Department of Energy. https:// www .nrel .gov/ docs/
      fy18osti/70414.pdf
Department of Energy (2015). Building America Case Study: Photovoltaic Systems
      with Module-Level Power Electronics. National Renewable Energy Laboratory,
      U.S. Department of Energy. DOE/GO- 102015-4755, 2015. https://www.nrel.gov/
      docs/fy15osti/64876.pdf
Department of Energy (2017). How to Estimate Demand Charge Savings from PV on
      Commercial Buildings. National Renewable Energy Laboratory, U.S. Department
      of Energy. https://www.nrel.gov/docs/fy17osti/69016.pdf
Department of Energy (2023a). PV Watts Photovoltaic Energy Production Calculator
      Version 8.1.0. National Renewable Energy Laboratory, U.S. Department of
      Energy. https://pvwatts.nrel.gov/index.php
Department of Energy (2023b). REOpt: Renewable Energy Integration and
      Optimization Tool. National Renewable Energy Laboratory. https://reopt.nrel.gov/
Department of Justice (2010). ADA Standards for Accessible Design. United States
      Access Board. https://www.access-board.gov/ada/
Department of Labor (2023). *Occupational Outlook Handbook.* Solar Photovoltaic
      Installers, 2021–2031. Bureau of Labor Statistics. https://www.bls.gov/ooh/
Dieziger, D. (2000). Engineering Tech Tips: Saving Money by Understanding Demand
      Charges on Your Electric Bill. U.S. Department of Agriculture. Publication

0071-2373-MTDC. https://www.fs.usda.gov/t-d/pubs/htmlpubs/htm00712373/index.htm

Energy Information Administration (2021). *State Electricity Profiles.* December 31, 2021. https://www.eia.gov/electricity/state/

Hanson, M. (2019). *The Inevitable Solar School.* Rowman & Littlefield Publishers. https://rowman.com/ISBN/9781475844207/ The -Inevitable -Solar -School -Building-the-Sustainable-Schools-of-the-Future-Today

International Energy Agency (2023). *Tracking Solar PV.* https://www.iea.org/energy-system/renewables/solar-pv

Lynch, M. (2022). The Twenty Five Oldest Colleges in America. *The Edvocate.* October 24, 2022. https://www.theedadvocate.org/the -25 -oldest -colleges -in -america/

Midwest Renewable Energy Association (2023). Solar Project Builder Finance Simulator Tool. https://www.solarprojectbuilder.org/

National Education Association (2022). Land Grant Institutions: An Overview. *NEA Research Land Grant Brief Number One.* https://www.nea.org/sites/default/files/2022-03/Land%20Grant%20Institutions%20-%20An%20Overview.pdf

National Science Foundation (2022). U.S. Institutions Providing S&E Higher Education. *Science and Engineering Indicators.* National Science Board. https://ncses.nsf.gov/pubs/nsb20197/u-s-institutions-providing-s-e-higher-education

Nemet, G. (2019). *How Solar Became Cheap.* Routledge. https://www.routledge.com/How-Solar-Energy-Became-Cheap-A-Model-for-Low-Carbon-Innovation/Nemet/p/book/9780367136598

Ramasamy, V., Zuboy, J., O'Shaughnessy, W., Feldman, D., Desai, J., Woodhouse, W., Basore, P., and Margolis, R. (2022). U.S. Solar Photovoltaic System Cost Benchmark. U.S. Department of Energy, National Renewable Energy Laboratory, 2022. https://www.nrel.gov/docs/fy22osti/83586.pdf

Solar Power Europe (2022). *Global Market Outlook for Solar Power.* Brussels, Belgium. https://www.solarpowereurope.org/insights/market -outlooks/global -market-outlook-for-solar-power-2022

Walz, K., & Christian, J. (2017). Engineering Design Projects for Community Colleges. *American Journal of Engineering Education, 8*(1), 1–11. https://clutejournals.com/index.php/AJEE/article/view/9958

Walz, K., & Shoemaker, J. (2017). Preparing the Future Sustainable Energy Workforce and The Center for Renewable Energy Advanced Technological Education. *The Journal of Sustainability Education, 17.* http://www.susted.com/wordpress/wp-content/uploads/2017/03/Walz-and-Shoemaker-JSE-March -2017_Future-Casting-Issue-PDF.pdf

Walz, K., Shoemaker, J., Scholes, A., Jiang, H., Sanfilippo, J., Silva, J., Zeltner, W., and Anderson, M. (2018). Experimental Field Trial of Self-Cleaning Solar Photovoltaic Panels. *ASEE Annual Conference Proceedings*, Paper # 22061. https://peer.asee.org/experimental-field-trial-of-self-cleaning-solar-photovoltaic -panels

Walz, K., Shoemaker, J., Ansorge, S., Gusse, A., and Hylla, N. (2020). Enlightened Education: Solar Engineering Design to Energize School Facilities. *ASEE Annual Conference Proceedings*, Paper #30133. https://peer.asee.org/enlightened -education-solar-engineering-design-to-energize-school-facilities

Walz, K., McMahan, A., Temple, G., and Alfano, K. (2022). Results of 2021 Energy Education Stakeholder Survey. *ASEE Annual Conference Proceedings.* https://peer.asee.org/results-of-2021-energy-education-stakeholder-survey

Walz, K., Hoege, T., Duensing, J., Zeltner, W., and Anderson, M. (2023). Field
    Tests of a Self-Sintering, Anti-Soiling, Self-Cleaning, Nanoporous Metal Oxide,
    Transparent Thin Film Coating for Solar Photovoltaic Modules. *Solar Energy
    Materials and Solar Cells*, *262*, 112560. https://www.sciencedirect.com/science/
    article/pii/S0927024823003811

14. Decolonizing post-secondary sustainability education in the Anthropocene

Kimberly M. Post

INTRODUCTION

I approached the theme of this publication from a particular perspective, so it seems important to position myself before I begin. I currently serve as the Associate Dean of Environmental Graduate Studies at Unity Environmental University's Pineland Campus, which is located on unceded Wabanaki territory in Maine, US. I have always felt a deep and profound connection to the natural world, a primeval, familial feeling that makes me love and nurture it as I would a member of my human family. It is my primary goal as an educator to teach others how to be in relationship with the Earth and live in kinship with all beings, be they human or more-than-human. We are living in profoundly challenging and divisive times, at risk of losing our identities, our communities, and this planet that sustains us. The escalating climate crisis is exacerbating the disparities created by enduring colonial injustices and its structures of dominance over land and Indigenous self-determination. I believe we need to learn how to dwell in reciprocity, and I believe this is vital to both human and environmental survival. With this lofty goal in mind, I posit that decolonization is a precondition for sustainable universities and colleges. If we change the dominant hegemonic narrative that excludes non-Western and more-than-human epistemologies and ontologies, universities and colleges need neither lead nor follow society, but collaborate as "pluriversities" toward a more just, resilient, and sustainable future.

THIS PLANET WE CALL HOME

Living in kinship with the world has not been the way for modern hegemonic history though, and much of my scholarship and research is in response to the mounting repercussions of anthropocentric thinking. Human and natural systems are facing challenges that are not only dauntingly complex and continuously evolving but are also an urgent call for attention and concerted action (Benatar, 2016; Dreier et al., 2019; UNESCO, 2022). We are witnessing and often complicit in unprecedented degradation of the natural world. Basic human needs are not being met for at least one third of the approximately 8 billion people on the planet – and there will likely be more than 10 billion people a generation from now (McCoy, 2017; UNESCO, 2022). Environmental sustainability and community resilience are fundamental frameworks that will shape how educators in all disciplines teach and equip students for the difficulties ahead (Satterwhite et al., 2016).

As human activities continue to negatively impact the planet, colleges and universities around the world have begun to embrace sustainability initiatives in various forms, leveraging them as catalysts for systemic change within academics, policies, and campus operations. While the last few decades have seen the development of sustainability-focused academic programs, this growing field of *sustainability education* (SE) remains broadly defined both in the literature, and in practice (Wals & Jickling, 2002). Internationally, SE is commonly referred to as *Education for Sustainable Development* (ESD), but use of the term *development* is increasingly criticized due to its colonial legacy and the associated assumptions about who or what needs to be developed (Imran et al., 2014; Jacobs & Narváez, 2022). Comparable programs in the US tend to use *Education for Sustainability* (EfS), but this too is problematic as its boundaries have spilled into the competing concepts and definitions of environmental education, environmental literacy, and ecological literacy (Santone, 2019).

Similarly, the definition of the term *sustainability* varies both in the literature and in practice. While it means different things to different cultures and regions of the world, it is still widely accepted as the term to best describe the preservation of natural resources to maintain ecological balance. The term gained prominence in 1987 with the publication of *Our Common Future,* a landmark report by the World Commission on Environment and Development (WCED). Also known as the Brundtland Report, the document declared the "three Es" of sustainability as **E**nvironmental regeneration and stewardship, **E**conomic prosperity, and **E**quitable societies (WCED, 1987). The Brundtland Report is the source of the most well-known definition of sustainability – "Meeting the needs of the present without compromising the ability of future generations to meet their needs" (WCED, 1987, p. 16). This also appears to be the point in which the term *sustainability* was first connected to the concept of *development* (Brandon & Lombardi, 2010; Kidd, 1992; Du Pisani, 2006). In the US, the Environmental Protection Agency (EPA) describes sustainability as:

> ...based on a simple principle: Everything that we need for our survival and well-being depends, either directly or indirectly, on our natural environment. To

pursue sustainability is to create and maintain the conditions under which humans and nature can exist in productive harmony to support present and future generations. (EPA, 2022)

It seems that the term *sustainability* has become rooted in the economic and social needs of humans at the expense of the natural world (Imran et al., 2014). Similarly, our understanding of sustainability education has been inextricably connected to this anthropocentric perspective. As planetary problems continue to increase, a growing body of educators and scholars are concluding that SE/ESD/EfS "actually undermines efforts to educate citizens about the importance of valuing and protecting the environment" (Washington et al., 2017, p. 38), in part due to its decidedly anthropocentric approach based on human exceptionalism that centers humans' interests and prioritizes development over ecosystem and societal health (Miller et al., 2014; Doak et al., 2015). Until we recognize nature's intrinsic value, a fully sustainable future is highly unlikely (Batavia & Nelson, 2016; Washington et al., 2017).

While SE is broadly defined in Western education, ranging from the specific "Education for Sustainable Development" (UNESCO, 2014) to the rather vague "pedagogical big idea, capable of complementing and connecting avenues of inquiry across the academic disciplines" (Sherman, 2008, p. 188), a persistent commonality is the Western hegemony of development (Cajete, 1994; Kerr, 2022; Kothari et al., 2019; Wals & Benavot, 2017). This emphasizes Anthropocentrism and reinforces power relations that favor Western knowledge and marginalize other ways of knowing (Hards, 2011; Jacobs & Narváez, 2022; Muraca, 2011). I propose that SE needs to move beyond its Western-centric perspective in recognition of "diverse geographic, social, cultural, and political contexts" (Kerr, 2022; Kothari et al., 2019). It is time to decolonize sustainability education.

As a settler academic living and working on unceded Wabanaki territory, I recognize that both my identity and my education are products of colonial processes and the subsequent sociocultural hierarchies they reinforced. I also recognize that decolonization must be led by Indigenous peoples, but I believe settler allies have important roles to play in this process. "Decolonization is a process for both the colonizer and the colonized" (Waziyatawin, 2011). Decolonizing sustainability education calls for many voices and I choose to use my voice by positioning myself in a critique of our hegemonic academy and calling for a transformational SE curriculum "that is more inclusive of the social, cultural and moral dimensions of sustainability" (Frandy, 2018).

This is how I come to this work. First, however, it is important to understand how the post-secondary SE field came into being and how the concept of development became intrinsically linked to sustainability.

A BRIEF HISTORY OF SUSTAINABILITY EDUCATION

Attention to post-secondary sustainability education began with the Talloires Declaration, a ten-point action plan for incorporating sustainability and environmental literacy in teaching, research, operations, and outreach in higher education. The Declaration was signed in 1990 by more than 350 university presidents and chancellors in over 40 countries, committing their institutions to sustainability (ULSF, 2017). This was followed in 1992 by the creation of Agenda 21 (also known as the Rio Declaration), the United Nations' action plan to promote Education for Sustainable Development (ESD) and establish sustainability educational policy and practices (United Nations, 1992). The emergence of these two initiatives emphasized the growing need for sustainability education at the collegiate level. As of this writing, the Talloires Declaration, now administered by University Leaders for a Sustainable Future (ULSF), has been signed by over 500 university leaders in over 50 countries (ULSF, 2017).

In North America, the 1990s also saw the proliferation of nonprofit and non-governmental organizations (NGOs) focused on sustainability in higher education. The National Wildlife Federation (NWF) established its Campus Ecology program, which became one of the leading conservation programs in higher education. In 2014, it transitioned to the EcoLeaders Program, a career development initiative for college students interested in sustainability leadership (Barcelo et al., 2012). However, its Campus Ecology Resource Center, a collection of conservation and sustainability resources for higher education, remains one of the largest collections in the United States (National Wildlife Federation, n.d.).

Learning for a Sustainable Future (LSF) was established in 1991 and charged with leading the Canadian response to the United Nations' Decade of Education for Sustainable Development (Learning for a Sustainable Future, n.d.). LSF was founded collaboratively between Indigenous and non-Indigenous peoples and continues the ongoing work to raise up Indigenous voices in sustainability education, voices that are currently not heard in other high-level programs and initiatives around the world (Association of Canadian Deans of Education, 2022). While primarily focused on the integration of SE into Canada's K-12 school systems, it is important to note that LSF, supported by Natural Resources Canada, is specifically focused on SE, rather than on broader support for sustainability integration across institutional systems.

In 1993, Second Nature was founded in Boston to help make the principles of sustainability fundamental to every aspect of higher education. While its primary focus is to "accelerate climate action in and through, higher education" (Second Nature, 2021), it also supports colleges and universities through advocacy and funding and provides sustainability education and leadership opportunities for students. Since its founding, Second Nature has worked with more than 4,000 faculty and administrators at hundreds of institutions to "help make the principles of sustainability fundamental to every aspect of higher education" (Second Nature, 2021).

The Association for the Advancement of Sustainability in Higher Education (AASHE) is the largest organization for higher education sustainability in North America. Launched in January 2006, it was the first professional higher education association for the campus sustainability community. Its roots can be traced back to the Education for Sustainability Western Network (EFS West), established by Second Nature in 1993, which served college and university campuses in the western US and Canada and provided resources and support for campus sustainability efforts (AASHE, 2022).

In 2010, AASHE was recognized by the North American Association for Environmental Education for Outstanding Service to Environmental Education Organization, Global Level. That same year AASHE launched the Sustainability Tracking, Assessment & Rating System (STARS) 1.0, providing a competitive framework for institutions to benchmark their sustainability efforts. The online resource library Campus Sustainability Hub was launched in 2016 for AASHE members to connect, share, and learn about sustainability in higher education. This remains the largest repository of resources for sustainability in higher education (AASHE, 2022).

By the turn of the century, hundreds of sustainability programs had emerged in colleges and universities around the world (Wright, 2004). These included sustainability-focused programs in the broader sustainability science field (Kates, 2011; Yarime et al., 2012; Lang et al., 2012) and sustainability-related programs in business, education, communications, law, and more (Johnson et al., 2019). But when the Sustainable Development Goals (SDGs) were articulated in 2015 by the United Nations General Assembly as the successors to the Millennium Development Goals (established in 2000), the terms *sustainability* and *development* became intrinsically linked (Sonetti et al., 2019). This appears to be the turning point for sustainability pedagogies and andragogies as well. With the prioritization of economic growth and marginalization of environmental integrity, most sustainability-focused educational programs have centered humanity, rather than the natural world, diverting attention from the true roots of the ecological crisis – anthropocentric thinking (Eisenmenger et al., 2020; Kopnina, 2014).

In *Transforming Knowledge*, educator and scholar Minnich writes, "… scholarship that refuses old exclusions and invidious hierarchies not only does not fit into any of the old fields, but also, for that very reason, has the potential to transform them all" (2005, p. 72). This transformation is the change that needs to happen if higher education is going to be relevant going forward, and the worsening planetary crisis is the catalyst. To decolonize sustainability, I propose two transformational steps. First, by understanding the colonial legacy and associated assumptions about who or what needs to be developed (Imran et al., 2014; Todd, 2016; Jacobs & Narváez, 2022), and recognizing that there are many ways of knowing and being in the world, we can begin to shift the narrative from anthropocentric to ecocentric. Second, if post-secondary SE can model Paulo Freire's praxis of "reflection and action upon the world in order to transform it" (Freire, 1972, p. 52), it can transform colleges and universities from siloed institutions to reciprocal collaborations, an ecopedagogical approach that joins campuses and communities together to work toward sustainability and resilience.

ECOCENTRISM: IN KINSHIP WITH THE WORLD

Ecocentrism asserts that humanity is in relationship with those both living and non-living (Arrows, 2016; Hettinger & Throop, 1999) and that "the land [is] relative and citizen" (Donald, 2009, p. 19). It reflects a "kincentric ecology" (Jacobs & Narváez, 2022; Salmón, 2000) in which "all living beings cooperate and co-create" (Moran et al., 2018, p. 73). This practice of experiencing the natural world as family is a relational view that counters the pervasive anthropocentric narrative (Bang et al., 2014). Rather than viewing humans as separate and, in many cases, superior to nature, there is no separation, no human dominance over nature (Washington et al., 2017). All beings are interconnected with each other and to the natural world. "Land is, therefore we are" (Bang et al., 2014, p. 45).

Ecocentrism is likely as old as the evolution of humanity and describes what may be considered the "original" sustainability ethos (Washington, 2015; Washington et al., 2017), the holistic ontological worldview of diverse cultures across the planet (Knudtson & Suzuki, 1992). Many Indigenous peoples engage in knowledge production practices that emphasize more-than-human relational ontologies (Panelli, 2010; Todd, 2016), center community and reciprocity between humans and nonhumans, and value environmental sustainability (Gadgil et al., 1993; Posey, 1999; Rappaport, 1999; Berkes et al., 2000; Berkes, 2008; Graham & Maloney, 2019). These worldviews often express and promote ecocentric values such as kinship toward living and non-living entities (Suzuki & Knudtson, 1992; Posey, 1999; Curry, 2011; Kimmerer, 2013; Vetlesen, 2019; Washington, 2019). The Indigenous Latin American relational ontology of *buen vivir*, simply translated as "good living", is one example. Buen vivir recognizes the interdependence between society and the environment and considers the idea of *community* not limited to people but encompassing the natural world as well (Kothari et al., 2014; Thompson, 2018). Similarly, the African *Ubuntu* emphasizes interconnectedness and belonging to a greater whole (Murove, 2009, 2014; Tutu, 1999), and valuing the ecological health of the community as well as the individual (van der Walt, 2010). Unlike colonialist Western epistemologies, there is no dichotomy of human and more-than-human in many Indigenous ways of knowing. "Everything in nature, including humans, enjoys equal status" (Aikenhead & Michell, 2011, p. 78).

In modern Western philosophy, ecocentrism can be traced to Aldo Leopold's "land ethic" (Belshaw, 2014; Leopold, 1949) and his assertion that "the economic parts of the biotic clock will [not] function without the uneconomic parts" (Leopold, 1949, p. 214). Like Arne Næss' deep ecology that recognizes the many diverse human and nonhuman communities that make up the living Earth (Næss, 1973; Smith, 2014), ecocentrism is considered "an ecologically informed philosophy of *internal relatedness*", in which all organisms are not simply interrelated with the environment but also *constituted* by those very environmental interrelationships (Eckersley, 1992, p. 49).

While the once human-centered field of environmental ethics now includes ecocentrism's intrinsic (rather than instrumental) value of all living organisms and their natural environment regardless of their perceived usefulness or importance to human beings (Hettinger & Throop, 1999), ecocentrism has yet to find its way into SE and Anthropocentrism continues to dominate the narrative (Washington et al., 2017). For example, both the 2014 and 2020 versions of UNESCO's Education for Sustainable Development roadmaps (UNESCO, 2014; UNESCO, 2020) fail to consider Indigenous worldviews, ethics, or ecocentrism. Scholars have since argued for a non-anthropocentric approach to SE and assert that questioning human domination over nature is a pedagogical imperative (Bonnett, 2002; Smith & Stevenson, 2017). Yet the fields of SE/ ESD/EfS remain largely anthropocentric and continue to propagate the colonialist ethos of development that is so antithetical to an ecocentric understanding of sustainability (Orr, 1994; Spring, 2004).

Ecocentrism centers interdependence by valuing the relationship between humans and nature (Darwin, 1859; Doherr & Baron, 2011; Doherr, 2015; Eliot, 2018; Leopold, 1942, 1949; Roszak, 1992; Soulé, 1985). While this "relationality" is a concept that is gaining interdisciplinary prominence as scholars attempt to understand complex phenomena in terms of relations (Walsh et al., 2020), relational approaches in SE remain somewhat marginalized. (Netherwood et al., 2006; Williams, 2013; Lange, 2018; O'Neil, 2018; Mcphie & Clarke, 2019; Taylor & Pacini-Ketchabaw, 2019). Relational theory considers humans and nature as part of one living system – interconnected, complex, and interdependent – an adaptive socioecological system in a constant state of flux (Walsh et al., 2020). It is a paradigm that defines humans and nature as co-creators with the nonhuman world (Abram, 2010). Integrating relationality into SE challenges the Western fixed meaning of what it means to be in relationship with the world. By recognizing that humans and nature are part of one living socioecological system and co-creators with the nonhuman world, SE becomes a pedagogy that acknowledges the spirituality and experiences that connect people, land, the living and non-living, those before us and those still to come (Abram, 2010; Datta, 2015; Walsh et al., 2020).

AN ECOCENTRIC EMPHASIS

Examples of ecocentrism in post-secondary sustainability education are unfortunately few and far between, but at Unity Environmental University (formerly Unity College), ecocentrism has been present since 2017 in the Distance Education Graduate curricula. The course *Human Dimensions of Natural Resource Management* was the first, incorporating TEK (Traditional Ecological Knowledge) throughout its original and all subsequent curricular iterations. The course explores components of TEK, contrasts TEK with the Western scientific knowledge, and considers the challenges and opportunities of incorporating multiple ways of knowing for improvement of wildlife management practices. *Conservation Ecology* soon followed, with learners studying ecosystem-level dynamics from both Western science and Indigenous TEK perspectives and learning how Indigenous perspectives can positively influence ecosystem restoration work. The newest course, *Climate Change Equity and Engagement,* delves into the complex intersection of climate change, equity, social justice, and community engagement and uses equity-based and decolonizing approaches for climate mitigation and adaptation. Additionally, Indigenous perspectives and local ecological knowledge are now imbedded in the *Ethical Practice and Policy* course, bringing ecocentrism into the Distance Education Graduate core curriculum (Unity Environmental University, 2023). Unity continues to create new courses that emphasize ecocentric perspectives, recognizing that the role of Indigenous knowledge production practices in sustainability work is increasingly valued.

With the 2022 adoption of the Kunming-Montreal Global Biodiversity Framework at the close of COP 15, the hope is that more ecocentric values will eventually make their way into mainstream SE. The new Framework recognizes Indigenous peoples and local communities, including collective rights and rights to their lands and territories, as well as their roles in and contributions to nature conservation (UN Environment Programme, 2022). This acknowledgment of the integrity and distinct nature of Indigenous and traditional territories will hopefully usher in a new era of both conservation and education.

ECOPEDAGOGY – WORLDING TOGETHER

The relatively new field of ecopedagogy examines Paolo Freire's critical pedagogy, a teaching philosophy that challenges teachers and students to examine structures of power and oppression (Fraser et al., 1997) through an ecological lens. It maintains the quintessential Freireian concepts of "the humanization of experience and the achievement of a just and free world" (Kahn, 2010, p. 18) while interpolating ecoliteracy and recognition of culturally relevant epistemologies "grounded in normative concepts such as sustainability, planetarity, and biophilia" (p. 18). Ecopedagogy attempts to produce a "revolutionary critical pedagogy based in hope that can bridge the politics of the academy with forms of grassroots political organizing capable of achieving social and ecological transformation" (Martin, 2007, p. 349).

Ecopedagogical theory evolved both directly out of Freire's work and indirectly through Latin American popular education (Gutiérrez & Prado, 1999; Gadotti, 2011) where his ideas have had significant historical influence. Freire intended to issue a book on ecopedagogy, which was superseded by his death in 1997. However, he left the following in a late reflection published posthumously in *Pedagogy of Indignation*:

> It is urgent that we assume the duty of fighting for the fundamental ethical principles, like respect for the life of human beings, the life of other animals, the life of birds, the life of rivers and forests. I do not believe in love between men and women, between human beings, if we are not able to love the world. (2004, p. 46)

Like ecocentrism, ecopedagogy reframes sustainability by embedding values and practices that emphasize reciprocity and recognize many ways of knowing. It also provides a framework for recognizing the systems of oppression and power at play in SE.

FROM UNIVERSITY TO PLURIVERSITY

In decolonizing post-secondary sustainability education, we must decolonize the academy as well. A vital first step is to acknowledge the historical roots of higher education in the US and its deeply entrenched systems of racism, power, and privilege. As activist and scholar Linda Tuhiwai Smith points out in *Decolonizing Methodologies* (2021), "Coming to know the past [is] part of the critical pedagogy of decolonization" (p. 38). Higher education in the US is primarily a patriarchal institution that was built by white European men of privilege on the backs of marginalized and often displaced peoples (Paton et al., 2020). European settlers initially praised Indigenous peoples for their community ethos and agricultural practices before shifting the narrative to one of savagery to justify their subsequent removal. These same stories rationalized the creation of what we now know as land-grant institutions, the backbone of research in the US, historically run by privileged land-owning white men and accessible only to them (Patel, 2021). In many cases these institutions were built by Black indentured servants, as were private institutions, the nation's first colleges and universities. We now know that profits from slavery helped fund some of the most prestigious schools in the Northeast, including Harvard, Columbia, Princeton, and Yale, and in many Southern states enslaved peoples both built the campuses and served faculty and students (Smith & Ellis, 2022).

The academy's Eurocentric roots have historically excluded non-Western epistemologies (Alvares & Faruqui, 2011). In a system of scholarship dominated by white male privilege, we have built institutions that consider Western male knowledge the only way of knowing (Minnich, 2005). Higher education has evolved into a system of silos, academics working in their own narrow fields of expertise with little if any multi- or interdisciplinary collaboration. The deeply entrenched and valued traditions of thinking built into the hierarchies of customs and eras provide many versions of knowledge, and the epistemologies that have emerged in our educational systems have only reinforced the root problem – the exclusion of marginalized (female, non-binary, oppressed male) voices from the creation of knowledge (Minnich, 2005). The development of the disciplines and their resultant curricula further perpetrates this exclusive knowledge mythos (Alvares & Faruqui, 2011; Minnich, 2005). Recognizing how we have constructed our knowledge systems and how we continue to think about them calls for an examination of curricula and disciplines as educational systems that continue to propagate this narrow yet prominent domination and narrative (Minnich, 2005).

Decolonizing post-secondary sustainability education means moving from the exclusive language of the "university" to the inclusive language of a "pluriversity." This metamorphosis needs to happen with community, in community, to equitably address the vital work needed to support resilience of our human and natural systems. "Pluriversities" can become collective hubs of co-learners – campuses in praxis with communities – to address the growing social, economic, and environmental impacts of a rapidly changing climate (Freire, 1972; Haraway, 2008; Ledwith, 2005; Palmer & Hunter, 2018; Shefner & Cobb, 2002). Everyone is a teacher, learner, and contributor, which creates multifaceted long-term relationships between campuses and communities. Higher education sustainability efforts can join with society toward resilience if we can reimagine an academy that represents all people and points us toward an ecologically and socially just future.

Decolonizing post-secondary SE in the Anthropocene is a multistep process, one that demands examination of terminologies, understanding of histories, questioning of dominant epistemologies, and recognition of multiple ontologies. In decolonizing both higher educational systems and the SE field itself, institutions neither lead nor follow, but model Freire's praxis of learning together in community and "reflection and action upon the world in order to transform it" (Freire, 1972, p. 52), while providing real-world, high-impact learning experiences as active and participatory community hubs. This requires institutions to share resources and expertise for society's benefit, but in return they are gaining experiential learning opportunities for students and researchers that extend far beyond the normal college classroom.

A PLURIVERSITY IN MAINE

Saint Joseph's College of Maine is at the beginning of its decolonization process, but the institution has been striving to model what it means to be a pluriversity. The campus is located approximately 20 miles northwest of Portland, the state's largest urban center, and has a long history of learning in praxis with community. It is a small private liberal arts institution situated on 474 mostly wooded acres, including 2,500 feet of waterfront on Sebago Lake, the second largest lake in Maine and source of the greater Portland area drinking water. The College's identity and mission as a Mercy institution are closely interwoven with the beauty and environmental quality of the Lakes Region, and maintaining these qualities is essential to preserving its identity and critical to the economic viability of the area. Environmental stewardship is an integral part of Saint Joseph's College's ethos and is expressed through its commitment to sustainability and community (Post & Lesher, 2022).

In 2018, the College established the Center for Sustainable Communities (CSC) to support social, environmental, and economic sustainability in the region. Founded upon the idea that colleges and communities should work together to improve the health and vitality of their regions, the CSC leverages interdisciplinary research and scholarship, community dialogue, human capacity, and innovation to advance social justice and sustainability, creating opportunities for innovation, leadership, and positive change (Saint Joseph's College of Maine, 2023).

A new kind of sustainability education is emerging from the CSC, one that blends values-based education with community-based education and research, and is grounded firmly in Freire's ecopedagogy. An example of this began in 2021, when the CSC facilitated a multi-year collaboration with CSC staff, students, faculty, and the Little Sebago Lake Association, which serves neighboring seven-mile long Little Sebago Lake (Post & Lesher, 2022). Saint Joseph's College and the Little Sebago Lake Association had worked on and off together over the last decade on various community-identified projects and problems, but this newest collaboration, in addition to assisting the Association with water quality measurements and overall assessment of lake health, identified a set of best practices (BPs) for sustaining reciprocal partnerships between learning institutions and community-based groups or organizations. The BPs, rooted in a decidedly Freirean ethos of honoring the voices of community members and centering community needs and values, were published in the peer-reviewed journal *Sustainability and Climate Change* (Post & Lesher, 2022). The six simple practices provide guidelines for colleges and communities to work together in reciprocal and equitable ways as they collaborate to address environmental sustainability and community resilience. They reflect the heart of ecopedagogy and Freire's assertion that it is humanity's responsibility to create a more just and equitable world (Freire, 1972). From "Protecting Little Sebago: A Model College-Lake Association Sustainable Partnership" (2022):

BP1: Outline Goals and Strategies Together

At the beginning of a campus–community relationship, emphasis must be on the collaborative process. By working together to identify the community's goals and discussing how they fit with student learning outcomes, a strong foundation can be laid for both the current project and any future collaborations between the campus and community. A clear and shared understanding of project goals and team member contributions will do much to further early progress, as diverging agendas for outcomes can unintentionally hijack community needs (Shefner & Cobb, 2002, pp. 275–276). Collaboration during the planning phase of a project is critical.

BP2: Share Power as Equitably as Possible

Once the collaborative process has been established, it is important to maintain this mutuality by working together to define the project. The community's voice is particularly important in shaping the research question or project direction. Sharing power can present challenges to college–community collaborations, so the campus partners must pay close attention to this aspect. When community members feel they have less voice in the relationship, the work is likely to be less valuable to them and the partnership may feel unbalanced and obligatory, rather than mutually collaborative as intended (Shefner & Cobb, 2002; Strand, 2000).

BP3: Be Clear, Deliberate, and Respectful in all Communications

Communication is an essential element of effective partnerships. Campus–community collaborations bring people together with different world-views, experiences, and perspectives, and require that they engage in conversations to accomplish often challenging and complex tasks. All participants must strive to understand and be understood, and this means avoiding what Freire called "alienating rhetoric" (Freire, 1972, p. 77) or disciplinary jargon, clarifying meanings, identifying assumptions and recognizing what might not be obvious to everyone involved, and "working to develop a common discourse that will make future partner interactions inclusive and productive" (Strand et al., 2003, p. 9).

BP4: Be Flexible and Accepting of Different Organizational Perspectives

Successful partnerships learn not only how to communicate across sociocultural divides, but they must recognize and navigate institutional constraints that could potentially impede a successful collaboration. "Community organizations and higher education institutions are very different in size, financial stability and cash flow, organizational structure and accountabilities, levels of bureaucracy, interorganizational relations, and reward structures" (Strand et al., 2003, p. 9). Campuses typically operate on semester schedules and have priorities that dictate deadlines and due dates, while community partners may be impacted by staff availability and time constraints. Both campuses and community partners may be navigating funding access or parameters. Although these factors can challenge collaborations, clear communication, recognition of differences, and flexibility will go a long way toward helping college–community collaborators work through challenges (Strand et al., 2003).

BP5: Remember that the Community Always comes First

The most obvious objective of a college–community partnership is to address an issue or solve a problem. However, academic and community needs and interests may very well diverge beyond their mutually identified goals. Faculty need to provide students with valuable learning experiences. They also recognize the inherent value of these learning experiences in both student recruitment and retention. Communities are seeking support, understanding, and positive change. They need good quality data, reports, or other products that are useful, and may also have to consider internal aspects such as community politics or financial obligations. For successful college–community relationships, the collaboration must meet the community's interests or needs, enhance organizational capacities, and focus on the mutual benefits of working together for the common good (Strand et al., 2003, p. 9).

BP6: Develop and Share a Mutual Long-Term Perspective

An important aspect of this work is the co-development of a future vision. This can be achieved by recognizing that short-term projects can make incremental contributions toward the future goal of positive and lasting change. Long-term goals typically fall into three general areas:

1. Helping the institution be both more relevant to the community and more effective in educating students to be active, engaged, and knowledgeable citizens (Shefner & Cobb, 2002, p. 293).
2. Helping communities gain more knowledge, access more resources, and become more resilient (Hayhurst et al., 2013, pp. 607–608).
3. Helping everyone acquire knowledge and skills that they can then bring to future projects, collaborations, and experiences (Strand et al., 2003, p. 10).

Since most one-time projects have modest impact, keeping a long-term perspective helps all stakeholders remain committed to the ongoing work needed for building sustainable and resilient communities (Post & Lesher, 2022).

FROM PLURIVERSITY TO PLURIVERSITIES

While Saint Joseph's College has embraced the pluriversity model of praxis with communities (Freire, 1972; Haraway, 2008; Ledwith, 2005; Palmer & Hunter, 2018; Shefner & Cobb, 2002), my scholarship journey had planted a seed of an idea that is just beginning to germinate. Colleges and universities are rich with intellectual capacity, curiosity, motivation, and in many cases, physical and monetary resources to drive toward the climate crisis. What if we could create a multi-campus hub to collectively address the growing impacts of our rapidly changing climate? This came to fruition in 2022, when the Center for Sustainable Communities at Saint Joseph's College, together with Maine Campus Compact, launched a new initiative to further support sustainability efforts in Maine. In a virtual summit with Gov. Janet Mills, a state-wide collaboration of Maine colleges and universities was announced. Aptly named *Maine Campuses Won't Wait* (MCWW), the initiative came together to support the state's climate action plan, *Maine Won't Wait* (Feinberg, 2022). MCWW holds the tenants of ecopedagogy front and center by bridging inter-institutional politics with grassroots organizing to achieve social and ecological transformation (Martin, 2007, p. 349). While this new collaboration has become a state-wide multi-campus hub for training and capacity building, particularly for campuses with limited capacities and resources, the hope is that by mobilizing student leadership and faculty/staff expertise, MCWW will advance a significant collective impact response to the climate crisis and together create more equitable and sustainable communities. With the support of Maine Campus Compact and the Center for Sustainable Communities, MCWW is proving that colleges and universities are valuable resources for their greater communities. In Maine, post-secondary SE is evolving into a collaboration of campus–community partnerships working together toward sustainability and resilience.

TOWARD RESILIENCE

The unfolding future is far from clear but what is certain is that we must recognize and honor all voices as we collaborate toward a just, resilient, and sustainable future. Knowledge is more than the "universal knowledge for humanity" (Mbembe, 2016, p. 37); it is open to epistemic diversity. We need a counternarrative to "the hegemony of modernity's one-world ontology" (Escobar, 2018, p. 4), a counternarrative that emphasizes humans and nature as part of one living interdependent system (Walsh et al., 2020). Abandoning or failing to acknowledge the importance of living in mutuality with the natural world means we lose sight of this place of wisdom and inspiration – our collective heritage. By reimagining sustainability as an interdependent web of symbiotic relationality, we acknowledge the fundamental sharedness of all life everywhere, human and more-than-human alike. Our practice of right relationship with the world turns kinship into a verb – a celebration of kincentric connection, reciprocity, and respect.

Decolonizing post-secondary sustainability education in the Anthropocene means working together to change the dominant hegemonic narrative that excludes non-Western and more-than-human epistemologies and ontologies (Cajete, 1994; Kerr, 2022; Kothari et al., 2019; Wals & Benavot, 2017). It means recognizing humanity's complicity in the great challenges we face and the devastating results of our anthropocentric thinking (Eisenmenger et al., 2020; Kopnina, 2014). Finally, it means reimagining the role of our higher education institutions. If universities can become "pluriversities" that represent all peoples and multiple worldviews, higher education can then lead *with* communities, *in* communities, collaborating toward a just, resilient, and sustainable future (Doppelt, 2017). This reimagining will become an active ontological process – a way we can go about worlding (Abram, 1996; Haraway, 2008; Kohák, 1984; Palmer & Hunter, 2018) together to heal our wounded communities and this planet we call home.

> In the world of the powerful there is room only for the big and their helpers. In the world we want, everybody fits. The world we want is a world in which many worlds fit. (EZLN, 1996)

REFERENCES

Abram, D. (1996). *The spell of the sensuous: perception and language in a more-than-human world.* Pantheon Books.

Abram, D. (2010). Becoming animal. *Green Letters, 13*(1), 7–21.

Aikenhead, G., & Michell, H. (2011). *Bridging cultures: Indigenous and scientific ways of knowing nature.* Pearson.

Alvares, C.A., & Faruqui, S.S. (2011). *Decolonising the university: the emerging quest for non-Eurocentric paradigms.* Penerbit USM.

Arrows, F. (2016). The CAT–FAWN connection: Using metacognition and Indigenous worldview for more effective character education and human survival. *Journal of Moral Education, 45*(3), 261–275. https://doi.org.ezproxyles.flo.org/10.1080/03057240.2016.1167026

Association for the Advancement of Sustainability in Higher Education. (2022). *History of AASHE.* https://www.aashe.org/about-us/aashe-history

Association of Canadian Deans of Education. (2022). *Accord on education for a sustainable future.* https://csse-scee.ca/acde/wp-content/uploads/sites/7/2022/03/Accord-on-Education-for-a-Sustainable-Future-1.pdf

Bang, M., Curley, L., Kessel, A., Marin, A., Suzukovich, III, E.S., & Strack, G. (2014). Muskrat theories, tobacco in the streets, and living Chicago as Indigenous land. *Environmental Education Research, 20*(1), 37–55. https://doi.org/10.1080/13504622.2013.865113

Barcelo, M., Cruz, Y., Escrigas, C., Ferrer, D., Granados Sanchez, J., Lopez-Segrera, F., & Sivoli, J. (Eds.). (2012). *Higher education in the world 4. Higher education's commitment to sustainability: From understanding to action.* GUNi series on the social commitment of universities. Palgrave Macmillan.

Batavia, C., & Nelson, M.P. (2016). Heroes or thieves? The ethical grounds for lingering concerns about new conservation. *Journal of Environmental Studies and Sciences.* https://doi.org/10.1007/s13412-016-0399-0

Belshaw, C. (2014). *Environmental philosophy: Reason, nature and human concern.* Routledge.

Benatar, S. (2016). Politics, power, poverty and global health: Systems and frames. *International Journal of Health Policy and Management, 5*(10), 599–604. https://doi.org/10.15171/ijhpm.2016.101

Berkes, F. (2008). *Sacred ecology: Traditional ecological knowledge and resource management* (2nd ed.). Routledge.

Berkes, F., Colding, J., & Folke, C. (2000). Rediscovery of traditional ecological knowledge as adaptive management. *Ecological Applications, 10,* 1251–1262.

Bonnett, M. (2002). Education for sustainability as a frame of mind. *Environmental Education Research, 8,* 9–20. https://doi.org/10.1080/13504620120109619

Brandon, P.S., & Lombardi, P. (2010). *Evaluating sustainable development in the built environment.* John Wiley & Sons.

Cajete, G. (1994). *Look to the mountain: An ecology of Indigenous education.* Kivaki Press.

Curry, P. (2011). *Ecological ethics: An introduction* (2nd edition). Polity Press.

Darwin, C. (1859). *On the origin of species by means of natural selection* (1st ed.). Murray.

Datta, R. (2015). A relational theoretical framework and meanings of land, nature, and sustainability for research with Indigenous communities. *Local Environment, 20*(1), 102–113. http://doi.org/10.1080/13549839.2013.818957

Doak, D., Bakker, V.J., Goldstein, B.E., & Hale, B. (2015). What is the future of conservation? In G. Wuerthner, E. Crist, & T. Butler (Eds.), *Protecting the wild: Parks and wilderness, the foundation for conservation* (pp. 27–35). Island Press.

Doherr, D. (2015). Alexander von Humboldt's idea of interconnectedness and its relationship to interdisciplinarity and communication. *Journal on Systemics, Cybernetics and Informatics, 13*(6), 47–61.

Doherr, D., & Baron, F. (2011). Humboldt Digital Library and Interconnectedness. *The Environmentalist.* Springer-Verlag. https://doi.org/10.1007/s10669-011-9369-y

Donald, D.T. (2009). Forts, curriculum, and Indigenous métissage: Imagining decolonization of Aboriginal–Canadian relations in educational contexts. *First Nations Perspectives, 2*(1), 1–24.

Doppelt, B. (2017). *Transformational resilience: How building human resilience to climate disruption can safeguard society and increase wellbeing.* Routledge.

Dreier, L., Nabarro, D., & Nelson, J. (2019). *Systems leadership for sustainable development: Strategies for achieving systemic change.* Harvard Kennedy School.

Du Pisani, J.A. (2006). Sustainable development: Historical roots of the concept. *Environmental Sciences, 3*(2), 83–96. http://doi.org/10.1080/15693430600688831

Eckersley, R. (1992). *Environmentalism and political theory: Toward an ecocentric approach.* State University of New York Press.

Eisenmenger, N., Pichler, M., Krenmayr, N., Noll, D., Plank, B., Schalmann, E., Wandl, M., & Gingrich, S. (2020). The Sustainable Development Goals prioritize economic growth over sustainable resource use: A critical reflection on the SDGs from a socio-ecological perspective. *Sustainability Science, 15*(4), 1101–1110. https://doi.org/10.1007/s11625-020-00813-x

Eliot, C.H. (2018). Ecological interdependence via constraints. *Philosophy of Science, 85*(5), 1115–1126. https://doi-org.ezproxyles.flo.org/10.1086/700600

EPA. (2022). *Learn about sustainability.* https:// www .epa .gov/ sustainability/ learn -about-sustainability

Escobar, E. (2018). *Designs for the pluriverse: Radical interdependence, autonomy, and the making of worlds.* Duke University Press.

EZLN (Zapatista Front of National Liberation). (1996). *Fourth declaration of the Lacandon jungle.* http://www.struggle.ws/mexico/ezln/jung4.html

Feinberg, R. (2022, February 2). *Maine colleges launch joint effort to address climate change.* Maine Public. https:// www .mainepublic .org/ environment -and -outdoors/ 2022-02-02/maine-colleges-launch-joint-effort-to-address-climate-change#

Frandy, T. (2018). Indigenizing sustainabilities, sustaining Indigeneities: Decolonization, sustainability, and education. *The Journal of Sustainability Education*, (18)March, 1–8.

Fraser, J., Freire, P., Macedo, D., McKinnon, T., & Stokes, W. (Eds.). (1997). Mentoring the mentor: A critical dialogue with Paulo Freire. *Counterpoints, 60.* Peter Lang.

Freire, P. (1972). *Pedagogy of the oppressed.* Penguin.

Freire, P. (2004). *Pedagogy of indignation.* Paradigm Publishers.

Gadgil, M., Berkes, F., & Folke, C. (1993). Indigenous knowledge for biodiversity conservation. *Ambio, 22*, 151–156.

Gadotti, M. (2011). Adult education as a human right: The Latin American context and the ecopedagogic perspective. *International Review of Education, 57*(1/2), 9–25. https://doi-org.ezproxyles.flo.org/10.1007/s11159-011-9205-0

Graham, M., & Maloney, M. (2019). Caring for country and rights of nature in Australia: A conversation between Earth jurisprudence and aboriginal law and ethics. In C. La Follette & C. Maser (Eds.), *Sustainability and the rights of nature in practice* (pp. 385–400). CRC Press.

Gutiérrez, F., & Prado, C. (1999). *Ecopedagogy and planetary citizenship.* Cortez.

Haraway, D. (2008). *When species meet.* University of Minnesota Press.

Hards, S. (2011). Ecologism. In D. Mulvaney & P. Robbins (Eds.). *Green politics: An A-to-Z guide* (pp. 132–134). SAGE Publications. https:// dx .doi .org/ 10 .4135/ 9781412971867.n44

Hayhurst, R., Dietrich-O'Connor, F., Hazen, S., & Landman, K. (2013). Community-based research for food system policy development in the city of Guelph, Ontario. *Local Environment, 18*(5), 606–619. http://dx .doi .org/ 10 .1080/ 13549839.2013.788493

Hettinger, N., & Throop, B.T. (1999). Refocusing ecocentrism: De-emphasizing stability and defending wildness. *Environmental Ethics, 21*(1), 3–21.

Imran, S., Alam, K., & Beaumont, N. (2014). Reinterpreting the definition of sustainable development for a more ecocentric reorientation. *Sustainable Development, 22*, 134–144. https://doi.org/10.1002/sd.537

Jacobs, D.T., & Narváez, D. (2022). *Restoring the kinship worldview: Indigenous voices introduce 28 precepts for rebalancing life on planet Earth.* North Atlantic Books.

Johnson, E., Edwards, D., & Simon, J. (2019). *The Falk School of sustainability and environment.* Chatham University.

Kahn, R.V. (2010). *Critical pedagogy, ecoliteracy, & planetary crisis: The ecopedagogy movement.* Peter Lang Publishers.

Kates, R.W. (2011). What kind of a science is sustainability science? *Proceedings of the National Academy of Sciences, 108*(49), 19449–19450.

Kerr, R. (2022). Unsettling the hegemony of "western" thinking: Critical reflection on my journey to understanding campesino-a-campesino pedagogy. *Societies, 12*(3), 76. https://doi.org/10.3390/soc12030076

Kidd, C.V. (1992). The evolution of sustainability. *Jounal of Agricultural Environmental Ethics, 5*, 1–26. https://doi.org/10.1007/BF01965413

Kimmerer, R.W. (2013). *Braiding sweetgrass.* Tantor Media, Inc.

Knudtson, P., & Suzuki, D. (1992). *Wisdom of the elders.* Allen and Unwin.

Kohák, E. (1984). The embers and the stars: A philosophical inquiry into the moral sense of nature. *International Journal for Philosophy of Religion, 17*(1), 88–90.

Kopnina, H. (2014). Revisiting education for sustainable development (ESD): Examining anthropocentric bias through the transition of environmental education to ESD. *Sustainable Development, 22*(2), 73–83.

Kothari, A., Demaria, F., & Acosta, A. (2014). *Buen vivir*, degrowth and ecological Swaraj: Alternatives to sustainable development and the green economy. *Development, 57*, 362–375. https://doi.org/10.1057/dev.2015.24

Kothari, A., Salleh, A., Escobar, A., Demaria, F., & Acosta, A. (Eds.). (2019). *Pluriverse: A post-development dictionary.* Tulika Books.

Lang, D.J., Wiek, A., Bergmann, M., Stauffacher, M., Martens, P., Moll, P., Swilling, M., & Thomas, C. (2012). Transdisciplinary research in sustainability science: Practice, principles and challenges. *Sustainability Science, 7*(1), 25–43.

Lange, E.A. (2018). Transforming transformative education through ontologies of relationality. *Journal of Transformative Education, 16*, 280–301. https://doi.org/10.1177/1541344618786452

Learning for a Sustainable Future. (n.d.). *About us.* https://lsf-lst.ca/about

Ledwith, M. (2005). *Community development.* Bristol.

Leopold, A. (1949). *A Sand County almanac and sketches here and there.* Oxford University Press.

Leopold, A. (1999). Biotic land use. In J.B. Callicott & E.T. Freyfogle (Eds.), *Aldo Leopold: For the Health of the Land: Previously Unpublished Essays and Other Writings* (pp. 198–207). Island.

Martin, G. (2007). The poverty of critical pedagogy: Toward a politics of engagement. In P. McLaren & J.L. Kincheloe (Eds.), *Critical pedagogy: Where are we now?* pp. 337–353. Peter Lang Publishers.

Mbembe, A.J. (2016). Decolonizing the university: New directions. *Arts and Humanities in Higher Education, 15*(1), 29–45. https://doi.org/10.1177/1474022215618513

McCoy, D. (2017). Critical global health: Responding to poverty, inequality and climate change comment on "Politics, power, poverty and global health: Systems and frames." *International Journal of Health Policy and Management, 6*(9), 539–541.

Mcphie, J., & Clarke, D.A.G. (2019). A walk in the park: Considering practice for outdoor environmental education. In J. Ringrose, K. Warfield, & S. Zarabadi (Eds.), *Feminist posthumanisms, new materialisms and education* (pp. 148–168). Routledge.

Miller, B., Soulé, M., & Terborgh, J. (2014). "New conservation" or surrender to development? *Animal Conservation, (17),* 509–515.

Minnich, E.K. (2005). *Transforming knowledge* (2nd ed.). Temple University Press.

Moran, U.C., Harrington, U.G., & Sheehan, N. (2018). On country learning. *Design and Culture, 10*(1), 71–79.

Muraca, B. (2011). The map of moral significance: A new axiological matrix for environmental ethics. *Environmental Ethics, 20*(3), 375–396.

Murove, M.F. (2009). African bioethics: An exploratory discourse. In *African ethics: An anthology of comparative and applied ethics* (pp. 157–177). University of KwaZulu-Natal Press.

Murove, M.F. (2014). "Ubuntu." *Diogenes, 59*(3–4), 36–47.

Næss, A. (1973). The shallow and the deep, long-range ecology movement: A summary. *Inquiry, 16*, 95–100.

National Wildlife Federation. (n.d.). *Campus Ecology Resource Center.* https://www.nwf.org/EcoLeaders/Campus-Ecology-Resource-Center

Netherwood, K., Buchanan, J., Stocker, L., & Palmer, D. (2006). Values education for relational sustainability: A case study of Lance Holt School and friends. In S. Wooltorton & D. Marinova (Eds.), *Sharing wisdom for our future: Environmental education in action* (pp. 249–259). Australian Association of Environmental Education.

Orr, D. (1994). *Earth in mind: On education, environment, and the human prospect.* Island Press.

O'Neil, J.K. (2018). Transformative sustainability learning within a material-discursive ontology. *Journal of Transformative Education, 16*, 365–387. https://doi.org/10.1177/1541344618792823

Palmer, H., & Hunter, V. (2018). Worlding. *New Materialism.* https://newmaterialism.eu/almanac/w/worlding.html

Panelli, R. (2010). More-than-human social geographies: Posthuman and other possibilities. *Progress in Human Geography*, *34*(1), 79–87. https://doi.org/10.1177/0309132509105007.

Patel, L. (2021). *No study without struggle: Confronting settler colonialism higher education*. Beacon Press.

Paton, M., Naidu, T., Wyatt, T.R., Oni, O., Lorello, G.R., Najeeb, U., Feilchenfeld, Z., Waterman, S.J., Whitehead, C.R., & Kuper, A. (2020). Dismantling the master's house: New ways of knowing for equity and social justice in health professions education. *Advances in Health Sciences Education: Theory and Practice*, *25*(5), 1107–1126. https://doi.org/10.1007/s10459-020-10006-x

Posey, D.A. (Ed.). (1999). *Cultural and spiritual values of biodiversity*. United Nations Environmental Programme.

Post, K., & Lesher, E. (2022). Protecting Little Sebago: A model college-lake association sustainable partnership. *Sustainability and Climate Change*, *15*(2). Mary Ann Liebert, Inc. http://dx.doi.org/10.1089/scc.2022.0012

Rappaport, R.A. (1999). *Ritual and religion in the making of humanity*. Cambridge University Press.

Roszak, T. (1992). *The voice of the earth*. Simon & Schuster.

Saint Joseph's College of Maine. (2023). *Center for sustainable communities*. https://www.sjcme.edu/centers/sustainable-communities

Salmón, E. (2000). Kincentric ecology: Indigenous perceptions of the human–nature relationship. *Ecological Applications*, *10*(5), 1327–1332.

Santone, S. (2019). *Reframing the curriculum: Design for social justice and sustainability*. Routledge.

Satterwhite, R., Sheridan, K., & Miller, W.M. (2016). Rediscovering deep time: Sustainability and the need to re-engage with multiple dimensions of time in leadership studies. *Journal of Leadership Studies*, *9*(4), 47–53. https://doi.org/10.1002/jls.21426

Second Nature. (2021). *2020–2021 Impact Report*. https://secondnature.org/wp-content/uploads/2021-Second-Nature-Impact-Report-Rev13.pdf

Shefner, J., & Cobb, D. (2002). Hierarchy and partnership in New Orleans. *Qualitative Sociology*, *25*(2), 273–297. http://dx.doi.org/10.1023/A:1015422902692

Sherman, D. (2008). Sustainability: What's the big idea? A strategy for transforming the higher education curriculum. *Sustainability*, *1*(3), 188–195.

Smith, G., & Stevenson, R. (2017). Sustaining education for sustainability in turbulent times. *The Journal of Environmental Education*, *48*, 1–17. http://doi.org/10.1080/00958964.2016.1264920

Smith, M. (2014). Deep ecology: What is said and (to be) done? *The Trumpeter*, *30*(2), 141–156.

Smith, S., & Ellis, K. (2022). History shows slavery helped build many U.S. colleges and universities. Shackled Legacy. APM Reports. https://www.apmreports.org/episode/2017/09/04/shackled-legacy

Sonetti, G., Brown, M., & Naboni, E. (2019). About the triggering of UN sustainable development goals and regenerative sustainability in higher education. *Sustainability*, (1), 254.

Soulé, M.E. (1985). What is conservation biology? *BioScience 35*(11), 727–734.

Spring, J. (2004). *How educational ideologies are shaping global society: Intergovernmental organizations, NGOs, and the decline of the nation-state*. Lawrence Erlbaum Associates.

Strand, K. (2000). Community-based research as pedagogy. *Michigan Journal of Community Service Learning, 7*(1), 85–96.

Strand, K., Marullo, S., Cutforth, N., Stoecker, R., & Donohue, P. (2003). Principles of best practice for community-based research. *Michigan Journal of Community Service Learning, 9*(3), 5–15.

Suzuki, D., & Knudtson, P. (1992). *Wisdom of the elders: Honouring sacred visions of nature*. Bantam Books.

Taylor, A., & Pacini-Ketchabaw, V. (2019). Learning with children, ants, and worms in the Anthropocene: Towards a common world pedagogy of multispecies vulnerability. In J. Ringrose, K. Warfield, & S. Zarabadi (Eds.), *Feminist posthumanisms, new materialisms and education* (pp. 125–147). Routledge.

Thompson, J. (2018). Joyfully living an integral ecology: Indigenous narratives and their contribution to the dialogue on well-being. *The Heythrop Journal, 59*(6), 969–982. http://dx.doi.org/10.1111/heyj.13019

Todd, Z. (2016). An indigenous feminist's take on the ontological turn: "Ontology" is just another word for colonialism. *Journal of Historic Sociology, 29*(1), 4–22.

Tuhiwai Smith, L. (2021). *Decolonizing methodologies*. Zed Books.

Tutu, D. (1999). *No future without forgiveness*. Random House.

ULSF. (2017). *What is the Talloires Declaration?* University Leaders for a Sustainable Future. http://www.ulsf.org/programs_talloires.html

UN Environment Programme. (2022). *Decision adopted by the conference of the parties to the convention on biological diversity*. Convention on Biological Diversity. https://www.cbd.int/doc/decisions/cop-15/cop-15-dec-04-en.pdf

UNESCO. (2014). *Roadmap for Implementing the Global Action Programme on Education for Sustainable Development*. UNESCO.

UNESCO. (2020). *Education for Sustainable Development: A Roadmap, ESD for 2030*. UNESCO Publishing.

UNESCO. (2022). *Reimagining our futures together: A new social contract for education*. UN.

United Nations. (1992). Agenda 21. *United Nations conference on environment development*. UN, Rio de Janeiro.

Unity Environmental University. (2023). *Academic catalogs*. https://unity.edu/about/leadership/administrative-units/registrars-office/academic-catalogs

van der Walt, J.L. (2010). Ubuntugogy for the 21st century. *Journal of Third World Studies, 27*, 249–266.

Vetlesen, A.J. (2019). *Cosmologies of the Anthropocene: Panpsychism, animism, and the limits of posthumanism*. Routledge.

Wals, A.E.J., & Benavot, A. (2017). Can we meet the sustainability challenges? The role of education and lifelong learning. *European Journal of Education, 52*, 404–413.

Wals, A.E., & Jickling, B. (2002). "Sustainability" in higher education: From doublethink and newspeak to critical thinking and meaningful learning. *International Journal of Sustainability in Higher Education, 3*(3), 221–232. http://dx.doi.org/10.1016/S0952-8733(02)00003-X

Walsh, Z., Böhme, J., & Wamsler, C. (2020). Towards a relational paradigm in sustainability research, practice, and education. *Ambio, 50*(1), 74–84.

Washington, H. (2015). *Demystifying sustainability: Towards real solutions*. Routledge.

Washington, H. (2019). Justice for nature. *Animal Sentience, 4*(27), 2.

Washington, H., Taylor, B., Kopnina, H., Cryer, P., & Piccolo, J.J. (2017). Why ecocentrism is the key pathway to sustainability. *The Ecological Citizen, 1*, 35–41.

Waziyatawin. (2011). *Understanding colonizer status*. https:// unsettlingamerica .wordpress.com/2011/09/06/understanding-colonizer-status/2011.

WCED, S.W.S. (1987). World commission on environment and development. *Our common future, 17*(1), 1–91.

Williams, L. (2013). Deepening ecological relationality through critical onto-epistemological inquiry: Where transformative learning meets sustainable science. *Journal of Transformative Education, 11*, 95–113. https://doi.org/10.1177/1541344613490997

Wright, T. (2004). The evolution of sustainability declarations in higher education. In P.B. Corcoran & A.E.J. Wals (Eds.), *Higher education and the challenge of sustainability: Problematics, promise, and practice* (pp. 7–19). Springer.

Yarime, M., Trencher, G., Mino, T. et al. (2012). Establishing sustainability science in higher education institutions: Towards an integration of academic development, institutionalization, and stakeholder collaborations. *Sustainability Science, 7*, 101–113.

Index

AASHE *see* Association for the Advancement of Sustainability in Higher Education
abductive logic 164, 165, 174
Abubakar, Sully Amin 144
academic travel impact 129
accessibility issues 17, 27–9, 258–9
accreditation schemes
    business schools 200
    schools of management 160–1
action-based research 239
active learning 227
activism 91, 239
ACUPCC *see* American College & University Presidents' Climate Commitment
adaptation, climate change 239
advocacy 192, 195
African universities 132–59
agribusiness sector 142–4
Agyeman, J. 60
aid organizations 136–7
Alexander, Bryan 11
Allegheny College 67–8
alliance, definition 134–5
alumni action 217–20
alumni careers 213–14, 217, 220
alumni clubs 85, 91
alumni networks 124, 150–1
alumni organizations 194
American College & University Presidents' Climate Commitment (ACUPCC) 44
andragogical approach 225–48
andragogy–pedagogy comparison 226
Anthropocene era 58, 275–96
Anthropocentrism 10, 60–1
Argiolas, Alessia 9
assessment methods, climate education 228–30, 233–5, 237, 243

Association for the Advancement of Sustainability in Higher Education (AASHE) 61, 66, 76–7, 128, 279

B-Lab 215, 222–3
Bamberg, S. 17
battery systems, electrical storage 255
Benamar, Said 9
benchmarking 61, 76, 88, 198–9
Benson, Thomas 8
Berg, Justin 41–2
best practices (BPs) 286
Biden administration 219
Birollo, Gustavo 8
Blue University case study 45–6, 50
book clubs 12
bottom-up approaches 26, 65, 67, 70–1, 140, 147
Bower, J.L. 208, 212, 220
BPs *see* best practices
Brown, Tim 209
Brundiers, Katja 8
Brundtland Report 276
BSIS *see* Business School Impact System
buen vivir 280
business coaching 149
business curricula, disrupting 207–24
business disciplines 9–10
business education 149, 184–206, 207–24
business ethics 210–11
business models 141–2, 145, 151
Business School Impact System (BSIS) 185, 199–201, 203
business school rankings 86, 94–5, 196–8
business schools 8, 82–104, 184–206
buy-ins, stakeholders 101

campus–community collaborations 286–7
campus sustainability 38–57, 128, 279

capacity-building mechanisms 163, 165, 169
capital budgeting 270
carbon audits 115
carbon emissions reduction 97–8, 238
carbon footprint assessments 87–8
carbon market 129
carbon taxes 232, 236
career advancement 213–14, 217, 220
career preparation 4–5, 124–6
case study approach 63, 84, 166
Castillo, Maria 8
Centola, Damon 53
charcoal energy 142, 144
Christensen, Clayton 208–9, 212, 220
circular economy sector 142–4, 147
clean energy technology 270–1
cleaner production (CP) initiatives 167–71
climate activism 239
climate change 58, 74, 96, 225–48
climate change impacts and crises 1
climate education 225–48
climate fatigue 101
climate misinformation 227
climate mitigation 238–9
climate policy 230, 232, 235
climate science 230, 231–2, 234, 237–8
climate strategies, stakeholders 82–104
cognitive bias 227
collaboration
    community–college 286–7
    definition 202
    for resilience/sustainability 70–2
    with stakeholders 70, 72, 86
    supra-HEI organizations 190, 192–3, 196, 199, 201–2, 204
collaborative initiatives 9, 12, 49–50, 52
college buildings, infrastructure 249–74
college campuses 38–57
college–community collaborations 286–7
colleges
    advancing sustainability of 249–74
    breadth/variety 2–4
    shared governance systems 256
    as transformational institutions 269–71
    transition to sustainability 202–3
Colombia 168–71
colonial legacy 147, 276–7, 281

commercial buildings 253, 256–7
communication element, partnerships 286–7
community
    nature relationship 280
    transforming 152
community–college collaborations 285–7
community engagement 44, 154
community initiatives 48, 192
community traditions 136
commuter students 116
complex contagions 53–4
composting 110, 115
confirmation bias 227
construction sites 258–9, 266
consultancy 164, 168, 173
corporate social responsibility (CSR) 84, 86–7, 92
corporate sustainability courses 117
corporations, legal definition 210
COVID-19 pandemic effects 94, 107–8, 112–13, 115–16
CP initiatives *see* cleaner production initiatives
creativity, definition 41
credibility, African universities 155–6
critical pedagogy 283
critical thinking 66–8
CSR *see* corporate social responsibility
Cullen, J.G. 161–2
culture 42, 43
cumulative advantage principle 41

DaPonte, P. 108
data types, BSIS assessment 200
de Bakker, Frank G.A. 8
de los Reyes, Gastón 10
decision-making culture 112–13
decolonization 275–96
demand costs, energy 253–4
development processes 42, 134, 276
development–sustainability link 276, 279
dialogue creation 202, 204
disciplines, variety of 3
disruptive change 207–24
disruptive innovation 208, 209–10
dissemination strategies 146–8, 151–2
diversity promotion 68–70
Dunfee, T.W. 211

E4Impact alliance 133, 135–9, 142, 145, 147, 148–9, 154–5, 156
Earth Day 48, 49, 51, 54, 67, 128
Ecocentrism 10, 280–2
EcoLeaders Program 278
ecological collapse 58
ecological conversion 106, 114
ecological sustainability 61
economic growth, Africa 133–4, 137
ecopedagogy 280, 283, 286, 288
education-information concept 69
Education for Sustainability (EfS) 276–7, 281
Education for Sustainable Development (ESD) 276–7
educational access, solar PV systems 257–8
educational subject areas, variety of 3
EfS *see* Education for Sustainability
electrical costs 250, 253, 255, 270
electrical training programs 263
Elkington, John 219
emissions reduction 97–8, 238
emissions trading 232, 236
empowerment 64–5, 68, 112–13
energy audits 68
energy conservation 113
energy consumption 252–4, 266
energy modeling software 254–5
engagement
    campus sustainability 51–2
    climate strategies 82–104
    community 44, 154
    students 69, 76, 93, 192
    see also stakeholder engagement
engineering design 252–63
enterprise business model 141
entrepreneurial influences 46–50
entrepreneurship education 132–3, 136–8, 140–1, 144–5, 151
environmental protection laws 219
environmental science studies 225–48
environmental stewardship 75–7
equity 20, 22–4, 27–8, 68–70
ESD *see* Education for Sustainable Development
Esper, Susana 8
ethics programs 84, 86–7, 210–11
event coordination 128
experience-based learning 165, 173

experiential learning 68, 76, 125, 285

facilitation
    change 17–19, 22
    leadership 64–5, 75–6
    organizational change 22
    synergistic connections 21, 25, 28–9
facilitatory stakeholders 65
faculty facilitation
    research programs 73
    student leadership 64–5, 75–6
faculty lines 214, 221–2
Farmdrive case study 142
fashion professionals 207, 213–14, 218
financial modeling tools 254–5
food pantries 111
food waste diversion 109–10
forest depletion 142
formative assessment 228–9, 237, 243
fossil fuel depletion 249, 250
Francis, Pope 42, 105–6, 108, 112, 115
Franklin University Switzerland 127–30
Freire, Paulo 280, 283, 285, 286–7
French business school study 8, 82–104
fund raising 155
funding sources, solar PV systems 268

garden modeling 109–12
GCNYC *see* Glasgow Caledonian New York College
GCSE *see* Global Council for Science and the Environment
GCU *see* Georgian Court University
Georgian Court University (GCU) 105–19
geothermal systems 253
Glasgow Caledonian New York College (GCNYC) 207–24
Global Council for Science and the Environment (GCSE) 8, 15–37
Global North–Global South differences 198
Global South
    Global North differences 198
    Green Office resources 126
global warming knowledge 231–2, 233–4, 236, 238

Globally Responsible Leadership
    Initiative (GRLI) 185, 193–6,
    201–3
governance structures
    business curricula 207–24
    solar development projects 256
    support/commitment of 52
    supra-HEI organizations 194
grants 137
Green College case study 43–5, 50
Green Gown Awards 190, 203
green initiative fee 44
Green Office Movement 120–31
greenhouse gas effects 232, 236, 238
greenwashing 86, 101, 219
Grenoble Agreement 96
GRLI *see* Globally Responsible
    Leadership Initiative

Haddock-Fraser, H.E. 184
Hart, S.L. 210–11
Heating, Ventilation, and Air
    Conditioning (HVAC) units 113
HEIs *see* higher education institutions
helioscope software 255
HESI *see* Higher Education
    Sustainability Initiative
HICs *see* high-income countries
high-income countries (HICs), SDG
    progress 1
High-level Political Forum on
    Sustainable Development (HLPF)
    190
higher education governance 52, 194,
    207–24, 256
higher education institutions (HEIs)
    defining sustainability of 4–7
    leading society 58–81
    promoting sustainability 187–8
    social change responsibility 240–2
    sustainability commitment 82–104
    transition to sustainability 184,
        202–3
Higher Education Sustainability Initiative
    (HESI) 185, 188–90, 202–3
Hiser, Krista 8
HLPF *see* High-level Political Forum on
    Sustainable Development
Homan, K.S.J. 115

human capital 133
human-nature relationship 281–2
hunches 164
Hurley, E.A. 74
HVAC units *see* Heating, Ventilation,
    and Air Conditioning units
hybrid business logics 142, 145, 151
hypothetic-deductive theory testing 172

Idea Journey model 40–3, 45–6
impact, sustainability programs 17, 27–9
impact categories, RML 162
impact entrepreneurship 138, 140–1,
    143–4, 150, 155
inclusion in higher education 20, 22–3,
    27–8, 68–70
innovation
    challenges to 52
    disruptive effects 208, 209–10
    facilitation 17
    promotion of 72–3
    role 39–42
    TD approach 163–4, 171
innovation adoption 38–57
institutional change 25–7
institutional policies 50
institutional support/commitment 52
institutionalization of sustainability 25–7,
    120, 124
integrated sustainability model 42–5
integrative approaches 25–6, 52, 59,
    63–7
interdisciplinary approaches 65–6, 71
Intergovernmental Panel on Climate
    Change (IPCC) 227, 234
internal relatedness theory 281
international mobility 96, 98
internships 67–8
interpretive displays 261
intuitive reasoning 164
IPCC *see* Intergovernmental Panel on
    Climate Change
isotopes 234

Jouzel Report 85
just sustainability 60
justice 20, 22–4, 27–8, 68–70

Kakkar, H. 54

key competencies in sustainability
framework 21, 23–4, 28
key performance indicators (KPIs) 93
Kim, Younsung 10
kincentric ecology 280, 289
King, Jordan 8
knowledge
disseminating 152
harvesting 146–8, 152
open nature of 289
knowledge production 163, 164, 172,
173
KPIs *see* key performance indicators
Kunming-Montreal Global Biodiversity
Framework 282

Laasch, O. 162
land-grant institutions 284
land sales 117
Laudato Si' university 9, 42–3, 105–19
Lawrence, E.L. 74
leadership 58–81
modeling behavior 7
organizational change 27
responsibility education 185, 193–6,
240–2
support/commitment 52
Leadership in Energy and Environmental
Design (LEED) certification 44,
116–17
Learning for a Sustainable Future (LSF)
278
LeBlanc, Jacqueline 10
LEED certification 44, 116–17
legitimization, African universities
155–6
Leopold, Aldo 281
LICs *see* low-income countries
Likert scale 231
living labs 62, 72, 82, 256
LMICs *see* lower-middle income
countries
local context, university alliances 155
local knowledge 147
long-term perspectives 288
Low-Carbon Pact 91
low-income countries (LICs), SDG
progress 2
lower-middle income countries (LMICs),
SDG progress 2

LSF *see* Learning for a Sustainable
Future

Maastricht University, Netherlands
121–2
macro-level strategies 17, 19, 26, 30
Madison College solar project 250–2,
259–65, 267, 271–2
Maine universities 285–9
management consultancy 164
management disciplines 9–10
management education 9, 160–83, 186
responsibility principles 87, 160–6,
171, 185, 190–3, 201–3
sustainable transformation 184–206
materiality analysis 88, 90, 148
media scrutiny 86
mental health 74–5
mentorship 73–4, 149
meso-level strategies 17, 19, 26, 30
Mexico 168–70, 171
micro-gardens 109–10
micro-level strategies 17, 19, 26, 30
Mills, Janet 288
Minnich, E.K. 279
Müller, M. 167
multi-actor collaboration 171, 175
multi-stakeholder initiatives 28, 186–8,
202

Næss, Arne 281
National Wildlife Federation (NWF) 278
natural resources, Africa 133
nature–humanity interconnection 275–6,
280
neoclassical economics 210
neoliberal development agenda 134
network skills development 140–1
New York State Fashion Act 219–20
non-governmental organizations (NGOs)
137, 278
non-profit organizations 189, 215, 238,
278
Nordhaus, William 238
NWF *see* National Wildlife Federation

O&M activities *see* operations and
maintenance activities
Ojiambo, Sanda 134

ONE *see* Organizations and the Natural
Environment
one-group pretest-posttest research
design 228, 229–31
online courses, Green Office Movement
120, 123
operational deficits 270
operational sustainability 241–2
operationalization principles 21, 23–4,
28, 160–83
operations and maintenance (O&M)
activities 263
organizational change 22, 25–7, 29,
160–83
organizational culture 51
organizational elements, partnerships 287
Organizations and the Natural
Environment (ONE) 6

PABs *see* Professional Advisory Boards
Pan African university alliance 132–59
Paris Agreement 115, 117
partnerships
African universities 145
business/management education 186
climate projects 238
communication within 286–7
development process 134
organizational elements 287
stakeholders 70, 202
supra-HEI organizations 194, 202
path dependence concept 41
Pawlish, Michael J. 9
pedagogy–andragogy comparison 226
peer learning 141, 195
peer networks 150
peer-reviewed knowledge production 172
photovoltaic (PV) technology 10, 113,
249–74
physical infrastructure 51
PIR *see* Positive Impact Rating
planning
RedES research 173
solar development projects 268
plastic waste 110
pluriversities 10, 275, 283–9
pollinator protection 110–11
Positive Impact Rating (PIR) 185, 196–9,
201–3
Post, Kimberly M. 10

post-secondary education, decolonizing
275–96
power consumption, demand costs 253–4
practitioner faculty 214, 221–2
praxis of learning 280, 285
pretest-posttest research design 228,
229–31
primary stakeholders 65
Principles of Responsible Management
Education (PRME) 87, 160, 185,
190–3, 201–3
problem-solving 66–8
process-oriented perspective 42
Professional Advisory Boards (PABs) 91
professional responsiveness 214–16
program design 16–18, 20, 23
program evaluation 16–18, 20, 23
prototyping strategy 52, 195
public access, solar PV systems 258–9
punctuated equilibrium theory 83
PV technology *see* photovoltaic
technology

qualitative data 200
quality strategies 17, 27–9
quantifiable data 200
quantity breeds quality principle 40

racial justice 69–70
reciprocity 275, 280, 283, 286, 289
recognition, student leadership 76
recycling 108–9, 115
RedES model 166–72, 173
reflection principle 126, 280
relational theory 281–2
relationality concept 281, 289
renewable energy 249–74
Research, Outreach Operations,
Teaching, and Students and other
stakeholders (ROOTS) 4–7
research promotion 72–3, 145, 156, 162
resilience 58–81, 112–13, 289
resource allocation process 209–10
resource scarcity 135
responsible business school rankings
94–5
Responsible Campus Network 87
responsible leadership education 185,
193–6, 240–2

responsible management education 87, 160, 185, 190–3, 201–3
responsible management learning (RML) 161–6, 171
Rio+20 conference 188
Rio Declaration 278
RML *see* responsible management learning
rootAbility enterprise 121–2
ROOTS *see* Research, Outreach Operations, Teaching, and Students and other stakeholders
Rubin, H.J. and Rubin, I.S. 107

Saint Joseph's College, Maine 285–9
SASB *see* Sustainability Accounting Standards Board
SCADA systems *see* Supervisory Controls and Data Acquisition systems
scale, definition 29
Schaltegger, S. 171
scholarship engagement 154
schools, advancing sustainability of 249–74
schools of management 9, 160–83
science-management-policy-ethics 240
SDGs *see* Sustainable Development Goals
SE *see* stakeholder engagement; sustainability education
Second Nature 278–9
secondary stakeholders 65
Senjem, Jason C. 8
sequential learning 228–9, 237
Seuring, S. 167
shade analysis tools 262
Sharing Information on Progress (SIP) reports 190, 192
Sharma, S. 210–11
Shrivastava, P. 12
silo system 280, 284
SIP reports *see* Sharing Information on Progress reports
Sivanathan, N. 54
small- and medium-sized enterprises (SMEs) 155, 167, 172
smart screen kiosks 261
SMEs *see* small- and medium-sized enterprises

Smith, Linda Tuhiwai 283
social capital 149
social change 240–2
social impact measurement 137, 139, 149, 151
social justice 44
social networks 53–4
social problems, Africa 132–59
societal impact 137, 139, 149, 151, 161, 171–4, 202–3
societal resilience 58–81
societal stakeholders 18
socioeconomic sustainability 123, 135, 156–7
solar photovoltaic infrastructure 10, 113, 249–74
"solarpunk" 11
SOS International *see* Students Organizing for Sustainability International
spirituality 114
staff facilitation, student leadership 64–5, 75–6
staff-led initiatives, on-campus 47–8
stakeholder engagement (SE) 82–104, 189, 197–8
stakeholder identification
    solar development projects 265–8
    supra-HEI organizations 191
    Transition 2026 88–90
stakeholder networks 51
stakeholder tables 265–7
stakeholder theory 59, 64
stakeholders 8–9
    collaboration with 70, 72, 86
    definition 83
    partnerships 70, 202
    recognition 76
    sustainability programs 18, 19–20
Starik, M. 12, 42
STARS *see* Sustainability Tracking, Assessment and Rating System
STEM disciplines 269, 271
strategic attributes, innovation 39–40
strategic commitments 207–8, 212–16
strategy 8
structural influences 50–2
structure 42, 43
student activists 91
student-driven approaches 120–31

student engagement
    assessment of 69
    climate strategies 93
    SDG achievement 192
student-led initiatives 47, 48, 93–5,
    120–31
student leadership 59, 64–5, 67, 68, 75–6
Students Organizing for Sustainability
    International (SOS International)
    122
Sulitest Association 189–90
summative assessment 243
Supervisory Controls and Data
    Acquisition (SCADA) systems
    262
supra-HEI organizations 185–206
sustainability
    boundaries of action 148
    definitions 2, 16, 276–7
    development link 276, 279
    institutionalizing 25–7, 120, 124
Sustainability Accounting Standards
    Board (SASB) 215
Sustainability and Management (and
    Business) 9
    recommendations 10
sustainability businesses 49
sustainability education (SE) 3–4, 10
    anthropocentric approach 277, 281
    definition 276–7
    historical perspective 278–80
Sustainability Impact Loop 208–9,
    216–20
sustainability justice 18, 21, 24
sustainability knowledge 146–8, 151–2
sustainability management 184–206
sustainability programs 120–31
    change areas 17–19, 22–9
    change drivers 17–19
    key competencies 21, 23–4, 28
    needs/opportunities 15–37
    student leadership 67
sustainability stakeholders 8–9
sustainability systems/strategy 8
Sustainability Tracking, Assessment and
    Rating System (STARS) 61, 66,
    76–7, 279
sustainability transitions 99, 184, 202–3
sustainable business education 207–24
sustainable development 60, 132

Sustainable Development Goals (SDGs)
    1–2, 45, 61–2, 115, 129, 132–3,
    188, 192
sustainable transformation 184–206
sustainable universities/colleges
    further research 10–13
    ROOTS ratings 4–7
symbols of sustainability 148–52
synergistic connections 21, 25, 28–9
systemic approach 49–50, 96
systemic change 19–22, 99
systems 42, 43
systems perspective 44

tacit knowledge 172
Talloires Declaration 278
Tascón, M.A. 69
TD *see* transdisciplinarity
TEK *see* Traditional Ecological
    Knowledge
Tereick, Miriam 125
top-down approaches 26, 70–1
Traditional Ecological Knowledge
    (TEK) 282
training commitments, business schools
    96–7
transdisciplinarity (TD) 161–6, 171–3
transdisciplinary framework 225–48
transdisciplinary modular approaches 10
transformative change 17–29, 279–80
transformative sustainability roles 83
Transition 2026 82–104
transportation footprints 5–6
travel impact 129
trees 144, 252, 266
triple-loop organizational learning 26
triple-win scenario 58, 64, 67, 76
trust relations 172

Ubuntu 280–1
UD *see* University of Delaware
UN Global Compact (UNGC) 87, 160,
    187–8, 190
UN PRME *see* Principles of Responsible
    Management Education
UNGC *see* UN Global Compact
universities
    advancing sustainability of 249–74
    breadth/variety 2–4

promoting sustainability 135
roles of 124, 135
shaping students 120
shared governance systems 256
as transformational institutions
269–71
transition to sustainability 184,
202–3
university alliances 132–59
University of Delaware (UD) 59, 63–7

value chains 147
values-based education 285
van Hoof, Bart 9
Vermeulen, W.J.V. 163
volunteer workers 125

Walz, Kenneth A. 10
waste policies 108–10, 142, 144
weather stations 262–3
Weber, S.M. 69
well-being 74–5
whole-institution approach 25–6, 65, 241
Witjes, Sjors 9, 163
Wolny, Julia 9
working group format 90, 93–5, 192
workshop format 67, 123, 164, 169
Wu, Jean 9

Yunus, Muhammad 207

Zaacol case study 142, 144
Zaal, Maartje 121